PRIVATE COMPTON

MY

EXPERIENCES IN THE WORLD WAR

OR

A BRIEF HISTORY OF THE THIRD BATTALION

111TH INFANTRY - 28TH DIVISION

A. E. F.

Written & Compiled

- By -

PAUL L. COMPTON

WENDY A. YESSLER

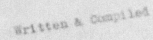

Private Compton: My Experiences in the World War Or

A Brief History of the Third Battalion 111th Infantry—28th Division A.E.F.

Cover design by Wendy A. Yessler

WAY Art & Life Design

ISBN: 978-0-578-50313-4

In Memory of

All those who served and gave their lives, both past and present.

"During these times of comparatively open fighting in the Argonne, when it was often
the case of 'every man for himself,' all barriers of rank were forgotten.
Our commissioned officers, always the picked target of the enemy,
were frequently disguised as privates.

Petty hates and jealousies vanished;
racial, religious and personal differences were unknown,
and everybody united in the common cause.

All men, doing their duty, were equal."

Private Compton

Previous page:

Troops at the American Red Cross Recreation Hut at Orleans, France, October 1918.
(Image courtesy of Library of Congress)

CONTENTS

Part 1

MY EXPERIENCES IN THE WORLD WAR
OR
A BRIEF HISTORY OF THE THIRD BATTALION
111TH INFANTRY — 28TH DIVISION A. E. F.

Part 2

Reflections and Ponderings

Foreword

It has been one hundred years since the Great War was fought and come to an end. When I first began working on this project, I did not realize this, but that realization added to my enthusiasm to share this historical manuscript.

Private Paul Compton was my great grandfather. I never met him, but I do remember meeting his wife Eva, my great grandmother, when I was a small child. They lived in Washington, DC.

The pages herein are scanned from a copy of Private Compton's original manuscript. I purposely did not retype it in order to keep a nostalgic and authentic feel. Part 1 contains the account of his experiences in the war, which is the majority of the book. Part 2 contains his poetic reflections and ponderings on various monuments, memorials, and life. He wrote and compiled the whole manuscript; however, he did not include a table of contents. I found a font similar to the typewritten copy, and organized a table of contents to make navigating the manuscript easier. The publisher required three or four poetry pages to be made clearer and I tried doing this without making a noticeable difference to the original manuscript.

A copy of the manuscript had been given to my brother by another family member, and it is not known when the copy was made. Private Compton's Preface mentions making mimeographed copies for those from company I who wanted them. I believe this was a mimeographed copy made near the same time period. Therefore, pages are as is, in original state. A few pages are slightly blurred, one slightly distorted, but original state. Photos in the poetry section were extremely dark. Duplicates of the originals were found and used; apparently postcards had been used.

Private Compton cited that he had gotten the District of Columbia War Memorial photo from Department of Interior, National Capital Parks. I was not able to locate the same photo, however, that organization referred me to the Library of Congress, and I did locate a photo that was almost exactly the same. Due to the foliage, clouds, and sky being the same, I believe it was taken on the same day by the same photographer, Theodor Horydczak, being created/published ca. 1931-ca. 1950.

Paul Compton stated that he attended the dedication of the War Memorial where John Philip Sousa was the band conductor for the ceremony. From the Library of Congress website, I have located and included photos from that day, cited as taken by Harris & Ewing.

I decided to try bringing Private Compton's experiences to life further by finding photos that would depict some of the things he was talking about. I researched the A.E.F catalogue collection of the National Archives, the Library of Congress website, newspaper archives, and historical books to locate photos. Whenever possible, I used photos from 111th Infantry, 28th Division. When this was not possible, I tried using photos depicting the places or events that he described.

Private Compton not only brings events to life, but his personality also comes to life through his writing. I hope you enjoy reading his manuscript as much as I did while working on it.

TO MY DARLING WIFE, EVA

Who is she, when things go wrong,
   I can take my troubles to?
Who is she to whom I cling?
   My little wife, she's you!

Who is she who darns my socks,
   Makes my coffee and my stew?
Who is she who keeps me clean?
   My little wife, she's you!

Who is she who is always there,
   Whose wants are but a few?
Who is she who comforts me?
   My little wife, she's you!

Who is she, when I am sick
   And I feel so very blue;
Who is she who is standing by?
   My little wife, she's you!

Who is she who makes my home
   And comforts others too?
Who is she who keeps me straight?
   My little wife, she's you!

Who is she who endures my faults?
   (And I have many, too!),
Who is she who understands?
   My little wife, she's you!

Who is she I hope to meet
   In that land beyond the blue?
Who is she I love so much?
   My darling wife, she's you!

- By -
PAUL L. COMPTON
4-5-56

M Y

EXPERIENCES IN THE WORLD WAR

O R

A BRIEF HISTORY OF THE THIRD BATTALION

111TH INFANTRY - 28TH DIVISION

A. E. F.

Written & Compiled

- By -

PAUL L. COMPTON

PREFACE.

To my comrades:

Over a decade has passed since the majority of us received our discharges from the U. S. Army at Camp Dix, New Jersey, bade one another "Goodbye" and started homeward to resume civilian life after doing "our bit" on the battle fields of Europe. While time can never efface from memory those vivid days of our army careers, especially when recalling those trying months under fire on the front lines, there are, no doubt, many who, as the years go by, will find that their memories are not so clear when endeavoring to relate the varied incidents that daily crowded our lives "Over There". It is, therefore, to place in your hands some permanent record of the activities, in France, of the Third Battalion, 111th U. S. Infantry, 28th Division, that this article is attempted. It is intended, primarily, as a simple narrative of the travels, on foreign soil, of one of the powerful combat units of the American Expeditionary Forces. We do not endeavor to relate all the many little happenings, humorous or otherwise, that took place, - not because we consider them of small consequence but because there are so many other incidents of greater interest about which we wish to write and there is so much to tell that, if it were attempted, we would not have space in one volume nor, for that matter, in several. These things are for the telling in the quiet hours of the winter evenings around the fire, at times when old members of the battalion come together (and reunite they will), and at times in the coming years when our memories may be less vivid than they are now and the tendency may be to lengthen the marches we made, increase the number of the enemy encountered, the difficulties surmounted, magnify our hardships and, generally, depart from the path of truth. It is our endeavor in this article to merely trace out, as accurately as possible, the activities in France of the Third Battalion, 111th U. S. Infantry, giving the names of places visited, events that transpired with corresponding dates, etc., so that in the distant future they may be readily recalled to mind and, in turn, bring with them memories of the battalion's part in the great World War, together with personal experiences both in camp and on the battle field.

It may interest my comrades and others to learn just how and under what circumstances this little history originated. One day in April, 1919, while the 28th Division was quartered at Le Mans, France, our Forwarding Camp, just prior to entraining for St. Nazaire, a Lieutenant in Company I of our battalion asked me if I would take down in shorthand and transcribe some notes he had prepared relating to the activities of that company in the A. E. F. (It seemed that each unit of the regiment had been instructed to write its particular history and to turn the same over to Regimental Headquarters for their records.) Although my knowledge along stenographic lines had become somewhat "rusty" over a period of about eighteen months' inactivity, I managed to take down the dictation which gave a chronological account of the company's movements during its participation in the war. Upon transcribing my notes that night at Regimental Headquarters, I made an extra typewritten copy which, at the time, I intended to keep as a sort of souvenir. After completing the task assigned me, I was thereafter regularly detailed to Regimental Headquarters during the remainder of our stay at Le Mans to assist in making typewritten copies of Sailing Lists, or rosters, covering the various units of our regiment soon to embark for the States. These lists gave the names of officers and enlisted men and the addresses of their nearest relatives or friends. Shortly after arriving home (perhaps a month), from the data obtained in the Lieutenant's history, I wrote another and longer article, going more into detail and relating numerous events which I thought would be of special interest to the men of Company I, 111th Infantry. Later, procuring a copy of the company's roster from one of its former officers, I got in touch with practically every I Company man who returned home on the SS Kroonland, advising them of the history which I had written. Subsequently, many demands for copies were received. These copies I had mimeographed and mailed to all desiring them, charging a nominal fee to reimburse me for the money I had expended. These histories proving so popular with my old comrades in Company I, the idea of a larger work occurred to me - a narrative embracing the activities of the entire Third Battalion, 111th U. S. Infantry in France, using my first manuscript as a basis or foundation upon which to build the present volume. I have accordingly herein related a story which, it is hoped, will be of real and vital interest to all survivors of our old outfit. No attempt is made to minutely describe each and every maneuver. It is believed, however, that with this record as a guide, each soldier who fought under the banner of the Third Battalion, or even with other units of our regiment, can trace out his own story of his individual part in the great conflict. The various engagements with the enemy would, of course, be described differently as to minor details, depending upon the personal experience of each man who participated.

In conclusion, I wish to say that I have endeavored in this article to give to the men of the Third Battalion, 111th U. S. Infantry, 28th Division, a more definite idea of where they were at stated times in France and, in the telling of our experiences, hope to convey to those who remained at home a little better impression of what befell their boys "Over There".

P. L. C.

ORGANIZATION.

The Third Battalion of the 111th U. S. Infantry, 28th Division, was originally formed by a combination of units of the Eighteenth Pennsylvania Infantry, National Guards, and the Sixth Pennsylvania Infantry, of the same organization. When the National Guard of the United States was called into Federal service, the various units were moved to their respective training camps and consolidated into different regiments which, in turn, were strengthened by the addition of more men. These regiments, subsequently, were divided into the various divisions and given new official designations. In this way, on October 11, 1917, various companies of the Eighteenth and Sixth Pennsylvania National Guards finally merged as units of the 111th Infantry of the newly organized Twenty-eighth (Keystone) Division, composed, until the arrival of additional troops from other States, entirely of regiments from the Pennsylvania National Guard. Training quarters were established at Camp Hancock, Augusta, Georgia.

Members of the Pennsylvania National Guard prepare to leave for Camp Hancock, GA
(Image courtesy National Archives)

New recruits learning to march in formation at Camp Hancock, GA
(Image courtesy National Archives)

CHAPTER 1.

LAST DAYS AT CAMP HANCOCK.

Troops comprising the Third Battalion, 111th Infantry, moved to Camp Hancook, Augusta, Georgia, in September, 1917, and after establishing themselves in squad tents pitched picturesquely along "Company Streets", began an extensive training program, under competent instructors in modern warfare, destined to be of some seven months' duration. Not many of the men will very soon forget those fatiguing weeks of close and extended-order drilling; the bayonet practice in the old "bowl" under the watchful eyes of our English instructors (imported for the purpose); the long endurance marches on which we were forced to shoulder heavy packs; our days of training at the rifle-range with "pup" tents for sleeping quarters while there - not to mention the severity of that particular winter spent in the "Sunny South" and our endeavors to keep "fires going" in quarters regardless of certain restrictions relating thereto! These, and many other like experiences equally as bad, together with certain events of a more pleasant nature, we will always remember when recalling our Camp Hancook days. We do not want to forget, in the telling of our camp life at old Hancock, those little slips of paper so liberally handed out to us, entitling the fortunate holders to nightly visits to the town of Augusta. We must admit that these "passes" came in mighty handy after a hard day's work on the drill field.

Finally, the winter months passed and Spring brought fresh hopes for all. Rumors about "packing up and sailing for France" were the usual topics discussed and upon which speculation was most rife. Additional troops from other camps throughout the United States came in to "fill up" our ranks to war strength, which fact seemed to substantiate many of the rumors. At last, in April 1918, all anxiety was definitely dispelled by the official order "Strike camp!", or words to that effect which then meant so much to the impatient men. The long-wished-for orders had arrived! We were to depart for oversea duty, perhaps to eventually engage in the World War - an event in our lives which, at times, seemed far distant or would never materialize. Our dreams had come true - we were to sail for France!

The last few days spent at old Camp Hancock were very busy ones - hustling times for those high in command down to the lowly "Buck" privates throughout the entire 28th. Old equipment had to be turned in for new; uniforms, extra clothing, etc. issued; (our Supply Sergeants were the most popular men in the whole camp during these busy days); barrack bags had to be properly labelled with the soldier's name, serial number, rank and outfit printed in large letters thereon; the Divisional insignia (a red keystone) stenciled on all baggage; a great

amount of clerical or "paper-work" incident to troop movements; the
Service Records of the men checked up; areas around all squad tents
properly cleared or "policed"; great excavations or, as the men termed
them, "graves" had to be dug in which were buried all refuse and discarded material.   In fact, after our ordeal of "policing" was over,
an overlooked cigarette stump left on the grounds would have been very
noticible.   Our last task, that of packing barrack bags and rolling
packs, was finally accomplished, and after successfully passing what
seemed the hundredth inspection, the great day arrived - Monday, April
29th, 1918, on which our battalion was scheduled to entrain.   Around
3:30 P. M. of that day, loaded down with heavy packs, a merry lot of
embryo "doughboys" joyfully (this time) responded as one man to the
command "Squads right!" and marched to the camp depot, where they
boarded the awaiting troop train bound, as rumor had it, for Camp
Upton, Mineola, Long Island, New York.

Camp Hancock, Augusta, GA
(Image from https://wynninghistory.com/tag/camp-hancock/)

CHAPTER 2.

OUR JOURNEY NORTH.

Our trip North was not without interest and it afforded the men
a much needed recreation from the monotonous routine of camp life.
The train ride was thoroughly enjoyed by all. Each car was in charge
of a non-com, whose duty it was to keep order and to see that no adventuresome "buck" took "French leave" at any of the stops along the
way. Every man was supplied with sufficient rations to last during
the trip and our Mess Sergeants managed to keep us served with hot
coffee at meal times. Card games helped to wile away the hours, enlivened by an occasional crap-shooting contest. Many of the men took
advantage of these leisure hours in writing to the folks at home,
while others amused themselves by tossing notes out of the car windows
when the train sped through some of the towns along the route. These
missives, in most instances only bearing a soldier's name and outfit,
were quickly snatched up by groups of fair admirers who crowded every
station we passed. They were acknowledged, at times, by a wave of
the hand or a hurriedly thrown kiss. On reaching Richmond, Virginia,
at which city we made a brief stop, the train was met by a committee
of ladies from the American Red Cross, who showered us with candy,
cakes, apples, cigarettes and postal cards. They also kindly offered
to mail any cards or letters we had written. By this time we were
beginning to feel like real heroes, having met with such rousing receptions so far in our journey North. At our next stop, Washington,
D. C., we found the Red Cross again "on the job" and here, after partaking of some refreshments, and led by our respective commanding officers, we walked around one of the nearby city blocks, which exercise
proved a decided relief after being confined to our rather crowded
coaches for so many hours. But, at Philadelphia, a real surprise was
in store for us. On pulling into Broad Street Station, our last stopping point before the end of the trip, we found the large train shed
packed with cheering civilians, many of whom were our relatives and
friends - all bent on one mission - to give "their boys" a rousing
"send-off" and perhaps, where possible, to shake a hand of some departing soldier, "sending him away with a smile". Many of the men
did meet their folks for a brief chat and a "Good-bye", as frequently
evidenced by the tear-dimmed eyes of some fond parent who happened to
spy their boy among that khaki-colored mass leaning out of the car
windows. The writer will never forget one parting scene he witnessed
that night between a mother and son. Indeed, we were now just beginning to realize we were on serious business and not on a pleasure trip.
Here, again, ladies of the Red Cross, burdoned down with heavy baskets
full of delicacies, held impromptu "receptions" at most every car
window, seeming to appreciate the wants of the men. They even entered the cars to make sure that not a man was overlooked in the hand-

-ing out of refreshments. Many also offered their services in conveying messages of love and good cheer to "the girl he left behind" somewhere in America. The men of the 111th will not soon forget those brief moments at old Broad Street Station. Subsequent events proved this was indeed a last farewell for many of the boys who chanced to meet their loved ones there that night. Amid wild cheering and a sea of waving handkerchiefs, we were again on our way, some feeling, perhaps, just a little sober as the train slowly steamed out of the Station and into the night on its journey North.

It was sometime during the early morning hours of May 1st that our destination - somewhere in New Jersey - was reached, for on arousing from our slumbers at day-break, we discovered that our train was on a siding in a station. Bright and early, not even taking the time for a meal, we gathered up our belongings and in Company formation marched a short distance to the awaiting ferries which conveyed us across the Hudson River to New York. Here, we were hustled into electric cars, and amid the shriek of many whistles from neighboring factories, tug-boats, etc., began the final stage of our trip to camp. In the matter of a few hours the entire regiment was housed in barracks at Camp Upton, Mineola, Long Island, N. Y., and, as usual, impatiently awaiting orders for the next move.

CHAPTER 3.

LIFE AT CAMP UPTON.

Camp Upton was the scene of busy activities for the officers and enlisted men of our Third Battalion. A great deal had yet to be accomplished during our few days' stay here preparatory to sailing. More equipment was issued, including our friend in time of need, the famous steel helmet, and upon donning these we already pictured ourselves in a front line trench "somewhere in France" facing the Hun! Several of the men having relatives or friends living in New York City, or in neighboring cities and towns, were granted short furloughs from camp in which to make visits upon their word of honor to return at a specified time. A number of their less fortunate comrades - not to be outdone - went A. W. O. L., much to the distress of their commanding officers. (For the benefit of those of my readers who are not acquainted with army terms - slang phrases as heard in the ranks - an endeavor will be made to explain them as we unfold our story.) A.W.O.L. are four much discussed letters pertaining to a soldier's life in camp and on a field of action. These letters stand for "Absent without leave", considered a very serious offense, especially in times of war when a prolonged A.W.O.L. might very readily be taken for desertion, which if occurring while in the face of the enemy, is punishable by Court Marshall and a possible verdict of the death penalty. All our men, as far as it is known, returned to camp, however, not wishing to take the chance of missing "that boat". At Camp Upton the battalion enrolled additional men in order to bring the various companies up to the required war strength of two hundred and fifty men to the infantry company. Here, as at Camp Hancock, the old "show-down" inspections were the order of the day, and woe to the unfortunate soldier who could not produce all equipment issued him, even down to a cake of soap or a tooth brush! These "show-down" inspections are always dreaded by all enlisted men. Every piece of clothing issued, all equipment, including toilet articles, etc., etc. must be arranged in a particular order for these inspections and strict accountability made to officers for anything missing or if not properly exhibited according to army rules and regulations. Companies were repeatedly commanded to "fall in" for inspection or some other reason equally dreaded by the majority of the men. Between inspections and the necessity of being within call at all hours of the day and night, we had very little time to ourselves. A few of the boys managed somehow to evade their ever alertful "Top Kickers" (First Sergeants) and to give the camp "the once over" before leaving. In the evenings large numbers of men would assemble in the Y. M. C. A. and K. of C. huts throughout the camp where they would give vent to their joyful spirits by making the night air fairly ring with war songs of the day. Such stirring melodies as "Pack up your troubles in your old kit bag", "Over There", "Kaiser

Bill", "Keep your head down Fritzie Boy!", "Hail! Hail! the gang's all
here" and a dozen other inspiring tunes will always be closely associated with our army careers.   These songs helped to brighten up
many a weary hour in camp or on the march, or wherever the troops
happened to be - on this side of the Atlantic or "somewhere in France"
in billets, on many a weary hike up to the front and were often sung
to the accompaniment of whistling shrapnel and whining machine gun
bullets!   Thank God for song!   Thus, for the impatient men, three
days dragged slowly by - our last days of camp life on American soil
before sailing for foreign shores.   We had time for little or no
sleep on the night of May 4th, which was spent in packing-up preparatory to leaving camp under orders which were then momentarily expected.
All were too excited to think of sleeping even if they had the opportunity.   During the bustle of that last night in America, a little
incident happened which at the time very few of the busy men noticed -
or if they did see it - thought nothing about it.   It has turned out,
however, to be quite a coincidence - or was it a premonition?   We
shall leave that question to be answered by the reader.   Seated upon
his barrack bag in a far corner of our quarters - alone - was a
soldier crying like a baby!   (It may seem like "stretching the truth"
but strangely enough the man's name was Crier and at that time was a
member of our battalion.)   It seemed that he had a horror of "going
over" - felt like something terrible would surely happen to him if he
did.   The writer learned only recently, through some buddies in his
V. F. W. Post, that Private Crier was killed in action during the war!

At midnight the battalion silently responded to the command "Fall
in!" and, marching under a dark sky, the long column proceeded out of
camp to the station where we again boarded passenger cars.   Every
car was literally packed to the doors and some of the men were obliged
to "bunk" in the aisles of the train, there not being a sufficient
number of cars available to comfortably accommodate the troops.

Needless to say, the early hours of that wonderful Spring morning,
Sunday, May 5th, 1918, will be an everlasting memory to all survivors
of the now famous 111th.   The long anticipated time had at last arrived!   The thought of bidding farewell to America (perhaps forever),
leaving behind all our loved ones, to engage in that terrible and uncertain struggle some three thousand miles across the sea, did not
seem to dampen the high spirits of the men.   On the contrary, it
seemed all rather enjoyed the prospects ahead - whatever fate had in
store.   In fact, it might be mentioned here, for the benefit of those
interested, that the average American "doughboy" was not fully satisfied until he found himself actually in the front lines "Over There"
and his quiries and speculations as to the great conflict definitely
answered by personal experiences.   Human nature, we guess!

CHAPTER 4.

THE S. S. OLYMPIC.

After a rather tiresome journey in the over-crowded coaches, at about seven o'clock, Sunday morning, May 5th, we reached Hoboken, New Jersey and the entire regiment crossed the Hudson River to New York on two ferry boats, which were packed to the rails, there being nearly two thousand officers and enlisted men on each boat. The majority were compelled to stand during the brief river trip but many relieved their aching backs by casting off their heavy packs and using these as seats. It was from the decks of our ferry boats that we obtained our first glimpse of the ship that was to take us across the broad Atlantic. All were very much impressed upon beholding the gigantic proportions of "our boat", the English White Star liner, the S. S. Olympic, as she quietly lay at anchor, towering far above all other nearby steamers. To give the reader an idea of its size, the S. S. Olympic was built as a sister ship to the ill-fated S. S. Titanic, whose immense dimensions are well known, both vessels having prominade decks measuring exactly one mile in circumference. We were all extremely happy that the voyage was to be made in a large vessel for more than one reason.

At about eight o'clock the first ferry boat landed at Pier No. 59 of the White Star Line. Shortly thereafter the other one tied up at the dock and unloaded the balance of the regiment. We then formed on the pier in the order our names appeared on the passenger lists, and as each man's name was called he responded "Here!" and marched up the gangway of the Olympic as his name was checked off the list. Thus, by eleven o'clock, our entire regiment was on board and assigned to quarters. General William Weigel, Commander of our Brigade, and his staff came on board and they were followed by two battalions of the 59th Infantry under command of Major Farrell.

The quarters aboard the Olympic for the enlisted men consisted of hammocks swung between decks. The officers, of course, were assigned to cabins - which goes without saying! The hammocks, while not quite as comfortable as the regulation army cots assigned to men in the camps, at least proved something of a real novelty to most of us and were the source of considerable amusement (when a buddy fell out) during the first night we occupied them. Our Third Battalion was very fortunate in being assigned to their section of the ship, as their particular section occupied a part of Deck "C" far above the water-line of the boat. Many of the men in other outfits had to be contented with hammocks swung just above their mess tables far down in the hold of the ship, where ventilation was very poor and conditions in general made worse on account of so many being crowded

together in such close quarters.   Hugh canvas funnels, reaching from
the upper decks down in the hold of the ship, were the only means of
conveying fresh air to the troops occupying that part of the liner.

At two o'clock, sharp, the gangway was hauled away and all men
ordered inside the ship.   At two-fifteen, the sound of the engines
and the dull throb of the ship told us that at last we were underway-
on that long anticipated voyage across the Atlantic!   Our leavetak-
ing, however, was entirely the reverse from that which the majority
of the men had mentally pictured it would be many times in the past.
No flags waved in the breeze, no bands played lively strains of music
in honor of the event, and instead of a wildly cheering multitude on
shore bidding the boys "bon voyage", the docks around our ship were
comparatively deserted, with the exception of a few embarkation officers left behind to continue their duties on Pier No. 59.   Many of
us, however, had overlooked the fact that, undoubtedly, these sailings
from America were kept a secret as far as possible owing to the fear
that German agents or sympathizers might be on the watch to post their
submarines, which at that period of the war infested the waters of the
Atlantic.   We were soon to be acquainted, however, with all the pre-
cautionary measures exercised for the protection of the troops on
board during the voyage.   All were anxious to get a "close-up" view
of the famous Statue of Liberty as we sailed out the harbor but, as
stated above, all men were ordered inside - below decks - and when we
were finally allowed to go out on deck, we could just make out that
symbol of Liberty outlined against the fast receding sky-line of New
York City.   All will recall how disappointed the men were!   It seemed
that the final stage of our journey towards "Over There" was well
underway at last!   It was a rather quiet and thoughtful lot of men
in the battalion that first night out as each man sought his hammock.
At last sailing for France!   What awaited us on the other side of
that vast stretch of sky and water?   Would we ever get to the front?
How long would it be before we returned home?   These and a thousand
similar questions presented somewhat of an obstacle to overcome before
we could close our eyes in sleep that first night out.

CHAPTER 5.

THE VOYAGE ACROSS.

An endeavor will be made to give the reader a brief account of our life aboard ship during the voyage. Time was our own to do with as we pleased, providing we did not violate certain rules and regulations soon made clear to the men. Of course, various and numerous details were organized, - such as K. P. duty (kitchen police, which covered duties in the kitchens of the ship helping the cooks prepare meals, peeling potatoes ("spuds"), washing dishes and similar culinary labor); and M. P. (Military Police), or guard duty, etc., but these assignments were all taken in turns and did not work a special hardship on any one man, with the possible exception of a few unfortunates who, on account of some act of disobedience, were compelled to pay penalties by performing extra duties. Card games were a popular pass-time but gambling for money in any of the games was strictly forbidden. More than one quiet little hand of poker or a crap-shooting affair was suddenly broken up by alert officers pouncing down on the unsuspecting participants. All were warned beforehand that they would stand the risk of their money being confiscated if caught in gambling aboard ship but the warning did not seem to have much effect. The funds thus seized went later toward rewards offered by the officers on board to winners in the numerous boxing matches staged for the amusement and benefit of all. Thus we passed the days - playing cards, reading, writing letters to the folks back home, debating on what the future had in store for us, or just lounging around, taking life easy and enjoying the sea breezes. The big steamer afforded ample space for plenty of exercise, and calisthenics usually started the day's program. Not a light of any description was allowed at night aboard ship - not even a lighted match or cigarette. Just before darkness settled upon the deep, all port-holes and decks were tightly closed and guards stationed throughout the ship to enforce orders regarding lights, or rather prohibited lights. All were forced to wear life-preservers continually during the day. We used these life-jackets for pillows at night, which recalls to mind our first night's experience sleeping in hammocks. All the men of our battalion turned in rather early that night. In fact, there was nothing else to do but to go to bed, or rather pile in hammocks. All decks were tightly closed, making our quarters so dark you could not see your hand pass before your eyes! Then the fun started! Men sleeping on the floor of the deck were stepped on by those endeavoring to climb up in their hammocks! Some fancy cursing, lots of laughter, many a tumble and some bruised joints marked the passing of our first night at sea! We slept in practically all our clothing, taking off shoes and blouses. "Abandon Ship" drills were given at least once a day and on the signal (one long blast of the steamer's whistle), the men quickly and orderly lined up to the respective life-boats previously assigned them, each group of enlisted-men being under the direct charge of an officer. A sharp lookout for submarines or floating mines was constantly kept by members of the ship's crew. Several big guns aboard were apparently ready for instant action, being manned by English sailors at all times - day and night. This last precaution probably diverted a serious mishap, as will be explained later. Considering the conditions under which this voyage was made, everything went very well with the enlisted men of the battalion except our daily meals or, to use the army term, mess. The enlisted men fared rather badly on this particular trip across as to that important item. Our food, for the most part, usually consisted of some thin concoction of water and carrots boiled together and not half seasoned. Our English cooks called it "vegetable soup". It will not do to put in print the name we soon substituted for that "vegetable soup". Both tea and coffee tasted, as many of the men complained, "like so much dish-water", little or no meat was served and we actually wanted for sufficient bread, although almost any day we could see whole loaves of bread being thrown over-board to feed the fishes, showing gross negligence somewhere. Most of the enlisted men on this voyage played havoc with their "iron rations" of hard-tack and corn beef in order to satisfy their hunger. Those in funds (and the number was very small) depended largely upon the canteens aboard ship in order to get enough to eat but even at these places the men were charged exorbitant prices for the little they got in return. In sharp contrast to this deplorable state of affairs for the enlisted men aboard, our own officers had an abundance to eat - even with the privilege of ordering what their appetites called for. Daily menus were placed at their tables! The writer, upon inquiry, was informed by a member of the ship's crew in these words: "They live like Kings", having reference, of course, to the meals served all officers. It is not in a vindictive sense at all that this little fact is mentioned in the telling of our experiences. The fault was entirely due to poor management on the part of our English crew, over whom our own officers had no jurisdiction. It is recited merely to point out in this story some of the many hardships, privations and suffering through which we passed during our services in the A. E. F.

The good ship Olympic made splendid time, being favored by a comparatively calm sea. The voyage, while uneventful to a sea-faring man in those troubled times, was full of the greatest interest to all of the doughboys and nothing escaped the watchful eyes of the men in our Third Battalion. On Thursday, the 9th, the ship began zigzagging in its course and all hands knew we must be in the danger zone. The men kept an anxious lookout for the dreaded "subs" we had heard so much about through the various newspaper accounts of the war. Some of the boys got sick from the motion of the big steamer as it zigzagged in that crazy fashion. Thursday was Ascension Day and Father Charles C. Conaty, then the Chaplain attached to the Brigade, said Mass in the Officer' Smoking Room. On Saturday morning, we were met by our escort, four American destroyers, which then kept pace with our ship, two destroyers on each side adding their protection against danger from submarines. We then realized that we were truly in the danger zone! That night most of the men had their packs made up with the expectation of landing Sunday. The exciting time, however, came about four

o'clock the next morning, at which hour we had an encounter with a
German submarine. Everyone was in quarters with life preservers on,
the life-boat guard and the watch were in their assigned places ready
to act if necessary. Immediately, however, with the greatest presence
of mind, the commander of the Olympic changed her course and succeeded
in ramming the submarine. This submarine was the German, "U-103".
Thirty-one survivors of their crew were picked up by an American des-
troyer. For further interesting details bearing upon this exciting
incident of the voyage, the following is quoted from George W. Cooper's
splendid history, "Our Second Battalion":-

"About four o'clock next morning, there was a crash and
then a shot rang out through the air, which awakened most
every man on board the ship. 'There's some excitement now,'
we all thought and exclaimed, as we jumped up and hurriedly
pulled on our clothes. In less than a minute, there was
another shot and we were sure that we were missing something
big. We ran through the corridors and up the stairs with
half our clothes on and the rest on our arms, but discovered
that we could not go out on deck. When asked what the
trouble was, the guards replied that we had rammed a submarine and that was all they knew. Seeing that we could not
go out on deck and there was no more shooting, we went back
to bed again and once more were awakened at seven o'clock
by another shot. This turned out to be one of our destroyers dropping a depth bomb. Whether or not they got a submarine, we never heard.

"A member of the crew described the ramming of the submarine by the Olympic, after the war was finished, as follows:
'It was just about four o'clock when the lookout man
picked out of the almost total darkness, the outline of a
lurking submarine, which was lying on the surface. Immediately after his warning shout, one of the forward guns
blazed out, and the ship, with her helm hard over, spun around
like a great racing yacht and crashed the enemy.
'The blow was, of course, not a clean one or there would
have been few survivors from the submarine. Judging from the
damage on the bow of the ship when dry-docked a few days later,
the blow cut off one end of the submarine. The rest drifted
past the stern of the Olympic and one of the gun crews on the
poop planted a six inch shell squarely into it. One of the
destroyers dropped behind and, by the light of star shells,
picked up 31 survivors, three of whom died on the way to port.
The total crew of the submarine was over 60.'

"Some time after the Armistice was signed, 1st Lieut.
N. J. Sepp , who had been Adjutant of the First Battalion,
wrote to Captain Hayes, who commanded the Olympic, and
received the following reply in the Captain's own hand-
writing:

"S. S. Olympic,
Southampton, March 9, 1919.

Dear Sir:

In reply to the above, the position was Lat. 49
degrees, 16 minutes N., Long. 4 degrees, 51 minutes
W. The time we rammed the German submarine - U-103 -
was 3:55 A. M., May 12th, 1918.

Yours very truly,

(Signed) Bertram F. Hayes."

"The American destroyers were just in the act of being
relieved by four English destroyers when all this occurred.
However, the American destroyers picked up the survivors
of the rammed submarine and took them to England."

The above incident will go down in history as our first victory
over the Germans! After this rather startling adventure, many felt
a genuine relief when at 7:45, the Isle of Wight was sighted in the
distance and we knew that the voyage was practically over. At 11:30
the engines stopped and we lay in the Harbor of Southampton, England,
being unable to dock on account of the low tide. The following day,
Monday, May 13th, 1918, we slowly steamed up the harbor and it was not
long before we were safely tied up at our pier. We were "Over There"
at last! Judging from personal recollections of the events of that
day and hour, it is needless to attempt to describe the feelings of
the men - only to say that all seemed to be in a most hilarious mood
as they began to disembark about two o'clock in the afternoon. On
leaving the ship, each man grabbed a barrack bag belonging to his outfit, and loaded down with these and our rifles, we made our way down
the gangway. After depositing these bags in piles on the pier, we
were lined up in company formation preparatory to boarding English
trains ready and waiting for the troops on the other side of the pier.

CHAPTER 6.

DOVER, ENGLAND.

Our Third Battalion was assigned to the first section to leave and the men were soon seated in the odd little side-door compartments of the train. We amused ourselves, while waiting to pull out, by "kidding" the little English newsboys who congregated at every car window to sell their papers. We later found out, however, that they had "kidded" us out of many a dime in good U. S. coin! Being ignorant of the prevailing rate of exchange, we paid for our newspapers many times over what they were actually worth! Those English urchins surely did reap a harvest that day! We were all amused at their style of accent and engaged them in lively conversations just to hear them talk. Our train pulled out of Southampton at about 2;30 P. M., the others following at regular intervals. By this time all knew we were bound for Dover, England, which place was reached that night after dark. Our journey aboard the queer little cars to Dover proved very pleasant and interesting. It gave us some idea of the far-famed beauty of English countrysides in the Spring of the year. We also passed through one little corner of London and were greatly amused by the sight of so many queer looking chimneys on the houses. At most every station the train passed through, there were gathered groups of English lasses on hand to give the troops a welcome. We can see them in memory today as they waved at the boys on the speeding train - rosy-cheeked country girls - the very picture of health and bubbling over with enthusiasm of youth at the arrival of "the Americans". Every precaution was exercised during our brief journey to Dover against danger from possible air raids by the Germans, which were at that time almost a nightly occurrence in that section of England. When darkness came, word was passed through the coaches not to strike matches unless the shades were drawn. Upon arrival at Dover, in assembling at the station, we were commanded to be as quiet as possible and not indulge in loud or boisterous talking, and above all, not to light matches. We found the town in total darkness and particularly noticed that every house in the place had its shutters tightly closed. The streets were comparatively deserted even at that early hour of the evening. The city, although thickly populated, seemed to us to be absolutely destitute of inhabitants as we marched through its streets. A long, steep and winding road finally brought us to our destination - English Rest Camp No. 2 - located on a high elevation overlooking the docks far below. This camp was later named "castle-on-the-hill" by the men. (We had, at last, a "castle" in England!) The section of the camp assigned to our troops consisted of a row of handsome residences which the English had converted into an "over-night" rest station to accommodate American troops enroute to France. The writer remembers toiling up three flights of stairs to a vacant room on the fourth floor in one of the buildings. If we expected beds that night, or even pallets made up on the floor, we were soon to be disappointed. But, here, we could at least relieve ourselves of the heavy packs and this, in itself, offered some consolation to the tired men. Many took out their blankets and rolled up in these for the night. All slept on the hard board floors, using their packs for pillows. At daybreak, matters took on a brighter aspect for all. We now had a chance to clean up a bit and were glad to take a chance of the opportunity thus offered. Breakfast was served in adjoining mess-tents by English war-workers (mostly women), and the boys of our Third Battalion agreed that "It wasn't so bad". All did full justice to that bread, butter, jam and tea set before them. We soon located an English canteen where cakes, hot chocolate, candy, tobacco, etc. could be bought. It was here that we were initiated into the "art" of learning the relative values of American and English currency. This, however, did not bother the greater majority of the men - who were "broke" anyway. We were just beginning to enjoy ourselves, forgetting for the time our months of hard training in camps back home, the many long hikes, first calls and other "joys" pertaining to the life of an American doughboy, when the dreaded command "Fall in!" was heard, and we were marched a short distance from camp and again reluctantly practiced "squads right" for an hour or so, much to the apparent interest of several British "Tommies" who watched the troops from a point of advantage nearby. Later on in the morning, we made the acquaintances of a number of convalescent English soldiers, who were quartered in hospitals in the vicinity of our camp. At these little gatherings, the principal topic of conversation was, of course, about the war. We listened to their many and varied stories of personal experiences with a great deal of interest not unmixed by a thrill or two. They related tales of German cruelty and treachery, hand-to-hand encounters with the enemy, stories about poisonous gas attacks, etc. These stories, in most cases, seemed true for they were told us by victims of the war who were then under treatment for having been gassed in action and by those who had lately lost a leg or an arm or two in some engagement with the enemy. We noticed, with sinking hearts, that some of these poor fellows were totally blind. Did a like fate await for us? Heretofore, we had merely heard of these things through reading newspaper and magazine articles and seeing them in the movies back home, but here was authentic information at first hand from men who had actually participated in the war! For the first time, perhaps, we fully realized just what war in all its terrible aspects meant and what we had to expect when our turn came to "go over the top"! It can be truthfully said, however, that these tales of warfare did not, apparently, lessen the enthusiasm of the men of our Third Battalion but, on the other hand, seemed rather to add to their desire to get into the thick of it and to find out for themselves something of the actual fighting. As we look back to those few hours spent in England, many of us will recall the somewhat sarcastic remarks addressed to us by several of the British "Tommies", to the effect, "What are you boys over here for? We have already won the war!" As to the truth of their statement, we certainly had our reasons later on for doubting it very much, as the following account will show!

Our stay in "Merrie Ole England" was brief. Shortly after 11 A. M., on Tuesday, the 14th, the battalion assembled, marched down the steep grade up which we had climbed the night before. We reached the docks in Dover about noon, where we literally piled into transports awaiting to convey us across the English Channel to France. The trip of twenty-one miles was uneventful but we noticed that even for this short distance we had the protection of four destroyers, two on each side of our transport. The air was damp and chilly, in other words - a condition of the climate quite frequent in that part of the country. We later often had cause to question the truth of that well-known phrase, "Sunny France!" However, the men out on the decks wore their overcoats during the trip. Their less fortunate comrades, packed together like so many sardines on the inside of the transport, did not object to the weather being a bit cold.

The first contingent of US troops arrived at Saint-Nazaire in France June 26, 1917. Lieutenant General John Joseph "Black Jack" Pershing, Commander-in-Chief of the American Expeditionary Forces (AEF), greeted the 14,000 infantrymen as they stepped ashore, declaring:

"They are sturdy rookies – we shall make great soldiers of them."

More than two million American soldiers would serve in WWI, 50,000 of whom would die in battle.

Above and left:
American troops arriving in France.
(Images courtesy of
National Archives)

Right:

The Quai Maritime At Calais.

At 2:45pm on May 14, a company of the 111th was the first of the Twenty-eighth Division to land at the docks opposite the Hotel de Chemin de Fer du Nord, in Calais. All the American troops were loaded at this port.

Image from
Pennsylvania in the World War: An Illustrated History of the Twenty-Eighth Division, Vol. 2, p. 500

CHAPTER 7.

CALAIS, FRANCE.

We reached the docks at Calais, France, at about 3:30 P. M. and upon landing, the first tangible evidence of those Boche air raids, about which we had lately heard so much talk, presented itself. A large building nearby, which at one time had been a hotel, was now in complete ruins. During our subsequent march through the town, we passed by building after building, each bearing marks of previous air raids. These scenes only served as mute reminders of one of the horrors of modern warfare and the terrible suffering it was inflicting on the peaceful civilians of France in towns miles away from the theater of war.

By four o'clock the entire regiment was assembled and we began our march through the streets of Calais, which took about an hour. Groups of ragged children - French and Belgium - were continually at our heels, begging for "souvenirs", tobacco, candy and chewing gum. In most cases, the extent of their English vocabulary consisted of but two words, - "Souvenir, Mister? - which meant anything we had to give them. Small boys were delighted on being handed American cigarettes and the little girls were equally pleased with a stick or two of "Wrigley's". We noticed, particularly, the great number of women wearing deep mourning, both here and on the streets of Dover, which offered additional evidence to what extent these townspeople had suffered through the loss of their dear ones in the war. Indeed, the first thing we saw while still aboard the transports was a military funeral slowly wending its way along a street near the docks. All in the procession were walking - a French custom - everyone but the corpse! Our our march, we passed by various prison camps maintained by the English and French and got our first glimpse of captive German soldiers, also many other different types of nationalities held at Calais by the Allies. All these sights proved intensely interesting and the men soon forgot the discomforture of "heavy marching order". At times our English friends, who accompanied us in some numbers, came to our assistance with words of advice and information in answer to the many questions we "fired" at them. One of our boys, who seemed anxious to get some first-hand information about the town, earnestly inquired of an English Sergeant, - "Say, buddie, do the Germans bombard this place much?" In reply, the Sergeant curtly said, "Wait and see"! In the matter of a very few hours we understood just what he meant!

Finally, our destination, English Rest Camp No. 6, was reached. "Rest Camp" was in the name only, as will be seen by a brief account of the battalion's sojourn at this place. Here, we were assigned to squad tents but instead of the time-honored army custom of putting eight men in a tent of this character, fifteen men, fifteen packs and fifteen rifles were housed under one small canvas! Imagine, dear reader, fifteen men with equipment in quarters originally intended for only eight men, and you will have some idea of our "hotel accommodations" on that, our very first night in France! So, right at the start, the words "Rest Camp" had the boys guessing - particularly on that word "Rest"! To offer some protection against pieces of flying shrapnel from exploding shells in case of an air raid on the camp, each tent was pitched over a "dugout" about three or four feet deep, and consequently stretching space was impossible for the men inside. So, at Calais, we had our first experiences with dugouts and while they were the target for many an oath that night (they seemed so unnecessary), later on in the evening we were only too glad to have these holes to crawl into!

Supper was soon ready in a large mess hall in the camp which accommodated several companies at a time. After our water trip and hike, we were not slow in answering mess call that evening and soon cleared off the tables and were clamoring for "seconds". It was not long after mess and we were back to our tents just about ready to "turn in" for the night, when our attention was attracted to the firing of a large field piece in camp and the sound of numerous bells and whistles in the City of Calais. During a lull in the firing of the cannon, we distinctly heard a peculiar noise resembling the swarming of millions of bees. This humming sound came from afar up in the air, seemingly right over our heads! Gradually, the sound got louder and louder and we then recognized the buzz of many aeroplane motors. At that time, we had not learned to distinguish, by sound, that now familiar humming of German planes, so consequently it was some minutes before we fully realized what was happening. At last it dawned upon every man - the Germans were coming over on one of their nightly air raids! The bells, whistles and the firing of that cannon had been signals to warn the citizens of Calais to seek refuge in their bomb-proof cellars! The men in camp were soon commanded to get "under cover" in their tents. We waited, with considerable excitement, the outcome of this new and startling adventure! Being located just outside of Calais and somewhat on an elevation, we had a fine view of the attack from the sky on the city, this being our first insight into this feature of Jerry's (as we called the Germans) method of carrying the war into the enemy's camp. The allied troops stationed in Calais and in our camp threw powerful searchlight rays on the German planes and when one was "framed", that is, exposed to view, we could hear the barrage from the "Archies" or antiaircraft guns barking away in an endeavor to bring a "Jerry" down to earth or to place a "fence" of bullets around him to prevent his advance over the town. This raid lasted for several hours that night. No bombs were dropped in the vicinity of our camp but while the planes were soaring over our heads, we expected any moment to receive one of Jerry's "calling cards", as some of the boys named them. Again, on Wednesday night, about the same hour, we were under another air raid. This time matters looked a little more serious. Several bombs were dropped so close to us that we could feel the earth shake. Frequently we noticed that shrapnel hit in our camp. This caused many of the men to crawl into their tents for some protection and to adorn their steel helmets for use at last! No casualties were reported among our troops. We learned later, however, that on the very next evening after we had vacated our camp near Calais, the Germans dropped a number of bombs into the area we had occupied, killing about twelve Chinamen who were being held there by the French.

Our brief stay near Calais was taken up, for the most part, in discarding all extra equipment and getting "stripped" of all surplus clothing preparatory to going into the interior of France - "up where the fun starts", as the men put it. So, on Thursday, we parted company with our barrack bags. Not a soldier regretted this in the least, as these bags were heavy and rather cumbersome to carry, especially when loaded with odds and ends of clothing and equipment. Several of the men happened to possess an extra pair of shoes and being in need of ready cash and not caring to carry the shoes further, sold them to the Chinese who daily visited our camp. These poorly-clad fellows seemed glad to get our heavy American hob-nails and paid anywhere from five to ten francs for a pair. Our section of the camp was continually crowded with ragged Belgium children of all ages and they quickly snatched up all discarded clothing and articles thrown aside by the men. On numerous occasions, when our backs were turned, they did not always confine their efforts solely to the rubbish piles! Indeed, we had to constantly keep a sharp lookout over our belongings and the men often remarked, "Nothing is safe unless nailed down." The writer remembers one little Belgium girl (a pretty little thing) who, when given a box of face powder, poured the entire contents out and proceeded to "powder up" until she was literally covered from head to feet. The envy of her companions was apparent! The men who were in funds (the number, by the way, was very few) had their American currency exchanged for Francs. A nearby canteen, maintained by the English and French, was usually the center of attraction during the intervals of the many commands to "fall in" for inspection or various other formations. Some, inclined to be more adventuresome than others, even managed to successfully engineer several excursions to the City of Calais, where their field for diversion was considerably broadened! On Thursday afternoon, the battalion marched to an English training camp, a distance of about four miles, where we were equipped with gas masks. It was here that many of the men had their first lesson in the quick and proper adjustment of these masks. Later, every man had to enter a gas chamber in order to test his new acquisition! Frequent drills with these masks were given at various times in order to prepare the men for possible gas attacks. On the way back to camp, we stopped at a Supply Base, where we turned in our rifles and ammunition and were issued fire arms and shells of English make. All will doubtless recall that hot afternoon's hike, terminating in being presented with a rifle full of grease which had to be thoroughly cleaned for an inspection scheduled in the near future!

FRONT AND BACK VIEW OF AN AMERICAN INFANTRYMAN, COMPLETELY EQUIPPED FROM HEAD TO FOOT AND READY FOR ACTION.

(Committee on Public Information.)

CHAPTER 8.

ON TO JOURNY.

At last orders came to "strike camp" and on Friday, the 17th, we fell in at 8:45 A. M. and at 9:30, the march to the railroad station began. The day was exceedingly warm and the march a long one through the burning rays of the morning's sun. As usual, heavy marching order was the style - each man carrying a pack weighing between 70 and 80 pounds, besides being burdoned with an overcoat and, of course, his rifle and gas mask. We had by this time taken off our summer underwear and put on woolens, as well as wool socks. We regretted this change more than once that warm Spring morning! The route took us back again through the streets of Calais and frequent stops were made along the way. These short "breathing spells" afforded great relief for the perspiring men. During the intervals the long column was resting, the people of the town came to our aid with wet towels to wipe perspiring faces, cool drinks and refreshments, and did everything possible to relieve the men from the effects of this fatiguing march. Reaching the railroad station at last, we deposited our packs on the ground and ran to a nearby canteen where we were served with sandwiches and a cup of tea preparatory to our journey via rail. (This bountiful repast was intended to include both dinner and supper.) Our so-called "mess" soon being over and seeing no possible chance for "seconds", we hurried back to our packs just in time to be counted off and assigned to our respective "Pullmans". And, here, a new experience awaited - that of travelling in the French box or freight cars! This method of conveyance, we soon learned, was a very popular one "Over There", especially in transporting soldiers of the A. E. F. from one place to another through France. We not only had to endure the usual filth, smell and dirt in these cars but, nearly everytime, were packed in like so many cattle being shipped to market. These cars were just about one-third the size of a standard American freight car, and on the sides of each was marked its capacity in French - "Chevaux 8, Hommes 40", meaning, of course, that the car could accommodate eight horses or forty men. (Most of these cars bore unmistakable evidence of having transported more Chevaux than Hommes!) In those days, it apparently made no difference to the railroad company who was to occupy these cars and because one set of passengers had recently ridden in them, did not, in the French mind, interfer with the cars being used by another and perhaps more discriminate set! On this particular trip, as was the case many times thereafter, fifty or sixty men with their packs, rifles and gas masks were assigned to each car. On the longer trips, it was consequently impossible to sleep with any comfort under these conditions. Indeed, at nights during the period of the war when we always travelled in total darkness, one considered himself lucky to get through the whole trip without being trampled on, or to have sufficient room to move a leg without hearing a loud pro-

Fifth Marines on way to training field, June 1917. Their first ride in the now famous "Hommes 40, Chevaux 8" (40 men or 8 horses).
In these "side door Pullmans" our soldiers traveled wherever they went, except at the front. Then they "hiked" or rode in trucks.
The "Hommes 40, Chevaux 8" furnished many of the famous jokes of the A.E.F.

Typical billet for American soldiers in France. 77th Division, Nordluinghem, France May 1918
(Images courtesy of National Archives)

test, generally in the nature of a healthy curse, from some molested neighbor who had probably received a kick in the stomach or face!

Shortly after twelve o'clock, we were on our way. Every man on the train, not previously informed, wondered where we were bound for this time. Some expressed their thoughts by lustily singing, "Where do we go from here, boys, where do we go from here?" - that well remembered refrain, the words of which many will recall as being so intimately associated with those days of uncertainty "Over There". Our train ride, which we were just beginning to really enjoy notwithstanding the conditions mentioned above, was not a long one. After passing through St. Omer, we reached Lumbres about 2:30 P. M., at which place we detrained. As some of the men expressed it - "the infantry had to live up to traditions by hiking it and it would never do to break that steadfast rule!" And "hike it", we did! This particular march, while not the longest in our many subsequent hikes via hobnails over French roads, was undoubtedly the hardest and most fatiguing one ever attempted, unaccustomed as we then were in being compelled to carry such heavy equipment, besides burdoned with over-coats and wearing garments entirely too heavy for that season of the year. Although frequent haults were made, many of the men were forced by sheer exhaustion to "fall out", taking chances on rejoining the column later. Others lightened their loads by slyly throwing away some of their equipment. A few even dropped their over-coats along the sides of the road, being careful, however, not to be caught in the act. When we reached the little village of Seningham about six o'clock in the evening, not more than 25 per cent. of the entire regiment was still in line. Here, billets were ready for us but, upon inspection, we found them so filthy and uninviting we decided, almost to a man, not to occupy them. Instead, we camped out in the open that night, not even taking the time or trouble to pitch shelter tents. We were already beginning to "rough it" and many will never forget those early experiences in France before we had become really hardened to them. After we were peacefully settled for the night and all was quiet, except perhaps an occasional disturbance caused by late arrivals trudging in to rejoin their companies, those of us who had not fallen asleep could hear in that still night air a distant and continual rumbling sound resembling the approach of a thunder storm - still very far away. Occasionally, we could make out quick flashes - like lightning - far away on the horizon. Some of the boys remarked that we were in for a storm. We were, but not the kind of a storm they had reference to that night. That rumbling noise we heard and the flashes we saw were made by the big guns up there on the Line! We were slowly but surely "getting there", as many no doubt realized that night while resting in the open, listening to that firing and contemplating on the future.

The next morning at 10:45, we resumed our march, somewhat refreshed by a night's rest but many still foot-sore and with aching backs from the previous day's hike. At noon, greatly to the relief of all, we were ordered to leave our packs in piles on the side of the road, to be picked up later by trucks which would convey them to our destination. This order was not issued any too soon for by this time our ranks had dwindled down to a comparatively few who still laboriously hung on.

Minus our heavy packs, the remaining few miles were soon covered.
About the middle of the afternoon found the regiment in the vicinity
of its permanent billeting area. We now divided, each battalion
marching to its respective camp site. Regimental Headquarters, with
Headquarters Company and Supply Company, was stationed at Alquines;
the First Battalion in Bouvelinghem; the Second Battalion in Haut
Loquin and Bas Loquin; and our Third Battalion found billets in
Journy. Our Machine Gun Company, along with others of the Division,
was stationed at Le Wast, these organizations being temporarily detached from their respective regiments and occupying training area
at one place.

CHAPTER 9.

IN TRAINING AT JOURNY.

It was around the middle of the afternoon on Saturday, May 18th, when our tired Third Battalion marched, or rather staggered, into the town of Journy. As we spent quite some time here, it might be well to relate a few of the many experiences through which we passed while quartered in this little roadside French village. It was at Journy that we gained our very first knowledge of that famous and much abused institution - the French billet! Under the French military law at that time, all barns, out-houses, stables, etc., the property of citizens, were taken over by the Government for the purpose of housing, or billeting, soldiers of the Allied Armies. (it seemed that the French preferred these filthy quarters - just so it was a building - rather than housing their soldiers in clean and sanitary tents.) It was undoubtedly at Journy that we acquired our first cootie, but we shall go into that later! So, upon our arrival at the village, the enlisted men of the battalion were immediately assigned to the various barns, stables, etc. scattered throughout the place. The officers, of course, were billeted in style, occupying dwelling houses of the inhabitants. The man who drew a stall in one of these stables considered himself lucky indeed, especially if the said stall happened to contain a good supply of hay or straw! It was no unusual incident for the original tenant of the premises, an old horse or cow, to wander home during the wee small hours of the morning only to discover his bed occupied by a sleeping doughboy! The result, we shall leave to the reader's imagination! Thus, stables were our homes for the three ensuing weeks - weeks of hard training with the British, under the supervision of Lieut. Colonel Stephenson, 16th Royal Scots. During these weeks, we had plenty of opportunities to observe and come into close contact with the famous British "Tommie", the Scotch "Kiltie" and last but not least, that grandest institution of the entire British Army - we refer to the "Sergeant Myger"! Who shall forget him? But we are anticipating a little in relating events at Journy as they occurred.

We had just about recuperated from the effects of our hike and had not enjoyed many days of leisure in which to inspect the little village of Journy and its environments when the entire battalion started its daily schedule of drill. Our drill field was located some two and one-half miles from camp which, of course, necessitated a daily hike of about five miles. The training schedule followed was rather a strenuous one, consisting of close and extended order drilling, bayonet practice, hand grenade throwing, instructions in the use of the British rifles, gas masks, etc. In the latter, we were drilled most thoroughly, even practicing digging trenches while wearing the darn things - a most trying and difficult ordeal, as any

American non-commissioned officers practice bayonet training in France in 1918. These men, having been taught by French soldiers before them, would then go back to their companies in order to train their fellow Soldiers.

Hand grenade training, showing different positions.
2d Bn., 329th Inf. (1st week) Le Manns, Sarthe, France. October 3, 1918
(Images courtesy of National Archives)

Above: Gas mask drill showing different movements in adjusting respirator. 2nd Battalion, 329th Infantry LeManns, Sarthe, France October 1918.

Below: American 77th Division receiving instruction in camouflage from the British instructor at Moulle, 22 May 1918.

(Images Courtesy of National Archives)

doughboy who has had this experience can readily testify! The art of handling and throwing those deadly hand grenades, with safety to ourselves and neighbors, was not exactly a parlor game, either! Woe to the unfortunate soldier if he should accidently drop his grenade after the pin was pulled! It would be just too bad - for the soldier and others standing near! The writer was always glad when that part of the drill period was over and, it is presumed, this goes for all the men. Later, we had a chance to "try out" our British rifles on a nearby rifle-range under the guidance of specially trained Sergeants of His Majesty's army. (These rifles were subsequently turned in and the U. S. Model 1917 issued in lieu thereof.) Also, we were one day invited to witness an exhibition drill given for our special benefit by a crack company of Britishers. The above conveys in brief form a general idea of our training program which was maintained, with little variation, from day to day. While on the subject of our drill schedule at Journy, we do not want to forget to tell about that "bright" doughboy - every company had one - who filled his pack with straw instead of the required blankets before his company marched to the drill field! The trick worked fine until caught "red-handed" in an unexpected field inspection! Who can forget how glad we all were to rest our tired and perspiring bodies under the shade of those ancient trees which completely walled-in our drill field! We wish to recall, too, those marches back to our billets, after the day's drilling was over - how we kept in step to the swinging tune of "Mademoiselle from Armentiers", sung with "a slight change" in the wording! Any doughboy will understand! With a regular daily drill schedule, the men were kept so busy that they had very little time to think about their troubles - real or imaginary.

Speaking about troubles, however, here we experienced a very real and serious one which affected every man, namely, the old complaint of ration shortage. It seemed that our Mess Sergeants depended upon the British for their supply of food and for some unaccountable reason were never able to draw the requisite amount. In fact, although each company of the battalion should have been allotted a supply sufficient to feed 250 hungry men, at many times our Mess Sergeants were up against the proposition of endeavoring to manage somehow on half-rations, that is, just food enough for about 100 men, which was even less than being on half-rations. After a scanty breakfast usually consisting of one small slice of bacon, bread cut so thin one could almost see through the slices, maybe some rice or prunes and a cup of black coffee, we were handed our mid-day lunch to be carried to the drill field, the distance being too great for the companies to come in each day for noon mess. (It might be mentioned that the one small can of "corn-willie" and a few "hardtacks" carried by each squad of eight men as their noonday mess did not add material weight to the usual equipment.) Then came the march, up one long hill and down the next, to our training area, followed by a hard morning's drill, after which we were allowed about half an hour for the so-called "mess" before resuming our afternoon's work. Recall generally sounded about 3:30 P. M., a signal most welcome to the tired and hungry men. Then, another hike back to our billets, where our cooks had prepared a meager supper owing to the usual shortage of food supplies. Who can remember those days when, on

Members of Company K, 111th Infantry, 28th Division, inspecting British rifles given them in exchange for their Springfield Model, Calais Pas de Calais, France. May 19, 1918.

Bayonet practice
(Images courtesy of National Archives)

coming in from a day's hard work on the drill field, we would almost
immediately "fall in" for mess, often not even taking the time to put
our equipment away?   Daily, it seemed to be a race to see who would
be first in the mess line!   Then came the problem of trying to ap-
pease our hardy appetites with a small allowance of "slum" (army stew),
a meager portion of bread, or in lieu thereof, some more "hardtacks",
and washing the whole down with a cup of that mysterious mixture we
called "coffee" for want of a better name.   In order to be on hand
for "seconds", many of the men upon receiving their first portion of
food would take their places at the end of the mess line, moving up
and eating at the same time until their turn again came to be served.
This performance was rather inconvenient but we felt full compensated
on receiving a second helping of grub.   There were times, however,
when we were just too late - arriving at the head of the line only to
see the last of the coveted "seconds" being carried away by the man
right ahead of us!   We can all recall those mealtimes at old Journy-
how we used to scramble to be first in line, how we contrived to
"reserve" our respective places by putting our mess-kits in line on
the ground, the general uproar ensuing from those in the rear of the
line when an over-zealous "buck" private would attempt to steal a
position well up front, and, particularly, the shortage of rations and
the various schemes resorted to by some in order to get, at mess, more
than was their rightful share.   This was successfully accomplished
sometimes by hurriedly eating our food, after which we would carefully
wash and dry our mess-kits and then "fall in" line again as though we
had not received our first helping.   If not tried too often, this
plan sometimes worked, providing, of course, one was not betrayed by
a supposed comrade!

All this reminds the writer of an incident which occurred at
Journy having a direct bearing on the subject under discussion - food,
or rather, the shortage of food.   It seemed that an enlisted man, a
member of one of the companies in our battalion, had broken into a
peasant's garden in the village and there appropriated some vegetables,
probably with the intention of being his own cook and Mess Sergeant,
thereby assuring himself of plenty to eat at least for one meal.   He
was caught in the act, his arrest followed, and as a punishment, at
Retreat that day was ordered tied to a tree on our parade grounds and
the entire Battalion invited over to witness the performance, which
was probably staged, not only for the humiliation and punishment of
the guilty man, but also as an object lesson or warning to the rest of
the men.   I might emphasize, however, that our sympathies were entirely with the prisoner and that not many relished the idea of further adding to their comrade's distress - no doubt realizing that they
would have done likewise if the chance had presented itself and if
pressed hard enough by the demands of an empty stomach.   In any event,
"object lesson" or not, this incident apparently was but a passing occurrence which did not have its desired effect, as subsequently many
were the complaints brought into Headquarters of plundered gardens,
stolen eggs, chickens mysteriously missing, etc.   Before the story is
concluded, however, it is the desire of the writer to quote from a
letter bearing on the matter which he received from Captain Robert M.
Keogh, formerly the commander of Company L, 111th Infantry, which
reads, in part, as follows:

"That part of your story relating to the
tying of the man to the tree, at Journy, amused
me.   The man referred to is Private Lester M.
Carson, Company L, 111th Inf. and he was tied
by my orders.   Later, Carson came back strong
and it was with great pleasure I recommended
him for a D. S. C., a decoration that was later
bestowed on him.   The punishment meted out to
Carson seemed to be very severe but when one
considers that we were preparing for a hard
game in which self had to be forgotten, it was
necessary to enforce rigorous discipline during
this preparation.   However, much as I disliked
to impose the punishment, I sincerely believe
that punishment was responsible for Lester
Carson winning that honor."

From the above, the reader will glean an idea of some of the many
hardships through which we passed in preparing for the big game ahead,
all of which were taken as part of the day's work and quickly forgotten in the exciting times which soon followed.   Perhaps, however this
is a rather broad statement to make if we take into consideration the
annoying presence of that little insect, so prevalent in France, com-
monly known as the "cootie", which put in its first appearance at
Journy and which remained our "bosom companion" for almost the balance
of our sojourn in its native clime.   Further references regarding
this pest will be found in the pages to follow.

Now that we have disposed of some of the disagreeable features of
our first camp life in France, an endeavor will be made to throw some
light on the brighter side and relate, in as brief a manner as possible,
a few of the happenings which helped in a measure to counter-balance
the bad.

On Sundays, of course, all training activity ceased and the men
given an opportunity to rest from their labors and to spend the day as
they desired.   Many improved their time by washing soiled shirts,
socks and underwear, or in trying to mend their torn garments. A few
sought nearby streams which afforded somewhat primitive facilities for
bathing but which answered all purposes.   Others, not so fastidious
as to their personal appearances but with a love for possible adventure,
found pleasure in taking long walks and in exploring the surrounding
country.   Some, who were in funds, visited a British canteen located
about five miles from Journy, bringing back supplies of tobacco, cakes
and bars of "Chocolat Menier" - that famous candy the advertisement
signs of which are to be seen all over France.   The writer recalls,
with a smile, the events of one beautiful Sunday morning when, accompanied by several comrades, he cheerfully hiked the whole ten miles
in order to lay in a supply of cigarettes and candy!   A real problem,
however, presented itself for solution on my arrival back to camp!
Where could I safely store my packages of cigarettes for future con-
sumption?   I knew that it would never do to leave them in the stable
where I was billeted, that is, if I wanted them to last for a reason-
able length of time.   Too many smokers around me were perpetually

broke to take that chance! Then, an idea dawned upon me! I walked over to the farm house nearby and rapped on the front door. The madam of the place answered my summons and then the fun started! I endeavored, by many gestures and contortions, to make her understand what I wanted. At first she seemed to be under the impression that I was making her a present of the packages of cigarettes! Finally, after much palavering, I succeeded in entering the front room of the house. There, by the door, I saw a row of shelves, on which I placed my cigarettes, showing her two packs which I put in my pocket. Much to my relief, she seemed to understand at last what I wanted. From that time on, until we finally left Journy, when I ran out of smokes, I would go over to see my "hostess" for a fresh supply! Fortunately, for me, the men folks of that household were in the war, otherwise I have my doubts whether the cigarettes would have been there on my subsequent visits! The madam evidently didn't smoke! The more religious attended meetings in the little village church, where services were conducted by our Chaplain. Journy did not boast of many pretty mademoiselles, hence any enjoyment we might have derived in the society of the fair sex was somewhat curtailed.

Thursday, May 30th, was Decoration Day in the States and likewise declared a holiday for the many thousands of Americans "Over There", unless we except our comrades who were at that time answering the call of duty on the borders of "No Man's Land" where, as the men of our Third Battalion soon learned, holidays were unknown. Many took advantage of a beautiful day and visited nearby towns, while others merely contented themselves by resting under the shade trees on the village green where, all day, groups of men could be seen swapping rumors, playing cards, "shooting" craps, and a few writing that long-delayed letter to the folks at home. We were informed that General Pershing would probably pass through the village on a tour of inspection, - consequently our day "at ease" was somewhat spoiled by an order which compelled every man venturing forth from the confines of his stable home to wear his heavy blouse. This, in itself, was quite a sacrifice for the men to make, as the weather that day was exceedingly warm. Later, after we had suffered this discomforture for most of the day, it was found unnecessary in that the General did not reach our billeting area, only getting as far as Brigade Headquarters.

About this time, we received our first mail from the United States, which will always be remembered as an outstanding event of great importance. On this particular occasion joy was especially rampant among the eager recipients of mail as many had not heard from home in weeks. Most of this first mail was addressed to us at either Camp Hancock or Camp Upton and had been forwarded in care of the A. E. F. A word or two at this point in our story regarding letters written by the men to their folks at home will not go amiss. All out-going mail was strictly censored by officers assigned to that duty. We were cautioned in writing them not to mention the position of troops, names of places, or anything having a bearing, directly or indirectly, on the movements in France of either our own companies or of others. In relating, then, where we were, the words "somewhere in France" frequently supplied the very vague information as to our exact locality - hence the origin of that famous war-time expression! On the upper right-

hand corner of all envelopes containing letters we would write,
"Soldiers' Mail" in lieu of attaching stamps. These letters were
then collected, unsealed, and turned into the company's office for
inspection. Here, with a letter in one hand and a pair of scissors
in the other, the censor officer would proceed to perform his task
most thoroughly by simply cutting out objectionable words or phrases -
quite effective, one must admit, but having its disadvantages (to the
writer and recipient) if a censored letter happened to be written on
both sides of one sheet of paper, as was often the case!

But the day on which we received our first mail was almost forgotten in the joy of the troops when "pay day" arrived, about June 4th.
Many up to this time had been greatly handicapped in not being in funds
and therefore unable to even purchase food on the days when our mess
was unusually light. Now, on being paid at the rate of about five
and one-half francs to an American dollar, every man felt like a
capitalist and matters, in general, seemed to take on a brighter
aspect for all. Those large and thin French paper francs, so different in appearance from American paper money, were the butt of many
jokes and "wise cracks" from the men. Some called them "wall paper"
and one man insisted that a thousand-franc note would make excellent
toilet paper! A little wine-shop, or cafe', located just across the
road from the quarters occupied by the fourth platoon of Company I,
was now the center of attraction. In fact, one of our principal associations connected with our stay in Journy will always be remembered
as that little bar presided over by a jolly mademoiselle whom the boys
called "Jennie". It was over Jennie's bar that many learned to distinguish between "vin rouge" and "vin blanc" with disastrous results
in one or two instances! The little village contained only about
three places which, for want of a better name, the man called "stores".
A "store" was usually maintained in the front room of some small dwelling and managed by the madam of the house who, as a rule, seemed to
think that all Americans were millionaires, judging from the prices
usually asked. In those days, we did not think anything of paying
about five francs (nearly a dollar in American money) for a handful
of nuts or a few dried figs and considered ourselves lucky at that if
half of our purchase was fit to eat! Nearby farms found a ready
market among the soldiers for eggs and milk. Bread, however, was
very difficult to purchase, the French inhabitants themselves being
limited to a supply sufficient only for their family needs. We
noticed that the French peasants bought their bread by a system of
tickets issued by the Government.

On Wednesday night, June 5th, almost the entire Third Battalion,
in groups of three or four, wended their way to Alquines, a distance
of about three-fourths of a kilometer, where an entertainment was
staged in the village square, opposite the church, in which men from
our regiment and the Royal Scots participated. Singing, reciting,
jigging, dancing, the playing on bag-pipes and pieces rendered by our
regimental band, as well as by the Scottish orchestra, were greatly
enjoyed by all. For the time at least, we almost forgot that there
was such a thing as a war going on, except when reminded of the fact
by that incessant roar of artillery which could be plainly heard at
all times and which seemed never to cease!

Thus, at Journy, we had our first real test of campaigning under conditions as they existed at that time in France. Later, these experiences were to become commonplace indeed, but at that time each passing event was a novelty in itself.

As we afterwards learned, from bitter experience, orders to pack up and move often came very unexpectedly in the Army, especially in times of war! So, on the following Saturday, June 8th, we received word that the battalion would evacuate Journy the next day, Sunday morning, the 9th, and to at once make preparations for departure. Where to? Well, no one seemed to know, that is, speaking for the enlisted men. Saturday afternoon was mostly occupied by a hike to Alquines, at which town we turned in our English rifles and ammunition and drew the U. S. rifle Model 1917 and the necessary ammunition. When the battalion returned to Journy, every man wondered "What was up?" Perhaps profiting by our past performance in carrying such heavy equipment on long marches, orders were received from Headquarters directing the men to roll an extra pack containing one blanket, an overcoat and an extra pair of shoes. These packs, we were informed, would be conveyed by trucks to our destination. Needless to add, this order was obeyed with alacrity, for all had by this time learned to know just what difference a few pounds less meant on long hikes!

CHAPTER 10.

IN THE VICINITY OF ANVIN.

Bright and early Sunday morning, June 9th, found our Third Battalion ready to move off at the appointed time. As the writer remembers, it was about 9 o'clock before the long column marched out of Journy. We passed through Alquines and then up the long hill to Harlettes, where we were joined by the balance of the regiment. Leaving Harlettes, our line of march took us through Coulomby and Neilles, at which latter place Division Headquarters had been located. General Muir and Staff reviewed us as we passed through the town. It was almost noon when we marched in review at Neilles. The day promised to be a warm one and some of the men already showed signs of fatigue. We marched twenty minutes and rested ten minutes out of every half-hour. This schedule was maintained during the whole journey. The entire hike consumed three days and we passed through many towns, large and small, on the way. Perhaps some of my comrades may recall a few: Waudringhem, Drionenville, Gloquant, Merck, St. Martin, Fauquembergues, Fruges, Lugy, Heyecques, Lisbourg, Equire and Bergueneuse. As a matter of historical interest, Regimental Headquarters was in Thiembronne the night of June 9-10; during the night of June 10-11, at Lisbourg, arriving in Anvin at 1:20 P. M., June 11th, and bivouacking there on the outskirts of that town. At about 4 o'clock in the afternoon of June 11th, our Third Battalion reached its destination, - an open field, situated about one mile from the little town of Anvin. Thus, another hike was at last finished. On account of lighter packs and the frequent rest periods along the way, the men managed to keep up in much better shape than they did on the march to Journy. The weather, during the time we were on the road, was somewhat inclement. In fact, it rained part of the time and slickers had to be worn. (Speaking of slickers, the United States Government certainly had "one put over" on them during the war by the manufacturers of these so-called army "rain-coats - at least the quality issued to the enlisted men! Instead of the water running off these slickers, it would soon soak in through the inferior goods, and after a man had been exposed to the elements for a few minutes, he was literally soaked to the skin! "Slickers!" They were probably named after the slickers who soaked Uncle Sam!)

On being assigned to our section of the field, shelter tents were pitched and the men prepared for a much-needed rest, the duration of which, however, none in the ranks could tell. The infantry companies of our regiment were now encamped in the same area, the First and Second Battalions on one side of a stream which divided the field, and our Third Battalion on the other. Our tents had not been up for more than an hour when, on account of enemy aerial activities in the vicinity, we were ordered to immediately take them down and to re-pitch them under cover of the nearby trees. This command was soon executed but not without much grumbling on the part of some who had just made themselves "at home", so to speak. Before the afternoon was over many had already bathed in the cool and inviting waters of the stream, and during our brief stay here, nearly every man grasped this rare opportunity for a refreshing plunge, not knowing when another chance would present itself. Facilities were also available for shower baths and the men lost no time in obeying orders to use them. Indeed, the men of the entire Third Battalion, with the exception of a few shirkers, devoted more or less attention to their bodily cleanliness during the few hours we were located in this ideal camp spot. Each organization had its "Company barber", usually some self-appointed comrade possessing the requisite tools of that trade serving in the capacity. His qualification as a tonsorial artist, in the majority of cases, apparently was a secondary requisite in the position to which he aspired, judging from the rather crude results of his handi- work! These men, at this time, reaped a harvest of francs and al- ways had a long waiting list of prospective customers "next" in line for a haircut or shave. The flaps to most "pup" tents throughout the entire battalion were drawn unusually early that evening and nothing occurred during our night's bivouac to disturb our much needed rest and slumber. The next day, we continued our activities with soap and water. We also oiled and thoroughly cleaned the barrels of our rifles and went over the balance of our equipment. Another de- livery of mail from the States helped to vary the monotony of our second day's encampment. Many found time in which to reply to let- ters received that day.

CHAPTER 11.

AT LE THILLAY, NEAR PARIS.

The men of our Third Battalion thoroughly enjoyed themselves
while encamped on such an ideal locality.   The stream, the lovely
green grass of early Summer and the cooling shade of the bordering
forest were all "just too good to last" as some expressed it.   And
every man knew it to be true!   So, we were not at all surprised
when, at 9:20 P. M., June 12th, the first organizations of the regiment began entraining, the first train leaving the station at Anvin
at 12:27 A. M., June 13th, - others following thereafter at regular
intervals, two companies to a train.   On Thursday, the 13th, the
exact hour of the day no record is at present available, the tents of
our Third Battalion were down, packs rolled, and the short march into
the town of Anvin had begun.   Here, we found our "parlor cars", the
familiar "Chevaux 8, Hommes 40", waiting for us, and it was not long
before the entire battalion was aboard, all by their hilarious actions
seeming glad to be once again "on the move".   We had been informed that
this particular trip via rail would be a rather lengthy one, and consequently every man endeavored to make himself as comfortable as possible under the usual trying travelling conditions.   No attempt will
be made to go into details concerning the journey other than to state
that, as previously experienced, the cars were small, some of them
extremely old and dilapidated, and all the coaches were filthy with
peculiar odors not exactly enjoyable.   Sufficient space, per man, was,
of course, not a redeeming feature of the trip!

The following day we passed through the suburbs of Paris and obtained our first glimpse of the famous Eifel Tower, which could be
seen in the distance as we slowly threaded our way through a maze of
railroad tracks.   Not long thereafter, our train came to a stop and
by this time we were prepared to obey the command, "All out!", which
was shorly heard.   Our destination proved to be Le Raincy, a few
miles east of Paris.   We arrived here 9 A. M., Friday, the 14th.
Then followed another hike, taking us through Les Pavillons, Boudy,
de P8d Aulnay, les Alouettes, Drancy, 6it out and La Courneuve, terminating at Le Thallay, a town of some size, which place we reached
on the afternoon of Saturday, the 15th.   Some of the other towns we
passed through on this march were Le Bourget, Dugny, Garges and
Bonneuil.   In Le Thillay, as in Journy, the Third Battalion, along
with Regimental Headquarters, Headquarters Company and our Supply
Company, were quartered in billets throughout the town, and all agreed
that our accommodations were, in most instnces, decidedly an improve-
ment in comparison to those which Journy afforded.   (It may be mentioned here, as a matter of record, that during the time our Third Battalion occupied Le Thalley, the First Battalion occupied Bonneuil; the

Second Battalion, Vaudherland, and the Machine Gun Company occupied Fort de Stain.) The above change of stations relieved us from training with the British Forces and brought us under the control of the French Army. After being assigned to our respective barns, stables, out-houses, etc. we had the balance of that afternoon to ourselves in which to become acquainted with the town. As stated, we found Le Thillay quite an important place in size, and consequently many things of interest claimed our attention, among which may be mentioned the numerous cafes, epiceries (Grocery stores), Boulangeries (bakeries), etc., and last, but not least, a fair sprinkling of the opposite sex, who seemed glad to welcome the Americans to their homes.

Sunday afforded an entire day of leisure in which to continue our sightseeing, and many broadened their field of explorations by taking walks into the neighboring towns of Bonneuil and Vaudherland, where, as above stated, our First and Second Battalions were respectively billeted. Some of the more adventuresome began walking toward Paris, a distance of about twelve miles, although strict orders had been received from Regimental Headquarters refusing any man permission to enter that city, that is, without a pass. An enlisted man had very slim chances indeed to procure these coveted passes! Those who were fortunate enough to successfully evade a small army of Military Police guarding all approaches to Paris, reached their destination by boarding street cars at Le Bourget into the metropolis. Others found their way into St. Denis, just outside of Paris, and considered themselves lucky to get so near the "Wonder City of the World" without being "hauled in" by their "friendly enemy", the M. P. As it turned out, however, all of those who went to Paris early in the morning and returned that night were not missed by their company commanders, there being no formations on Sunday after Reveille. Had this been known beforehand, many would have endeavored to follow the lead of their more daring comrades! For those remaining within the limits of the town, entertainment was provided by a concert in the afternoon given by the Regiment band, which was largely attended by many Parisians, who were in the habit of making weekly excursions into the nearby countrysides. At this gathering the boys had a chance to meet many fair mademoiselles (some not so "fair") and it was then we regretted our inability to converse in the language of the land! Subsequently, English-French dictionaries were in great demand, and with the aid of these books, we rather laborously endeavored to make ourselves understood - with comical results! We soon discovered that many of the inhabitants had a fair knowledge of the English language, and more than one doughboy, in trying to learn something of the French speech, often found, at Le Thillay, a willing teacher in some patient mademoiselle.

At this point, the writer wishes to bring in one or two little incidents which he personally observed at Le Thillay and which will, perhaps, illustrate a little more clearly the pleasant relationship that existed at this place between the American soldiers and the French. A picture is brought to mind of several husky doughboys (members of Company I) playing at "jumping rope" with a group of town belles! Another and familiar scene would be a sort of "school" being conducted by some mademoiselle as teacher, her doorstep the

class room, with French as the major study and some lucky doughboy as
her attentive pupil!   Then, we recall, the children of the town - how
they would gather around the soldiers, begging for first one thing and
then another!   The writer remembers one little girl about ten or
twelve years of age who seemed to be taking quite an interest in a bag
of candy he was fast consuming.   The expression on her face as she
saw that candy being rapidly devoured, piece by piece, was really
painful to watch!   I could see that she wanted some very badly but,
unlike many of her little comrades, was too timid to approach me.
Going over to a nearby shop, I purchased a fresh supply which I carried back and handed her.   Then, somewhat to my surprise, she made a
low and graceful curtsy and said some word in French which I presumed
was a word of thanks.   Before running away, she presented me with a
little button with the picture of Marshal (Papa) Joffre thereon and
seemed tickled to death when I pinned it on my blouse.   Now, for the
"catch" to this bit of romance!   In about a minute that little ras-
cal reappeared accompanied by a small army of reinforcements which to
supply with candy would have taken nearly a month's pay!   Luckily,
a doorway was conveniently near, into which I retreated and remained
"under cover" until the enemy had evacuated that particular sector!

Many of the men had expressed a doubt that we would do any drilling at Le Thillay, but all speculation on this important subject was
settled on Monday morning, shortly after mess, when we reluctantly responded to the old command, "Fall in!" and were conducted to our drill
field, just outside of town.   Then followed a daily training
schedule for the remainder of our time at this place.   Our drill
grounds were located on rather a high knoll which commanded a splendid
view of the surrounding country, including the distant outlines of
Eifel Tower.   Considerable time was spent in gas mask drills and
bayonet practice, the two most dreaded ordeals of our entire training
program!   Here, also, we received our first Chauchat rifles and
learned to use them.   Recall was usually sounded at 3 P. M. and we
had the balance of the day to ourselves.   The mess wagons, or kitchens, of some of the companies were stationed quite a distance away
from where the men of these organizations were billeted.   Consequently,
many of the men spent most of their spare time in going to and from
mess three times a day.   Good "eats", well prepared, were served at
this time and the boys had no cause for complaint on that score.
Thus, our Third Battalion put in a week of drilling at Le Thillay -
a week of hard work mingled with pleasanter diversions - until Saturday, June 22nd.

Le Thillay, France (Image from www.geneanet.org)

Chauchat Light Machine Rifle & Bipod

(National Archives)

CHAPTER 12.

ST. DENIS-LES-REBAIS.

Sundays seemed to be our favorite "moving day", for on the 23rd, in accordance with orders received from Division Headquarters, we left Le Thillay at about 8 o'clock in the morning, this time being transported by auto trucks driven by Chinamen. This method of conveyance was, in itself, a distinct innovation from that heretofore experienced, and although each truck was literally jammed with men, packs, rifles and equipment, we never-the-less enjoyed our ride over the smooth roads and fine boulevards for which France is noted. Our route took us through Roissey-en-France, Le Amelot, Meaux, Annette, Lagny, Rebais, and then into the little village of St. Denis-les-Rebais, our destination, which place we reached in the late afternoon. We found some outfits of our regiment already in bivouac on the open fields in and around the town. Shelter tents were soon up and the men ready for mess. But, here, a new difficulty arose. It had taken us but a few hours to make the trip, whereas our wagon trains composed of kitchens, ration and water carts, travelling at a much slower speed, were, of course, left far behind. It took them three days in which to make the trip. During these three days, "iron rations" of canned meat and "hardtack" constituted our mess. Thus, it was at this time that many of the men learned their first bitter lesson and changed their opinions on the subject of carrying along "iron rations". (After three or four more months of campaigning, men who at one time would have thrown their "iron rations" away at the first opportunity, could not secure enough to carry on their backs. The amount of food they took with them when going into the lines was only limited by their carrying capacity!) During the three days without our kitchens, raw meat was issued as part of our rations which, of course, we had to prepare and cook in our mess-pans as best we could. Several of our comrades, who had been butchers in civilian life, were now called upon to exercise their skill in cutting portions of steak for the men of their respective companies. Each man constructed his own cooker, a simple device, usually consisting of two stones laid about six inches apart between which a fire was started. Resting our mess-pans, containing a piece of meat and some bacon fat, on these stones and by working hard to keep a steady fire going, resulted in a meal - for some! Others, less patient or by carelessness, found to their sorrow that to even properly cook a small piece of meat, under these conditions, required a certain amount of skill! The man who was the better cook had a decided advantage over his less fortunate comrade - for these three days at least!

On Monday, as usual, drilling was resumed, this time under the direct supervision of our own officers. While at this place, we received another large consignment of mail from the United States - always an event of great rejoicing. The ardor of many was somewhat dampened, however, by an order from Headquarters restricting the men in frequenting the cafes in town, where bottles of vin blanc, vin rouge and sparkling champagne were temptingly displayed and on sale! Guards were stationed at the entrances to these places with instructions to arrest any would-be customers! It seems that this drastic measure was taken on account of several cases of disorder among the troops reported to Headquarters when the regiment was stationed at Le Thillay. About the middle of the week, an order which greatly pleased every man was received, namely, to turn in our overcoats and one blanket. These were accordingly stacked in piles around the village church in the center of the town and were later carried away on trucks. The weather was beginning to warm-up and none regretted getting rid of those heavy army overcoats and woolen blankets! On Friday, we had an assimilated Division maneuver in a Southwestern direction through Rebais, where Division Headquarters were located.

An entire week of hard drilling and very little play dragged slowly by until Saturday, the 29th. At 8:30 A. M. of that day the whole regiment was once more assembled and we left St. Denis-les-Rebais via hob-nails, the battalions marching in their numerical order in a Southeasterly direction. About noon we reached the little town of Orly, where we rested and consumed another hurried meal of "iron rations".

About this time an important incident occurred which bears relating. While it pertained more particularly to our First Battalion, indirectly it affected the entire regiment and was the subject of much discussion throughout the entire 111th. Word was rapidly passed down the column that Colonel Shannon, under orders from the Brigade Commander, had just dispatched one platoon from Company A and another from Company B up to the front line to serve with the 153rd French Infantry, part of the 39th French Division under the command of General Pougin, and that the Colonel had every reason to believe that before long our entire regiment would be called upon to defend the sector! The platoon from Company A was in command of Lieut. Cedric C. Benz and the platoon from Company B was in command of Lieut. John H. Shenkel. As these two small units of our regiment were the first of the Division to enter the lines, the outcome, of course, greatly interested every man.

It seems that during the afternoon of July 1st, these two platoons participated in a grand attack on Hill 204, near Chateau Thierry, inflicting heavy losses on the enemy. The platoon from Company A took 38 prisoners. The two platoons rejoined the regiment on July 2nd, having suffered in this initial operation a casualty list of 39 men. Thirteen of our comrades were killed, five from Company A and eight from Company B. Later, the platoon commanders were awarded the Croix de Guerre, as well as the Distinguished Service Cross by our own Government. Each platoon was also decorated with the Croix de Guerre as a unit, and several enlisted men were individually decorated for heroic action under fire. Thus, briefly, is recorded the first baptism under fire of some of our boys - and after learning of all its horrible details, the enthusiasm of their comrades anxious to begin fighting sank several degrees!

Colonel Edward Martin, in his history of the 111th Infantry, gives under a chapter entitled "The First Action" a rather good account of this attack. We shall therefore quote the entire chapter as it appears in Vol. No. 2, "The Twenty-Eighth Division in the World War".

"On June 29, Regimental Headquarters and Headquarters Company marched to La Vapre Farm on the highway from Chateau Thierry to Meaux. The Machine Gun and Supply Companies were one-half mile away and the battalions at farms nearby. Just after the head of the column had halted for a noon rest, orders were received by Colonel Shannon directing that he select two platoons to proceed to Bassevelle, from which place a guide would conduct them to the station of the One Hundred Fifty-third French Infantry, which, under its commander, Colonel Mattern, planned to attack Hill 204 on July 1st.

"Colonel Shannon was at a loss to know which platoons should be designated and, quick action being necessary, Captains Williams and Lynch, whose companies were leading the column, were ordered to report to him. To them was explained the urgent nature of the order and each captain was instructed to delegate a lieutenant and one platoon from each company for the mission. A near riot was caused in the two companies by men who were not going. Men made all sorts of claims as to their being entitled to participate. 'Captain, please let me go, I've been in the Guard ten years.' 'Captain, may I go in Tom's place? He has a wife and baby at home and I'm not married.' Those platoons were envied by all.

"The platoon from Company A was commanded by First Lieutenant Cedric C. Benz, and that from Company B by First Lieutenant John H. Shenkel, each platoon consisting of fifty-eight men. They proceeded according to orders and reached their destination on the evening of the 30th, going into the trenches the same night and remaining there until the time for attack, which had been set for 6:00 o'clock on the evening of July 1st.

"The Keystone Division had been on French soil since the middle of May under many varying circumstances and at last some of its units were to meet the enemy face to face. The platoon from Company A was assigned to the left flank of the attacking forces and that from Company B to the right flank. Of the one hundred sixteen men of the two platoons who entered the battle thirty-nine were killed or wounded, nine making the supreme sacrifice on the field of battle, and another, Private Leon C. McCuiston, Company A, mortally wounded, died on the following day. The men who gave their lives in this initial combat were: Sergeant George A. Amole, Corporal Steven Graves, Privates Ensel Maxwell and Mattio Vacchono, all of Company A, and Corporals Ralph W. Uhlman and Raymond Wohllman and Privates Finley B. Taylor, Wilbur

Mannering and August J. Scholz, of Company B. Both platoon
commanders were decorated with the Croix de Guerre, and
later received the Distinguished Service Cross. This
decoration was also given to a number of enlisted men of
the platoons and each platoon was, as a unit, awarded the
Croix de Guerre.

"About 9:00 o'clock that same evening a staff car pulled
into La Vapre bringing three wounded men from Company A, all
badly injured but able to talk. They gave the fisst account of the action that reached the Regiment, the news
spreading like wildfire that Companies A and B had met the
Germans hand to hand and knew how to fight. Lieutenant
Brooks, of the Machine Gun Company, and Sergeant Thorpe, of
the Trench Mortar Platoon, were standing together looking at
the wounded men when Lieutenant Brooks said, 'I envy those
men their wounds.' 'So do I, Lieutenant,' answered the Sergeant. One week later the sergeant gave his life on almost
the same ground where these men had been wounded, and two
months later Lieutenant Brooks stood up in order to draw the
enemy fire that he might locate its position and so paid with
his life. What the French commander thought of these platoons is told in a letter sent by him to Colonel Shannon, and
afterwards published in bulletin form. This was read to the
Regiment while in bivouac in the Grande Foret, on the evening
of July 4, 1918.

"The bulletin is as follows:

Twenty-Eighth Division,
American Expeditionary Forces,
France, July 4, 1918.

BULLETIN

1. On the afternoon of July 1, two platoons of the
111th Infantry participated with the 153rd French Infantry
Regiment in the attack on Hill 204. The following letter,
written by Colonel Matter, commanding the 153rd French Infantry Regiment, tomthe Commanding Officer, 111th U. S. Infantry, is published for the information of the command:

'I have the honor to inform you that the detachment of
your regiment which you have been so good as to put at my
disposal for the attack of July 1, has shown in its baptism
of fire an admirable attitude.
'The detachment was placed with the Second Battalion
of the 153rd, which had as its mission the taking of the
woods on Hill 204.
'The platoon from Company A operated on the eastern
edge of the woods; the platoon from Company B on the western
edge. At the hour 'H' (6:00 P.M.) the assaulting troops
left the trenches where they had been staying in order to
allow artillery preparation on Hill 204.
'From the beginning of the attack the American detach-

ments were marked by their ardor, bravery and their enthusiasm.

'In spite of the firing of the enemy's heavy and light machine guns, trench mortars, riflemen placed in trees, these men bravely threw themselves on their adversaries.

'A fierce hand-to-hand contest immediately took place in the thick and almost impregnable woods, where each man sought his man. The combat was violent, and your men never ceased during all the operation to arouse the enthusiasm and admiration of their French comrades by their magnificent behavior.

'Lieutenant Shenkel, especially, distinguished himself during the combat, making a great impression on his own troops and our soldiers. Led on by his ardor, with seven men, the lieutenant found himself surrounded on all sides. The detachment cut its way through by using the butts of their rifles and bayonets on the enemy's flanks, and succeeded in rejoining their comrades; Lieutenant Shenkel himself killing, with a pistol shot, a German officer.

'The attitude of all American ranks, especially the non-commissioned officers, was also noticeable. Of six non-commissioned officers participating in the attack, five have fallen gloriously, killed or wounded. All officers, N.C.O.'s and privates were superb in their enthusiasm and courage.

'I would appreciate very much if you would bring to the knowledge of your regiment, the splendid conduct of your men, who fought for the first time with us, and let everybody know that with such admirable soldiers as yours, and ours, the defeat of the Germans is certain in the near future.

'(Signed)   Matter.'

"The Commanding General of the 39th French Division adds:

'I join with all my heart the sentiments of admiration which Colonel Matter expresses for the valiant troops which have just given to ours a splendid example of bravery. I join my salutations and respect to the brave men who have fallen on the field of honor, the number of which is, unhappily, too great.

'(Signed)   Pougin.'

"The Division Commander desires to congratulate the two platoons participating in the attack of July 1, upon the receipt of such splendid commendations from the Regimental and Division Commanders under which they served. He believes that the action of these men is but an example of what the whole Twenty-eighth 'Keystone' Division will show when opportunity offers.

"By command of Major General Muir.

"Edw. L. King,
"Colonel, General Staff,
"Chief of Staff."

Colonel Edward C. Shannon, commanded the 111th infantry throughout operations in France.
(Image from Pennsylvania in the World War: An Illustrated History of the Twenty-Eighth Division, Vol. 2, p. 490, 1921)

CHAPTER 13.

BASSEVILLE AND THE CALL TO ARMS!

Getting back to the activities of our Third Battalion, from Orly
we continued our march which finally terminated at Basseville about
four or five o'clock on the afternoon of Saturday, June 29th. Here,
the entire Third Battalion was soon settled in and around the little
group of farm houses called a village. Some of the men occupied barns
while others, who were sent to farms where billets could not be procured,
made their temporary homes in "pup" tents. Several platoons from
Company I were at first assigned to billets but later, on finding these
already occupied by a detachment of Italian troops, were greatly relieved on receiving orders to pitch their tents in a neighboring orchard.
We particularly noticed the extremely filthy appearance of these sons of
Italy! All seemed to be suffering from ugly looking sores and judging
from the general unkempt condition of these soldiers, we feared that
they were bearers of our common enemy, the cootie! This fear was very
soon substantiated by witnessing the tell-tale antics of the Italians
as they frequently and vigorously scratched their bodies! It will,
therefore, go without saying that those of us who were at first allotted barns, stables and sheds just recently vacated by our Italian
allies, were very much relieved on receiving subsequent orders to pitch
tents instead. We had no desire of adding to our already increasing
number of these body lice! These soldiers, we were informed, had
been employed in repairing roads in the vicinity of Basseville and
shortly after the arrival of the American troops, many of them moved
elsewhere, leaving inviting quarters which, however, remained unoccupied
for want of an American tenant!

We now occupied a position immediately behind the lines, and it
was at Basseville that we heard the first shell on its mission of destruction from the mouth of the enemy's cannon until its swift journey
suddenly terminated in a loud explosion somewhere within our lines!
For us, the war had at last really begun!

Sunday, June 30th, afforded a day of complete rest, at least for
most of the enlisted men, which by this time every man needed. Nothing
occurred during the day to mar our usual camp life and the men found
ample time in which to "catch up" in their delayed correspondence. No
doubt many of the boys were anxious to get word to the folks at home
that they were at last actually "under fire" somewhere in France, giving little thought, perhaps, that such a message would not tend to
gladen the hearts of their loved ones so far away.

On Monday, as usual, our regular program of drilling was commenced. As some of the men remarked, "They would drill us even

though the Kaiser and his whole damn army were looking on!"   Our
maneuvers were frequently interrupted by enemy aeroplanes, some of
them coming over during the time we were on the drill field. Guards
were continually on the "look out" for these planes and when one was
sighted, two blasts on a whistle would be our signal to run, as quickly
as possible, under cover of nearby trees or to stand perfectly still
until the plane was out of sight, after which, upon one blast of the
whistle, we would resume our drilling.   While on the subject of aeroplanes, it was at Basseville that some of us witnessed a real air-
fight at close range - an American aviator, Lieut. Pitman, being
brought down after an exciting encounter with a German airman!

Many of the men realized that our Third Battalion must be pretty
close to the Line.   Upon inquiry, we learned that our regiment was
now about fifteen miles Southwest of Chateau-Thierry and it looked as
though we were headed right toward that city!   About that time,
Chateau-Thierry spelled "fighting" with a capital letter!   All indica-
tions seemed to point to the fact that from Basseville we would be
ordered at any moment up to the lines - where we did not know or care
much - and we were told to hold ourselves in readiness to move on an
instant's notice.   While here, all Regimental, Battalion and Company
commanders were conducted, at various times, by French officers up to
the lines on the South bank of the Marne River in order to grasp the
general plan of defense of that particular sector and to gain some
experience preparatory to moving their respective troops.   On Tuesday
and Wednesday, several officers from our Third Battalion spent part of
these days in reconnoitering the position which we were expected to
take over.

Our thoughts about this time, with the approach of July 4th,
naturally turned back to other Fourths spent in the United States - to
past celebrations at home of Independence Day!   Many of our men wondered not a little in just what manner and under what conditions they
would face the 4th of July, 1918!   Indeed, to say the least, our
prospects for a "quiet Fourth" were not very bright, as we knew only
too well that "Jerry" would obligingly supply the requisite "fire-
works" if, by that time, we were ordered up to the front line!

It was, therefore, with some misgivings as to what the next few
hours would bring forth when the men sought their shelter tents on
the night of July 3rd.   We could now distinctly hear the firing of
the heavy pieces on the lines and occasionally could even make out the
plaintive whine of some shell as it sped on its mission of destruction
and, perhaps, death.   It is safe to say that the majority of the tired
men were fast asleep when, suddenly, they were awakened by the shrill
blasts of Sergeants' whistles, accompanied by that dreaded but expected
command of "Outside and roll packs!"   On looking at our watches, we
saw that it was exactly 4:15 A. M., and more than one doughboy grimly
remarked, as he hurriedly got into his clothes, "Well, boys, we are
S. O. L. for a quiet Fourth of July this year!"   (Just what meaning
"S. O. L." conveyed, I shall leave to those of my readers, not
familiar with doughboy expressions, to guess!)

After that first alarm, it was only the matter of a few minutes before the little hamlet of Basseville and vicinity was the scene of busy activity. All the men had a feeling that "something was in the air" and doubtless, every man there entertained a secret desire to be on hand "when the fun started!" We felt that our period of inactivity had lasted long enough, that we were sick and tired of drilling (we could do that much back home) and, it is safe to venture, that each individual soldier of our Third Battalion wanted a change of some character even though that change meant actual fighting, at close quarters, with the enemy! So, as we jumped into our clothes, took down tents and rolled our packs during that early morning hour of July 4th, 1918, any casual observer watching the busy men would have thought that they were going on some kind of a pleasure trip instead of possibly being bound for the front line! In a comparatively short space of time, the entire battalion was assembled on the road and while it was still dark, the column of men marched out of the village. We could not restrain ourselves over the joy we felt at the prospects of possible excitement just ahead and we began to sing and whistle in unison. We had not covered more than a kilometre or two, however, when orders came down the line to maintain absolute silence. This command only added to our suppressed excitement! Could the Germans be so near as that? We wondered!

At 6:45 A. M., the Third Battalion (now joined by the entire regiment) reached our position, Le Mesnil, in what was then known as the Charly-Nogent Line of Resistence. Nearby flowed the Marne River, the town of Charly being on its northern bank and the town of Nogent on the southern side of the river. We understood that we were now just about eight miles behind the front line at that point and that the line there must be held at all costs in the event the Germans broke through at Chateau-Thierry, at which place it was expected the enemy would make an attack at any moment. We remained in this position until about 2:45 that afternoon, when we marched into the town of Nogent where the whole regiment was assembling. During all the forenoon, we had been comparatively comfortable resting in the cool woods along the banks of the Marne River. We were somewhat reluctant, therefore, to leave these woods! However, it appeared that "the army was on the move again" and, under the rays of a burning sun, the entire regiment began its march in an easterly direction. We shall not soon forget that march on that hot afternoon of July 4th, 1918! How perspiration and words freely flowed! How we cussed the Germans or whoever was responsible for this seemingly needless hike on such a hot day! We were peeved, too, that we had not had a chance, thus far, to even fire just one shot at Jerry by way of properly celebrating the Glorious Fourth! And here we were hiking - no one knew where to - just hiking, hiking and again hiking - the penalty evidently inflicted because we joined the infantry! "We would rather stand still and fight any day!", we thought, as we wearily trudged onward, our packs seeming to increase in weight as that hot sun began to take its toll! After about three hours of torture, we/the Grande Forest, where the entire regiment went into bivouac. How inviting those large trees looked! Here, at last we could rest and cool off!

We had not been in the forest long before trucks began to assemble on the road nearby and a rumor soon went around that these trucks were to convey us up to the front line that night! Our cookers also arrived and shortly thereafter mess was ready, to which we did full justice! Packs were then unrolled and in a little while the entire area around presented a war-like picture dotted with our tents. Many of men, worn-out from the day's activities, at once sought rest and sleep within their tents. Others gathered in groups to discuss current events and to exchange ideas as to the possibility of seeing some real fighting in the very nesr future. Some of the men, realizing the uncertainty of what the next few hours might bring forth or where this adventure might lead them, used the few remaining hours of daylight in hurriedly writing to the folks at home, telling them that our battalion was then lying just behind the lines expecting orders any minute to advance in the face of the enemy. While his command was thus occupied, Colonel Shannon was called away to Brigade Headquarters and that, in the excited minds of all, was most significant! Surely, we would soon receive orders to advance! We impatiently waited! It was just getting dark when the Colonel returned and he immediately called an Officers' meeting. Soon afterward we learned, to our disappointment, that the regiment would not move in all probability until the next morning. It seemed that all our hard hiking that day had been in vain! Orders to bivouac here for the night were given and those of us who had kept awake to hear the latest "low down" on the situation now sought their tents or just stretched out on the ground, using packs as pillows. Thus, July 4th, 1918, passed into history with the men of the 111th! Other Fourths may come and go unrecalled in years to follow but it is safe to say that the events of that day in the year of 1918 will not soon be forgotten by the men of our Third Battalion!

About 5:30 the next morning, July 5th, after partaking of a hasty breakfast, tents were taken down, packs rolled and soon the march back to our orchards in Basseville was under way. The men could hardly realize that we were returning to the place from which they so gayly sallied forth just a few hours ago! We reached the familiar camp site during the middle of the fore-noon, or about 10:30 A. M. Old quarters in billets and tents were again occupied and many took occasion to "cuss the luck" that had deprived them of a peaceful Fourth spent in France as our holiday, only to be sent "on a wild goose chase" through the hot summer's day! And here we found ourselves back to where we started from with apparently nothing accomplished! Who started "this man's war" anyway?

CHAPTER 14.

HILL 204.

After taking possession of our former quarters in and around the little hamlet of Basseville, the men of our Third Battalion settled down for the next move, every man hoping that very soon his outfit would be called into action - not action in the sense of useless hiking but the activity all craved and, at this time, looked forward to - some real fighting with those Germans we had heard so much about! Other units of the regiment were not idle, however, for on July 5th, the Trench Mortar Platoon of Headquarters Company was ordered to join the 153rd French Infantry. The platoon rejoined the regiment on July 7th, with casualties of three men killed.

On July 7th, our Third Battalion came into its share of this excitement! One platoon each from Companies L and M was assigned to duty with the 153rd French Infantry, 39th Division, under General Marchand, in command of the operations around what was then known as "Hill 204". On July 9th, Companies I and K were called into action by serving with the 146th French Infantry around Vaux and Hill 204. These moves brought us under very heavy enemy shell fire and necessitated seeking cover in the trenches previously occupied by our French allies. The weather, which up to this time had been fair and somewhat warm, now changed to rain and we all can recall how disagreeable these trenches were! Some were very poorly constructed affairs - mere holes dug in the ground - and mud was everywhere! (Regimental Headquarters, previously established at Vatrie on July 5th and later moved to Fosse Ardois at 8:45 P. M. the same date, was now located at Le Mesnil.) By this time, the entire 111th was thrown in on the reserve line!

The period from July 7th to 18th, inclusive, in our operations around Hill 204, witnessed many events of stirring activity affecting not only our Third Battalion but all units of the 111th. Two infantry companies from a battalion would be called to the front line to "stand to" while the other two companies would be held in reserve a little back of the line in readiness to relieve their comrades when called upon. It rained steady on Wednesday, Thursday and Friday, July 10th, 11th and 12th, during which time Companies I and K were on the line. Our Machine Gun crew, appropriately named "the suicide legion", evidently saw some real action about this time according to the following quotation from a history of that organization: "Leaving at night, we marched to the same positions we occupied on July 5th and dug machine gun emplacements and, upon completion, our guns controlled a large field of fire along the Marne River. During the evening of July 14th, the third platoon, under command of First Lieut. Wainwright, was ordered to Chezy sur Marne, with the second battalion of our regiment, and the following day, the 15th, we received our first real shelling, causing three casualties, all gas burns in our company and about thirty-six casualties in F Company of the second battalion. Leaving Chezy sur Marne, we joined the remainder of the company that was on its way to the front. We marched quite a distance and finally reached the wood where the 30th Infantry had suffered heavy losses, and there we were placed in small dug-outs. This wood is located along the Marne River near Graves Farm and Crezancy, and later named 'Dead Horse Wood' by the Americans, owing to the large number of dead animals laying around the ground. We entered this wood under an American barrage and we were not all under cover when the Bosche started his counter barrage. It was here we lost our first man, wounded by shell fire. We were shelled almost continuously the entire time located there. On the 20th, we were to place our guns in position along the Marne, but orders were changed and we were withdrawn to Grande Bordeau Farm and here our men, who had been burned with gas, were sent to the hospital with the additional ones who were burned while in the wood."

During these times, a number of changes were made in the lines of the allied armies but at no interval were the men of our regiment stationed in a quiet zone! Our Third Battalion, while in the vicinity of Nogent Artaud, was under a particularly heavy barrage from the enemy's guns. In fact, we were compelled to literally live like so many moles in the ground, for to venture forth from our dug-outs meant, possibly, instant death! From our elevated position on Hill 204, with the aid of field-glasses, we were able to command a large area of the surrounding country without much danger of being seen by the Germans, if exercising extreme care to keep well under cover. The naked eye disclosed what appeared to be little patches of light blue scattered in the valley below but, by the aid of our glasses all guess-work concerning the nature of these little blue spots was settled. They proved to be the dead bodies of French soldiers who had fallen in defense of the position we were now holding!

On July 15th, the second battalion of our regiment reported to the Commanding General, Third Division, in the vicinity of Pertibout Fme., relieving the 30th U. S. Infantry, operating along the Marne River between Fossoy and Crezancy. On July 16th, the first battalion was ordered to Viffort and taken by truck from that point and reported to the Commanding General, Third Division, and used in support of our second battalion, which had taken over the front line of the 30th U. S. Infantry. On July 17th, the Regimental Commander was ordered to report on the following day to the Commanding General, Third Division, with Headquarters and Machine Gun Companies.

On Thursday night, July 18th, Companies I and K returned from duty with the French Army and rejoined the Third Battalion at Petite Noues. The writer will long have occasion to remember the events of that night's march from the front line! It was nearly eleven o'clock before we were relieved by the French. A heavy rain was falling and it was so dark one could hardly discern the outlines of the man next to him. Aided by a French guide, the two companies began their hazardous march. We experienced considerable difficulty in walking as the down-pour had made the ground very slippery. The inky blackness of the stormy night, coupled with the necessity of maintaining a strict silence (our French guide talked in whispers), added greatly to the perilous nature of this night's march from the lines. Indeed, it was so dark that it was with difficulty the men, marching in single file, managed to keep on the narrow, slippery and winding path through the maze of trees and underbrush. To facilitate matters, each man grasped the pack of the comrade in front of him so as not to become separated and thus break-up the column and lose those in the rear. All went fairly well until, in the center of a labyrinth of rocks, trees and brush, the path was intercepted by what was apparently a steep incline - possibly a large shell hole - we could not make out through the darkness. At any rate, in crossing over, the column was broken up and each man was left to proceed as best he could! The confusion which resulted can be imagined! The writer, who had lost the man in front of him, remembers giving one big jump off into space with the forlorn hope of making a safe landing on the other side. I felt that, at all hazards, I must catch up to that column ahead! To be lost in those woods filled with Germans would be just too bad! There was little time to calculate as the situation called for some quick action! Just before I leaped, I heard several comrades around me struggling to their feet and hurrying off, at the same time, uttering low curses as if they had fallen. My turn "to make it" came and loaded down with that heavy pack on my back besides carrying my rifle and gas mask, I jumped! Instead of a "happy landing", I felt myself falling into the unknown - a most unpleasant sensation especially when not being able to see your hand before you! The next thing I remembered was seeing all kinds and colors of star-shell-lights as the barrel of my rifle struck a hard blow across my face when I landed in a heap at the bottom of the ditch, shell hole or whatever it was! When I came to (the blow had rendered me unconscious), I quickly scrambled to my feet at the same time spitting out what remained of several perfectly good teeth! Hurriedly climbing out of the place, I stumbled on ahead with only one thought in mind - to rejoin that column! I caught up to my comrades just in time and was one of the last men to "fall in" as the column resumed its march! During our hike from the lines, which lasted the balance of that rainy night, I felt blood trickling down from the bridge of my nose and chin onto my slicker! When it got light enough to see a little, the man next to me said: "Compton, for Christ sake wipe that mud off your face!" Later, as the first signs of the sun appeared on the horizon, my admonisher was greatly surprised to see that what he had thought was mud, turned out to be blood - and plenty of it! Later on in the morning, when we came to a small stream of water, my wounds were patched by one of the battalion's first-aid men and subsequently healed without the necessity of my going to a field hospital for treatment, although the cut on the upper portion of my chin penetrated entirely through to my lower teeth. I still bear slight scars on my nose and chin as mementos of that night's march - not mentioning the missing front teeth! The above incident proved to be but one of the many unpleasant experiences of the night's activities and is related somewhat in detail as an example of many similar adventures through which we later passed under similar or even more trying conditions.

Luckily, our movements that night were not discovered, for had the Germans opened fire on us in those woods many would have perished before morning. We were on strange ground whereas the enemy, undoubtedly, was familiar with every foot of the territory. To make a long story short, Companies I and K succeeded in rejoining the balance of the Third Battalion at Petite Noues about 9 A. M., crossing the Marne to Nogent, where we assembled. At this place we had a few hours rest in French barracks. From here, we returned to our first position in the woods where we were loaded on trucks and hauled to St. Eugene. These movements were not accomplished, however, without casualties throughout the battalion! By this time, we were beginning to realize something of the horrors of war from personal observations! At St. Eugene, K Company suffered their first losses - five men being hit by the explosion of a shell! At this place, several patrols were sent out by the battalion.

In closing our remarks concerning the Third Battalion's share in the defense of Hill 204, our work while in this sector was later complimented on by the Commander of the French regiment under whom we served.

CHAPTER 15.

CHATEAU THIERRY.

The same date (July 18th) on which we rejoined our comrades at Petite Noues, the Regimental Commander, with headquarters and Machine Gun Companies, reported to the Commanding General, Third Division, and was directed to proceed by marching to Grieves Fme., where guides would be met to conduct the troops to the position of the 30th U. S. Infantry. At 1:15 A. M., the troops reached the position of the 30th U. S. Infantry, and the Regimental Commander took over the command of the sector, relieving Col. Edmund L. Butts.

Leaving Le Petite Noues via auto trucks at 9:30 P. M. on the evening of July 20th, we arrived at Charley-Saul-Chevy, a town of some size, at about 2:00 A. M. on the morning of the 21st. Regarding the use of motor trucks in transporting troops from one sector to another during the war, a word or two might be said of interest to those of my readers not familiar with the A. E. F. "taxi" - the large and powerful automobile Army truck. It had one redeeming feature in that it would generally "get you there" in short order but as to one's physical condition at the journey's end - well that is another story! In the first place, as one man so aptly put it: "Why in Hell can't these trucks come to the men instead of the men having to hike a mile or so to the damn things?" This quiry was, no doubt, at times shared by all, for it seemed that each time automobiles were used they were usually stationed along some road several kilos away when, apparently, they could just as well have been driven up to the tired men, thus saving an extra hike! This is but one of the many mysteries of the World War as yet unsolved - from the doughboy's viewpoint at least! It was in boarding these trucks that the "fun" started! Like our box-car experiences, it seemed there was no limit to the carrying capacity of these motor vehicles! Men and equipment were packed in until there remained, apparently, absolutely no space for another man. However, literally taking as the truth that old adage, "There is always room for one more", another man or two would pile in - "SRO" - standing room only - it was for each truck load. Sardines in a can didn't have a thing on the boys in those days - boats, trains, automobiles - forever packed in! So, dear reader, you can readily see that auto trips were not exactly "joy rides", hampered as we were with heavy packs, rifles and other equipment! Never-the-less, a certain spirit of high glee always accompanied these auto "excursions", the men evidently preferring cramped positions for a few hours rather than "hiking it" for possibly many hours over the hard, dusty and oftimes muddy roads of France. Then, too, we never knew exactly where we were bound for on these trips or just how long the ride would take. There was always a certain amount of excitement in the air when we started out, which

Infantry about to move by truck to the Chateau Thierry Sector

A view of the city showing the ruined houses. Chateau Thierry, France, August 1918.

(Images Courtesy of National Archives)

made the men forget just how uncomfortable they really were!

After that tiresome trip via auto trucks even the shell-wrecked houses which lined the principal thoroughfare of Charley, looked very inviting to the men. These houses, at least, afforded splendid billet accommodations, we thought. However, on this as well as many other occasions we were doomed for a bitter disappointment! Instead of receiving orders to locate billets for the remainder of the night, the dreaded command of "Fall in!" was heard as we unloaded and the battalion quickly wended its way through the dark and deserted streets leading out of the town into the open country beyond!

Our rather hasty departure out of Charley was made necessary due to an order received from an aide to General Muir, Division Commander, directing that the regiment move from Grande Bordeaux Farm, which position it had occupied on being relieved during the night of July 20th. The Third Battalion, having been detached in the meantime, was ordered to rejoin the regiment in bivouac near Brasles, north of Chateau Thierry - hence no time was to be lost in unnecessary "layovers". That forced march in the hours that followed after leaving the town of Charley will clearly be recalled by the men of the Third Battalion, accompanied as it was by dangers almost too numerous to mention. We were now passing through a country being continually shelled by the enemy - and heavily shelled both day and night at that! We had to be constantly on guard against both deadly shrapnel and poisonous gas! It was at this time that the battalion, as a unit, suffered more casualties than ever before experienced! This was due, in part, to the fact that the men had not become accustomed to the proper wearing of their masks or neglected to adjust them in time when the warning cry of "Gas!" was heard. Some of the men who got gassed on this march had taken their masks off before the signal "All clear!" was shouted down the line. These masks were miserable things to wear for any great length of time, anyway. Imagine putting a tight-fitting rubber bag over your face, a pair of smeary glasses to see through, a rubber hose in your mouth to breathe through and good strong tweezers pinching your nose - all at one and the same time - and you will have a slight conception of just how comfortable (?) these masks were! Small wonder the men hated to wear them and would rather take the risk of being gassed in order to remove these instruments of torture! Let us all pray that there will not be any more wars but, if another war does come, let our prayers be "for a humane gas mask!"

Our route took us through the city of Chateau Thierry and while passing through that maze of wrecked houses, blown-up streets, shelled walls, felled telephone poles, wires, etc., etc., and in crossing the Marne River on a pontoon bridge, we had every reason in the world to agree with General Sherman's viewpoint regarding war! Though harrassed on all sides by German shells, shrapnel and gas, we heroically continued our advance, unmindful of the dangers which completely surrounded us! Above the din of bursting shell, that dreaded cry of "Gas!" could be heard, it seemed, every few minutes. Needless to add, every man of the entire Third Battalion, from our most active officer down to the laziest "buck" private, came into his full share of arm exercise in adjusting and taking off gas masks! Our marching order

111th infantry, 28th Division, stopping for rest at Chateau Thierry, France, July 21, 1918.

Wrecked bridge over Marne River and ruined buildings where machine gunners of 3rd Division held ground. 150th Regt. F. A. (formerly 1st Regt. F. A., Ind. N.G.), July 25, 1918. Chateau Thierry, France. Part of the 150th Regt. F. A. on way to front to relieve men of the 26th Division. (Images courtesy of National Archives)

was the "five-paces-apart" formation, the men being thus separated so that if a shell happened to fall within the column the resulting casualties would be reduced to a minimum. It may be said, without fear of contradiction, that our entrance into and exit from Chateau Thierry were both marked by plenty of excitement for all! In fact, those who had at one time or another grumbled or complained about being kept in a "quiet zone" now agreed to a man that they were at last satisfied and some of the more timid even hinted that they had had enough of it! Even the most highly excited man in our battalion at that time noted and admired the scenic beauty of the country around Chateau Thierry as it unfolded in panoramic splendor around us. While, of course, the city itself had long since suffered the ravages of war (scarcely a building had escaped being hit), it nevertheless presented a pretty picture nestling there on the banks of the beautiful and peaceful Marne. It was difficult indeed for the most fanciful mind to associate such a scene with warfare and the shedding of human blood!

On July 22nd, after exciting times for all, our Third Battalion succeeded in its movement and rejoined the regiment in bivouac near Brasles, north of Chateau Thierry. Late that afternoon, the regiment moved in t the Bois de Barbilon and bivouaced. At 1:30 A. M., July 23rd, 1918, Field Orders No. 9, dated Headquarters, 56th Infantry Brigade, 23 July, 1918, were received which directed the regiment to move by the road in the Bois de Barbilon to Verdilly, thence by route of the 112th Infantry, which was indicated in the order, to the Grande Rue Farm. While enroute, verbal orders were received directing that the Commanding Officer of our regiment report to the Commanding General, 26th Division, upon the arrival of his troops at the Grande Rue Farm. Headquarters Company, our Machine Gun Company, second and third battalions were bivouaced in woods east of Grande Rue Farm and our first battalion in woods north of Grande Rue Farm. At 9 A. M., the Commanding Officer reported to the Commanding General, 26th Division, and was directed to hold his force in readiness to support the troops of the 26th Division on the line. In the afternoon of that day, he was directed to reconnoiter the position held by the 101st and 102nd Infantries with a view of relieving them with two battalions of our regiment. The relief of the position above mentioned was begun at dark with the second and third battalions, under command of the Regimental Commander, Lieut. Col. Bertram L. Succop remaining in command of the first battalion, Headquarters Company, and the Machine Gun Company.

While the relief was in progress, orders were received at 3:30 A. M. to be prepared to make an attack the following morning at 6:15 A. M., July 24th. Our Third Battalion occupied the right of the sector with two companies in the front line and the second battalion occupied the left of the sector with two companies in the front line, each battalion having two companies in support.

The attack started on time and proceeded without opposition for a distance of about 800 yards when a French cavalry patrol, moving along our left flank, reported to the Commanding Officer that the enemy had evacuated Epieds. The advance was immediately stopped and this information sent by a runner to the Commanding General, 56th Infantry Brigade, who had established his P. C. at Beruet, with a request that the artillery barrage which was to be put down be immediately stopped. In a short time a message from the Commanding General, 56th Infantry Brigade, was received which directed the advance be continued until strong resistance by the enemy was met, with La Croix Rouge Farm as the objective.

Upon receipt of this order, the advance was started with two companies of each battalion leading with their elements in line of platoon columns, followed in close support by the other two companies in the same formation, with instructions to march by compass, bearing North 15 degrees East. The advance continued and when the leading element of the right sector was opposite Epieds, it moved to the right flank and contact was lost with it for the time being. The balance of the column continued to advance until opposite Beauvardes when considerable machine gun fire developed from that town. The advance was halted and a patrol from Company K was sent to reconnoiter and it was reported that the French were conducting an operation against that town. It was decided to continue the advance, leaving that town on our left, through the Foret de Fere. Owing to the dense growth of the forest, it became almost impossible to keep contact with the units and the column was reduced to a column of files with Companies E, H, I and K. The right Sector became disengaged at this time and, as later developed, were held up on the southern edge of the forest. The units above-mentioned (Companies E, H, I and K) continued the advance through the forest and about 4:00 P. M., Company H, which was leading, was held up by machine gun fire. This opposition was overcome by automatic rifle teams which were sent out to the right flank and the advance continued until about 700 yards from the La Croix Farm where an intense machine gun fire was laid down by the enemy. (At the time Company H was held up by that enemy machine gun fire, it caused more than 25 casualties in just ten minutes' time!)

One platoon at a time was fed into a hurriedly established line until two companies were engaged when the opposing fire was reduced. The column was again formed and an attempt made to make a further advance but the fire from the enemy immediately reopened and it was impossible, owing to the dense forest and the heavy fire to make a further advance. The action above-mentioned caused losses of five (5) killed and fifteen (15) wounded!

An officers' patrol was sent to the left of the position with a view of obtaining information as to the strength of the enemy and in about one-half hour information was received from this patrol that the enemy was in force in the vicinity of La Croix Rouge Farm.

About 500 yards in the rear of the position where this action took place was a clearing in the forest of about 400 yards square and a sunken road ran along the southern edge of the clearing. It was decided that as the hour was growing late, it was best to establish a position and hold the ground gained. With this end in view, Company K was placed in the front line, the other three companies of the detachment echeloned in depth in the forest to the rear. The organization of the position was completed and all units in position before dark. The establishment of this position was accomplished under con-

gun fire and later intense artillery fire which was

he entire night. Patrols were sent out from the

in information as to the troops on the right and left

early evening contact was gained with the French on

wards morning contact was also gained on our right with

detachment which had worked up through the forest on

advance, a staff officer of the 26th Division ac-

Commanding Officer of our regiment and when it was de-

nize the position, this officer, with two runners, left

mation as to our location and condition to the Commanding

Infantry Brigade. Prior to this, messages had been sent

me to time to the old P. C. of the Commanding General, 56th

ring information as to the progress of the advance but owing

that the P. C. had been changed, most of our messages fail-

him. of course, developed later. At the

This fact, information was in his hands as to the

supposed that full At 5:00 A. M., July 25th, no word having

of the detachment.

ved from the Brigade Commander as to the supporting troops,

it. Jean M. Siaux, 54th Chasseurs, French Army, who was at-

the regiment, volunteered to convey a message to the Brigade

and with two runners left the position, found the Brigade

and gave him the first information as to the condition and

of the detachment. The position was a strong one and easily

the force occupying it.

ter on that day, a message was received from the Brigade Com-

advising that the detachment would be relieved by the 167th

Infantry, 42nd (Rainbow) Division. At 8:40 P. M., the same

the relief was made and the detachment was marched South through

ods to Courpoil, where the detachment was reported to the Brigade

nder and thence to the Trugny Woods, where the rest of the regi-

had been assembled and bivouacked. (The two companies of our

Battalion, on being relieved, retired to Fere de Tardenois, where

emained until darkness, later rejoining the regiment in bivouac at

de Trugny.) It was while making this advance that we suffered

of our first privations of war, the battalion going without rations

seventy-two hours, due to inability to get provisions up to the men!

Concerning the activities of our Machine Gun Company from July

st to 29th, inclusive, the writer again quotes from a brief account

his possession, as follows: "On the 21st of July, orders came to

ove to Chateau Thierry and while on the march we lost four more men

rom the effects of gas received in the wood. We entered Chateau

Thierry during the afternoon of the 21st and proceeded to cross the

river. The machine gun carts wrre drawn by hand across a pontoon

bridge for a distance of three kilos past the city to the outskirts of

the town and there we were billeted in evacuated German stables. We

remained in the stables until about 11 P. M. the night of the 22nd of

July, then started to march North along the lines of the 26th Division.

We marched all day the 23rd and made camp in the wood where the Marines

had fought, and here our French instructors left us. We marched all

day the 24th, passing through St. Germaine and Epieds. Stopped at

Courpoil this night and were shelled quite heavily, causing us to move

hot July sun!   Somewhere we had read about "the Marne running in blood" but on that afternoon such a thought never entered our minds! The war, for a time, was forgotten!

On our marches in the vicinity of the Marne and around Chateau Thierry, we frequently met on the road pathetic sights - groups of French women and children carting away to a safer zone as much of thei household belongings as they could possibly carry along. Sometimes ol and feeble men would be seen accompanying these groups but very seldom did we notice any of the younger men who, apparently, were at the time defending their beloved France.   It was certainly a sad and pitiful sight to see these poorly-clad women and children with their few belongings being compelled to thus leave their homes and remaining property at the mercy of German shells, - knowing that when they returned they would find all in ruins!   These poor wretches always brightened-up when they met "the Americans" on the way up to the front.   Many times they said something to us in French as we passed - probably some word of encouragement but, by their smiling faces, we knew that they were glad to see us going up to aid their men in driving the enemy off of French soil.

The following incident is recalled and, while it is somewhat of a personal nature, it may be well to bring it in at this point in our story as it will, undoubtedly, serve to revive old memories of all comrades having a similar experience while "over there".   It happened along the Marne, near Chateau Thierry.   We had marched into a village of considerable size, the name of which escapes the writer's mind. Everyone seemed to think that we would surely remain in the town over night and the men began to seek quarters in the shell-wrecked houses and barns throughout the place.   About noon, just after mess, the writer located an inviting barn in the hay-loft of which there appeared to be a good supply of nice clean straw!   Climbing up a ladder, I soon satisfied myself that here was an ideal spot for an afternoon's siesta! After a long hike all the morning through the burning rays of a July sun and having just eaten rather heavily, to rest here and possibly sleep for the remainder of the afternoon would, indeed, be heavenly! Then too, as my barn was somewhat isolated, perhaps I would not be discovered and would escape some nasty details!   Taking a blanket out of my pack, I made myself a very comfortable bed on the floor of the barn and, after undressing, was soon "wrapped in the arms of Morpheus". The last thing that I remembered was hearing the old familiar grunts and exclamations coming from a group of crap-shooters who had gathered in a circle just outside of the barn door.   (We shall draw the curtain as I peacefully slept - denoting the passing of time!)   I awoke with a start and looked around!   Not five feet away was a comrade "sawing wood" in good fashion.   I wondered when he found the place.   How quiet everything was outside!   I ran over to the door of the loft and looked out.   Not a soldier could I see or hear!   And that sun! When I entered the barn, the sun was just overhead but now it had nearly completed its day's trick!   What time was it and where were my comrades?   I hastened back and aroused my sleeping companion. Neither one of us possessed a watch!   We quickly dressed, made up our packs and were soon down on the ground.   Not a soul could we see!   The outfit had marched off and left us behind!   Night was rapidly approaching!

Knowing that the regiment was headed for Chateau Thierry, we set out down the road in that direction, following the military signs posted along the way. Just as it was getting dark, we met a detachment of American artillery and fell in with these troops. We marched along with them for a spell and when they went into bivouac for the remainder of the night, we pitched our tent in some woods near their cooker. The next morning we had mess with the artillerymen and, upon telling what outfit we were from, some of their men informed us that "the 111th was in bivouac just over there", pointing to another section of the same woods where we had just spent the night. We thanked them for our breakfast and the information, and it was not long after that before we located our respective companies. Never will the writer forget, however, that strange feeling which came over him when it was realized that he had been left behind!

The locale of the following escapade may have been Chateau Thierry (the writer is under the impression that it happened at that place) but, anyway, it occurred in the Marne sector with I Company men as the principal actors. Our outfit arrived in town minus our cooker and the chances for an early mess seemed very slim indeed to the hungry men. After being dismissed from ranks, we had ample time in which to explore the many wrecked homes throughout the place - long streets of them. In nearly every house we entered there was evidence of the hasty departure of the late occupants. All the heavier furniture was left behind - great French bedsteads with thick mattresses and bed linen which looked so inviting to the tired men; tables, bureaus with drawers full of linen; wardrobes full of clothes of all kinds and description; pianos, chairs, china and glassware - all left behind at the approach of the German army! While some of the boys were going through these houses, others had been busy ransacking the many gardens located in the rear of these homes, gathering up whole armfuls of all kinds of vegetables - carrots, beets, potatoes, tomatoes, beans, etc., etc. Seeing that there was prospect ahead for a treat of vegetable soup, one of our men in a spirit of high glee dressed himself up in a complete suit of full dress or evening clothes which he had found in one of the houses - high silk hat included! Thus attired, he voluntarily served the laughing men with a tray in one hand and a towel thrown over his left arm. The writer can see him now, dressed in that comical and ill-fitting suit, as he played "waiter" for the boys as they ate that soup served in such style - thanks to the plentiful supply of chinaware, knives, forks and spoons which the town afforded! It is regretted that the name of our "waiter" on this auspicious occasion cannot at this time be recalled but all I Company men will undoubtedly remember the incident.

Briefly summarizing the activities of the entire 111th Infantry in the Marne Defensive, we shall close this chapter with a review as given in Colonel Edward Martin's history of the Twenty-Eighth Division. The Colonel writes as follows:

"Following the engagement at Hill 204, the Regiment continued its training. At this time the regimental, battalion and company commanders were conducted by French Officers to the ground on which was established a reserve line, on the south bank of the River Marne, for use in case of further advance of the German forces. At midnight of July 3-4, the Regiment was ordered to occupy this line, the occupation being completed at 6:30 A. M., July 4, Regimental Headquarters being at Le Mesnil. At noon of the same day, it being seen that no German attack would be forthcoming, the Regiment was ordered to march to Grande Foret, arriving there at 6:00 P. M. and bivouacking for the night. At 5:30 the next morning, the Regiment marched to its former billets in the Bassevelle area, with Regimental Headquarters at Le Vapre. Later, on the 5th, Regimental Headquarters and Headquarters Company were moved to Fosse Ardois, and the whole Regiment moved to areas north of the Chateau-Thierry-Meaux road, going from Army to Corps reserve. On the 6th, the Trench Mortar Platoon of Headquarters Company, under the command of Lieutenant W. P. Snow, took part in an attack on Hill 204, rejoining the Regiment on July 7th. In this engagement, there was a loss of three killed and one wounded, Sergeant Samuel Thorpe of Headquarters Company being the first man in that unit to fall. He died a few days later in a German hospital. This was the first use of trench mortars made by any unit of the Division. On the 7th, one platoon of Company L and one from Company M were sent to serve with the French near Hill 204. These platoons were under Lieutenant W. A. L. McDowell, whose men would literally follow him through hell and high water. Later, Companies I and K served with the One Hundred Forty-sixth French Infantry in a sharp operation near Vaux.

"On July 8, the entire Regiment, less two companies and two platoons of the Third Battalion, again took up the reserve position along the Marne with Regimental Headquarters at Le Mesnil, occupying this sector until July 15th. During this period, a number of changes were made in the line owing to the detachment of several units of the Regiment. The line was subjected to considerable enemy shell fire, particularly in the sector occupied by the Second Battalion and later in that occupied by the Third Battalion in the vicinity of Nogent l' Artaud. During this week a number of the officers went forward for observation to the front-line positions occupied by French and American forces in the vicinity of Chateau-Thierry.

"On the evening of July 14, Bastille Day, all forces received orders to be on the alert for the long-expected German 'peace drive' and the troops on the Marne were moved to the right. The position of the One Hundred Eleventh was just outside of the artillery zone.

"On the afternoon of July 15, the Trench Mortar Platoon reported to the French Commander near Vaux, and the Second Battalion, under the command of Captain W. R. Dunlap, was ordered to report to the commanding general of the Third Division in the vicinity of Pertibout Farm. Here orders were received for the Battalion to proceed to Bois d'Aigremont, and upon arrival there, it reported to Colonel Butts, of the Thirtieth Infantry, at 3:00 A.M. on July 16th. Positions were taken in the trenches previously constructed by the Thirtieth Infantry, where the men were subjected to intense shell fire in which gas, shrapnel and high explosives were used.

"On receipt of information that the enemy proposed to attack at 4:00 P. M. on the 16th, the Second Battalion was directed to counterattack from its position at the northern edge of Bois d'Aigremont and

clear the entire sector to the Marne River between a line running
north and south through Crezansy on the right, and a north and south
line just east of Fossoy on the left.   The first wave, consisting of
Company G and two platoons of Company E, under command of Captain
Schlosser, went forward at 2:00 P. M. by crawling in thin lines through
the wheat field toward their objective, the Metz-Paris road, which was
to be reached at 4:00 o'clock.   One platoon of Company G worked its
way along the ravine running in a northeasterly direction toward
Crezansy, the object, which was accomplished, being to clear and hold
the town.   At 4:00 o'clock the artillery laid down a creeping barrage,
under cover of which the first wave crossed the Paris-Metz road, clearing the woods to the railroad, where positions were taken up.   Another
platoon advanced to a point from which good observation of the river
was had, remaining there until dark, when combat patrols moved forward
covering Mezy and the south bank of the river to the dam.   The supporting troops, consisting of Companies F, H and E (less two platoons),
were held in support in the woods about five hundred yards south of the
railroad, where they entrenched for better cover.   These positions
were held until the Regiment was withdrawn on the 20th, and the positions
taken over by the Seventh and Thirty-eighth United States Infantries.

"The First Battalion went into Bois d'Aigremont in support of the
Second Battalion on the night of July 16-17, taking up its positions on
the hill, some of the troops being protected by the old aqueduct which
furnishes a portion of the water supply for the city of Paris.

"On the 17th, the commander of the One Hundred Eleventh was ordered
to report next day to Major General Dickman, of the Third Division,
taking with him Headquarters, Machine Gun and Supply Companies.   On
July 18, Companies I and K returned from duty with the French and re-
joined the Third Battalion at the Petites Noues.   The same day Col.
Shannon reported to the commander of the Third Division at Pertibout
Farm, and was directed to proceed to Greves Farm, where guides were
met to conduct the troops to the position held by one battalion of the
Thirtieth Infantry and the Second and First Battalions of the One
Hundred Eleventh.

"At 12:40 A. M., July 19, Colonel Shannon arrived at the headquarters of the Thirtieth Regiment near Greves Farm and at once took
over the command of that sector from Colonel Butts.   While going into
this position there were a number of casualties due to heavy enemy
shell fire, the first man to fall being little Walter L. Weldner,
Colonel Shannon's striker.   About this time Lieutenant Colonel Sucoop
rejoined the Regiment and remained continuously until after the Armistice.

"The location near Greves Farm will ever be known to the One Hundred Eleventh as 'Dead Horse Hill.'   The entire transport of the
Thirtieth Regiment was in the woods at this point when the German attack started on the morning of the 15th, and practically all the horses
had been killed.   The companies that were not in the immediate front
line were set to work burying the few soldiers that their comrades of
the Thirtieth had not been able to bury, and also the dead animals.
(1)
"The counter-attack made by the American and French forces near

Pontoon bridge constructed by American soldiers over the Marne at Chateau Thierry, France, July 1918.

American and French soldiers constructing pontoon bridge across Marne River for use of artillery. Chateau Thierry, France, July 21, 1918.

(Images courtesy of National Archives)

Soissons on the 17th and 18th had compelled the retirement of the Germans from the banks of the Marne, and it was now possible to draw upon the Allies' defensive line along the river to furnish troops for other sectors. On the night of the 20th and morning of the 21st, the One Hundred Eleventh was withdrawn from this sector, being relieved by elements of the Seventh and Thirty-eighth Regiments of the Third Division, which later continued the push toward the Vesle.

"On leaving 'Dead Horse Hill' a night march was made to Grande Bordeaux Farm, where the troops arrived between midnight and 4:00 A.M., immediately going to sleep, and it was the first time in five days that they had been able to sleep without their gas masks being at Alert.

"An incident of the stay at Grande Bordeaux Farm was a severe lesson in the effects of gas. One of the companies of the First Battalion had been among the last to leave 'Dead Horse Hill', which at the time was drenched with mustard gas. A steady rain was falling and the slickers were soaking wet. On arriving at Grande Bordeaux Farm, the exhausted men threw themselves down in any place and when they awoke in the morning many of them could not see, the fumes of the gas having taken effect as the men slept. As a result of their experience, thirty-five men, temporarily blinded, were taken to the hospital that morning.

"Early on the 21st, the Germans vacated Chateau-Thierry, the apex of the Marne salient and the highwater mark of their advance on Paris, and on the afternoon of the same day the Twenty-eighth Division, once more united under its own commander, was ordered to cross the Marne. At 3:30 P.M. the One Hundred Eleventh Infantry started marching through the battered village of Nesles into Chateau-Thierry, where the Regiment crossed the river on a pontoon bridge.

"This pontoon bridge had been thrown across the river by the French, assisted by American engineers, shortly after the Germans moved out, and was designed for foot travel only. When the Machine Gun Company and One Pounder Platoon of Headquarters Company arrived with their guns and ammunition carts, they proceeded to unhitch the mules and lead them across. A French sentinel protested vehemently, using the same slogan made famous at Verdun two years before. Two irate captains used diplomacy instead of force, and the Machine Guns and One Pounders of the One Hundred Eleventh were the first in the Division to cross the Marne. The last of the One Hundred Eleventh crossed at 8:00 P.M. on July 21, the Regiment bivouacking that night in the village of Brasles. Here the kitchen and ration carts joined the Regiment after making a very circuitous detour through Nogent l' Artaud. The 22nd was spent at Brasles and that night the Regiment proceeded to the Bois de Barbillon, northeast of Chateau-Thierry, for a few hours' rest under the trees and in a pouring rain.

"Things were getting hot along the front. The Twenty-sixth Division had attacked in a northwesterly direction to the left of Chateau-Thierry and had been very roughly handled in its attack of the 21st, making it necessary for the Fifty-sixth Infantry Brigade, with Brigadier General Weigel in command, to swing over to the left and take position in the line with such units of the Yankee Division as

remained effective.   With this in view, early in the morning of July
23, the Regiment proceeded to the Grande Rue Farm in a northwesterly
direction from Chateau-Thierry, reporting at 9:00 A. M. to Major
General Edwards, commanding the Twenty-sixth Division, and going into
bivouac in the woods to the east and west of the Chateau-Thierry-
Etrepilly road. On reporting to General Edwards, Colonel Shannon was
directed to hold his forces in readiness to support the troops of the
Twenty-sixth Division then in the line, and shortly after noon was
directed to reconnoiter the position held by the One Hundred First and
One Hundred Second Infantries with a view of relieving them with two
battalions of the One Hundred Eleventh. The relief of the position
was begun at dark with the Second and Third Battalions under the command of Colonel Shannon, Lieutenant Colonel Succop remaining with the
support in command of the First Battalion, Headquarters and Machine
Gun Companies.

"While the relief was in process orders were received at 3:30
A. M. to prepare to make an attack at 6:15 A. M., July 24th. The
Third Battalion was to occupy the right of the sector and the Second
Battalion the left, each battalion having two companies in the front
line, and two in support. The attack started on time, proceeding
without opposition for a distance of about eight hundred yards, when
a French cavalry patrol on the left flank reported to Colonel Shannon
that the enemy had evacuated Epieds, and the advance was stopped.
General Weigel, then at Bezuet, was advised, and a request made that
the artillery barrage which had been ordered should be immediately
stopped. In a very short while General Weigel directed that the advance be continued until strong resistence by the enemy should be made,
La Croix Rouge Farm being the objective.

"From Epieds the advance was started with two companies of each
battalion leading, their elements being in lines of platoon columns
followed in close support by the other two companies in the same formation, the instructions being to march by compass, bearing north
fifteen degrees east. The advance continued and when the leading
element of the right sector was opposite Epieds it moved to the right
flank and for the time being contact with it was lost. The balance
of the column continued until opposite Beaubards, when heavy machine
gun fire developed from the village. The advance was halted and a
reconnoissance patrol from Company K reported French troops to be
conducting an operation against the village. The advance was resumed,
continuing through the Foret de Fere, leaving the town on the left.
On account of the dense growth of the forest it became almost impossible to maintain contact between the units, and the column was reduced to a column of files consisting of Companies E, H, I and K. The
right sector became disengaged at this time and was held up on the
southern edge of the forest. Companies E, H, I and K continued the
advance through the forest, and at about 4:00 P. M. Company H, which
was leading, was held up by machine gun fire. The opposition was
overcome by automatic rifle teams sent to the right flank and the advance continued to a point about seven hundred yards from La Croix
Rouge Farm, where an intense machine gun fire was laid down by the Boche.

"Two companies hurriedly established a line and reduced the enemy
fire, after which the column was again formed and attempt made to ad-

Above: Emplacement of 380 M/M German gun in woods east of Epieds, France, 26th Division.

Below: Showing tracks used in bringing gun in and out. Germans succeeded in getting gun out in their retreat. In woods east of Epieds, France.

(Images July 28, 1918, courtesy of National Archives)

vance, but the enemy fire immediately reopened and it was impossible, owing to the density of the underbrush and heavy fire, to advance further. An officer's patrol sent to the left of the position reported the enemy to be in force in the vicinity of La Croix Rouge Farm. As it was growing late and support was very uncertain it was decided to establish a position and hold the ground gained. Company K was placed in the front line, the other three companies being echeloned in depth in the forest to the rear, all units being in place before dark. In the early evening contact was gained with the French on the left and toward morning liaison was gained on the right with a small French detachment that had worked up through the forest.

"At 5:00 A. M., on July 25th, no word having been received from the Brigade Commander as to the supporting troops, First Lieutenant Jean M. Sioux, Fifty-fourth Chasseurs, French Army, a most capable and gallant officer, who was attached to the Regiment, conveyed a message to General Weigel at Courpoil, giving him the first information as to the condition and location of the detachment. These positions were held throughout the 25th, each side keeping up a desultory rifle and machine gun fire.

"While Colonel Shannon was advancing to the position at La Croix Rouge Farm the First Battalion, Headquarters and Machine Gun Companies had followed through Epieds and Bezu-St. Germain to the village of Courpoil, bivouacking in the woods to the right of the village. Companies F, G, L and M, after being separated from Colonel Shannon, joined the First Battalion at this place.

"Late in the afternoon of the 25th word was received that the One Hundred Eleventh would be relieved by the One Hundred Sixty-seventh Infantry, Forty-second Division. The relief was effected by 9:00 o'clock that night and the detachment with Colonel Shannon marched south through the woods to Courpoil and thence to the Trugny Woods, where the rest of the Regiment had been assembled earlier in the night.

"The casualties during the advance to La Croix Rouge Farm were five killed and fifteen wounded, and the total casualties of the Regiment up to this time were: killed, officers two, men fifty-five; wounded, officers three, men three hundred fifty-nine. Among those killed at La Croix Rouge Farm was Sergeant Andrea, of Company G, who had earned his D.S.C. at Crezanzy."

CHAPTER 16.

IN PURSUIT OF FRITZ.

Sunday, again, proved to be the "moving day", for on the 28th, about 6 A. M., found the entire regiment in column ready to march off. None were at all surprised in this sudden turn of events. Indeed, the majority of the men had anticipated that Sunday would see the "outfit on the road again".

The morning was well spent before the long column finally got under way. Frequent stops of long intervals were made during our advance that Sunday - much to the satisfaction of all. At six o'clock that evening, after being on the road for eight hours, we reached the Foret de Fere, and had covered only about six kilometres! It seemed to the men that the regiment had been cautiously "feeling its way along" that day! There was an air of suppressed excitement throughout the troops! Every man seemed to sense that we were on serious business!

Under shelter of friendly trees in the Foret de Fere, the 111th Infantry again went into bivouac. Here we found numerous dugouts which showed unmistakable signs of having been recently occupied by German troops. Many a man in our battalion, especially the "souvenir crank", in handling old German blankets, clothing and parts of uniform, equipment, etc. found in these dugouts, had reason later on to regret it! The unfortunate soldier very soon discovered, to his dismay, that he had only succeeded in adding to his already increased accumulation of cooties! In these woods, also, a new problem confronted the men, many suffering from an attack of dysentery, - hence soon the place was known as "Dysentery woods". On Tuesday night word was received from a French artilleryman that Fritz had been pushed back so far that he was out of range of the French guns, which were located just to our right. While in these woods a rumor somehow started that Germany was at last willing and ready to make peace with the United States. By this time, however, we had learned our lesson about believing all such rumors and consequently paid little or no attention to this one. At nine o'clock Thursday night an alarm was given that an enemy aeroplane was overhead. This warning was very soon substantiated by the now familiar sound of the dreaded German motors. Advice was received that about that time a bomb was dropped on some troops of either the 109th or 110th Infantry, lying somewhere in our rear, injuring a number of their men. It was told us that a squad of men playing cards in a "pup" tent had been hit, - that the enemy plane had located the troops by a small light thoughtlessly used by the players. Full details of this disaster never reached the writer. No incident of particular importance occurred during Friday. On Saturday, August the 3rd, we received orders that we would move out that night.

About 7:30, the regiment was "on the move" again! The hike that night proved to be one of the most miserable marches we had ever before experienced! Rain, which kept up continuously and violently practically all night, greatly added to our difficulties. Our slickers offered little or no protection in that down-pour! They reached to the top of our leggings and, consequently, the water dripping off these slickers ran through our leggings and into our shoes. Our feet were soon soaked! At each step, we could feel that cold water oozing up between our toes - a most disagreeable sensation! Packs were soon soaked which greatly added to their weight! Our progress was very slow on account of so much traffic on the roads - trucks, wagons, machine guns, mules, - all moving onward through that stormy night. We crossed the Ourcq River and marched through the town of Courmont. It was indeed a sad lot of weary soldiers on the march that night! Frequent stops were made and some of the more tired and sleepy during these intervals of rest would lie right down in the mud and water seemingly unmindful of possible serious effects from this exposure. Others would almost go to sleep standing on their feet until brought back to the stern reality of the situation by that often repeated and low command of "Forward!" So, altogether, it was a night long to be remembered by all, the events of which were frequently afterwards recalled by the men when relating some of our more trying experiences.

It was just getting light when we passed through the town of Cierges and the cold, dismal dawn of the new day seemed to reflect the feelings of the tired and wornout troops as they slowly trudged onward - ever onward! It was at this place that the 110th Infantry had such a hard and costly encounter with the enemy just a few days previous. While for many reasons we were glad to see morning, the sights which met our gaze when the shadows of the night were dispelled sufficiently to discern objects shall never be forgotten! Both sides of the road were literally strewn with bodies of dead Germans - many horribly mutilated and in various stages of decomposure. It soon became evident that the American dead had been buried for, except in one or two isolated cases, we did not come across a body in the familiar kakhi - much to the relief of our boys. Many of the bodies had swollen and turned black from exposure. The odors wafted to us on the morning's breeze were anything but pleasant! Doubtless every man of the 111th who passed along that road has, to this day, an indellible picture traced on his memory of some horrible spectical which confronted him in the cold, gray dawn of that terrible morning! The writer, speaking for himself, shall never forget his feelings on beholding so many of the dead - each prosterate body having a strange facination and bearing some mute evidence of the fatal shot or shrapnel! Of the many horrible scenes witnessed that morning, one in particular arrested my attention as I emerged from a strip of woods. On my left, just at the edge of a growth of underbrush and near the road, lay two of the fallen foe in a position which plainly suggested the circumstances under which at least one had met his death. The familiar red cross band pinned on the arm of one of the men told that old war story as plain as if it had been told in words. Here was a comrade who had gone to the aid of a mortally wounded pal only to be

himself killed!   Both were very tall men and, judging by their powerful and well built bodies, were probably members of the famous Prussian Guards who had lately operated in that vicinity.   The body of
the Red Cross man partly covered that of his comrade as if, while in
the very act of rendering first-aid, a piece of shrapnel had ef-
fectively ended his errand of mercy.   On closer inspection, this
seemed substantiated by observing the cotton bandages still grasped in
one of his outstretched hands.   The faces of both men were clearly
visible from the road.   It required only a quick glance to see that
the first to fall had been hit in the stomach.   The clothing from
that part of his body had been cut away, leaving a ghastly wound exposed to view!   The Red Cross man had practically the entire top of
his head taken off by shrapnel.   It was as if a razor had been used
to sever his head just above his ears!   Nearby lay his helmet half
filled with blood!   The whole bloody scene presented a most sickening and grusome sight!   Subsequently, during our march that morning
and on many occasions afterwards, it befell my lot to witness other
scenes of a like nature but somehow or other that particular picture
stands out more prominently than all the rest!   I must admit, however,
that the sight of our own dead made an everlasting impression on me!
It somehow gave a man a peculiar feeling to see lying at his feet the
still form of a buddy, especially when that buddy had been in animated
conversation with you but a few seconds before!   It is not the intention of the writer to dwell at length on scenes similar to the above.
To those of my readers who fought in the World War such descriptions
are already written perhaps too vividly on the pages of their memories!
To others, whose fortune it has been to thus far escape these unpleasant experiences, sufficient has already been related to convey to
them incidents covering the bloody toll of war!

The sun had been up some hours err the long column was brought to
a halt in an open field northwest of Villome.   The command was given
to "Fall out and pitch tents!"   This order, always most agreeable,
was that morning a God-send to the muddy, hungry, sleepy and nearly
exhausted troops.   Tents were erected as rapidly as the wornout men
could throw them up and many of the boys at once "turned in" to rest
their aching bodies and perhaps snatch a few hours sleep, taking
chances of getting mess which, we were informed, would be served as
soon as possible.   A hasty breakfast was at last prepared to which
all did full justice.   Some of the men at this meal expressed their
doubts that the regiment would remain in its present position for a
very long period.   Their doubts were well founded for, about noon
while the men were lined up receiving another handout of grub, orders
were passed around for the troops to move at once.   Mess was hurriedly
gulped down, tents struck, packs rolled and in a surprisingly short
space of time we were again ready for the road and wherever it led us!

Rumor had it that the Germans "were on the run" and we knew that
it was up to us to see that they were kept running!   Although not
fully recovered from our recent labors of the previous night, this
news was at least encouraging and served to brighten up the spirits
of the men considerable.   However, the "chase", as some of the boys
called it, proved of short duration.   About one kilometre was covered
when, greatly to the surprise of many, a "right-about-face" was given

and the men were marched back to their old location in the open field. It later became known that the Fourth Division had received and were moving under the same orders which we had at first received and, consequently, our services were not needed - at least for the present. None regretted the "false alarm", however, and eagerly looked forward with pleasant anticipations to a night of refreshing sleep!

The following morning, August 5th, about 11 o'clock, the entire regiment was again on the move and during the afternoon of that day reached the woods Northwest of Dravegny, in the vicinity of Bois Chenet. Here, we were held for several days with nothing much on our minds to worry about except exercising an unusual amount of precaution due to the heavy enemy barages centered on these woods. Jerry always managed to make things lively for us! He could be relied upon for that! While not engaged in dodging shells, another occupation at this time proved to be a most popular sport and perhaps while not as exciting, it at least gave the men something to do - profitably employing their spare time! Our short sojourn in the wilds of Foret d' Fere, as above stated, had resulted in annexing to our ranks a considerable number of new recruits - cooties! While, of course, these little enemies had not been entirely unknown to us heretofore, evidently the reinforcements just lately received were vigorously acting under orders to "dig in!" Their added numbers and persistent activities now caused the men some concern. We found this foe very stubborn and loath to abandon operations on his chosen sector - our poor bodies! In fact, although frequent onslaughts were kept up day and night, their ranks seemed to increase rather than diminish! "Shirt-reading parties" were organized in the hope that concentrated efforts along these lines would route the enemy from his strenghold! The mystified and uninitiated reader hereof is informed that to "read one's shirt" back in the days of 1918, was a term used by the doughboys meaning to shed that garment and minutely examine the same, incidently picking off and killing, with one's two thumbnails, the cooties seen lurking in the folds of said shirt - underwear, socks or whatnot! The procedure, while not exactly pleasant, was soon universally adopted as the most effective way to, temporarily, rid our bodies of these annoying vermin.

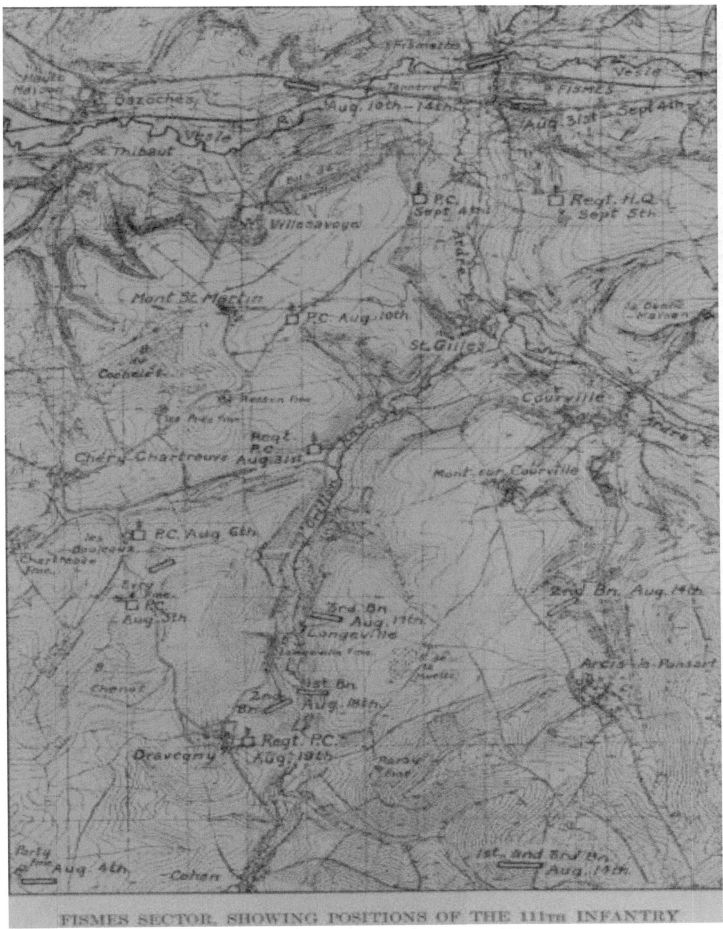

Taken from Twenty-eighth Division: Pennsylvania's Guard in the World War Volume 2, Page 332, 1924, By Colonel Edward Martin

Doughboys moving into action near Fismes, 1918.
(Image courtesy Library of Congress)

Ruined streets and buildings in Fismes, August 12, 1918
(Image courtesy of National Archives)

CHAPTER 17.

FISMES AND FISMETTE!

On August 8th, 1918, the First Battalion and one-pounder platoon of Headquarters Company were sent to the support of the 112th U. S. Infantry, which regiment had relieved troops of the 32nd Division on the Vesle River.   On August 9th, the Second Battalion was sent as further support to the 112th Infantry, and on August 10th the command of the sector was taken over by the Commanding Officer of our regiment, and the entire 111th placed in position.

Thus it was that during the evening of August 9th, our Third Battalion was called upon to take an active part in operations around the little town of Fismette, located just across the Vesle River from its sister-village, Fismes.   Both places had been Jerry's stronghold for sometime and the scenes of long-contested battles with the French. In marching to our position we were continuously harrassed by a terrific barrage of shell and gas, causing the battalion many casualties. At this time we had to contend with and endeavor to overcome the effects of high explosive shells which the Germans sent over by way of variation for our entertainment!   These shells, upon bursting, would not only broadcast the usual amount of deadly shrapnel but would send forth terrible fumes, the effects of which while not as diasterous as poisonous gases, caused the men to cough and sneeze excessively.   The continuous falling of these shells within our lines made it only a question of a short time when the men were unable to wear their gas masks.   Knowing our predicament, the enemy would cunningly proceed to lay down a barrage of mustard or some other gas equally as dangerous, catching us unawares with masks off!   Many a man breathed in the deadly vapor thinking at the time it was only the fumes from high explosive shells!   Man after man, in that advance up to Fismes, fell in his tracks, being almost overcome and unable to keep up the steady pace maintained by the battalion.   Some of the men just temporarily "dropped out", rejoining their companies later.   Field hospitals took care of the more serious cases and some of the gas victims were not able to report back for duty until many days afterwards.   Taking everything into consideration, our march up to the front that night was one long to be remembered by all!

Shortly after midnight on the 10th of August, we reached the town of Fismes and were greeted there by an expectant barrage, the enemy sending their shells into the village at almost regular intervals.   In single-file and five paces apart, we proceeded down a dark and deserted thoroughfare which was obstructed in many places by the wreckage of shell-torn buildings.   The demolished houses took strange and fantastic shapes in the darkness, while the silent uninhabited streets

spoke more of death than life! We had been warned by our officers
of the near proximity of the German forces. All conversation was
ordered to cease and the commands of our officers were conveyed in
undertones! The seriousness of our mission, accompanied as it was
by perils seen and unseen on every hand, seemed to be fully appreciated by each and every man of our Third Battalion that night!
We kept close in the shadows of the buildings and were compelled to be
constantly on the alert to guard against stumbling over any obstacle,
fearing that in so doing we would perhaps give our position away to
some German spy or sniper hidden, maybe, in one of those buildings!
Several times the column was brought to an abrupt stop and we remained
motionless in our tracks until an enemy star-shell light, or "flare"
had died out. (These lights were often used by both the German and
the allied armies in signalling work at night and for the purpose of
keeping a surveillance over the enemy's position.) They were shot
off or discharged very much like a sky-rocket and while slowly descending to the earth would throw off hundreds of little stars which brightly illuminated quite an area. The darkest spot would thus be exposed
in a brillance resembling the light of a noon-day sun. To proceed
under the light of these rockets was decidedly hazardous and due precautions were exercised down the long column of marching men whenever
Jerry would send one up. This was our first experience in this particular phase of night warfare and many comments regarding it were afterwards exchanged. On this night, however, any remark or query had to be
postponed until a more opportune time!

We had proceeded but a short distance down one of the streets
when - crash! - a shell hit in one of the buildings just across the
way! This was immediately followed by another and another until it
seemed that Jerry had surely discovered our movement. Some of the
men were apparently becoming panic-stricken - darting out of the
column and running aimlessly ahead - but the sharp commands of our officers brought them back and the troops proceeded in an orderly formation.   Under a terrific barrage, literally hurling upon our ranks
brick, stone and motar from the shelled buildings, we slowly advanced
through what remained of the Town of Fismes, receiving word there to
cross the Vesle River and reinforce our Second Battalion. In moving
into position the Third Battalion, it is needless to add, suffered
many casualties. Dawn found our battalion divided, only a portion of
the men succeeding in crossing the Vesle into the Town of Fismette
under cover of the preceding night. Only seventeen men from Company
I succeeded in crossing that bridge into Fismette, where they were immediately ordered to join forces with the Second Battalion in a desperate effort to break up the German attack.

For three days and nights the battle raged, during which time the
combined forces of the Second and Third Battalions firmly held their
ground, successfully repulsing three enemy attacks.   It was in this
engagement that the fighting assumed almost a "hand-to-hand" encounter! (At other times, on approach of the Americans, the Germans
had retreated without much ceremony but here they were most persistent
and seemed determined to regain their lost territory in Fismette!)
A number of our men met horrible deaths at this time, the enemy employing "flame-throwers", besides the dreaded German hand-grenade, or

"potato-masher" as nicknamed by the Americans. These grenades were
mounted on sticks about a foot long and could be easily thrown with
accuracity a great distance. Captain Thompson of our troops met a
horrible death during the first morning's fighting in the streets of
Fismes - near the bridge - his head being blown to pieces by one of
these "potato-mashers"!

While holding-down this sector, we occupied the many wine cellars
found throughout the two villages. In these cellars, we were comparatively safe from shell fire and German snipers but at any moment
expected an exploding shell would block up the entrances to these
under-ground vaults and imprison us! These cellars, luckily for us,
were very strongly constructed of brick and stone securely arched and
afforded a splendid refuge from the flying debris and whistling shrapnel on the streets outside. It must not be construed, however, that
we spent all our time resting peacefully under ground and out of harm's
way! None of this for the men of our Third Battalion! Many were assigned to various details, both day and night, such as trips to and
from ration and ammunition "dumps", acting as battalion and company
runners, going out on special patrol duty, litter-carriers, etc., etc.-
all of which necessitated the crossing and recrossing of that bridge
between the two towns which was constantly under heavy shelling from
the German guns! The enemy had cunningly bob-wired the Vesle River
at this point and it was impossible to cross over except by means of
the bridge which was swept by machine gun fire and bombarded by heavy
artillery!

Thus, for three terrible days we held our ground - days long to be
remembered by the men of our Third Battalion! Here, our very first
cases of "shell-shock" developed! The nerves of the strongest were
tried! The second night we occupied these towns, the Germans sent
over a powerful gas attack! The writer at the time happened to be
in a small cellar then occupied by other members of his squad. We
first heard the terrific concussion of the exploding shells in the
street just above our heads. We looked for the ceiling of the cellar
to come tumbling down at any minute! Very soon some of the men began coughing and sneezing! Taking warning, we hastily adjusted our
gas masks! The fumes from these shells rapidly descended and filled
our close quarters with the deadly vapor! Just about this time, a
detail of men was being organized to man a machine gun commanding a
certain street nearby. The writer, experiencing considerable difficulty in keeping his mask on owing to excessive coughing and sneezing, quickly responded to the call for volunteers to stand guard over
the machine gun which, at least, was out in the open where the gas was
not as thick. Between the two evils - a gas-filled chamber on one
hand and exposure to shell fire or snipers on the other - I did not
hesitate to choose the latter! Anything to be out of that hole and
be able to breathe! On regaining the street, I had no trouble in
keeping my mask on, the gas not being so dense in the open. I had
crept just about three houses from our cellar when I stumbled over
some object lying on the sidewalk in the shadow of the buildings. A
hurried glance and I hastened on to join the detail. It was just
another American doughboy lying there in the streets of Fismes - killed
by shell or snipers - one of the many I had lately seen! Our detail

relieved the tired machine gun crew just as a bursting shell took
away a portion of a brick wall across the street from where the gun
was stationed!   Truly, a hot welcome!   The night was clear and
from our position the moonlight afforded an unobstructed view of the
long and desolate street ahead.   The machine gun had been placed in
the shadow of a corner building.   The minutes seemed hours as they
dragged slowly by.   As regular as clock-work, Jerry sent over his
deadly missives into the village, many coming too near to make our
detail feel exactly comfortable!   We had received orders, on taking
over the gun, not to fire until given the command by a Lieutenant who
had been placed in charge of several machine guns located in the
vicinity.   Word was later passed down the line that at a certain
time (the exact hour was made known to us) an American patrol would
be sent out to reconnoiter and to let them pass unchallenged.   An hour
passed.   The Germans were now shelling a distant part of the town.
Quiet reigned in our immediate neighborhood - much to our relief.   A
slight breeze served to refresh the atmosphere somewhat and we risked
taking our gas masks off.   Presently and without warning a flare illuminated the scene around us.   We crouched down close to the ground
and remained perfectly motionless while that ball of fire slowly
descended.   By its light, we hastily "took in" the situation.   We
could now plainly see the havoc recently wrought by those German shells.
Where only a few hours ago stood a large building, nothing now remained
but a pile of brick, timber and stone!   Prosterate forms on the sidewalks and in the roadway told of more human blood spilled during our
occupancy of the town!   Not a living thing could we see down that
long street commanded by our machine gun.   Were German snipers lurking
in those dense shadows ahead?   Were they, too, taking advantage of
that flare and looking for us?   The flare reached the ground and died
out.   How dark and dismal it now seemed!   A whispered word of warning from the corporal in direct charge of our particular detail!   That
was the American patrol going out - don't open fire!   Two more hours
on that gun!   The early morning air was chilly - penetrating.   How we
longed for a snatch of sleep between warm blankets!   Three o'clock
and our relief came!   They were first told about the patrol on duty
and the exact time it was due to return.   We then hastened back to
our quarters (now almost entirely free from gas), stretched out upon
our blankets and prepared to spend the remaining hour or so before
dawn in a much needed rest and sleep.

During the next day, rumors of being relieved sometime that night
spread throughout the ranks of Our Third Battalion.   These rumors
were substantiated by our own officers late in the afternoon.   Only
a few more hours to remain in that hell hole!   Several minor incidents occurred during the day.   The battalion made no attempt to advance further into the enemy's territory but firmly held the ground
captured dispite the heavy shelling and an occasional machine gun barrage.

Several of our men, during the hot afternoon of that August day,
risked their lives in going after water to refill canteens.   They had
located a pump in the rear of a shelled ruin situated some blocks away.
The lure of a cool, refreshing drink was hard indeed to resist regardless of the danger incurred by this unnecessary exposure to enemy fire.

The writer, with several comrades, made a dash for the pump which we reached without mishap. Quickly taking a drink and filling our canteens, we made the run back to our wine cellar in record time - the race enlivened by one of Jerry's "love tokens" which, it seemed to us, was sent over especially for our benefit - just to make the adventure a bit exciting! Luckily, the shell fell "short" and, out of breath but with full canteens, we rejoined our comrades, victorious!

Relief at last! On the night of Tuesday, August 13th, our position was taken over by a part of the 77th Division. After marching from the front lines nearly all that night under heavy shelling, the battalion arrived in the vicinity of Abby d' Igny, where we went into bivouac.

Our short stay in the woods just above Abby d' Igny was uneventful but extremely restful after those exciting days in Fismes and Fismette. During this brief period of relaxation, we were constantly "entertained" by the frequent booming of big guns comprising part of the 55th Coast Artillery Corps not far away. The enemy shelled the woods every night and morning, leaving us quite unmolested at other times. Our kitchens were again "on the job" and after being deprived of real food for several days on a streach, we hovered around them at all hours for "a hand out". The men now had a chance to shave and clean-up a bit. The weather was fine but somewhat warm.

Concerning the activities of our Machine Gun Company during its first occupancy of Fismes, we close this chapter by quoting a few notes made by an officer of that important unit of the 111th. The account reads as follows:

"On August 1st, we left this wood and marched all night during a very heavy rain and part of the next morning, until we reached our new area. Here the entire regiment was quartered in an open field living in shelter tents. Late in the afternoon of the 2nd, we were ordered to move forward and, after going a short distance, we were ordered back as the 4th Division had moved into position ahead of us. We returned to the position we had just left, remaining there until the morning of the 4th, when, we left on an all day march and once more we entered the wood, setting up this time our guns for anti-air-craft work. We remained in this position until the night of the 6th, when orders came to relieve the 112th. That later was recinded and on the 7th, we were again ordered to relieve the 112th. While in column that day, shelling wounded several of our animals. The day of the 8th was spent in cleaning and preparing the guns for front line work. Early on the morning of the 9th, we made ready to move into position but did not move until evening. Roads were being shelled heavily at that time with high explosives and gas, and during the march we lost one man wounded. We unloaded equipment at the junction of the main and sunken roads. Guns and ammunition were carried a distance of two kiles or more into the town of Fismes, where we relieved the 112th Machine Gun Company through a

heavy bombardment of the town. The day of the 10th, we
spent in sniping and later picking out different objects
and positions for firing upon. Our casualties were then
increasing continually. This night the German shelling
increased and caused considerable losses to our regiment.
The morning of the 11th, we spent in sniping and harras-
sing fire and in the afternoon orders came for a machine
gun barrage to be fired at 1:05 P. M. The officers and
Sergeants layed the guns and gave fire orders for same,
the results of which were successful. Having only men
enough to man seven guns in three platoons, we disposed
of nearly 40,000 rounds of ammunition. The morning of
the 12th, we were in position when orders came to evacuate the town. We left the town about twelve noon and
moved over a road that was subject to heavy shelling but
during our march no casualties resulted. Marching until
late afternoon, we arrived in a wood above Abby d' Igny,
where we joined the remainder of the regiment. We remained in this wood until the 18th of August, when we
again moved forward into reserve position near St. Gilles
and proceeded to establish a line of resistence. Here,
the shelling was constant and we were compelled to wear
gas masks a great deal of the time. Some of our men were
sent to the rear, being badly gassed with mustard gas. We
were also subjected to bombing by German planes that came
over most every night. Remained here, digging trenches
and gun emplacements."

Men of the 28th Division camp in the woods near Fismes, out of sight of the German airmen.

(Image courtesy of National Archives)

CHAPTER 18.

ON "THREE GUN HILL" AT LONGUEVILLE FARM.

On Sunday night, August the 18th - a night made brilliant by a
full moon, we again hastily rolled our packs and by eight o'clock were
on our way. The guns of the enemy were strangely quiet along our
sector that night. The troops, however, exercised every precaution
during the march keeping, as far as possible, in the dense shadows afforded by an occasional stretch of woodland. When obliged to cross
open fields flooded by moonlight, we quickened our steps, observing
at the same time the usual "safety distance" of five paces apart.

Finally, without mishap, our Third Battalion reached the side of
a small group of hills located at a place called Longueville Farm,
about three-quarters of a kilometre northeast of Dravegny. Our battalion was soon assigned to its bivouac site on the side of a long and
precipitous hill, which we found to our delight already honey-combed
with numerous dugouts capable of accommodating from one man to five or
six. After we had received the order to unpack, there followed a
general scamper among the men to obtain the most desirable dugouts.
Corporals, however, were ordered to keep their respective squads together, if possible. Our kitchens were stationed at the base of this
hill and we were reasonably assured of our regular meals while occupying this position.

It now seemed that our Division had been retained in the Fismes
sector to establish a line of resistence. We had not been "relieved"
at all in the true sense of the word - and we knew it! Only fooled
again! At any rate, we were not on the front line but in reserve -
and that was something to be thankful for! While some troops were
holding Fismes and the sector on its immediate right, trenches were
ordered to be dug a short distance behind Fismes. Each battalion of
the two regiments of our brigade was to take its turn in Fismes of
four-day stretches. The 112th Infantry was at this time doing its
"turn" in Fismes and the men of our regiment were sent up each night
to dig trenches. During the days, we were permitted to rest. The
boys of the Third Battalion nicknamed their present location "Three
Gun Hill" on account of the three large guns belonging to the 55th
Coast Artillery which were stationed at the foot of our hillside dugouts. At times our position was heavily shelled by the enemy and on
the 25th Company I, alone, suffered five casualties, one of which
proved fatal.

The days spent on "Three Gun Hill" all had their interesting
stories, some of which we shall endeavor to relate. On account of
the very sandy and precipitous nature of the ground, we experienced

considerable difficulty in maintaining our dugout homes in habitable condition. The least jar, occasioned quite frequently by a misstep of some clumsy man occupying a dugout above our's, would cause the loose earth to tumble in on us - much to our consternation and to the amusement of the trespasser! But, we had another and more formidable disturber of the peace and wrecker of homes with which to contend. Every time one of the huge guns nearby opened fire, the resultant vibration caused our whole hillside to tremble, releasing stones of various sizes which, starting on their wild career at the top of the hill, would roll down the steep incline, often caving in numerous dugouts in their path. We were compelled to be constantly on guard at all times. One one occasion, a very large boulder came crashing down, barely missing a dugout in which a group of men were at the time playing cards. In its wild and disastrous journey, the huge stone caused considerable excitement, as well as havoc, but fortunately no one was hurt. The writer, with several other men of his squad, had taken possession of a dugout located near the crest of the hill and consequently had little to fear in the way of a "cave-in" or particularly the danger of a descending boulder.

We were not on "Three Gun Hill" many hours before the battalion got its first assignment at trench digging. Right after mess that evening, picks and shovels were furnished and as soon as night spread its black and protecting mantle over the countryside, the entire battalion set out, leaving a small detail behind to stand guard over our camp. After marching a short distance (much shorter than many of the men had predicted), we reached the scene of our nocturnal labors. Here, we found the ground already marked for digging, white cords denoting the desired lines of trenches to be dug. Taking off our blouses, we (the privates) set to real work with pick and shovel while the noncommissioned officers had the more desirable jobs of "bossing" the operation. (The writer owes a debt of gratitude to "Shorty" McCue, at that time his Corporal. "Shorty" proved to be a very lenient "boss" on that digging job, whispering in the ears of his men, "Take it easy, boys!" What is more than that, he often pitched-in and did some digging himself! Good old "Shorty" McCue! May he someday read this "memorial" perpetuating his good deeds to a grateful squad!)

The night was somewhat cloudy but occasionally the moon spread her pale light over the fields relieving, for brief periods, the inky darkness and greatly assisting the men at their labors. All conversation was carried on in low tones and, except for the sound of the implements at work and an occasional spark or two from a pick when it came into contact with a stone, a distant observer would never dream that hundreds of men were busily engaged in digging trenches there. Smoking was strictly prohibited as an added precaution. We worked in four-hour shifts although these periods varied quite frequently. While some of the men were engaged in the actual digging, others would be sent out on details to the nearby woods to cut and gather branches from trees. This foliage was carried back to the unfinished trenches and carefully distributed over the newly dug earth before we left for the night - thus camoflouging, or hiding from view, the trench-work from any German plane which might otherwise observe the newly dug trenches during the daytime. While engaged in digging, we were unmolested by enemy fire which undoubtedly was due to the many precau-

-tions taken.   Had they known the work we were engaged in, their shells
would have greatly aided (?) in plowing up the earth for us!   What a
pity!

Two or three uneventful days passed.   The greater part of the
time the men were allowed to rest and take it easy but sound sleep was
almost impossible on account of exposure to the hot August sun, the un-
mercible rays of which fairly baked the open and sandy hillside.   Our
dugouts afforded little or no protection, especially during the after-
noons.   Flies, too, were numerous and bothered the men considerably.
Due to the extreme heat, causing our bodies to freely perspire, the
presence of the cootie was generally and unmistakably felt!   In fact,
our old occupation of "shirt reading" was one of the most popular diversion of the day!

One afternoon, a squad of men was picked out to establish a
liaison post some four kiles away from camp, the object being to maintain a connecting-link or station of communication between the 111th
Infantry and a regiment of another Division - probably the 77th
Division at that time.   As the writer happened to be a member of this
squad, we shall go somewhat into details and relate our experiences -
experiences shared, no doubt, by many a man of the Third Battalion.

We quickly made up our packs, obtained several days' rations from
the company's cook and, under charge of Corporal McCue, the little detail set out.   Upon reaching the post, ideally situated in a grove
of trees and thick under-brush on a slight elevation, we set to work
with a will and much merriment erecting our pup-tents - anticipating a
life of ease and comfort for a few days anyway - "far from the maddening crowd", as it were!   What a relief to be away from that sun-
baked hillside!   Here we could really rest and sleep under those
splendid trees, the thick foliage of which offered such an abundance
of shade.   We pitched our tents under the largest trees so that they
could not be seen from an enemy plane.   It seemed that this spot had
been used for a similar purpose before.   A rough table had been put
up and we even found two or three chairs!   It was nearly dark before
tents were erected and our first mess at the post eaten.   One man at
a time was to stand an hour's guard duty during the night.   Some con-
tention arose as to which hour each man was to be assigned but the
argument was soon satisfactorily settled by drawing numbers.   The
lucky numbers, of course, drew the best hours - after midnight being
considered bad!   Guard duty was to start from ten o'clock that night.

The days at the post flew by all too quickly!   We were our own
"bosses" and did pretty nearly as we pleased.   A plentiful supply of
food fresh from the company's kitchen was daily delivered.   We soon
located not far distant a small French village - Dravegny - where the
Red Cross maintained a canteen.   To this town we made daily trips -
taking turns - bringing back tobacco, candy, cakes, writing paper, etc.
The weather still remained very warm but, under shade, we had no cause
to really suffer from the heat like our unfortunate comrades back on
the hillside.   If it hadn't been for the confounded flies drawn by
the lure of food (molasses), life at the post would have been heavenly
compared to what we had been through!   We soon discovered that a

French fly was every bit as pestiferous as its American cousin! On making explorations nearby, we came across several large dugouts scattered throughout the woods and made up our minds, should the bosch shell the place, we would abandon our tents and seek shelter in these dugouts. We had no occasion to make this change, however. While the Germans did shell our woods, none of these missives fell at what we considered "a dangerous distance" and, consequently, we stuck to our tents, laughing at Jerry's mistaken range! The nights here were wonderful - a glorious moon bathing the fields below in a soft, mellow glow. How peaceful everything seemed! What a contrast to those nights of terror spent in Fismes! It seemed impossible, gazing out upon the quiet countryside around us, that bloody war was in the land and especially that we had an active part in the raging conflict! But, far away, could be heard the continual booming of heavy artillery and upon the distant horizon, for miles around, the eye could catch that quick flash, resembling lightning, as some cannon was fired. It was here, by the way, that the writer of this narrative passed his twenty-ninth birthday, August 21, 1918, observing the event by an extra "treat" at the canteen and by writing a letter home. More letters were written by our squad that week than for many weeks in the past!

Our "little picnic", as we called it, was destined to come to an end and that very unexpectedly! One afternoon, about the 24th or 25th of August, a detail was sent up to relieve us - much to our dismay! We hated to leave the post where we had enjoyed a few days of comparative independence to go back on that hot hillside again - there to roast during the daytime and to dig trenches at night. But orders were orders! So, we struck tents, again rolled packs and reluctantly we marched back to rejoin our battalion. We had hardly settled again in our old dugouts on "Three Gun Hill" when all were pleasantly surprised by a bit of good news! With the battalion, we were to march back to Abbe d' Igny, about four kilometres in the rear, there to get a hot shower bath, new summer underwear and our clothes put through a steam "de-cootiezer" while we bathed! Upon hearing this, it all seemed too good to be true and we were somewhat reconciled in having to leave our liaison post for this treat. Many will recall that hot afternoon's hike, followed by a much-needed bath, a change of clothes, good eats and reading matter at the Y. M. C. A. station, or hut, at Abbe d' Igny. The swimming pool, too, was crowded to capacity! This was the first chance we had to really get a good bath since lying along the Marne between the 5th and 8th of July. Needless to add, we made the most of it - not knowing when we would again have this rare opportunity. The "de-lousing" process was the first we had enjoyed since landing in France and it goes without saying that all were greatly benefited thereby, having by this time accummulated more than our full quota of cooties! It was a happy bunch of clean men that late afternoon marching back to camp on "Three Gun Hill". We little dreamed then what was in store for us in the very near future!

CHAPTER 19.

FISMETTE RECAPTURED.

On August 30th, the order came!   The Third Battalion was to take over the Fismes sector for the second time!   That night, we left Longueville Farm, marching along a camouflaged road which led into St. Gilles and thence into Fismes.   We were to relieve the 112th Infantry which had lost, the day before, two companies in Fismette!   What a prospect!

The advance was made under difficulty, the enemy shelling the road with their usual accuracy and sending over a large amount of gas - just to make it interesting for us!   We were compelled to wear masks a part of the time, consequently adding to the discomfort of the marching companies.   At last, after a few "near" casualties, our Third Battalion marched into the town of Fismes.   What a scene of destruction was spread out before us!   We hardly recognized it to be the same place that we had left not many days before.   Fismes was practically levelled to the ground and shells were still falling like rain!   As on our previous occupancy, we were assigned to quarters under ground, - the now welcomed wine cellars - and for the second time we found ourselves face to face with death in that shell-wrecked village!

For four days and nights our battalion was subjected to the heavy shelling, causing many casualties.   On the afternoon of September 5th, the 110th Infantry passed through in an attack on the German lines and our battalion followed in support with orders to hold the bridge-head North of the Vesle River.   This advance took us across the Vesle, where we took up a position in Fismette, holding the bridge against the onslaughts of the enemy.

We shall remember for the balance of our lives those terrible nights spent on duty at the bridge.   Details were organized to convey the wounded from the town of Fismette, across the Vesle River, through Fismes and thence to a first-aid dressing station located in the cellar of a large house on the edge of that village.   Our path from Fismette to the hospital in Fimes was constantly under fire from German sharp-shooters, snipers, machine guns and the enemy artillery.   The rescue work - a large part of it - was carried on at nights but even under cover of the darkness, this proved to be a most perilous duty, as the enemy seemed to know what we were doing and forthwith proceeded to make it "hot" for us!   A great many flares sent up from the German lines dispelled the darkness at unexpected times and made the work in carrying the wounded an exceedingly dangerous undertaking.   To make matters worse for us, the bridge across the Vesle River after a day or two of shelling had been reduced to a single beam about a foot wide, over which

Main bridge between Fisme and Fismette as left by the Germans. Fisme, France August 26, 1918.

The town of Fismette after repeated shelling by both sides during the war.
(Images courtesy of National Archives)

we had to convey the wounded on stretchers - a most difficult feat and a very dangerous one, exposed as we were to enemy fire.   Luckily, the river at this point was very narrow - a mere stream - otherwise our casualty list would have been materially increased.   Two incidents of a personal and somewhat humorous nature transpired at this time which may prove entertaining in the telling.

It was during my second night on the litter detail.   I had been assisting in the work of carrying the wounded from a small first-aid dressing station located adjacent to the bridge-head in Fismette, thence over the Vesle River, through the town of Fismes to the temporary field hospital, mentioned above.   After several round trips, I was just about "all in".   Our path through Fismes was obstructed in many places by debris from shelled buildings on both sides of the narrow street which led to the hospital, fallen telephone wires, poles, deep shell holes, etc., all of which made walking extremely difficult, especially when burdened with a litter upon which reclined a wounded comrade - and some of the wounded were very heavy men!   In cases where the wounded man was considered a heavyweight, four men were assigned to the litter but quite frequently I had made the trip that night with only one comrade assisting at the other end of the stretcher. I was waiting my turn in the darkened enclosure of a court-yard for another wounded man to be brought up when I dimly discerned through the dark what appeared to me to be a pile of army blankets heaped up in one corner of the yard.   The pile was about four feet high and, in my almost exhausted condition, looked very inviting.   What a soft place to rest my weary body while awaiting my next turn on a litter! Yes, it surely was a pile of blankets alright!   Now for it!   I looked around for my buddy, who had been on the litter detail with me that night, but I could not find him.   "Maybe he was 'gold-bricking' too," I thought.   Quickly making for that stack of blankets, I was in the act of throwing my aching limbs upon this newly found bed, when suddenly there came through the darkness a loud and excited exclamation, the words of which I shall always remember.   "Hey you!   Keep off that!"   I looked around and standing there beside me was a burly Sergeant. Where he came from or how he got there without my knowing it, I give up!   "I just wanted to rest here awhile", I remarked. "What, on top of a bunch of dead men?", he retorted!   Just at that moment a German flare lighted the interior of the court-yard and one quick glance revealed the awful truth of the Sergeant's statement! What I had thought to be nothing more than a pile of blankets was, in fact, the dead piled there on top of one another, the whole ghastly sight being partly covered by several army blankets and shelter-halves! Before the flare died out, I caught a glimpse of protruding feet which, in the darkness, I could not see.   The faces of the dead were covered up.   To say that I was horrified, puts it very mildly!   I mumbled some remark to the Sergeant about "not being able to see in the darkness" and hurriedly left the spot -maybe to do my stunt of "gold-bricking" elsewhere!

The other incident occurred that same night.   My buddie and I had made one round trip on the litter detail, successfully conveying our man through the shell-torn streets of Fismes to the field hospital. On arriving back at the bridge-head in Fismette, our attention was attracted by the cries and moans of a wounded man awaiting his turn to be carried to the rear. Between pleas for speedy assistance, he assured us that he was very badly wounded in one knee and that it was impossible for him to stand up - much less walk. (All wounded men who could possibly make it on foot to the hospital were ordered to do so, thus allowing the small litter detail to quickly handle the more severe cases.) He was quite a heavy man but after some difficulty - he seemed perfectly helpless - we got him on the stretcher and commenced our perilous errand of mercy - our burden moaning and groaning every step of the way. "Don't jar me, boys!", he frequently pleaded. Shells started to come in fast and furious but we steadily advanced with our litter dispite the often repeated warnings of its occupant. We had noticed that his cries of pains had suddenly ceased after we had crossed the Vesle River. A distant whine of a shell, growing louder and louder as it seemed to be heading right for us! Bang! We were engulfed in the flying debris of a nearby building, that is, my buddie and I! Our severely wounded (?) man, even before that shell struck across the street, had apparently been blessed with a miraculous and speedy cure, for he certainly displayed remarkable agility in leaping from the litter and running at top speed into a house close by! Needless to add, my buddie and I wasted no time in looking for that Prince of Gold-brickers but, gathering up our litter, we returned to Fismette, there to offer our services where they were really needed. We put the affair down as a pure case of "gold bricking" but resolved to profit by the experience! On future trips that night, all our wounded were very badly crippled men! We could safely vouch for each case! (While on this work, I had noticed that the more silent a wounded man proved to be, the more serious were his injuries - while many times the reverse was the case. The man who yelled the loudest most likely had only a slight flesh wound while some poor devil who said nothing was, perhaps, in a dying condition! Of course, there were exceptions but it is safe to say that this was true in the majority of the cases we handled that night up in Fismes.)

For four days and nights, under a terrific shelling, we held the line but at a great sacrifice of human life. Many met their death at the bridge and in the streets of Fismes. We were constantly menaced, especially during the daytime, by German sharp-shooters, or snipers, who had secreted themselves at advantageous points throughout the town, "picking off" our men when duty called them upon the streets. One of these snipers, who had been left behind to harass the Americans, voluntarily gave himself up as a prisoner of war rather than engage in this kind of warfare. He was treated kindly by our officers and later proved his gratitude by giving out valuable information concerning the probable locations of his comrades on sniper duty in and around Fismes and Fismette.

During the night of September 4th, two platoons of Company I, 111th Infantry, crossed the newly constructed bridge over the Vesle River and entered Fismette - our objective! (This bridge had just been built by our Engineers, the old one having been shelled to pieces.) We found the town evacuated but nevertheless we maintained a sharp lookout for snipers, having learned our lesson while occupying Fismes.

The men were quickly assigned to quarters in the buildings and, where possible, took refuge from possible shelling in the many wine cellars. Like Fismes, most any dwelling of some size had its wine cellar. The enemy fire had practically leveled the town but fortunately at this time the heavy shelling had somewhat abated, for which all were truly thankful. Only a necessary gas guard was maintained during the remainder of the night in order to afford the wornout men a much-needed rest and sleep.

My squad took possession of a cellar located under a house about the center of the town. On entering and striking matches,(after first taking the precaution of hanging a blanket over the shell-wrecked entrance leading to the street above) we discovered that this cellar was "luxuriously" furnished with a small wooden table, several broken chairs, a piece of carpet and a small oil lamp! The latter was soon lighted and by its feeble glow, we greedily devoured a goodly portion of our "iron" rations of "corn willie" and "hardtack", after which packs were unrolled and everything made ready to snatch a few hours' sleep for the remainder of the night. About three o'clock in the morning, I was called by my Corporal to stand my turn of guard duty outside. At the very first indication of a gas attack, I was instructed to awake and warn my sleeping buddies. Grabbing my rifle with fixed bayonet, I reluctantly relieved the sentry then on duty, taking my post just outside the house (or rather what remained of it) in which my comrades were sleeping. All was very quiet. Only occasionally a man or two would be seen upon the street. No shells were coming over, that is, close at hand. The first faint light of the new day enabled me to dimly discern the long rows of shelled houses on both sides of the thoroughfare. Suddenly, there appeared about a hundred yards down the street the figure of a man approaching very slowly. He must have just emerged from one of the nearby dwellings. At first, I took him to be one of our men. On looking closer, however, I saw that he had on a French helmet, a German blouse and that his leggings were of the French blue. He carried a small bundle on a stick over his shoulder. I permitted him to advance within about ten yards from where I was standing, holding my rifle in readiness. Upon my command, "Halt!", he promptly obeyed and threw his bundle to the ground. On the alert against any possible treachery, I walked up to him and my suspicions were affirmed. He was a German, alright! That frightened expression gave him away! Ordering him (by gestures) to gather up his bundle and go with me, I escorted him to our quarters and called my Corporal. The disturbance also awakened some of the other men. Our prisoner by this time appeared badly frightened, especially upon noticing the menacing attitude of some of our men. He was a mere boy - not over sixteen or seventeen years of age. At first he evidently tried to make us believe that he was French, pointing to his helmet and leggings. It so happened, however, that one of our men was of German parentage and could speak and understand that language. After much to do, we finally got the truth out of him. He said that he purposely staid behind to give himself up to the Americans, - that he was tired of fighting and preferred the life of a prisoner of war. Some were for taking him out and letting a bullet end it all right there, but wiser heads prevailed and milder treatment was accorded the boy. He was later taken to Regimental

Headquarters and there turned in as a prisoner of war.

During the early morning of September 5th, the remaining two platoons of Company I entered Fismette. In the afternoon, the 110th Infantry regiment passed through in an attack on the German lines with the 111th Infantry in support. The enemy was now retreating toward the Aisne and the entire 111th was again assembled and ordered to advance. With the Second Battalion as advance guard, we marched once more through the demolished town of Fismes, proceeding eastwardly up the Rheims Road until almost near Villette, when we crossed the Vesle River, still maintaining an eastwardly direction. All along the Rheims Road we passed many dead Americans.

Briefly reviewing the activities of the entire 111th Infantry Regiment during the month of August, 1918, during which period our Third Battalion played so prominent a part, we shall again refer to Col. Martin's record, which reads as follows:

"Two miserable, rainy days were spent in the woods at Trugny, and on July 28th, the regiment marched to the Vente Juan Guillaume near Le Charmel, where it was held in corps reserve until August 3rd, that night proceeding through Cierges, Sergy and Courmont to Villome Farm, northwest of Coulanges-en-Tardenois, crossing the Ourcq River without knowing it. That night seemed like the blackest since the beginning of time, for it was almost impossible for the men to distinguish their companions to the right or left. One day was spent at Villome, the Headquarters of the regiment being moved on August 5th to Evry Farm, an old prison camp, the regiment being in the Bois Chenet.

The Vesle.

"On August 6th, 1918, the 111th became the Brigade Reserve, the One Hundred Twelfth Infantry having relieved the 32nd Division in its sector of the line on the Vesle River. The order making this designation provided that the 111th be held in the vicinity of Les Pres Farm, but an inspection of this vicinity showed that all suitable grounds were occupied by other troops. Headquarters Company advanced to the cross roads at Les Pres Farm, between Chery-Chartreuve and Mont St. Martin, the Second Battalion being in the Fond de Mexieres, the First Battalion in the Bois de Ger, and the Third Battalion and Machine Gun Company being on the southern edge of the Bois Chenet, with the Supply Company at Evry Farm; the P. C. of Col. Shannon was at Les Bouleaux, just south of Chery-Chartreuve. On the evening of the 7th, the One Pounder Platoon was sent to Fismes in support of the 112th Infantry, whose One Pounder Platoon had been shot to pieces. Later in the evening, a request was made for one battalion to reinforce the left flank of the 112th Infantry, and the First Battalion left the Bois de Ger at about 9 o'clock, reporting to Col. Rickards, of the 112th Infantry, at 1:30 A. M., August 8th, and was placed in reserve near his P. C. at the junction of the roads near Mont St. Martin. The remainder of the regiment remained in bivouac.

"Early in the evening of August 8th, Col. Rickards advised Col. Shannon that he would probably need additional support and requested that one battalion be held in readiness to move on short notice. The Second Battalion was sent forward at 10:45 P. M., reporting to Col. Rickards about midnight. General Muir, early in the morning of the 9th, in company with General Weigel and Col. Shannon, visited the P. C. of Col. Rickards, and while there directed Col. Shannon to arrange for the relief of the 112th.

"A reconnoissance of the positions occupied by the 112th having been made, the First Battalion relieved the troops of the right sector, Company A leading and being the first unit to cross the Vesle. The Second Battalion went to the left flank. Some delay was caused in getting the troops into position on account of erroneous information having been furnished as to the exact position of the troops supported by the First and Second Battalions of the 111th. This delay to the troops caused Company A to do a very daring and dangerous thing in crossing the Vesle on what was left of a footbridge. Shells were flying thick and Captain Williams realized that the use of the extended marching formation would result in a very heavy casualty list, so they were closed up and crossed quickly and without the loss of a man. Within a minute after the last man was across a shell exploded at the edge of the bridge. It was on this same bridge that Father Simoni, Chaplain of the Third Battalion, stood, bullets whistling all around him, helmet in his hand, runners yelling at him, and calmly asked his immortal question, 'Is there any danger?'

"As the battalions moved into Fismes, the Third Battalion came up under cover of darkness to the position of reserve along the Chery-Chartreuve-Fismes roads to the north of Resson Farm, the Machine Gun Company joining the First Battalion. The Signal Platoon was split up between the three battalions, the Trench Mortar Platoon was acting as runners and the Band had volunteered as a unit to act as stretcher bearers after they had been denied the privilege of joining the front line with rifles.

"The relief of the left sector of the 112th was accomplished without delay during the evening of the 9th of August. The relief of the right sector was considerably delayed by the constant shell and machine gun fire on Fismes and the bridge-crossings between Fismes and Fismette. While the relief was in process, orders were received to organize an attack beyond Fismes to find out the strength of the enemy and to establish a line beyond the town, the companies of the First Battalion augmented by Companies I, L and M of the Third Battalion, being designated for that purpose. Companies B and C, under the command of Captain Lynch and Lieut. Horner, led in the attack, with Company A, under Captain Williams, as the clean-up company. The artillery barrage began at the zero hour, but was not close enough to the town of Fismette to reach the enemy's advanced machine gun nests. The advance of B and C was immediately met by an intense fire from the Boche machine guns and a counter barrage, and they were forced to retire with heavy casualties to the town of Fismette. The artillery barrage under which this attack was made was augmented by a machine gun barrage in which between one hundred fifteen and one hundred twenty-five guns took part, practically all of the companies from the 107th, 108th and 109th Machine Gun Battalions taking part in it. Over 50,000 rounds of ammunition were fired by the Machine Gun Company of the 111th Infantry,

under Capt. Pollock.   When the companies of the Third Battalion were
sent to assist the First Battalion in the attack on the morning of the
10th, Major Alan G. Donnelly, commanding the Third Battalion, proceeded
to Fismes to take over the command from Major Kelley, of the First, who
at first had been given charge of the attack, but was unequal to the
task.   Major Kelley's P. C. was in Fismes, and, until the afternoon of
the 11th, it was impossible to get from him information as to the condition of the troops in Fismette, communication between Fismette and
Fismes being impossible except by runners, several being killed while
bearing messages.

"At 1:00 P. M., on the 11th, Major Donnelly was ordered to arrange a surprise raiding party of two companies and send them forward
at 5:00 P. M. to capture prisoners, machine guns and material located
in the ravines and sunken roads leading south from Mont de Perte and
La Fosse Auloup.   Companies L and M were selected for this and had to
fight their way to the position designated as the jumping-off place,
which was occupied by the enemy.   Beyond this they were unable to advance, owing to the strong opposition, and consequently suffered heavy
casualties.   They withdrew to Fismette, where Major Donnelly organized
the defense of the town and sent the first authentic information as to
the conditions existing therein.   Fismette was held by Major Donnelly's
troops until their relief by the 109th Infantry on the night of August
13-14, and during the entire time they were subjected to heavy machine
gun and artillery fire.   Much hand to hand fighting took place in the
streets of the village, there also being an attack with liquid fire.
During the entire time the troops occupied Fismette, it was almost impossible to evacuate the wounded, and, on the night of the relief, arrangements were made for carrying details, who brought all the wounded
across the Vesle prior to the troops leaving Fismette.

"As mentioned above, the Second Battalion under the command of
Major Dunlap relieved the left flank of the 112th on the night of the
9th.   Three companies of the Second Battalion, after crossing the
Vesle on a foot bridge constructed by the 112th, occupied a position
in Le Grand Savarf, the front of their line being along the railroad
at that point with the Fifty-ninth U. S. Infantry (old companions on
the "Olympic") on their left flank.   During the 10th, strong patrols
discovered that the woods northwest of their position and toward
Chateau du Diable were infested with the enemy in considerable strength,
principally machine guns reinforced by some infantry.   On the morning
of the 11th, the battalion was directed to push forward to the Reims
Road.   Capt. Schlosser, of Company G, had prior to this time succeeded in filtering his men across the railroad, additional troops from
Companies F and H later being sent to reinforce Company G.   The attack advanced parallel to the railroad, driving the enemy before it and
capturing thirty enemy machine guns in the advance.   Two platoons of
Company H and two of Company F advanced on the right of the railroad
with Capt. Cain and two platoons of his company between Capt. Clarke
and the river.   When the attack was about completed, a barrage from
friendly artillery came down, coupled with one from the enemy, and
the shelling became so heavy that it was impossible to hold the position
gained, the forces gradually falling back and, after being reorganized
at the railroad, made a successful attack and gained the road, which

position they continued to hold during the night of August 11-12th. Company K, of the Third Battalion, had been sent up in support and placed in a position to protect the left flank of the Second Battalion. On account of the Fifty-ninth having failed to maintain liaison with the left flank of the Second Battalion, it was deemed advisable to have additional support at this point and, as no other troops were available, the First Battalion of the 109th Infantry furnished two companies for the position, being later reinforced by one company from the 108th Machine Gun Battalion and one platoon of Company B, 109th Infantry, which covered the right flank and threw a fire in a northwesterly direction across the front of the Second Battalion. This support from the units of the Fifty-fifth Brigade was without the official sanction of their Brigade Commander, which, however, was later received.

Relieved.

"On August 13th, orders were received to the effect that the battalion on the left sector would be relieved by units of the 153rd Infantry Brigade, 77th Division, during the ensuing night. The relief was to have been started at 10:00 P. M., but was much delayed owing to a misunderstanding, and the last of the Three Hundred Fifth Infantry did not reach its position until daylight. As this organization was going into line for the first time, and the relieved battalion, to evacuate its position would have to cross open ground exposed to artillery fire, it was deemed advisable that they be held in position until the following evening, there being ample room for all. This action was approved by General Weigel, and Major Dunlap's battalion remained in position during August 14th, turning it over to the Three Hundred Fifth during the night of the 14th-15th of August.

"The One Pounder Platoon, the first troops of the 111th to reach the Vesle, remained during the entire time the 111th was around Fismes. The little 'cigarette guns' did splendid work; the men all secured rifles and engaged in sniping to their hearts' content. A note from Lieut. Poffenberger to Capt. Johnston said, 'Every man has at least two notches on his gun, and I have four.'

"On retirement from the Vesle, the First Battalion bivouacked on the northern edge of the Bois des Cinq Pilles, the Second Battalion at La Garenne, the Third Battalion, Regimental Headquarters, Headquarters Company, Machine Gun and Supply Company in the woods north of Abbaye d' Igny.

"The fighting on the Vesle was particularly severe, for in their retreat to this point the Germans intended to make a definite stand and were prepared to give the Americans the strongest kind of resistence. During the engagements between the 8th and 15th, the losses were: Killed, six officers and one hundred eight men; wounded twenty-one officers and five hundred twelve men; missing, one officer and one hundred eleven men (all of those reported as missing were later fully accounted for), making the total of casualties twenty-eight officers and seven hundred forty-eight men. Capt. Edmund B. Lynch, of Company B, was killed while attempting to rescue, almost single handed, two platoons that had been cut off by the enemy, and for which he was post-

.humously awarded the D.S.C.; Capt. John M. Clarke, Company F, after
having made a successful advance with other units of his battalion, was
killed after getting to shelter, and Capt. Orville R. Thompson lost his
life leading a charge on the afternoon of the 11th. Lieut. Bush, Company E; Lieut. Woodbury, Company A; Lieut. Gundlach, Company L, and
Lieut. Glendenning, Company B, made the supreme sacrifice in the operations prior to the leaving of Fismes. The total of wounded company
commanders was equally as heavy, Capt. Schlosser, Company G, received
one of the three wounds borne by him before meeting his death in the
Argonne, and Lieut. Horner, Company C, Capt. Williams, Company A, and
Capt. Johnston, Headquarters Company, received wounds necessitating
their removal to the hospital. Lieut. Horner later rejoined the Regiment in time for the operation north of Thiaucourt and received his
promotion to captain.

"A large number of citations were received on account of bravery,
but a list of all awards will be found elsewhere in this work. A number of officers and men also received foreign decorations such as the
Croix de Guerre, Order of Leopold, from the Belgian Government, and
decorations from the Italian Government. It is impossible to give an
account of the many deeds of valor performed. Too much cannot be said
of the valor and daring of the runners, who as a rule were boys under
twenty with no sense of fear, and no matter what time of day or night
a message might be handed them to be delivered in any point where shelling might be the hottest, they always started and were never known to
stop until their destination was reached or they had fallen in their
tracks. History can never pay too high a tribute to these boys and
their many deeds. An unrewarded act was that of Lieut. Harrop, Headquarters Company, who pushed a coil of wire over an open field in sight
of the enemy and put the first telephone in Fismes.

"Mention must be made of the splendid work done by the detachment
from the One Hundred Third Field Signal Battalion, under the command of
Lieut. Harry A. Souders, who was ever vigorous in maintaining communication between Regimental P. C. and the Division and Brigade officers to the rear.

"The Regiment remained in the vicinity of Abbaye d'Igny until the
18th of August, when it was moved to the support line in the vicinity of
Dravegny, where the men dug in preparatory to an expected attack, as information had been received that the Boche were assembling eight divisions in the vicinity of Le Chemin des Dames, beyond the Aisne. This
position was held with two battalions alternating in the front line on
the Vesle until September 4th."

CHAPTER 20.

OPERATIONS FROM SEPT. 1 - 8 SUMMARIZED.

By way of summarizing the activities of our troops on the Fismes-Fismette front and at Courlandon, thereby ending the Chateau Thierry Drive, we shall now quote the following from material at hand.

Machine Gun Company - 111th Infantry.

"We again moved into positions on the right of Fismes and action there had quieted considerable since our last relief. The Bosch were now directing the majority of his artillery fire to the back areas where the large naval guns were stationed. We remained in this position until the night of September 1st, when we returned to practically the same positions we had occupied near St. Gilles. We remained there until the day of the 4th, when we again moved into Fismes and we were located there until the afternoon of the 5th, when we moved into position on a hill, a short distance from Courlandon. We remained in this position until 1:00 P. M., the afternoon of the 6th, when we went over the top with the attacking infantry. The infantry moved to the right and the French on our right moved to the left. The second platoon, under Lieut. Brooks, filled in the gap made by this movement and here we had four men killed and twelve wounded, Capt. Pollock being wounded and Lieut. Brooks being killed. The Supply Train was stationed about six kilos from the front line and during the counter barrage they suffered two casualties from gas. We remained in this position during the day of the 7th and were relieved early the morning of the 8th by the French. We marched back to St. Gilles and arrived there at 8:00 A. M. Guns and equipment were carried as far as Villette, where they were left beside the road and later picked up by one of our limbers."

Company I, 111th Infantry.

"In the meantime, the enemy having regained its position in Fismette, a small village just across the Vesle River from Fismes, and having had patrols in Fismes, we were again ordered to relieve the 112th. Our company occupied the front line in Fismes for the second time. For four days and nights our position was heavily shelled, which caused us many casualties here, but our patrols entered the German lines in Fismette and on the night of September 4th, two platoons of our company

crossed the newly constructed wooden bridge built by the
111th Engineers, (the old bridge having been shelled to
pieces) and entered the town, capturing one man and
causing the enemy to retreat.   The next morning, the remaining two platoons of I Company crossed the river, and
our company, with the balance of the battalion, pushed
on to the Fosse de Diable, where we again met stiff resistence, being constantly exposed to heavy shell and
machine gun fire.   Indeed, this particular time of the
war will never be forgotten by the boys of the 111th and
will go down in history as being one of our "hottest"
periods Over There!   While in the town of Fismes, and
not out on special details, we lived in wine cellars under
the houses and expected any minute to be cut off from the
outside world by an exploding shell which might cause an
obstruction in the narrow entrances to these cellars.
Houses were literally falling down all around us and a man
took his life into his hands to walk on the streets.   German sharp-shooters were also stationed in many of the
buildings, but notwithstanding this the men of I Company
proved loyal and when duty called, they faced the fire
both day and night, seemingly unmindful of the impending
dangers.   Details were organized here to convey the wounded
from the town of Fismette across the river and through Fismes
to our first-aid dressing station.   Even under cover of
darkness this was a most perilous duty, as the enemy seemed
to know what we were about and at once proceeded to make it
interesting for us.   They would send up flares which, while
slowly descending, would brightly illuminate the country
around, and the darkest night would thus be changed into a
brillance resembling daytime.   Our path from Fismette to
the hospital in Fismes was constantly under fire from their
guns.   To make matters worse, after a day or two, our only
means of travel between the two towns was reduced to a single
beam across the Vesle River, over which we had to take long
chances in conveying the wounded.   The name 'Fismes' will
always be symbolical to that of 'Hell' in the minds of the
men of old I Company, 111th!   We had to take a position
here in an old stone quarry, known as 'Devil's Gulch' by the
men and were subjected not only to the usual heavy shelling
and machine gun fire, but also had a taste of German gas,
the three proving a bad combination and again causing many
hardships and casualties throughout the company.   On the
afternoon of September 8th, our objective being obtained,
we gladly received the news that the French would relieve
us that night.   After being relieved, we were ordered back
to St. Gilles, where we spent the night."

Company K, 111th Infantry.

"We left Longueville Farm and moved to the front line,
relieving the 112th Infantry, 28th Division, which had lost
the day before two companies in Fismette.   Within one hour
after relieving the 112th, the Bosch put down a heavy bar-

rage on our positions but fortunately no losses were suffered. Our position here we occupied until the 5th of
September, sending out patrols nightly who performed their
duties in excellent manner and secured valuable information.
On the afternoon of September 5th, the 110th Infantry regiment passed through us in an attack on the German lines and
our regiment followed in support with orders to hold the
bridge-head North of the Vesle River. This advance took
us across the Vesle River, where we took up a position holding the bridge-head. Here, we were relieved on September
6th, moving back, and after having a good meal, moved up to
the village of Villette, east of Fismes. Here, we were held
in support for two days."

Companies L and M, 111th Infantry.

"Reentered Fismes, August 31st, 1918, with Company K on
the right, Company I on the left, Company L immediately in
center (though acting as battalion support) and Company M
two kilometres in woods in the rear as battalion reserve.
Fismette captured by Company I, September 5th and pursuit of
enemy taken up by the 76th Division. Third battalion relieved morning of September 6th and same afternoon, sent to
Courlandon as Regimental support, being used as holding
troops in the Fosse de Diable, the ridge having already been
captured by the First and Second Battalions, 111th Infantry."

Operations 111th Infantry, Sept. 1st-8th, 1918, in Memorandum from E. C. Shannon, Colonel, 111th Infantry, to the Commanding General, 28th Division, copied from George W. Cooper's book, "Our Second Battalion".

"During the night 31st August-1st September, 1918,
the Commanding Officer, 111th Infantry, took over command of
the line of resistence of the sector occupied by the 56th
Infantry Brigade, the 3rd Battalion of this regiment occupying the outpost zone, 2nd and 1st Battalions, resistence
line. On 4 September, 1918, the general advance of the 55th
Brigade on our right and the 77th Division on our left having
been ordered, Company K of this regiment, which occupied the
sector east of Fismes, 206.6-286.8 to 207.3-286.8, joined the
advance to the left of the 110th Infantry, crossed the Vesle
River and established a bridge-head at 206.6-287.0. The
balance of this battalion being stationed in Fismes proper,
had strong patrols advancing toward the Vesle River and while
the general advance was in progress they accomplished a crossing and occupied Fismette. These positions were held during
the night of the 4th-5th September, 1918, by this battalion,
while the balance of the regiment was moved to the ravine
205.0-285.3. The Commanding General, 56th Infantry Brigade,
directed that the battalion in Fismes and Fismette clean up
these towns, burying all American dead and assembling any
German material of value. The Commanding Officer of this

regiment made an inspection of both of these towns during the morning of 5 September, 1918, and upon his return from this inspection about noon, found a memorandum which directed him to prepare his regiment to advance in the direction of Concrevaux and secure the line La Grande Hameau-Bouregard Fme. and Maizy, with the further information that a detailed order would be furnished soon and also verbal orders directing the withdrawal of the 3rd Battalion from Fismes and Fismette, these towns having been occupied by troops of the 77th Division.

"Field Orders No. 31, Hdqrs., 56th Infantry Brigade, dated 5 September, 1918, were received about 2 P. M. Paragraph 3 of this order directed the advance by way of the St. Gilles-Fismes-Fismette-Baslieux - 193.4 road, but contained no information as to the approximate location of the right of the American line and the left of the French line. An officer was dispatched to obtain, if possible, from the Commanding General, 55th Infantry Brigade, these locations, and further, to ascertain if there was a bridge crossing available in the vicinity of Villette. The information obtained showed that the left of the French line was at about 210.3-287.7, and that there was a bridge crossing north of Villette. With this information and with permission of the Commanding General of the 56th Infantry Brigade, who was present, verbal orders were immediately issued to the assembled Battalion Commanders directing the advance of the regiment north on the St. Gilles-Fismes Road, thence east on the National Highway, 31, thence north across the Vesle River, thence in a northeasterly direction toward the La Fosse au Diabl. The advance guard was composed of the 2nd Battalion with Machine Gun Company of the 111th Infantry, 800 yards in the rear of the 1st Battalion with Company B, 109th Machine Gun Battalion. The advance guard commander was directed to proceed via the road indicated, sending out strong patrols to gain contact with the French left and the American right. On account of shell fire the entire advance was made in column of files. The advance guard moved out at 3:30 P. M., and while the main body was passing through Fismes a message was received from the Division Commander that there was apprehension of a counter-attack from Romain by way of Gde. Hameau and that we were to connect up with the American right flank so as to repel any such counter-attack. Copy of this message was immediately dispatched to the advance guard commander, who received it at 5:45 P. M., and he was directed to push on and connect up with all possible dispatch. Message dated 6:40 P. M. from the advance guard commander gave the information that they were in contact with the French left and another message dated 7:35 P. M., that they had gained contact with the right of our 109th Infantry, and further message dated 8:06 P. M. gave the information that in connection with the French, the advance guard commander was closing the gap between the two lines by placing two companies on the line

and two companies in close support. The 1st Battalion was
moved up to about 209.7-288.4. The 3rd Battalion, Headquarters Company and Companies B and D, 109th Machine Gun
Battalion were placed in Les Bois Haut de Courlandon and
Regimental P. C. established at 209.2-287.5. At 11:17
P. M., a message was sent by runner to the Commanding Officer, 109th Infantry, advising him of the disposition of
the several units of this regiment and requesting that runners be exchanged so that liaison could be maintained.
Through the progress of these events the movements were made
under almost constant enemy shell fire. These positions
were maintained during the night 5th-6th September, 1918,
the front line being subjected to considerable machine gun
fire from the enemy. The morning of the 6th September,
1918, the Commanding Officer of the 111th Infantry called
on the Commanding Officer, 109th Infantry, meeting him as
he was on his way to the P. C. of the 55th Infantry Brigade.
The general situation was discussed and the Commanding Officer, 109th Infantry, was of the opinion that no more than
one Battalion of the 111th Infantry was necessary to
strengthen his line between his right and the French left.
He also stated that his mission to his Brigade P. C. was to
receive orders covering the general advance of the whole
line and that he would advise me as soon as he had definite
information as to what was to be done. At 12:25 P. M., 6
September, 1918, the following message was received from
the Commanding Officer, 109th Infantry:

'From No. 1 Solo.
At 288-209.3.
Date: 6 September, 1918. Hour 12:15 No. 2 Runner.

To C. O., 111th Inf.
We advance, general attack at 1 o'clock. Artillery
preparation begins at 12:56, progress of the attack
100 meters to 4 minutes, at first line on the crest
of the hill running northeast and southwest, the
crest being immediately in your front, halt 30 minutes for covering fire on that line. Next advance
to be at 100 meters in 5 minutes, next line halt
about one kilometer in advance on a parallel line
through La Grand Hameau and co-ordinate 290-210.
Halt on this line for one hour with covering artillery fire for the entire line, then progress at the
rate of 100 meters in 5 minutes, following the artillery barrage as fas as possible. I am directed by
the Brigade Commander to call on you for one battalion of two companies in the first line and two in
support and keep in contact with the French on your
right. Answer.

Ham, Colonel.'

"This message was immediately dispatched by runner to
the Commanding Officer, 2nd Battalion, this regiment, with.

the instructions to carry out the order and if necessary,
he could call on the 1st Battalion which was in support for
any help that might be needed. The above message was
received by him at 12:45 P. M., and receipt of message of
Commanding Officer, 109th Infantry, was acknowledged, advising that the force requested would be furnished. This
Battalion (2nd) joined in the attack and advanced about 300
meters beyond the position originally held by them, when
they met strong opposition which drove back the left of the
French, exposing our right. Our line held and broke up
two counter attacks made by the enemy, and the French then
moved forward and joined to the right of our line. The
counter-attack was sufficiently strong and our casualties
were so heavy as to cause the Commanding Officer of the 2nd
Battalion to call upon our 1st Battalion for help, and he
further requested that the 3rd Battalion, this regiment, be
moved up to closer support in case it might be needed. The
report of Major Dunlap, attached hereto, gives more minor
details of the action.

"When the call was made for the 3rd Battalion to move
up, the Commanding Officer of this regiment temporarily
moved his P. C. to that of the Commanding Officer of the
2nd Battalion in order to better judge the conditions existing. Major Dunlap had the situation well in hand, his
dispositions were such as to repel any further counter-
attacks and steps were immediately taken to evacuate the
wounded, bring up reserve ammunition and food for the men
in the advance positions. The entire Headquarters Company
was detailed for this work. All the work of evacuation,
ammunition and food supply was started about 4:30 P. M.,
6 September, 1918, and continued during the night of the
6th-7th September, 1918. The approach to the position occupied by the troops was through a deep valley which was
constantly shelled by the enemy, who used a large amount of
gas, and the work of these carrying parties was extremely
difficult. During the morning of the 7th September, 1918,
the writer visited the P. C. of the Commanding General, 55th
Infantry Brigade, making verbal report of the operation and
showing distribution of troops. Information was obtained
there that the regiment would be relieved during the night
of 7th-8th September, 1918, by French troops. Later in
the day the formal order was received and the relief by the
307th French Infantry was completed at 3 A. M., 8th September, 1918, the regiment withdrawing in small parties to
ravine at 209.0-283.0, 203.0-279.7, and 202.8-281.95.

"During the attack, nine German prisoners were taken,
two of whom were badly wounded. These were given first-
aid and forwarded with the wounded of this regiment. The
other seven were marched under guard and turned over to
the Commanding General, 55th Infantry Brigade. They were
all from the 20th Bavarian Infantry and one of them stated
they had just taken their position in the line before the

attack. The casualties during the period named were as
follows: Officers, killed, 4; wounded, 5. Enlisted men,
killed, 32; wounded, 362; missing, 53. Of the 53 missing,
it is believed that none were taken prisoners and that all
will eventually be returned to their command.

E. C. Shannon,
Colonel, 111th Infantry."

The report of Major Dunlap, above referred to, reads as follows:

"Hq., 2nd Bn., 111th Infantry,
American Expeditionary Forces, France,
10th September, 1918.

From: Commanding Officer, 2nd Battalion, 111th Infantry.
To: Commanding Officer, 111th Infantry.
Subject: Report of tour of duty from September 5th to 8th,
         1918, inclusive.

"Per V. O. C. O., pursuant to Field Orders No. 32,
Headquarters, 56th Infantry Brigade, dated 5 September, 1918,
this Battalion left its station (Ravine one kilometer south-
east of Fismes) at 3:30 P. M., as advance guard to the regiment, mission being to get contact with the left flank of
the French and the right flank of the 55th Infantry Brigade,
U. S., their lines being, from available information, at
points north of Courlandon. Contact with the French left
(4th Regiment, 9th Division Infantry), was obtained by
patrol at 6 P. M., 5 September, 1918. Contact was maintained and our patrols to our left guard gained contact with
the 55th Brigade, U. S. (109th Infantry), at 7 o'clock P.M.,
5 September, 1918. Our column advanced to a line between
point at 209.8-288.7 to 210.2-288.3, where two companies
were deployed closing the gap between the French and our
55th Brigade, which was our mission. The two remaining
companies of the battalion were placed in close support.
These positions were maintained throughout the night and
until 1 P. M., 6 September, 1918.

"At 12:45 P. M., 6 September, 1918, a memorandum
received from Colonel Ham, 109th Infantry, requesting that
the battalion participate in a general attack to take place
at 1 P. M., 6 September, 1918. The battalion went over
the top at 1:02 P. M., two companies (F and H) under Capt.
Robert S. Cain and one platoon, Machine Gun Company, 111th
Infantry, under Lieut. Daniel W. Brooks in the first line,
and Companies G and E, under Captain Arthur L. Schlosser,
and one platoon, Machine Gun Company, 111th Infantry, under
Lieut. Edwey X. Wainwright, in the second line. Companies
A, B, C and D being placed at my disposal by the Commanding
Officer, were placed in support. The attacking line advanced to a line from 209.9-289.2 to 210.4-288.9. The
enemy counter-attacked in force at 2 P. M., 6 September,

1918, counter-attack being made by the 20th Bavarian Infantry. Companies A and D were sent forward to reinforce our lines and request was made to the Commanding Officer that companies of the 3rd Battalion be placed at my disposal in the event of enemy counter-attack breaking through. French troops withdrew about 200 yards in the face of the enemy counter-attack. Our troops, assisted by the fire from 111th Machine Gun Company, broke up the enemy counter-attack and held our position, after which the French line advanced to its original position and maintained contact with our right. The 3rd Battalion with Company B, 109th Machine Gun Battalion, under Lieut. Strickler, arrived and was placed in the position occupied by our troops prior to the attack. These dispositions were maintained until relieved by the 307th French Infantry, relief being completed 3 A. M., 8th September, 1918. Our troops were withdrawn to St. Gilles.

"Number of prisoners taken, 9; casualties: officers, killed, 4; wounded, 5; enlisted men, killed, 30; wounded, 240.

William R. Dunlap,
Major, 111th Infantry."

Operations 111th Infantry, Sept. 1st-8th, 1918, quoted from Colonel Edward Martin's history, "The Twenty-Eighth Division in the World War".

"Colonel Shannon, during the night of August 31-September 1, had taken over the command of the line of resistence of the sector occupied by the Fifty-six Brigade, the Third Battalion being in the outpost zone with the First and Second Battalions on the resistence line.

"On September 4 the general advance of the Fifty-fifth Brigade to the right of the One Hundred Eleventh and a unit of the Seventy-seventh Division on the left having been ordered, Companies I and K, of the One Hundred Eleventh, which occupied the sector east of Fismes, joined the advance on the left flank of the One Hundred Tenth, crossed the Vesle and established a bridgehead. The two other companies of the Third Battalion (stationed at Fismes) advanced strong patrols toward the Vesle, and as the advance progressed, accomplished a crossing and occupied Fismette, which they held during the night of September 4-5, while the balance of the Regiment moved to the ravine one and a half kilometers south of Fismes, near the St. Gilles-Fismes Road. The members of the Third Battalion after reaching Fismette were able to bury many of those who had lain in 'No Man's Land' since August 10, among them being the body of Captain Thompson.

"Colonel Shannon made an inspection of Fismes and Fismette on the morning of September 5, and on his return to the P. C. about noon, found a memorandum directing him to prepare the Regiment to advance in the direction of Concrevaux and secure the line La Grande Hameau Bouregard Farm and Maizy, with the information that a detailed order would follow and also verbal orders directing the withdrawal of the Third Battalion from Fismes and Fismette, which had by this time been occupied by troops of the Seventy-seventh Division.

"After Captain Gill had found that there was a bridge crossing at Villette, Colonel Shannon issued verbal orders directing the advance of the Regiment north on the St. Gilles-Fismes Road, thence east on the National Highway 31, north across the Vesle River at Villette and then in a northeasterly direction toward La Fosse au Diable.

"The advance guard was composed of the Second Battalion and the Regimental Machine Gun Company, Company B of the One Hundred Ninth Machine Gun Battalion following eight hundred yards in the rear. On account of shell fire, the entire advance was made in column of files which much delayed the movement. While the main body was passing through Fismes, a message was received from General Muir that there was apprehension of a counter-attack from Romain and that the One Hundred Eleventh should connect up with the American right flank to repel the expected attack. By 8:00 o'clock in the evening, the Second Battalion had carried out General Muir's instructions and had connected up with the French on the right and the One Hundred Ninth Infantry on the left. The First Battalion moved up in support of the Second, and the Third Battalion, Headquarters Company and Companies B and D, of the One Hundred Ninth Machine Gun Battalion, together with the Regimental P. C., were established in Le Bois Haut de Courlandon, all of the movements being made under almost constant enemy shell fire.

"The above positions were maintained during the night of September 5-6, and until shortly after noon on the 6th. For the benefit of those unfamiliar with military orders, there is here copied the order that was received by Colonel Shannon from the commanding officer of the One Hundred Ninth Infantry. (See copy of Colonel Ham's order herein written.)

"The Second Battalion was instructed to carry out this order and if necessary to call on the First Battalion, then in support, for any needed help. The Second Battalion, with five minutes' notice, joined in the attack, advancing about three hundred meters beyond the position originally held by them, where they met strong opposition which drove back the left of the French, exposing the right flank of the Second Battalion. Two counter attacks were made by the enemy which were held up and broken by magnificent work on the part of the Machine Gun Company, the French then moving forward and joining the right of the One Hundred Eleventh's line. The counter attacks were of such strength and the casualties had been so heavy that the First Battalion was called on for help and the Third Battalion moved up to closer support, Colonel Shannon temporarily moving his P. C. to that of Major Dunlap in order to better judge the existing conditions. It being seen that the situation was then well in hand and that the dispositions were such as to repel any further counter attacks, Headquarters Company immediately began to evacuate the wounded and bring up reserve ammunition and food for the men in the advance positions. The ration supply was difficult of access, being through a deep valley, under constant enemy shell-fire and saturated with gas, and the work of these carrying parties was extremely difficult. The fighting had been almost continuous and toward the close the men worked and fought in the hope of promised relief that was slow in coming. Men can go days without rations, but when the water supply runs short the height of human agony and endurance is reached. On the 7th, information came forward that the Regiment would be relieved during the night of the 7th-8th by French troops, which was effected by the Three Hundred Seventh French Infantry at about 3:00 A. M., September 8, the One Hundred Eleventh withdrawing in small parties to St. Gilles. (2

"The casualties during the September operations on the Vesle were: Killed, officers four, men thirty-two; wounded, officers five, men three hundred sixty-two. Headquarters Company and the Supply Company lost a number of men on account of gas. Lieutenant Michael Keith, the much-beloved regimental chaplain, was so badly gassed that he died in a hospital in Paris on September 8th. Lieutenant Dan Brooks, of the Machine Gun Company, stood up to draw the enemy fire and made the supreme sacrifice; Captain Fielding, Company E, received notice of his promotion from first lieutenant to captain and thirty minutes later had gone to the Great Beyond; Lieutenant Ettinger was the second commander of Company A to fall within three weeks; Captain Robert Pollock was wounded so severely that he was never discharged from the service, and died almost three years later in the Walter Reed Hospital in Washington, D. C. Captain Cain, Company H, was another company commander added to the wounded.

"In the operations of the Regiment with the French near Courlandon, the men of the One Hundred Eleventh were brought in close contact with the French troops, and the following letter sent to the commanding officer of the Second Battalion indicates the regard in which the Americans were held by their French comrades:

'I personally ask your Major permission to tell you how I have been happy and proud to go over the top with your valiant men. Their fearlessness of death and their gallantry have excited the greatest admiration of my brave soilders.

CHAPTER 21.

BEUREY.

It seemed that the Regiment had been ordered to close a gap in the positions between the right of the 109th U. S. Infantry and the left of the French troops operating north of the Vesle River in the vicinity of Courlandon. This was accomplished on the night of September 5th, and on the afternoon of the 6th, a general advance in the entire line was made, which resulted in a brisk engagement, with rather heavy casualties, as related in our previous chapter.

The ground gained was held and on the night of September 7-8, the regiment was relieved by troops from the 307th Infantry, 62nd French Division and marched to St. Gilles, at which place the Third Battalion spent the balance of the night. On September 9th, the regiment was moved, by marching, to Bois de Reims. The following day, September 10th, the regiment again was on the march which terminated at Bois De La Boulcy, our Third Battalion occupying Eperney Woods, at which place we rested in bivouac until September 12th, when we boarded trucks for Beurey.

This proved to be a seventy kilometer trip, made in French camions, with Sengalese drivers. As usual, the trucks were over-crowded and all will recall that night's ride over rough roads. Sleep, under these conditions, was out of the question. In fact, many of the men were forced to stand during the entire trip. Nevertheless, the men were all in high spirits and took the situation good-naturedly. Of course, as was always the case on these trips during the period of the war, we had no idea of our destination. It was quite sufficient to know that we were at last relieved from front line duty and that very probably the ride would terminate at some rest area far in the rear! Consequently, the men were very happy and during the entire journey they filled the night air with songs, jokes and laughter. Little did they dream of what awaited them in the very near future!

Just about dawn we reached a small town, the trucks stopped and the order, "All out!" came down the line from our officers ahead. Our "joy-ride" was over! On alighting, we learned from a military sign posted on one side of the road that we were in Beurey. (The other two battalions of our regiment were driven to the towns of Mogneville and Contrisson.)

The work of assigning the men to quarters was soon underway. All were billeted in houses and barns throughout the village. Beurey had suffered very little from German shelling and it was a decided relief to be in a town that was inhabited and where the buildings were not falling upon us! We had had quite enough of that in Fismes and Fismette to last us for some time to come! Before the morning passed our

Third Battalion was completely housed.   Orders shortly thereafter were issued for-bidding the men to go beyond the town's limits and instructing all to keep in constant contact with their respective companies.   Another order, which caused some dismay, was to the effect that the next day a drilling program was to be started and to be continued during our stay in Beurey.   After mess, at noon, we started out, in groups of merry doughboys, on a tour of inspection of the town. The little French shops and bars were soon crowded with men eagerly grasping this opportunity to purchase sweets, tobacco and drinks.   Each "saloon" had its bar-maid, ranging in years from the petite Mademoiselle of sixteen to the gray-headed Madam of sixty or more.   It goes without saying that as soon as "the Americans" arrived in town prices everywhere and for everything took a magical jump!   The boys, however, gladly paid out their francs and, soldier-like, bought what they wanted regardless of the cost! Many a doughboy went "broke" in Beurey and "borrowing until next pay-day" was the subject of many an earnest discussion!   At Beurey, too, the sex appeal led many a man off "the straight and narrow"! The town boasted of Mademoiselles aplenty in wild and maddening numbers - some very "easy on the eyes" and some, of course, not so attractive.   Numerous small "stores" scattered throughout the place were merely conducted as blinds for immoral purposes. A doughboy might enter one with the sole idea of making a purchase and leaving.   A pretty girl, a wink, a sweet smile and one little word - the trick was accomplished!   Then followed the real business of the place transacted in one of the rooms back of the "shop" or upstairs! During our second day in Beurey, if the writer may again engage in some personal reminiscences, I entered a small shop for the purpose of buying some chocolate candy I saw temptingly displayed in the window.   I approached the counter but no one seemed on the premises, although a bell hanging over the door rang loudly as I entered.   After waiting for some minutes and hearing no sound, I thought I would take a look around and endeavor to arouse the proprietor of the place.   That particular afternoon I was "candy hungry" and had set my mind on devouring the entire contents of that tray in the window!   I noticed a small door in the rear of the shop which probably opened up into a back room of the house.   It was partly glassed and two lace curtains were draped over the glass portion.   Curiosity getting the better of me, and desiring to be waited on if possible, I went over and gazed into that back room . What I saw, dear readrer is unprintable here! Seeing that my chances to get waited on - for candy - were small indeed, I hastily made a graceful exit - not without hearing a none too cordial greeting from the pair in that back room whose "business" I had seemingly interrupted!

The writer at this place enjoyed what proved a rather unusual experience.   During my wanderings around the town on our second day there, I came to some army barracks which were occupied by men from my old Division, the 79th.   Upon inquiry, I found that they were just preparing to go into action on the front lines - to receive their baptism of fire!   I did not envy them! I endeavored to locate some of my former comrades in the 313th Infantry - "Baltimore's Own" - but learned to my sorrow that that particular unit of the division was stationed some miles away.   In talking to some of the men, they questioned me closely about what to expect "up front".   I did not

paint a very glaring picture of our experiences on the front lines.
But, did this dampen their enthusiasm? I should say not! That bunch
of rookies acted as though they were going on a Sunday school picnic
back home and, sick at heart, I left them in their joyful ignorance!
I wonder, as I write these lines, how many out of that group of happy
doughboys lie buried today "somewhere in France!"

Beurey was situated close to a railroad. One afternoon, in my
saunterings on the outskirts of town, I noticed a number of soldiers
gathered around some box-cars on a siding. Nearly every man in the
group held a jar of jam and a box of crackers, the contents of which
were being greedily devoured. Upon arriving on the scene, my
curosity was soon satisfied. They had broken into one of the freight
cars and, to the joy of all, found it loaded with various kinds of jam,
jelly and excellent crackers (not the army variety - hardtacks) galore!
"Come on over, buddy, and eat!" I did not need a second invitation!
Though it may be my good fortune to sit at many banquet tables in after
years, I shall never forget that afternoon's feast in Beurey! The unexpected "eats" were indeed most welcome for our kitchens had not as yet
caught up and we had been fed on "corn-willie" and small portions of dry
bread. I would not undertake to say at this writing just how many
boxes of those crackers I did consume or how many jars of jam and jelly
I sampled! However, I can say that at least one doughboy in the outfit went to sleep that night but not on the usual empty stomach!

Before we close reciting the little experiences - personal and
otherwise - incident to our stay in Beurey, it may be well to explain
that situated not many kilos away was that large and thickly populated
town of Bar le Duc. It did not take the men long to learn of this
fact! Despite strict orders prohibiting soldiers to leave town except on passes, many successfully evaded the dreaded M. P. along the
route, found their way into Bar le Duc and came back to their companies
with glaring tales of the wonderful times had there. To the poor unfortunates who could not steal away, stories were told and retold of
"wine, women and song" - all three attractions, of course, much more
desirable than could be found in the "hick town of Beurey!" As the
writer happened to be one of the "unfortunates", it is regretted that
he is unable to describe just what did take place in Bar le Duc when
our boys got there. Some comrade reading these lines can, perhaps,
supply the deficiency!

On Sunday, September 15th, the regiment received its first batch
of replacements - soldiers to take the place of those killed, wounded
and otherwise missing. These new men, some of whom had never as yet
been under fire, were quickly assigned to the different companies
throughout the 111th. A large majority of this replacement came from
Western states, my outfit (Company I) getting several men hailing from
Oregon and Washington. The "rookies", as we nicknamed them, kept us
busy answering all sorts of questions as to what to expect when their
turn came to "go over the top". Our word-pictures, it goes without
saying, were highly colored but after the experiences in Fismes and
Fismette, were not so very far from the truth after all! Many of
these "rookies" expressed the desire to undergo their first baptism of
fire, to go "over the top" and on to conquer new territory from the
arch enemy, "Old Kaiser Bill". Their hopes were to be realized -
sooner than expected!

Above: Congestion on supply roads to Argonne offensive 1918. American troops moved into position for the Meuse-Argonne offensive under the cover of darkness. Remarkably, over 600,000 American soldiers moved into position without alerting the enemy.

Below: American troops, riding on top of French-built Renault FT-17 tanks, going forward to the battle line in the Forest of Argonne. September 26, 1918. (Images courtesy of National Archives)

CHAPTER 22.

THE ADVANCE TO THE ARGONNE!

Our Third Battalion had not been many hours enjoying the hospitality of Beurey before we read in the newspapers about the reducing of the St. Mihiel salient by the American Army. By the aid of maps, we discovered that our regiment was now directly in back of St. Mihiel. On realizing our position, we judged that in perhaps a very short time we would be taking our turn on the front line as was the case in the Chateau Thierry Drive. Subsequent events, following in rapid succession, proved our theory to be correct!

On Monday, September 16th, our battalion went out, as usual, for its seven-hour drill period. About three o'clock in the afternoon, an order was received from Headquarters calling the companies off the field to report to their respective quarters in the town. All felt sure by this time that "something was in the air" and a wave of excitement spread through the troops. It was not long before the expected orders were issued. "Pack up and be ready to move off right after mess!" Long before supper that evening, most of the men were ready and anxious to leave. After mess our entire Third Battalion had all packs rolled and, impatiently, awaited the command "Fall in!" Goodbyes in the best French we knew were extended to our friends in the town. Many a love-sick doughboy stole away from his comrades to spend a few precious moments in bidding farewell to some sorrowing Mademoiselle!

At about eight o'clock the long column was assembled on a road at the edge of the town. The night was very clear. By the light of the full moon, one could almost read the fine print of a newspaper. Shortly, the command "Forward!" was heard. We were on our way! The men, ready for new adventures, were in jovial spirits. The more experienced cautioned more than one man in the ranks of our replacements not to hum too loudly as we marched along. Fresh from camps at home — many not even thoroughly trained in the handling of their rifles — little did those poor devils that night realize that they were marching into the very jaws of death! What a blessing, at times, the future is unknown to us!

Our entire regiment was again on the march, the other two battalions of infantry and our machine gun company having joined us on the road shortly after we left Beurey. The order of advance was twenty minutes of marching followed by rest periods of ten minutes duration. Under this schedule, the long column proceeded on its wearisome tramp through the night. We noticed that, during the early morning hours, the sky had become overcast with threatening clouds. Upon reaching

the Bois de Laheycourt, about 3:30 A. M., Tuesday, September 17th, a
gentle rain had set in, - cold and penetrating in the early morning
hours.   We had now covered about twenty-three kilometres and were to
rest in these woods for the balance of the night and perhaps longer.

All were very tired and foot-sore and when the order finally came
down the line to "Fall out!", packs were hastily unrolled and preparations made to snatch, if possible, a few hours sleep before continuing
the hike.   A few of the men, reckoning on the rain which was steadily
increasing, pitched their pup-tents in the woods.   Others merely contented themselves by rolling up in their shelter halves, - too weary
apparently to bother about erecting tents.   My buddie and I, however,
decided to put up our tent for the night.   Accordingly, we selected
what we thought to be an ideal spot and finally, under many difficulties working in the inky darkness of the woods, had our tent up at last
and prepared ourselves to spend the remaining hours before dawn in restful slumbers.   Unfortunately for us, though, we had unknowingly pitched our slter -halves directly over a small ditch or gully which served
as an excellent drain for the rain.   Consequently, it was not long
before the accumulating water in our tent made things rather interesting for us!   We could feel its cold fingers as it slowly but surely
crept in and touched our bodies but we were too tired, sleepy and worn
out to bother about such a trifle!   Upon awakening in the morning,
after a sound sleep, we discovered ourselves lying in a small size
swimming pool and, of course, thoroughly drenched to the skin! By this
time, however, my buddie and I had become good sailors as well as
soldiers and, except for the vexation of having water-soaked blankets
on our hands, we passed the little incident off as a joke, remarking
as we wrung the water out of our clothes the next morning, "Its a great
life if you don't weaken - this army stuff!"

During the day, spent in the Bois de Laheycourt, the various companies of our regiment made hot coffee, the men having taken turns on
the march in carrying along the necessary pots for this purpose.   Our
field kitchens had not as yet caught up with the troops.   That hot
drink of coffee proved to be a veritable God-send to the men, chilled
as they were to the very bone after a cold, rainy night spent in those
woods!   Many tried various ways in which, by hook or crook, they
could manage to get an "extra" helping of that life-giving fluid! (Personally speaking, I have often known the times in France, especially on
cold, rainy mornings after a hard night's march or "stand to", when I
would have gladly given anyone the equivalent in francs of five good
American dollars for just one steaming hot cup of coffee - yes, minus
sugar and cream - and army coffee at that!)

After an entire day's rest in the Bois de Laheycourt, the 111th
continued its march at about eight o'clock that night, our Third Battalion leading the way.   About midnight we entered some woods.   Although we were not aware of it then, this wild section of country with
its thick under-growth and many tall and stately trees was the Argonne
Forest!   The stage was set!   The actors were ready! How little did
we know then what a prominent part our battalion would be called upon
to play in that particular scene!

Many will undoubtedly recall that first night in the Argonne, the weary march through the dense woods; the road which kept winding and winding through the black forest, at times quite wide and more frequently but a narrow lane; how tired we were of it all; the number of men who "fell out" along the way - all these unpleasant memories, and more besides, will forever be associated to that night when, as soldiers of the A. E. F., we first entered the Argonne Forest!

About four o'clock on the morning of September 18th, our regiment came out of this particular section of the forest and entered the town of Futeau. Our visions of a rest at this place soon faded away as we continued on our weary way through the village. Many of the men by this time had fallen by the wayside completely exhausted. Some of these later caught up with their respective outfits and others were picked up by the Military Police along the route to be turned over to their company commanders. Rain was falling as we passed through Futeau and many would have fallen out here had not our officers assured us that we would stop just a short distance on the other side of the village. That "short distance" proved to be a good kilometre past the town. We then marched over a field and finally the long column was brought to a halt on the side of a hill. This spot we called "the hills of Futeau." We had marched a good twenty-five kilometres under extremely bad marching conditions. The strain told on the most seasoned trooper, too!

Were we to rest at last? This question was on the lips of every tired doughboy. Already we had lost about half of our replacements in the two nights' grind. These new men simply could not stand the pace much longer. The question all wanted answered was soon settled, for about six o'clock word was passed around that the march was to be resumed that night. Promptly at eight o'clock in the evening, the battalions were again on the march, our Second Battalion this time leading the column. Le Neufour was reached about four o'clock on the following morning, the 19th, after a hike of another twenty-five kilometres. Shortly after we reached our destination, it started to rain again. Near Le Neufour, the 111th went into bivouac. We were informed that our companies were only nine kilometres behind the Line - a most cheerful bit of news after that fatiguing march to receive!

The next day, the 20th, our kitchens caught up with us - a most happy event for all. Our "Iron" rations could not have lasted much longer and we were sick and tired of cold "corn willie" and hardtack! How we appreciated that liberal helping of hot "slum"! "Seconds" were cheerfully dished out to the hungry men by accommodating Mess Sergeants! The Mess Sergeant was King that day! God bless him! We remained here, taking life comparatively easy, until Saturday night, the 21st, when we moved up through the woods a couple of kilometres, stopping at a point about three kilometres Northeast of Le Neufour. The following day, Sunday, the 22nd, the various Chaplains throughout the entire regiment held Catholic and Protestant services in the woods for the benefit of the men. These services were well attended although it had started to rain. With several comrades, the writer thoroughly enjoyed listening to our Chaplain that Sunday morning as he addressed that khaki-clad congregation. After singing several old and familiar hymns, in which all joined with a will, the Chaplain began his sermon.

It was really more of a fatherly talk than a sermon, however. He did
not mince his words in the least but made the men understand that duty
was very soon to call them into new dangers, that they must face, like
good soldiers, whatever the future held in store for them, trusting in
their God to see them safely through.   He dwelled at some length upon
the loved ones back home in the States, told us that they were with us
in their prayers and that they expected "their boys somewhere in France"
to speedily end the bloody conflict - this terrible sacrifice of
precious human life.   After he finished talking many hardened hearts
were touched and many eyes were dim with tears - not that his sermon
was particularly sad but, under the conditions at the time, it somehow
affected the men.   Several more hymns were sung and after a short
prayer by the Chaplain the services were concluded.   All derived a
great amount of comfort and renewed courage by attending these services.
Somehow the future, though very dark and uncertain, assumed a brighter
aspect!

The next day, Monday the 23rd, rumors about an impending drive
were heard on all sides. The particular sector we were now occupying
had heretofore been known as a "quiet sector", the line remaining
stationary at this point since 1914.   As to how "quiet" it was remained to be seen!   We knew that part of the 112th Infantry was holding
down the trenches and reasoned, of course, that our turn would probably
come next!   Our position now was shelled but very little. It was a
new experience to be so near the Front Line and have things so quiet
and peaceful around us!   (To give some idea of the strength of the
German position at this point on the front, which they had held since
practically the beginning of the war, it may be said that the French
maintained that the German lines could not be taken.   Both sides were
conducting warfare in this locality on the policy of "Don't you shoot
and I won't" arrangement!)   All movements of the American troops were
made with the utmost secrecy and under cover of darkness.   When reconnoitering parties were sent out to look over the ground before the
attack, it was necessary for each man of the detail to wear a French
helmet and uniform in order that the Germans might have no idea that
Americans were in the neighborhood!

During these hours of "watchful waiting" we had noticed the great
activity of allied artillery around us.   Enormous shell dumps could be
seen on every hand and the big guns were placed in position almost hub
to hub.   As to the length of this formidable firing line, we heard
that it extended along the front for a distance of forty miles! Judging from these preparations, we knew that a big drive of some sort was
shortly to be made and that, very likely, the advance of the infantry
would be covered by a barrage from these guns.

CHAPTER 23.

THE MEUSE-ARGONNE DRIVE.

Wednesday night, September 25th!   Just a date, to be sure, but one long to be remembered by the men of the 111th!   Our Third Battalion was encamped under pup tents on the slopes of a hill in the vicinity of Neufour with the balance of the regiment in bivouac nearby. Except for an occasional distant booming of a cannon, the early hours of the night were unusually quiet.   In fact, too quiet, we thought!

I now recall that it was with a feeling of some uneasiness when I sought my tent to "turn in" that night.   Something seemed to warn me that my slumbers would be interrupted!   My bunkie evidently shared the same premonition, judging from his remarks as he reclined on his side of our tiny quarters.   After talking the matter over, we decided to sacrifice comfort for any emergency which might arise during the night. Accordingly, we crawled into our blankets - shoes and leggings untouched - two modern "Minute Men" ready for anything at any time!

The whole camp was soon asleep.   Lying there in my tent, I could even hear the tramp, tramp, tramp of the nearest sentry on guard as he paced up and down on his lonely post.   Silence - an ominous silence - seemed to pervade over all!   I tried to shake off that restless feeling and to join my buddie in a refreshing sleep but to no avail.   The hours dragged slowly by.   Nine o'clock!   I heard the guard on duty being relieved.   Ten o'clock - another spell of tossing, counting imaginery sheep, etc. to bring on those precious hours of unconsciousness.   It surely must be midnight now!   I looked at my comrade's watch - a wrist watch with an illuminated dial.   Five minutes to eleven!   It did not seem possible that so many men could be huddled in one spot and everything be so quiet.   Not even a distant boom of a cannon could I hear - only that guy in the next tent snoring his head off!   What was that?   Someone was asking the guard to be directed to our First Sergeant's tent!   I plainly heard every word.   Then followed a brief interval of intense silence which was suddenly broken by a shrill blast of the "Top's" whistle!   "Outside and roll packs!"   The sharp command was shouted to the sleeping men of Company I.   In a few seconds every man was on his feet, aroused not only by the Sergeant's whistle but also by a terrific thundering of heavy artillery which had just opened up.   All was now a scene of busy activity throughout the entire camp.   We could feel the ground tremble as hundreds of allied guns close at hand belched forth their large shells.   The "Big Drive" was on!   (It was later estimated that over 3,500 pieces took part in this "Million Dollar Barrage" - the heaviest ever put down at any one time in the history of war-fare!)   Thus, after a short period of inactivity, our Third Battalion suddenly participated in that famous

Left: Engineers of the 302nd Engineer Regiment repairing a roadway over a trench and soldiers of the 92nd Infantry Division (Buffalo Soldiers) in a trench headed into action in the Argonne Forest, France, 1918.

Below: 80th "Blue Mountain" Division advancing in the opening of the battle.
(Images courtesy of Library of Congress)

drive - known now as "The Argonne Drive". The men, although somewhat excited, kept their nerve and in a remarkably short space of time our battalion, with the balance of the regiment, was ready to move off. We carried in the top of our packs the reserve rations issued that day, consisting of four boxes of hard tack and a two pound can of roast beef. We had been cautioned that these rations were to last us for two days!

It was exactly 11:30 when the entire regiment moved out of the woods. We found ourselves on a very muddy road - so muddy in fact that it was with the greatest difficulty we managed to keep on our feet as, loaded down with packs, rifles, ammunition and rations, we trudged along. The night was extremely dark. A heavy mist permeated the atmosphere. For miles around, we could see the quick flashes of fire from hundreds of guns as they boomed away in the night. Some were stationed almost in our path and the sudden explosion would nearly knock us off our feet as we marched for some distance along the firing line. The noise was terrific! French guns, American artillery, large pieces and smaller pieces of every description, including great naval guns, - all hurling their deadly missives right into the German lines! It was impossible to carry on conversation for we could not hear the words of the man next to us unless shouted. It is difficult to convey a true description of that terrifying roar of cannon. Personally, I can only add that I had never heard anything just like it before nor do I ever expect to again! We had started off in an easterly direction, later changing our course by turning to the right. At 3:30 on the morning of September 26th, we reached some woods where the whole regiment lay until the afternoon of that day.

With the advance of the 111th Infantry, above described, the campaign of our Third Battalion in the Meuse-Argonne had commenced! From the evening of September 25th, 1918 until relieved by the 82nd U. S. Division on October 9th-10th, events transpired in such rapid succession that it would be difficult indeed to describe each and every happening with any degree of accuracy. Therefore, I can do no better at this time than to again quote from various accounts which, in a general way, will tell our story of the Argonne. After a few quotations, I shall reminisce somewhat and recall some of the many incidents so intimately associated with those never-to-be-forgotten days in the Argonne.

From September 26th to the 30th, our Third Battalion was designated as Brigade Reserve and the balance of the Regiment as Division Reserve. During this period in reserve, we occupied what was then known as Hill 263. This position in the Argonne later proved to be anything but a "quiet zone".

About this time, our fortunes were shared more or less with the Second Battalion of our regiment and the writer will now quote, in part, from George W. Cooper's "Our Second Battalion" as follows:

"The rest of our Division on our right had advanced considerable and it could not be understood why 'Our Second Battalion' could not advance its line. The Germans who were opposing us certainly must have been cut off from the rest of the enemy, who were being pushed back on our right, or else they were ordered to hold that position and hold up our advance while the rest withdrew. The result was that Major Dunlap received an order to withdraw his troops while attempting to take the trench in front, but he refused to do so, replying that to withdraw would open the flanks of both the 112th and 77th Division. When the authorities in the rear learned that 'Our Second Battalion' was meeting such strong resistance, they sent a message that we were to advance in conjunction with the 77th Division and, after reaching our objective - the trench in front of us - the Third Battalion would leapfrog over us and take up the advance. During the night, Captain Haller, who was then commanding the Third Battalion, reported his battalion to Major Dunlap and the situation was explained to him, while his troops were put in position in the rear of our troops.

"Towards morning, Major Dunlap received a message from the Captain commanding the battalion of the 77th Division on our left, saying that they were to advance that morning (Saturday, the 28th) and wanted to know what we would do, and the Major sent the reply, 'I will advance with you.'

"At six o'clock, our barrage was put down, under cover of which the trench was reached, but the 77th Division did not advance with us. Scouts were sent along to explore the trench in front of the 77th Division and they reported back that the trench was all clear. This word was sent to the 77th Division by Captain Schlosser and they refused to believe it and further refused to move up to the trench at that time. A little later, an officer from the 77th Division was seen going through the trench in front of their position, with pencil and pad, making notes of the different guns and material in that sector.

"The Third Battalion then jumped over us and we remained in the trench awaiting further orders. Orders were received in the afternoon for the Battalion to march to Varennes to report to the Chief of Staff of the Division for instructions, and Lieut. Rice, then acting as a M. P., and who was killed a few days later, led us through the Forest to Varennes. Just before we started, a tank explosion occurred on the road just a few hundred yards in back of us as the second of two ambulances went over a little bridge, but no damage was inflicted. Along the road we took into Varennes were some big Howitzers, which the Germans had not had time to take back with them, and just outside of Varennes, we came to a bridge which was mined.

"We rested a little on the outer edge of Varennes, while Major Dunlap reported to the Chief of Staff and received orders to proceed up further to the Commanding General, 55th Brigade, for disposal. We started through that town and never did we see such a congestion of traffic. It seemed as though everyone was on the move, automobiles,

Above, American troops during the Meuse-Argonne Offensive, 1918.
(Image courtesy of Library of Congress)

Below, Meuse-Argonne Allied offensive in France, a U.S .Army 37-mm gun crew man their position.
(Image courtesy of National Archives)

that the eyes of the United States Army were upon him!   As the night
wore on, we came to the conclusion that the zero hour would be at day-
break.   It seemed to the men, however, that under cover of darkness was
an excellent time to make the attack, if one was to be made, but this
feeling was not evidently shared by those in command.   What if we were
discovered by the Germans during the night?   Perhaps even now they were
preparing to attack us!   All through the night, every once and awhile,
a Boche machine gun would bark away.   Some, we knew, were very close at
hand - others at some distance - but our battalion seemed to be surrounded!   None of these guns opened fire for any great length of time-
only four or five shots from a piece every now and then.   It appeared
that Jerry was taking no chances himself that night in being surprised!

After a wearisome night of "standing to", during the long hours of
which we momentarily expected to be attacked or commanded to take the
offensive, the dawn of Tuesday, October 1st, saw our Third Battalion at
last in action!   Le Chene Tondu was assaulted by Company K, which was
followed up by Company L.   The latter company then consolidated with
Companies K, I and M.   Our entire Third Battalion then maneuvered into
position for a general attack upon the enemy, pushing forward through
the lines held by the 112th Infantry.

Resuming our quotations from various data collected relative to the
activities in the Argonne of the respective companies in our Third Battalion, we find the following:

Company I

"On the evening of October 4th, two platoons of Company I
and one from Company L, amid heavy machine gun fire, made a successful attack on a sunken road held by the enemy.   We captured a few prisoners and killed many who offered resistence.
During the night, our small force holding this road was subjected to two unsuccessful attacks on the flank by the enemy.
In the morning, however, the remaining forces of our platoons
were able to move forward and, together, we established a
strong line of resistence along the sunken road.   Jerry, evidently seeing the futility of endeavoring to break through,
later retreated.   We were then relieved on the afternoon of
the 5th by our Second Battalion, taking a position in support
until the evening of October 9th, at which time our regiment
was relieved by a unit of the 82nd Division.   (NOTE) On the
morning of October 1st, our fighting strength numbered about
240 men.   On the 5th, after being relieved by our Second Battalion, the ranks of Company I were reduced to the number of
82 men!   These figures speak for themselves!"

Company K

"The advance (Argonne) commenced at day-break and from
then on, the fighting was the fiercest with K Company in the
thick of it!   From this time on, it was a case of fighting
until the men were exhausted and could advance no further;
then relieved by another outfit for a time and then back into
the lines again.   This continued for fourteen days, during

which time Company K saw the hardest fighting they had seen so far in the war. Particularly deserving of mention was the attack on Hill 244. This hill was attacked on October 1st and for five days the fighting raged around it with no gain and little, if any, advance. On October 5th, a portion of the German line was broken through and pushed back. Seizing the opportunity, the Company came through the break and succeeded in taking the road on the hill. During this fighting (five days), Company K lost more men than during the rest of the entire time that they were in action! It was in taking Hill 244 that Captain James A. Groff was severely wounded in one leg (later amputated) and Lieut. Harold W. Painter was killed. On October 6th, we were relieved and moved back in support. After a day's rest in billets, formerly occupied by German troops, the Company moved up again, this time as 'moppers-up'. The advance continued over Hill 244, which had at last been captured. We finally stopped near Apremont, at which place we were relieved. During this period as 'moppers-up', the Company did a great work in clearing many dugouts of Germans who had hidden and were firing on the rear of our advancing men. German snipers, by the score, were also taken prisoners or were killed by the vigilant soldiers of Company K. On the 9th of October, 1918, our men were relieved by troops of the 82nd Division."

Companies L and M

"Company L, withdrawn from the Line on September 29th, used, in patrols, to locate the 77th Division. Formed a machine gun support for one platoon. Duty in the sector of the 35th Division, where many of the enemy threatened to break through the Lines. Rejoined regiment same date and took position that night at the base of the Le Chene Tondu, Argonne Sector. Le Chene Tondu was assaulted by Company K on October 1st and was followed by another assault by Company L. The latter company then consolidated Line with Companies K, I and M, the entire battalion taking a position on the Line preparatory to a mass attack on the enemy. One platoon, Company L, assaulted enemy center, 6:01 P. M., October 4th, taking the position formerly occupied by the Germans. This platoon also included members of Companies K and I, who desired to participate in the assault. Company M was too far on the left to take an active part in this assault, though it did splendid work in moving its Line forward in the face of enemy fire. The entire Third Battalion participated in the repulse of the enemy's counter-attack the next day and was relieved same date."

111th Machine Gun Company

"During the evening of the 25th of September, 1918, the second platoon, under command of Lieut. Jacob Mertens, Jr., was ordered to relieve the French. The balance of the Company remained in the wood until 11 P. M., when they also moved forward. Upon relieving the French, the second platoon advanced with the infantry while the remainder of the Company was held in reserve. On the night of the 26th, we were ordered to go into position on the left of Varennes but orders were changed so we remained in the evacuated German trenches. On the night of the 28th, the second platoon returned to the Company and the first and third platoons were ordered in positions South of Montblainville, where they remained until the morning of the 29th, when our first platoon moved into support with the 35th Division which was advancing on our right. It was here that the 82nd Division relieved the 35th and as they moved forward the Bosche sent over a heavy barrage, of which we were the recipients of a great part! The first platoon was ordered back to the Company, as the entire regiment was to move into a fort forest. The day of September 30th, we moved into evacuated German dugouts with entrances facing the enemy, who were about 500 yards from us! Here, we were subjected to the fire of snipers who infiltrated through the Lines that night. On the morning of October 2nd, these German snipers succeeded in wounding one of our men- our first casualty in this forest. At 12:00 midnight, we were informed to be prepared for a German counter-barrage that was certain to follow our barrage - our barrage scheduled to start about 1:30 or 2:00 A. M. The second German shell of this barrage fired in our area was a direct hit on the dugout of our second platoon, killing twelve men and wounding six, three of whom died later in a hospital! That evening, we buried the dead and later were ordered into the front line and during the move, the path we were advancing on was shelled with trench mortars. The Company was now reduced to a small number, hardly enough men to man four guns. On the 4th, one gun was sent with K Company of our regiment and the other three with our Second Battalion. Upon the Third Battalion being relieved, the one gun with Company K was returned to us and we then advanced over heavily mined roads to Hill 244, a distance of nearly three kilometres, where we met with bitter resistence that held us in this position over night, we being on the right flank of the Second Battalion. On the morning of the 8th, we moved to the rear of the Second Battalion, occupying a position in support of that unit of our regiment. We were relieved at 4:30 A. M. on the 9th of October by the 82nd Division and marched a short distance to the rear, where we went into camp. Here, many of our men who had been slightly wounded in previous engagements returned to us."

An excellent summary of the activities in the Meuse-Argonne of our entire regiment appears in Colonel Martin's history and, as our Third Battalion is prominently mentioned throughout, we shall again quote from the Colonel's book. The account reads as follows: (3)

"The regiment rested in the towns of Mogneville, Contrisson and Beurey until the night of September 16th, when
orders were received to move to the vicinity of Neufour.
Marching by night, the regiment reached the Bois la Hey-
court at 5 A. M. on September 17th, bivouaced, took up the
march that night, arrived in the vicinity of Futeau at 3
A. M. on September 18th, remained in the woods for the day
and took up the march the same night, finally arriving in
the vicinity of Neufour at 12:15 A. M., September 19th. On
the night of September 21st, the regiment marched to the
ravine Grand Rupt, Foret d' Argonne, their bodies knee deep
in mud, where it rested and prepared for the attack until
the night of September 25th.

"Colonel Shannon temporarily turned over the regiment
to Lieut. Colonel Succop on the 17th and went back to Major
Iland's Field Hospital for a much-needed rest, but rejoined
the regiment the morning of the 25th.

"The general plan, so far as the 111th was concerned,
was about as follows: In the preparation for the attack,
it was the policy of the higher command to keep secret from
the enemy any information that the American troops were moving into the sector. To further this concealment, the front
lines were to be held by the French troops until the night of
the 25th, while the American troops moved up in close support under cover of darkness. When the 'D' day had been
announced, the Americans were to relieve the French in the
front line positions and form for the attack. The Third
Battalion was designated as Brigade Reserve, with one company relieving the French forces occupying the front lines.
The 112th was to form for the attack just in the rear of
these positions and, following the barrage in the initial
attack, was to pass through the front line troops. The
company from the Third Battalion was to rejoin the battalion
in the reserve as soon as the 112th should pass through.
The rest of the regiment was designated as Division Reserve.

"In compliance with the above plan, early in the evening of September 25th, Company K, under command of Captain
James A. Groff, was sent forward to relieve the thin line
of French troops that were then holding the front positions,
the balance of the Third Battalion moving up in close support of the line acting as Brigade Reserve. At 10:18 P.
M., September 25th, the order was received that the attack
would begin at 5:30 A. M., September 26th. In compliance
with orders previously received, the Regiment, less the
Third Battalion, moved to the ravine North of Etang du Molly,
arriving there at 5 A. M. on the 26th. In moving to this
position, the troops were conducted through the artillery
positions in the rear of the infantry lines, and, as the
artillery preparation had begun at 2:30 A. M., the men had
the novel experience of marching forward under the elevated
muzzles of their own high calibre guns. The advance to the

final positions was over a road designated for one-way traffic and that in the opposite direction. Captain Gill, late in the afternoon of the 25th, had discovered that it was possible to use this road, for the Military Police were withdrawn at dark and as long as there was no one to prevent it, the 111th could go ahead.

"The Argonne is decidedly hilly. Had the course of the Aire been straight and the valley come down symmetrically to the river, the 28th Division would have had straight open fighting, which is satisfactory to brave men, whatever may be the cost. To the left of the 28th Division was the 77th, for whom the direct frontal attack was mandatory, but this was out of the question for the Pennsylvanians! Fully realizing that the true defense of the forest was on flanks, the enemy developed a strong resistence in front of the 28th in the first day of the engagement. The resistence was all the more strenuous because of the position of Varennes, where the road crosses the river in sight of the surrounding hills. Varennes was a central storehouse and distributing station for the German lines, and naturally the valuable place to retain.

"Daylight of the 26th saw the beginning of America's greatest battle, and although the 111th had been designated as a reserve, it was not long until it was called upon, Company K being the first unit designated. The 305th of the 77th Division very early in the engagement began to close in to its left and a gap of over a mile opened between the 112th and 305th. Captain Groff had a hard time locating the right flank of the 305th and later getting in communication with the left of the 112th. Company K remained with the left flank of the 112th, acting as emergency troops until they joined the Regiment on September 30th at Varennes. The other three companies of the Third Battalion, under command of Major Haller, were in support of the 112th until September 30th.

"On the afternoon of the 26th, the Second Battalion proceeded to the left of the 112th to close the gap and reestablish liaison with the 77th. A narrow gauge railroad was followed until the contact was gained with the enemy, this being on what had been the 3rd German trench. The battalion remained in this position during the night. On the 27th, at 6:00 A. M., the Second Battalion made an attack under a counter barrage and later in the day was prevented from taking a trench 300 yards distant by enemy trench mortar and machine gun fire.

"An examination of a map showing the relative positions in the Argonne will reveal that on the evening of the 27th, the line of the 28th Division represented a reversed L, the right angle at the base being on the road to the North of Pte. Bourevilles, and had advanced but a little over two kilometres since the initial attack on the morning of the 26th.

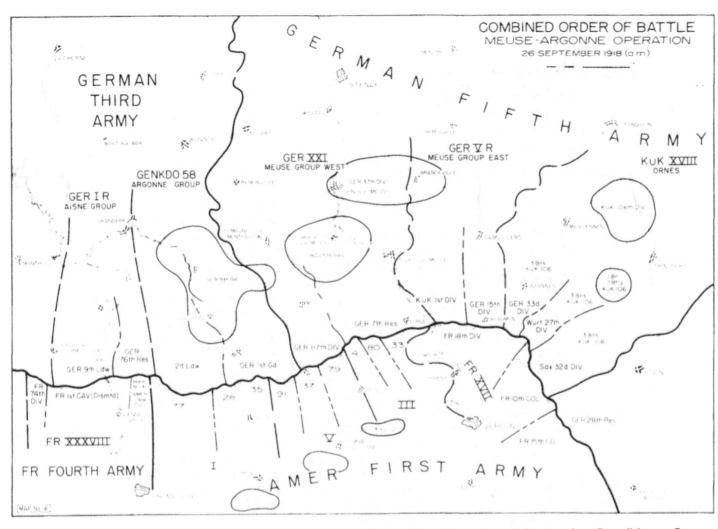

Above image from: United States Army in the World War 1917-1919: Military Operations of the American Expeditionary Forces, Vol. 9, Page 133, Center of Military History, United States Army

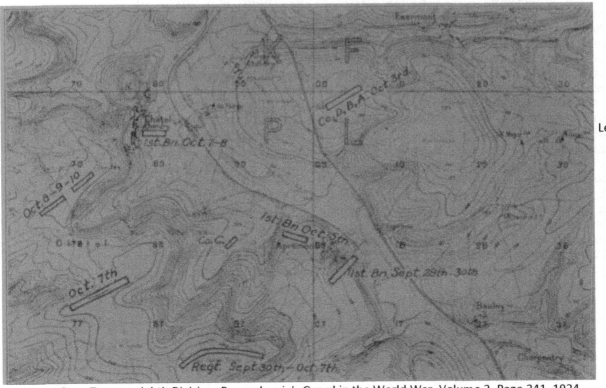

Left: The 111th around Chene Tondu and Chatel-Chehery. Showing Successive advances by the regiment and also positions of First Battalion.

Taken from Twenty-eighth Division: Pennsylvania's Guard in the World War, Volume 2, Page 341, 1924
By Colonel Edward Martin

"The schedule for October 1st, called for a battalion
of the 112th to make an attack on Le Chene Tondu through the
center of the line held by the First and Second Battalions
of the 111th, with the Third Battalion acting as supporting
troops.   The 112th failed to arrive on time and the Third
Battalion had to make the initial attack but it was unable
to advance beyond the line already held by the other two
battalions on account of the intense machine gun fire.

"The companies and platoons availed themselves of every
possible opening where the enemy's fire was relatively weak
and gradually forced their way forward.   Finally the artillery got within range and again the troops of the First and
Second Battalions attacked Le Chene Tondu in the vigor of
renewed courage and the light of the knowledge they had
gained of the enemy's positions.   A footing was gained and
then another attack and their efforts became incessant as
they made more bites at close quarters and struggled for
complete mastery.   The Germans infiltrated back between
their units, and the 111th reciprocated with the greatest
enthusiasm.

"The push beyond Le Chene Tondu was partly accomplished
under barrages thrown by the heavy mortars from the Division
Trench Mortar Battery.   The One-Pounder Platoon could not
be used on account of the ammunition having a nose so sensi-
tive that it exploded on contact with the smallest twig,
making it about as dangerous for the gunman as for the enemy.
The Regiment was also augmented, without much success, by the
gas and flame sections that came from somewhere in the rear,
nobody knowing or caring very much.

"October 3rd, saw conditions and the position of the
troops unchanged until about 10:00 P. M., when the Chief of
Staff telephoned that a heavy artillery fire would be laid
down on the enemy positions, and that all the troops must
take what cover was available to protect them from the expected retaliatory fire.   All the Battalion P. C.s were ef-
ficiently connected by telephone with the Regimental P. C.
and the word was passed along.   The Regimental P. C. was in
a frame building that had been erected by the enemy on the
northern slope of the ravine, south of Le Chene Tondu.   The
Machine Gun Company was being held in reserve in a similar
building east of and next to the Regimental P. C.   Back of
all these buildings on this slope were very good dugouts, in
which the troops were ordered to go before midnight.   About
11:30 o'clock a large caliber enemy explosive shell landed
in the building occupied by the Machine Gun Company, killing
twelve and wounding six, and a piece of this same shell came
through the Regimental P. C. severely wounding Adjutant
Ballent, the French liaison officer on duty with the Regiment, and knocking off the back of Colonel Shannon's chair.

"October 4th saw the beginning of the second phase of the

Meuse-Argonne Offensive.   The First Corps, holding the left of the American line, and of which the 28th Division was a part, had not made the heavy advances made by the Third and Fifth Corps on the right, but the First Corps had not failed to keep the enemy moving backward, particularly since the veteran First Division had relieved the 35th on the right of the 28th.   Although there was heavy fighting to the right, conditions remained unaltered on the front of the 111th. During the earlier fighting the German forces were composed of older men but as the fight progressed they had brought up many of their very best reserve divisions composed of younger men, and the struggle became all the more intense.

"The 109th and 110th Regiments had been having terrific fighting on the right flank of the Division and it became necessary to withdraw the Third Battalion on October 5th and send it to reinforce what was left of the 55th Brigade.   The ground vacated by the Third Battalion was occupied by the First and Second Battalions which extended their lines to the right and left.

"The 6th saw no change in the front until late in the night, when the 103rd Trench Mortar Battery placed its mortars back of the Second Battalion and the 112th went into position to attack Chatel-Chehery and Hills 244 and 233, in an attempt to clear the forest and effect the relief of the 'Lost Battalion' of the 77th Division.

"At 5:30 A. M. on the 7th the trench mortars laid down a heavy barrage on the enemy positions and the attack of the 112th began, which, after magnificent work on their part, caused the enemy to retreat, and the First and Second Battalions of the 111th made an advance of four kilometres before they were stopped, by heavy machine gun fire, at about 4:00 o'clock in the afternoon.   The Third Battalion had rejoined the Regiment on the morning of the 7th and was left in reserve on Le Chene Tondu.   In the advance the First Battalion was on the left and the Second Battalion on the right.   Late that afternoon, the Second Battalion joined up with the left of the 112th and dug in for the night.

"October 8th saw a fatigued, tired, almost dead on their feet, but not disheartened outfit, make another attack, which was taken part in by the Second Battalion but little ground was gained and the casualties were heavy. Veteran regiment that the 111th was, it had about spent its strength.   Not all casualties are due to bullets, shells or gas, and no form of torture can be more severe than hunger, thirst and almost total loss of sleep.

"The 111th Infantry had spent fourteen days of as near hell-on-earth as any man could ever wish, and it was with the greatest satisfaction that at 11:15 P. M., on the 9th,

Above: Battery A, 108th Field Artillery in action, firing toward Chatel Chehery, Ardennes. This battery was under fire of enemy gas shells at the time the photo was taken, October 3, 1918, Varennes-en-Argonne, Meuse, France. Almost 4,000 guns were in action.
"The Meuse-Argonne Offensive was the largest operations of the American Expeditionary Forces (AEF) in World War I, with over a million American soldiers participating. It was also the deadliest campaign in American history, resulting in over 26,000 soldiers being killed in action (KIA) and over 120,000 total casualties."

Below: Line of German prisoners who were captured by the Americans in the Argonne. 28th Division P.C. LaForge, Meuse, France, October 4, 1918. (Images Courtesy of National Archives)

Colonel Shannon received word that the 326th Regiment of the 82nd Division would relieve the Regiment at 2:00 A. M. on the 10th. The relief was late in arriving and it was not completed until 7:15 under cover of a heavy fog. No one in the Regiment will ever forget Captain Rafferty's restaurant on Le Chene Tondu. 'Meals at all hours – We aim to please' was its motto. Nor will be forgotten the Regimental Headquarters in an old German rest camp, which was splendidly fitted up with bunks and cooking facilities.

"The fatal casualties in the Argonne were less than those on the Vesle, for, although the fighting was fully as severe, experience, particularly among the older men counted. The casualties in the Argonne were: Killed, four officers, 128 men; wounded, eleven officers, 563 men. Captain Arthur L. Schlosser, Company G, was killed on September 29th. Lieut. Wilhelmus Rice was killed on October 2nd, Lieut. Poffenberger, Headquarters Company, died in the hospital about October 10th, and Lieut. Harold W. Painter, Company K, was killed on October 2nd. Captain James Groff was seriously wounded on October 1st, and his leaving marked the departure of the last commander of a combat company who had crossed on the Olympic."

We have endeavored in this chapter to relate, as accurately as possible, the activities of our Third Battalion in the great Argonne Drive. Associated with our campaign in that now famous theatre of action are many incidents which befell the actors who played such prominent roles on that historic battlefield of the World War. Each and every man who survived the terrors of those days will, undoubtedly, recall stories of personal danger, of untold hardships – happenings exciting, sad and amusing – which he, alone, can best recite. Therefore, in closing this chapter the writer will confine himself to one or two little narratives in which he personally figured, leaving the deficiency to be supplied by comrades with vivid memories.

Every man of our Third Battalion will recall the opening days of the Argonne Drive when we entered No Man's Land of four years standing. Many strange and interesting sights here arrested our attention which may be well to describe. One night the battalion camped in a sector literally honey-combed by hugh French dugouts (some thirty and forty feet under ground) which completely occupied one side of a big hill. The Line at this point had not been moved for four years. The French troops, consequently, had found ample time in which to construct underground homes – all practically shell-proof. It was in this spot that the battalion's "souvenir cranks" reaped a golden harvest of countless French and German equipment found in these dugouts and scattered everywhere upon the ground.

It was in the late afternoon, during the early days of our Argonne adventures, when we marched into an immense camp-site deep in some woods which had just recently been evacuated by the retreating German army. Here we found a veritable store-house of food – bread, meats, vegetables, wines and even honey! Appropriating a cooker which our host had obligingly left behind, it was not many hours before the hungry men had a steaming hot supper ready consisting of excellent vegetable soup. As the weather was chilly and damp, this soup greatly aided in warming both body and spirit of the cold and hungry men. Others enjoyed fried rabbit for mess that night, finding the caged animals in the camp upon arrival. Honey, also, was found in large quantities and every hive (luckily evacuated) was soon completely ransacked. None of the men, however, seemed to care particularly for the German bread, loaves of which were left behind by the enemy in retreat. As the boys remarked, "Saw-dust could taste no worse!" Upon sampling a slice myself, I fully concurred in the general opinion expressed by my buddies.

We were duly warned by our officers about taking the risk of eating food which we chanced to find in these camps recently occupied by the enemy but it was difficult indeed to resist the temptation and come down to old army hard-tack and corn-willie when more desirable food was so plentiful. However, none of the men were poisoned, although we really took long chances, as cases were known where Jerry had purposely set traps baited with poisoned food and water, knowing that sooner or later his camps would be occupied by the pursuing Allies.

While in this locality, exploration parties (composed mostly of souvenir-hunters) had the time of their lives inspecting the long, underground passages which connected some of the larger dugouts. Most of these tunnels and under-ground quarters were securely boarded up so that danger from a cave-in was reduced to a minimum. In fact, many of our men, upon finding out that these places were equipped with bunks - some even supplied with mattresses and blankets - were tempted to occupy them as their sleeping quarters. A closer inspection, however, revealed these beds to be infested with rats, cooties and creeping creatures of every description! Consequently, those who were at first inclined to bunk in these places wisely changed their minds and slept in the many shacks scattered throughout the camp or in their own pup-tents. The ventilation, or rather lack of ventilation, was also a bad feature down in these dugouts. Presence of the deadly mustard gas permeated the foul air. Each entrance to a tunnel leading down into the larger dug-outs was equipped with a signal device - some with electric wiring attached to sirens - which had been used by the Germans to warn comrades below in dugouts that a gas attack was coming over. All of our men who ventured under-ground were cautioned not to handle these signal devices or to open any packages or boxes found, our officers again fearing some trickery at the hands of the enemy.

For three days in the Argonne, the front line of our Third Battalion was located within less than thirty yards from machine gun nests of the enemy. This portion of the forest was covered by very thick under-brush and many trees. While affording our men some protection, this foliage likewise provided Jerry with ideal locations within which to secret his numerous machine guns. And Jerry did not lack machine guns in the Argonne! The woods were full of them! In holding the Line here, we were at all times under heavy machine gun fire. While we, of course, exercised every precaution - day and night - many of our boys met their deaths or were badly wounded from that almost continual rain of bullets!   Jerry's machine gun bullets were particularly noted for the nasty wounds they could inflict!   During these never-to-be forgotten days, we were forced to literally hug the ground, not even so much as disturbing the foliage around us for fear of drawing fire from one of Jerry's guns located, we knew, just a few yards ahead.

While I do not desire to inject in this article too many yarns of a personal nature, it is believed that what I have to relate at this point in our story will be appreciated by all who participated in making Argonne history.   I shall never forget the sight as long as I live!   My platoon had just gained its position along a narrow ravine running through the woods.   I was in the act of taking off my pack, the word having been passed along that we would probably occupy the ravine for some hours at least.   Inwardly, I congratulated myself that I had safely reached this haven of shelter.   Many of my comrades had fallen in coming through the woods to this position!   I had no sooner dismissed the thought when, on looking up, I saw a lone doughboy walking toward where my comrades and I lay crouched on the ground.   As all our men at that time were accounted for, we concluded that he must be a 112th man - perhaps a runner.   We frantically motioned for him to get down on his hands and knees and crawl, realizing his great danger from that machine gun hid up there in the woods - so close at hand and now so ominously quiet!   Too late, however!   The Germans had undoubtedly spotted their prey!   The poor fellow was just about to step down to where we were lying when that gun opened up!   A bullet hit him squarely in the throat!   Blood fairly gushed from the wound as he lunged forward almost on top of the writer.   The next few minutes were too horrible to attempt here to describe!   That mortally wounded man was terrible in his death struggles!   We tried to keep him as quiet as possible, fearing that he would give our position away to the enemy.   It took several men to hold him down.   His agonized expression - that blood flowing from the wound - the struggling men - all remain indelibly pictured in the writer's mind.   We did everything we possibly could for the poor devil (no first-aid man was available at the time) but our efforts were in vain.   He died as he was being taken back to a first-aid dressing station.   We had improvised a litter for this purpose made of two shelter-halves.   The man, whose name we never learned, was a company runner from one of the units of the 112th Infantry operating in that vicinity.

The fourth platoon of Company I, 111th Infantry, under the command of Lieut. Charles A. Gillespie, occupied positions in the ravine above referred to.   The men were comparatively safe from enemy machine gun fire as long as they kept close to the ground.   If any moving about had to be done, we were forced to crawl on our hands and knees, and very cautiously at that!   Indeed, every time Jerry sent over a shower of bullets, we could see the bark flying from trunks of trees that were hit - barely two or three feet above our heads!   To stand erect, during the daylight hours, was sure suicide!   And we all knew it!   The sad fate of that runner from the 112th had proved the seriousness of the situation!   If the writer's memory serves him right, it was about nine o'clock on the morning of our first day's occupancy of the ravine, October 1st, 1918.   Privates Clarence H. Calhoun, Frederick C. Mason and myself were engaged in a whispered conversation with

earth!   In the Argonne, one was fortunate indeed to have been born a
dwarf!

During these times of comparatively open fighting in the Argonne,
when it was often the case of "every man for himself", all barriers of
rank were forgotten.   Our commissioned officers, always the picked target of the enemy, were frequently disguised as privates.   Petty hates
and jealousies vanished; racial, religious and personal differences were
unknown, and everybody united in the common cause.   All men, doing
their duty, were equal.   At camps back home many a domineering "Top"
Sergeant's life had more than once been threatened.   "Wait until we
get him up on the front lines", was the whispered oath in many an outfit!   But a few months later when we actually found ourselves on the
front lines, all these former threats were forgotten.   Some of the
toughest disciplinarians wearing a "Top's" chevrons turned out to be
very meek under fire!   So perhaps, after all, that change of attitude
had something to do with the change of heart of the lowly buck private!
War - that melting pot of all human grievances both real and imaginary -
overshadowed all and the well-oiled war machine, of which each man was
an important cog, hit perfectly on all cylinders!

In the battle of the Argonne, we were beset by another foe - noted
for great military prowess on many a front - our old enemy, the tiny
cootie!   Those first days of October were rather warm and the pesty
creatures seemed to take a special delight in launching their offensives upon perspiring bodies.   A certain buck private of Company I -
the writer - was reported as "missing" one day in the early afternoon.
During a lull between Jerry's fire-works, I managed somehow to elude the
watchful eyes of our officers and, at the risk of being spotted by the
Germans, crept on all fours some twenty or thirty yards back of our
position in the ravine being held by my outfit.   I knew that if I remained at my post, I would be expected to "stand to" for the remainder
of that warm afternoon.   The cootie attack had gotten my body in a
feverish heat - brought on by much scratching - and I decided then and
there to conduct an extensive offensive campaign of a strictly private
nature!   Finding a sheltered nook down in the woods, I took off every
stitch of clothing that covered my perspiring and itching body.   One
by one, between my two thumb-nails, the enemy met their Waterloo!   By
way of satisfaction, I kept a faithful count of every cootie caught.
When the casualty list had totalled one hundred killed in action, I then
declared an armistice in the hostilities.   My two thumb-nails - the
battlefield - ran red with the blood of the enemy!

Just before reluctantly forsaking my leafy retreat and crawling
back to rejoin my comrades, I took advantage of the seclusion afforded
and attended to a matter of nature which had been bothering me all that
morning.   This last confession, dear reader, may seem uncalled-for on
my part and could very well be omitted.   However, I relate it only to
satisfy inquiring minds who might well ask: "How could the men attend
to themselves huddled in that ravine for so many days when it was so
dangerous to go any distance away for fear of attracting Jerry's attention?"   The answer to that question is very simple.   They did not
go away!   When the demands of nature could no longer be denied, the
soldier dug a hole a few feet from the spot where he had been "standing

to", the depth of which depended upon the amount of energy he cared to put into the work. In some cases, the "amount of energy" was almost nill and even the dullest mind can comprehend the result! This was my opportunity and I took it! If any further apology is due for my rather candid remarks throughout this story, remember, dear friends, that it is primarily the policy of the writer to disclose, as far as possible, many of the incidents, great and small - pleasant and unpleasant, which daily regulated the life of the average American doughboy in France during the World War - incidents which from lack of wide publicity should appeal to all those who honestly want to know. In this volume, therefore, a doughboy feebly endeavors to satisfy inquiring minds! Putting on my clothes, I crawled back to the ravine. I had been gone nearly the entire afternoon. Some of the boys thought that I had been "knocked off". When I told them what I had been doing, one or two more of our little group up there in that ditch were subsequently "missing" from their squads!

In relating these various experiences which occurred in the Argonne, we do not want to overlook the fate which befell one of I Company's greatest "souvenir" collectors, Watson R. Pepperman. Little good his bag of German helmets, etc. brought him, however! Poor Pepperman was knocked off by machine gun bullets during one of our engagements with the enemy, and at the time he was loaded down with a large assortment of German trophies. The writer did not see him killed but was informed of the sad occurrence a few minutes after it happened. Personally, I cared very little about burdening myself with German equipment! Many times, it was all I could do to carry along my own heavy pack, rifle, ammunition (including about six hand grenades) and gas mask without being compelled to "fall out" on some long march! One day, however, up in the Argonne Forest, I almost stumbled over the body of a dead American soldier - a 112th man, I now recall. Someone had evidently been through the poor fellow's pack for it lay open nearby and toilet articles, etc. belonging to the man were scattered about the body. Seeing a shaving brush which looked comparatively new, I picked it up and tucked it within the folds of my pack. I happened to be alone at the time and recall to this day my somewhat guilty feeling as I left the spot. Somehow, I felt that I was taking something which I had no right to appropriate, even though the owner had no further use for it! However, I consoled myself with the thought that if I hadn't taken the brush somebody else would! This brush, by the way, I am using today, and it constitutes the single "souvenir" of my Argonne days!

So ends the writer's contribution to that great list of incidents which happened in the Argonne Drive. No doubt, comrades who may read these lines will have more to add to the number. As stated in our Preface, however, these stories are for the telling when old members of the battalion unite!

George W. Cooper's "Our Second Battalion" gives an accurate account of the movement of our entire Brigade upon being relieved in the Argonne sector, and I, again, take the liberty of quoting from that excellent work, as follows:

"Our last night in the Argonne was a very chilly one.
At 7:30 on the morning of October the 9th, the line was
taken over by a unit of the 82nd Division, and, under cover
of the heavy fog we started to march to the rear. While
on this march, we were subjected to heavy shelling. Jerry
seemed determined to give us a good 'send-off'. Our kitchens had moved up and when we reached them, we got a cup
of hot coffee and then proceeded on the march. After hiking about eight kilometers, we reached a part of the
Argonne Forest, where we were to stay for the day and night.
We were not sure yet that we were entirely relieved from the
drive, for we were still within shelling distance and could
be moved up to the Line in a hurry again, but we had only a
small number of men left and hoped we would keep on going
to the rear. It was about eleven o'clock when we got to
the woods and about the first thing we did was to take off
our shirts and undershirts and begin to kill the cooties,
which had accummulated on our bodies in the past few weeks.
The kitchens followed us back and in the afternoon we were
served the first hot meal we had had for two weeks.

"While lying in these woods, we were told that we would
start out the next morning at 7:30, march a few kilometers
and then board trucks. The next morning (the 10th)we
started out through the woods, but were met by Captain Gill,
the Regimental Adjutant, just as we reached the road. He
told Major Dunlap that we would have to walk a little further than was intended at first. About eight o'clock, the
regiment got on it way and we passed through Mountblainville.
A little distance past this town, we were given hard tack
and canned roast beef, and then we followed the narrow gauge
railroad into Varennes again. It certainly was a hard march
and the only thing that kept so many of us from falling out
was the thought that we might miss the trucks, which were to
haul us 'somewhere'. We knew not where, and, as a matter
of fact, cared less.

"We kept proceeding along in column of file at a slow
pace, yet it was strenuous. The whole Brigade was on the
march and, according to another soldier who saw us coming
out that morning, it was one of the most pitiable sights he
had seen. We were dirty and ragged and our beards were
long, for we had not gotten a chance to put any water on our
hands and faces for two weeks, let alone try to shave. Nearly everyone was carrying a German cane or some other souvenir
that had been picked up in the Argonne.

"After we left Varennes, we turned to the left on a
little road and then turned to the right on the long road,
which eventually led us to just outside of Clermont, where
we boarded trucks driven by Chinese, after marching over
twenty kilometers. We rode and stopped and finally, at
about three o'clock the next morning, which was Friday, we
were told to get off the trucks and go over in the field
next to the road and lie down until morning."

CHAPTER 24.

EUVILLE.

The sun was well up on the morning of Saturday, October the 12th, when our Third Battalion marched into a town of considerable size and the men assigned to billets. This town proved to be Euville, situated some ten or twelve kilometers away from the City of Commercy. (The locations at this time of the various units of the regiment were as follows: Regimental Headquarters and Headquarters Company at Rangeval; the Machine Gun Company, First and Second Battalions in Jouy-les-Cotes; the Third Battalion in Euville and the Supply Company at Corneville.)

After being assigned to our respective quarters in barns, stables, out-houses, etc., we spent the balance of the day (Saturday) in resting and looking for the arrival of our kitchens. Some of the men busied themselves in cleaning equipment. Others, interested more in their personal appearances, endeavored to remove the abundant supply of dirt and whiskers accummulated during during the past week or so. We were all too tired and hungry to do much "sight-seeing" that first day in Euville.

By Sunday Mr. Doughboy felt more like his old self again! A night's sound sleep between four walls and a roof over our heads worked wonders! The day was spent in looking the town over and getting acquainted with our French hosts. Some of the more religious attended church services in the morning at the town's principal house of worship located (as usual in France) in the center square of the village. During the afternoon, our Third Battalion received its quota of replacements, this time from the 86th Division. These new men took the place of our former comrades who were either killed, wounded or missing in action during the Argonne Drive. With the addition of these replacements, our Third Battalion was again on the war-strength basis! We wondered, not a little, when these new men would be called upon to join us in another attack upon the enemy!

On Monday, we were issued new underwear and overcoats. We were all supposed to take a cootie bath, but there was only room for about fifteen men at a time and consequently, very few men got bathed!

It looked as though we were going to get a real rest at Euville, for an officer was to be sent to Paris for the regiment and get the trunks of all our officers stored there. Training programs were made out and on Tuesday, the 15th, the drilling was begun again, but before noon had come, orders were received to prepare to move by trucks that day, and the troops were marched back to their billets and prepared to move.

In looking back over the events incident to our short stay at Euville, I recall one or two little stories which I will endeavor to relate, believing that they will prove of special interest to my buddies of the old outfit, Company I. It is my opinion that former members of the other companies comprising our Third Battalion will likewise enjoy and appreciate these reminiscences. No doubt, in reading over these lines, they will recall similar stories associated with their respective companies while "at rest" in this particular area.

We found Euville to be inhabited, chiefly, by the female sex, their men folks being away at the front. The shopkeepers literally robbed any man wearing the uniform of the United States Army! Many of us were forced to submit to their demands or else fall back on iron rations pending the arrival of our kitchens which had not as yet caught up. All these women were not so mercenary, however. One treasured memory of Euville still lingers in the writer's mind and, in justice to a kind-hearted old French mother, it gives me pleasure to here relate the story. Perhaps some buddy of mine, in reading this, will recall that he, too, was one of the players in this little drama of the brighter side of the World War. Personally, I am unable at this late date to recall the names of the men from Company I who participated. It happened just before our kitchens arrived in town. The weather was very chilly - a penetrating chillness - with just enough intermittent rain to make it all the more disagreeable. A small party of I Company men had bought a supply of eggs, some raw meat and a few potatoes. Not wishing to advertise the purchase of these provisions too widely (for obvious reasons), we made our way around to the rear of some houses on one of the side streets of the town with the intention of building a fire and doing a little private cooking on our own hook. Wood, however, was very scarce and it was sometime before we managed to find even a few dry sticks with which to build our fire. These sticks we piled up over some paper and straw (a nearby barn furnished the latter two items), a match was applied and then that rain, which had up to this time stopped, began falling again - harder than ever - soon quenching our tiny flame, and hopes! After several more unsuccessful attempts, accompanied by some fancy cursing, we were about to give up in disgust and return to our billets when we heard a feminine voice exclaim: "Ah! les Americains!" We looked up and there standing in the doorway of a nearby dwelling was a rather portly woman beckoning for us to come over. The first thought that flashed through the mind of the writer was that our little band was in for a "call down" for, on looking around, I saw that we had begun operations in the lady's back garden! Such was not the case, however. She invited us, by a few well chosen gesticulations, into her nice warm kitchen where a roaring fire was doing its duty in an immense stove. Continuing her "sign language", punctuated at intervals by a few words in very bad English, she soon made her good intentions known. In a short time (how too quickly it passed) our supply of eggs, meat and potatoes were cooked and seasoned to a turn over that hot kitchen stove. But this was not all! She added to our menu a plentiful helping of food from her own pantry and gave us a meal that I shall remember to the end of my days! Without a doubt that repast, topped off by hot coffee with plenty of cream and sugar, will live forever in the minds of that little band of tired, wet, cold and hungry doughboys! So will the memory of that kind-hearted old French mother never be effaced! We offered to pay her but she refused to take a franc! She spoke enough English to make us understand that she had a boy in the French army and was expecting him back home on a furlough very shortly. Needless to say, each man of our little group thanked her profusely for her kindness. On the way back to our billets, we were strangely quiet. Perhaps, at that time, more than one of us thought of a certain mother far away over the ocean waiting for her boy to come safely back home! It was the first real home atmosphere we had breathed for many a long, dreary day! Personally, I shall never forget the kindness of that dear old French mother! God bless her!

We had not been in Euville long before we had exhausted our interest in the small town and felt the urge for a hike to the City of Commercy which, we knew, lay some ten or twelve kilometers away. However, we learned that passes were required of all entering Commercy and we were further informed that it was impossible to get by the Military Police without exhibiting the coveted slips of paper! Some of our men succeeded in obtaining these passes but many (including the writer) were unable to do so. Finding the time hanging rather heavily on our hands, on Sunday we (those without passes) decided to hike to Commercy and there take our chances with the Military Police guarding the road into the city. All went well until we gained a short bridge just on the border of our objective. Here, we were haulted by two burly guardians of the law and were ordered, in sharp commands, to show our passes! This, of course, we were unable to do and we were then told to report back to our outfits. In vain we pleaded - explaining the great difficulty in procuring passes, the long hike we had taken and how anxious we all were to spend a few hours in Commercy. Our entreaties, however, were useless! "We have our orders and intend to obey them", was the only answer we received. Thorough disgusted, we started our return journey back to Euville, which now seemed twice the distance. A few of the disappointed group endeavored to get by the Military Police stationed at another point, but there met defeat also! They rejoined the main group before we reached Euville. Together, we made it "hot" for all M. Ps. in general and those guarding Commercy in particular! If words could have killed, many would have fallen that day under our heavy barrage!

It was at Euville that we heard the very first of the many rumors to follow about an armistice and the ending of hostilities. One day, I believe it was on Monday, the 14th of October, a French dispatch carrier rode through the town on a motorcycle, stopping just long enough to inform a group of soldiers and townspeople who quickly gathered around that "le guear" would soon be over! Of course, none of our men took much stock in what he said, dismissing this bit of information as just another wild rumor. (From the time our division landed on English soil up to the present, we had been constantly "fed up" on rumors - rumors of advancing, rumors of going back for a rest, rumors of a change of clothing, rumors of a thorough de-lousing, etc., etc.) This, however, was the first rumor to reach us about an armistice and, as I have stated, we treated it like all the other rumors we had heard. Time, alone, would soon verify it, we all hoped - a vague sort of hope!

On Tuesday, the 15th, our kitchens caught up and many enjoyed their first hot meal they had had for several days. We also received a long over-due batch of mail from the States - the first distributed since before the great Argonne Drive had started. It rained practically all that day - a day which would have been dreary indeed if we had not been kept busy in packing and policing up; in discussing that topic of the hour, "Where do we go from here?"; reading letters received from our folks back home and endeavoring, between our various detail duties, to write as many letters as we could ourselves. Thus busily engaged, that rainy day passed all too quickly. This was especially the case for the usual number of "gold-bricking" bucks on "sick roll" in quarters and sound asleep!

Packs were now made up and the men told not to leave their billets. (This last order was hardly necessary for by nightfall a hard and steady rain had set in.) We were only too glad of the opportunity to remain in our respective barns - we at least could rest and take things easy. Some of the men proceeded, by guarded candle light, to "read shirts" - a slow but sure de-lousing process; others engaged in that ever popular army pastime, shooting craps and the more talkative gathered in small groups where lively discussions were carried on as to when the army would be "on the move" again, intermingled by that old chorus, to which reference is made in the above paragraph, namely, "Where do we go from here, boys, where do we go from here?" Many joined in singing that refrain.

A shrill blast of the First Sergeant's whistle, accompanied by the cry, "Outside and fall in!" suddenly brought every man to his feet. The dreaded but expected summons had arrived! Every billet in town was now the scene of busy activity - men everywhere quickly shouldering their packs, grabbing their rifles, ammunition and gas masks - then silently assembling in squad formation just outside of each billet - through it all that steady down-pour of a cold October night's rain! Uncle Sam's army was indeed on the move again! Where to, we knew not and cared less!

By 8:30 P. M., October 15th, (the writer recalls asking his Corporal the hour), our Third Battalion marched out of Euville - into the blackness and that persistent rain storm. As usual, we were compelled to tramp some distance before we finally reached that long train of motor trucks which were to convey us - where? We could never quite understand, during our A. E. F. days, just why we were always obliged to hike several kilometres prior to these "joy rides"! It seemed that the trucks could just as well have been driven up to us instead of we marching many a weary mile in order to board them! Arriving at a neighboring village (Gironville), we found the long line of motor vehicles awaiting their usual load of human cannon fodder!

CHAPTER 25.

THIAUCOURT SECTOR - PANNES - BENEY - BOUILLONVILLE - XAMMES -

BOIS DE NONSARD.

Our destination, as usual, was shrouded in mystery but this important fact we did know, namely, that we were bound "for the front" again! There could be no mistake about that!

The motor ride - not exactly a "joy" ride for we were packed-in like so many sardines in a can - ended about two o'clock the following morning, October 16th. It was still raining when we unloaded at Pannes, a small village, or rather, what remained of a village. The entire town had been literally shot to pieces. About the only building in the place that boasted of a roof, as far as we could make out in the darkness, was a church located in the center square of the village and that appeared to have suffered a great deal from Jerry's shells. We could now distinctly hear, amid the roar of heavy artillery, machine gun firing which told us plainer than any words that we were not very far away from the front lines!

Immediately after unloading at Pannes, we marched through the rain until we reached another village. Military signs posted along the road informed us that this shell-torn spot was known as Beney. Here, we rested for a brief period and were given time to partake of a light breakfast - too light, in fact, for most of us. We hesitated about going into our iron rations too heavily, not knowing how long they would have to last us. From Beney, the column marched on to Bouillonville, a town of considerable size, located in what was then known as the Thiaucourt Sector.

We, of course, were not at the time aware of the fact that the Thiaucourt Sector was destined to be the final scene of the World War drama in which our Third Battalion would be called upon to play its role. At midnight, October 16th, we relieved the 37th Division occupying the front lines near the little village of Xammes. Our Second and Third battalions took over the front line position with our First Battalion in reserve at Thiaucourt.

Events of vital importance affecting the fortunes of our Third Battalion now began to crowd each passing hour. At this point in my story I shall again refer to and quote from various data collected concerning the activities of the several units of our Third Battalion on this - our last - front. In each case, the action will be brought up to the time when our battalion went into barracks in the Bois de Nonsard.

111th Machine Gun Company.

"We left our position on the morning of October 10th, and after a march of 22 kilos, we loaded on trucks and rode to Jouy-les-Cotes, arriving there the morning of the 11th. We camped in the field until 8 P. M. when we marched to Rangeville, a distance of three kilos and there we billeted in barns.

"On the afternoon of the 14th, we received 75 replacements from the 86th Division. We left there by truck at 6:30 P. M. of the 14th and rode to Pannes, where we unloaded the next morning and marched through Essey to Boullionville. On the 16th, we relieved the 37th Division at 12:00 midnight and moved into the trenches at Xammes, where everything was comparatively quiet until the 21st of the month, when a raiding party was ordered out from the First Battalion. Judging from results later, the enemy was well informed of the proposed raid owing to the fact that his barrage preceded ours by at least one half an hour. During this we suffered five casualties, four killed and one wounded.

"Upon being relieved, November 5th, we withdrew to the town of Xammes and remaining there until the 7th, we marched to Nonsard and rested until the 10th, when we again marched to Xammes and made ready for an attack with the infantry, the attack to be made on the morning of the 11th, but later this was cancelled and we were ordered back to Nonsard."

Company I

"On gaining our objective (Xammes in the Thiaucourt Sector), Company I had its share with the other units in the Third Battalion in holding down the front lines. The Company sent out many successful patrols and raiding parties.

"In relating the experiences of Company I during these closing days of the war, I recall at this point how one Joseph Arliecavage, formerly a member of my squad, was killed under rather peculiar circumstances. It happened sometime during the night of October 22, 1918. Joe and I were two of a detail picked from among several other members of Company I and designated to take turns at standing guard during our outfit's occupancy of a certain stretch of woodland on the Xammes front.

"At this time our lines were being harrassed by enemy shelling which kept up, intermittently, all during the night and the early morning of October 22nd. About dawn, my trick of guard duty being over, I went over to awaken Joe who was scheduled to relieve me. I found him rolled up in his blanket and apparently sound asleep. It was still very dark in the woods as only the first hint of a new day appeared on the horizon. Reaching over to shake him by the shoulders, my hand came into contact with a wet spot on his blanket. Even then I did not suspect the truth. Not receiving any response to repeated shakings, I thought it rather strange that he should be sleeping so soundly, and I looked closer. Joe was dead - killed by a piece of shrapnel as he peacefully slept during his relief period from guard duty! I could hardly believe the evidence of my own eyes, for at no time had Joe been out of my sight and I had not heard a single sound from him. I then recalled a particularly heavy barrage sent over into our lines shortly after Joe had been relieved and, undoubtedly, it was in that barrage that the poor fellow met his instantaneous death!

"On the 24th of October, we were relieved by Company L of our battalion and took a position in support until the night of the 27th, at which time our battalion was relieved by the First Battalion, 111th Infantry. During this period, our casualties numbered about ten killed and many wounded - some very seriously. Here, we were kept constantly on the go trying to keep in touch with Jerry, sending out reconnoitering parties, conducting nightly raids, etc. and, at all times, subjected to heavy enemy artillery barrages.

"Speaking of heavy shelling, a particular experience through which we passed at about this time may well be worth the telling. Located about four kilometers outside of the town of Xammes and on our line of advance is a very steep range of hills. However, before we could gain the base of these hills, we had to cross an open and exposed plateau in full view of Boche planes. This field offered no protection whatever from the shells of the enemy. Marching in the formation of five paces between men, our Company had covered about half the distance when, suddenly, the German artillery sent over "all they had", as many of our boys later expressed it! These shells ranged from the little "one pounders" to shells of larger dimensions! Evidently, Jerry had sighted us from one of his planes and had signalled our exact position to his artillery! An order came down the line to "Double-time", which order all obeyed with considerable alacrity! Morris Harris, of Baltimore, Maryland, a young Jewish member of Company I during those trying times, probably owes his life that day to his steel helmet. A bit of shell hit the rim of his head-gear and inflicted a slight scalp wound. Private Harris was taken back for treatment and later rejoined his outfit - thanks to his precious steel helmet! (It is presumed that Harris has cherished that old helmet throughout the intervening years. If so, he can offer a substantial proof of this story.)

"It literally rained shells as our Company doubled time

Above: BENEY-THIAUCOURT AREA Looking north, northeast from Euvezin, across the Rupt de Mad, p. 207

Below: BOIS DE BENEY-XAMMES AREA Looking northeast from vicinity of Lamarche-en-Woevre, p. 306

Images from United States in the World War 1917-1919: Military Operations of the American Expeditionary Forces, Volume 8, Center of Military History

for the protecting shelter of those wooded hills just
ahead! The writer now recalls that during those few minutes (which at the time seemed hours), he broke all personal records, past and present, for a 100-yard-dash!   On
gaining the foot of this particular range of hills, we at
once began digging-in and each man soon had his own dugout
within which to at least offer his head and shoulders some
protection.   About this matter of digging-in, brawn counted to a large degree.   The stronger the man, the sooner he
had a hole of some sort within which to crawl!   This work
went pretty hard on men who, back in their civilian days,
were of the "white collar" class!   But, when shrapnel was
whizzing thick and fast, even these "white collars" made
the dirt fairly fly!   "Self preservation is the first law
of nature", or words to that effect, were certainly seen
put into action that day!   As long as the Germans did not
change their range of fire, we were comparatively safe on
the wooded hillside.   We noticed, with satisfaction, that
the greater danger lay out there on the open field over
which we had just crossed.   But, we had no sooner congratulated ourselves when we were confronted with a new
danger!   Some blunder over signals and we had our very
first and unpleasant experience of being under fire from
our own long-range guns!   American shells were falling
"short" and dropping around us at a very uncomfortable distance!   This serious error, however, was soon corrected.
To the writer's personal knowledge, no casualties resulted
the few minutes we were under fire from our own guns.

      "Another incident - exciting while it lasted - hap-
pened about this time and it may be well to record it while
on the subject.   It was all over in a fraction of a second
but that particular fraction of a second seemed a lifetime!
We were all hard at work on our respective dugouts.   The
writer and several comrades were at the time taking a brief
rest from our strenuous labors and were watching the effects of that rain of bursting shells out there on the open
field.   Suddenly - it seemed from out of a clear sky - a
shell landed not five yards away from the spot where we were
standing!   Luckily for us it proved to be a "dud" (dead
shell) and, of course, failed to explode.   Had that shell
exploded - well perhaps this tale would never have been
written, at least by the author!   Needless to add, after
that close shave, the little group went back to work at renewed vigor!

      "As was usually the case, we had no sooner dug our-
selves in when an order came down the line to move.   We
were to advance up the slope of the hill.   The ground here
was pretty rough with a large amount of thick under-brush
and many small trees.   The latter, however, afforded some
protection against enemy planes.   Upon reaching the crest
of this hill, another large field, or plateau, spread out
before us.   Its area covered many kilos.   Directly ahead

and a long distance away, we could make out a village, for towering above the houses was that ever-present church steeple so intimately associated with all French villages. Without the aid of field glasses, we could see groups of men - evidently German soldiers - as they ventured forth on the edge of the town. The foe was entirely too far away for rifle practice on our part. We then wondered if an order would shortly be given to capture the town. We anticipated this with some misgivings for, in order to take the village, we had that open field to cross in full view of the enemy! However, our worries were soon over, for about three o'clock that afternoon Company I received an order to evacuate the position and fall back in reserve. The sector was then taken over by another infantry unit of the 111th - much to the secret relief of many, no doubt! The men of old Company I will always remember Jerry's artillery efficiency on that particular front!

"Speaking a word at this point in our story relative to the work of German artillery, it is desired to bring out another incident which will demonstrate the cunning of our foes along that line of warfare. While the particular incident did not happen on the Thiaucourt Sector (the exact location at present being unrecalled by the writer), it will serve to illustrate that Jerry certainly had this phase of modern warfare down to perfection. "Your address is all that they need", was the common expression of our boys when discussing the effectiveness of Jerry's big guns! But to proceed with our story!

"Our Third Battalion and, in fact, practically the entire regiment had enjoyed for several days a much needed rest under the protecting foliage of large trees in a certain stretch of wooded country. Shelter tents were pitched, our mess wagons were on the job and during our stay in these woods, we had been "living the life of Riley", so to speak! One fine afternoon, just about four o'clock (it was in the month of August and the sun was well up), we received orders to strike our tents, pack up and get ready to move out. These orders were received with some surprise. Surely we would not march until after dark! During our sojourn in these woods we had not been bothered by German artillery. It was evident that our position had not been discovered. If any had entertained hopes of not evacuating the woods before nightfall, these hopes were soon blasted! By 4:30, our outfit was on the move again!

"On leaving the woods and getting out into open, we noticed in the distant sky a couple of German observation baloons! To the naked eye, they appeared like mere specks but, from their location, we knew they must be enemy baloons. Our regiment had not advanced more than a hundred yards when we were greeted by a torrent of shells! What happened was this: Our movement had apparently been sighted by the enemy

stationed in those two observation baloons and armed with
powerful field glasses. A signal had been flashed to their
artillery, giving the exact range, and Jerry had lost no
time in "sending 'em over". It looked as though we were
"in for it" with a vengeance! The writer vividly recalls
the excitement of the next few minutes. An order came
to "double time". At this moment a number of I Company men
and men of other companies in our Third Battalion had what
may be called "a lucky break". Just ahead, we saw a stone
wall enclosing an old French cemetery. Sections of this
wall had long since fallen down and on our approach we saw
that the place was literally honey-combed with dugouts.
Our officers evidently quickly took in the situation too,
for orders to get under cover were given. We needed no
second invitation! The writer remembers sharing a rather
large dugout with several comrades, thus keeping comparatively safe from the shrapnel which was flying thick and fast
around that old burying ground. We remained in the cemetery until after nightfall. When we finally did get orders
to continue the advance, our troops moved forward - not on
the open road again, for the moon was very bright that night -
but marched along keeping close to the wooded side of the
road. To accomplish this, we were compelled to advance for
a time in "Indian file". The German guns which had so
ardently greeted our troops as we emerged from the woods
that late afternoon were now silent. Strict silence was
observed as we cautiously advanced and when a man did speak
to his neighbor, he did so in very low tones. German
artillery and the big cannon of the Allies were booming
away on some distant front, as we could see by those quick
flashes of light which, intermittently, illuminated the
sky for miles around. The sound of the cannon was but
faintly heard. Now that the excitement was all over, we
jokingly "wise-cracked" about the quick scamper all made to
find a dugout. The whole affair - particularly that "double
time" so willingly executed - reminded the writer of those
old pioneer days as depicted in stories and the movies, with
visions of fleeing men, wagons, mess-kitchens, mules, etc.
and a band of Indians in hot pursuit! This, and many
other experiences, proved to the Americans on every front
where they fought during the World War the great efficiency
of German artillery.

"But, we will now conclude our story of the part played by Company I, 111th Infantry, on the Xammes front. The
company's occupation of this sector was from October 17th
to the night of October 27th-28th, inclusive. Every night
during this period the Germans and the Allies sent over
their heaviest barrages, usually starting about nine o'clock.
Jerry sent over many gas shells and, consequently, we were
compelled to wear gas masks for hours at a time. The men
of Company I, when recalling those days on the Xammes front,
will always associate them with heavy shelling, gas, plenty
of rain and mud, cold weather and, many times, the lack of
sufficient warm food!

"On the night of October 27th-28th, the Second Battalion of our regiment was relieved by the 64th Infantry of the Seventh Division, and the First Battalion and Machine Gun Company of the 111th relieved our Third Battalion. It was just before dawn on Monday morning, October 28th, that the weary men of Company I first entered the Bois de Nonsard, after a march during part of the night of about fifteen kilometers."

Company K.

"The Division assembled and went into camp for a day's rest and the next day started back to a promised rest, which by the way, turned out to be promised, only. We were to march four kilometers to a point where trucks were awaiting us and from there were to be moved back to rest billets where the regiment was to take a much needed rest, baths, change of clothing and receive replacements. Bitter disappointment awaited us, however, for instead of being four kilometers, the trucks were twenty kilometers away, waiting for us on a hillside back of the town of Aubreville.

"From this point, which was three kilometers from Verdun, we moved by trucks to the village of Euville, about twelve kilometers from the City of Commercy. Here we were to be de-cootied, receive new clothing, replacements to fill our decimated ranks, and receive a general rest with just enough drilling to keep us in trim. Again, we were disappointed. We received the replacements but not the clothes nor the promised cootie baths, and after just getting peacefully settled in billets, received orders to move. This trip ended about two in the morning. It was very dark and rainy. We unloaded at Pannes. Needless to say, we were at the front again as the shelled shocked appearance of the town showed and the sound of the big guns told us. Immediately after unloading from the trucks, we marched to the village of Beney, and from there to Bouillonville, in the Thiaucourt Sector, arriving there on the morning of the second day. The night we relieved the 37th Division in the front lines in front of the village of Xammes. K Company occupied the front lines for seven days and was relieved by Company M, and took up a position in support of Xammes. It was during these seven days in the front lines that K Company captured a German prisoner, who gave such valuable information that we were advised that he was the most valuable prisoner that the Division had ever taken. The information given by him led to the conduct of numerous raids along the entire Divisional front, which met with such success that three citations were received from General Bullard, commanding the Corps, commending the work which had been done.

"From the front line, the Company moved back to Xammes

and was placed in support for six days, sending out patrols and raiding parties with successful results. During the night of October 27th-28th, K Company was relieved by the first battalion of the 111th Infantry and moved back to a German artillery camp in the Nonsard Woods, where we at last began our long-promised and badly needed rest. Here we were housed in old German billets and began to reorganize and get into our former shape."

Continuing quotations from data at hand, Col. Martin's History, under the sub-title "Thiaucourt Sector" reads, in part, as follows:

"After relief on October 10th, the Regiment moved to Pont de la Lune, where it remained during the night. On October 11th, it marched 18 kilos between 6:00 A. M. and 3:00 P. M., with one loaf of bread to every two men, and finally reached Parois. From there, the Regiment moved by trucks to a new area. (The locations at this time of the various units comprising the 111th have been previously quoted from the Colonel's history.) On the 13th, 1600 replacements joined the Regiment. On October 15th, the 111th moved by trucks to the Thiaucourt Sector, relieving the 37th Division, which, much to the delight of all, left a bountiful supply of rations. The Second and Third Battalions took over the front line position (formerly occupied by a brigade of the 37th Division) with the First Battalion in reserve at Thiaucourt. The regiment faced the town of Rembercourt, in the old St. Mihiel salient.

"While facing Rembercourt, the First Battalion in reserve was housed in cellars of the town of Thiaucourt with the Supply Company in Bouillonville. The Second Battalion was on the right of Thiaucourt around Jaulny with the Third Battalion at Xammes. The Machine Gun Company was split between the two forwarded battalions, as were the One-Pounders. The sector was supposed to be a quiet one, but the 111th was too accustomed to action to allow anything to remain quiet and soon livened it up with raids on the German trenches, bringing in a number of prisoners.

"During the night of October 27th-28th, the Second Battalion was relieved by the 64th Infantry of the 7th Division, and the First Battalion and Machine Gun Company of the 111th relieved the Third Battalion. The Second and Third Battalions were bivouacked in Bois de Nonsard, with Regimental Headquarters and Headquarters Company at Nonsard."

We shall now proceed with our story of The Third Battalion, beginning with camp-life in the Nonsard Woods. Our introduction to this - that long-anticipated "haven of rest" was anything but pleasant. Weary, cold, foot-sore and hungry after our hike from the lines, we trudged along a very muddy road (it had recently rained - a cold, penetrating October drizzle) until, suddenly, the column left the main highway and turned off into a narrow side lane. We had not marched but a short distance through a strip of woods when several huge frame structures loomed ahead of us through the haze of that drear October morning. These buildings, we learned, comprised what was once a German artillery camp and had been occupied in times past by both German and French infantry. Some of the structures were quite small - mere sheds - others were larger in size. The larger buildings, we soon discovered, were stables. The tired and sleepy men were soon assigned to quarters. The writer quickly appropriated a stall in one of the stables which was designated for the use of I Company. The filthy place, which at one time had been the abode of a horse or mule, seemed like a palace after that grinding hike through the mud and rain! Anything to be able to take that heavy pack off and to snatch a few moments of complete rest! The men soon had fires going in their respective buildings - thanks to a plentiful supply of dry wood found in several of the smaller sheds nearby. Our kitchens were set up and before noon the entire camp was thoroughly organized. There was plenty of "detail duty" and none escaped - not even the most seasoned "gold-bricker"! We soon saw that if we expected to get that long-promised rest at this place, all had been very much fooled!

It was not many hours before "we were put to drilling once again and the place assumed the conditions of a regular camp. We had all the calls blown, from First Call and Reveille in the morning to Taps at night. The drilling was carried on from eight to eleven-thirty in the morning, and from one to four in the afternoon on the fields just outside of the woods. Numerous aeroplanes would come over, but once again, the long blast of the whistle would be blown announcing the coming and two blasts, the passing of the aeroplane. It rained practically all the time we were in these woods and when it began to rain rather violently, we were brought into our barracks." (These last few sentences are quoted from George W. Cooper's "Our Second Battalion".)

The writer is positive that the memory of that first night spent in Nonsard Woods will never be forgotten by the boys of Our Third Battalion! The entire camp was infested with huge rats. The rodents seemed to take a special delight in running over our bodies after we had retired for the night! We would not have minded it so much, however, if the creatures had contented themselves with merely "running over" our prostrate forms. It was when they boldly nibbled at our toes or came too near our faces that we seriously objected! Many were the curses heard that first night and many were the casualties reported the following morning in the rat family! After that first night's battle with hob-nail shoes as weapons, we were careful in the future to keep candles burning near our bunks. Fearing, however, that Jerry might spy even a candle-light during the night, the men were very careful to make sure that all crevices in their buildings were covered. We had not been in camp long when one day, instead of going out to drill as usual, every available man was organized into "rat-exterminating" squads with an appointed corporal in charge of each detail. Rats were so numerous that even in broad daylight they over-ran the place! Armed with stout sticks, each squad went "over the top" that morning with splendid results! Large sections of flooring in the stables were torn up in a search for the enemy stronghold. By noon's mess, the battlefield was strewn with bodies of the dead - not a very appetizing sight as you, my dear reader, must admit!

Members of 16th Infantry, 1st Division getting news of victory in the rustic city built by the Germans in Bois de Nonsard where the Germans lived for four years. Nonsard, France, September 13, 1918.

Rustic huts in Bois de Nonsard. This is where the Germans made ready to spend the winter. Nonsard, France, September 12, 1918.

(Images courtesy of National Archives)

German canteen in woods near Nonsard, rustic town in which Y.M.C.A. made quarters and immediately line formed for free "eats" and cigarettes. 1st Division, Nonsard, France, September 13, 1918.

Kitchen in the Bois de Nonsard, 1st Division.
Mess Sergeant Paddy Ryan, Headquarters Co. 2nd Field Signal Battalion. Nonsard, France, September 13, 1918.

(Images courtesy of National Archives)

Between fighting rats and the ever-present cooty, we found plenty to occupy our leisure hours at Nonsard. Many of the men found time after mess in the evenings to catch up in their correspondence. Letters were received from the folks back home telling of the dreadful flu epidemic then sweeping the States. It was at this time that the writer received news of several deaths among his relatives. Of course, all had their share of guard duty which kept up in shifts throughout the nights. About this time, too, furloughs were granted the men in turns. Some of the more fortunate obtained the coveted passes to go on a ten-day leave to several of the rest arears then established by the A.E.F. in various sections of France. A few even obtained permission to visit relatives in some of the neighboring countries, chiefly England and Italy. More about these furloughs will be related in another part of our story. Life for the average doughboy in the Bois de Nonsard maybe summed up by a few familiar phrases - Plenty of rain - lots of mud - hard drilling - lonely guard-duty - some sickness - and not forgetting our old enemies, the rats and cooties!

At this point, for the special benefit of any old I Company man who has had the courage to wade through my story thus far, I shall now re-cite a little happening which perhaps he may, with a smile, recall. Remember, comrades, "Mess-Kit-Dick"? How he came to take command of Company I during those dreary November days at Nonsard? I say you do! To those of my readers not familiar with the tale of just how this "nick-name" came about, I shall endeavor here to enlighten. About this time, many of our old officers were changed - some through promotion and going to their new commands, some through transfer by choice, or otherwise, etc. One cold November day, word went around through the ranks of Company I that its new commander in the person of Captain Richard H. Waldo had arrived in camp. Shortly thereafter, the outfit received orders to "fall in" for inspection. We now had a good chance to give our new commander "the once over". We all remember how spick-and-span he looked in that great fur-lined overcoat - so warm and comfortable, we thought! So, here was the man to take over the command of this dirty and lousy bunch of soldiers - men in worn-out, shabby and ill-fitting uniforms soiled with the filth of weeks at the front! Many, judging the Captain by his swell attire, immediately catalogued him as a "swivel chair" officer! This seemed verified at inspection by the rather awkward manner in which he received and returned our rifles. Our really first personal contact with the new Captain occurred that day at mess. Now we come to the point of our story. As the men of I Company lined up at the bugle call, Captain Waldo stationed himself near the field kitchen and watched closely as each mess-pan received its share of food. Was the Captain on the job to see that every man received his full helping of grub and to OK the food and service? Was he so much interested in that? Or, was he there merely to inspect our mess-kits - to see if they were spotlessly clean? Many of the men thought the latter! In any event, Captain Richard H. Waldo, among certain members of the "inner-circle", thereafter became known as "Mess-Kit-Dick"! It may interest my readers to learn that during the few months Captain Waldo commanded our company (November 14, 1918 to February 5, 1919), he soon endeared himself to every man in the outfit. Upon leaving us to accept a new command, he gave all a cordial in-vitation to visit him at his place of business in New York City.

Persistent rumors soon became current that we were not to remain
in camp at Nonsard much longer. During the still hours of the nights
there, we could distinctly hear the continual booming of cannon up on
the lines. We instinctively felt that our battalion would be called
upon sooner or later to go up! Sure enough, before dawn on the morning of November 4th the order came! We were to advance to the little
town of Beney in support of the First Battalion on a reconnaissance!
We moved out of the Bois de Nonsard with some misgivings. On the way
up, a heavy enemy barrage was laid down through which it was necessary
for us to pass! This was, without doubt, the worst barrage ever put
down on our battalion. Company I had one man killed and five wounded
in this advance. K Company fared better according to the following
data: "*** due to the fact that a distance of eight paces was kept
between each man and that the company moved straight forward through
the barrage, not a man was hurt. This movement was executed under
direct observation of the enemy, who was firing at a range of 2,000
meters." The contemplated attack in which our battalion had been
scheduled to play its part was cancelled and, during the afternoon of
the same day, November 4th, the Third Battalion returned to its original
position in the Bois de Nonsard. Concerning the activities of this
day, Colonel Martin writes that "***over fifty men of Company C were
lost by running into a very nasty machine gun trap. On the same day,
the First Battalion and Machine Gun Company were relieved from their
positions in the front line by the 112th Infantry and bivouacked in the
Bois de Buxieraubois, southwest of Nonsard." It seemed that our objective had been a very difficult one to take without a great sacrifice
of men in the endeavor. This can be more readily understood when taking into consideration the nature of the country around the Xammes Sector. The Germans had all the advantage over our troops owing to the
peculiar geographical lay-out of the surrounding territory. After we
returned to camp, we then understood why our battalion had previously
spent one entire morning in the fields near Nonsard rehearsing for the
contemplated encounter.

Our Third Battalion remained in the Bois de Nonsard until Sunday
morning, November 10th, when around three o'clock in the morning we
again received orders to prepare to move into the lines at once!
Breakfast was eaten at 4:30, and at five o'clock we started marching,
reaching St. Benoit at 10:30, at which place the battalion rested for
about two hours. We then moved through Xammes, taking a position in
support of our Second Battalion which had been ordered up to support
the First Battalion of our regiment in an attack on Dampvitoux, zero
hour being 2 P. M. This attack proved unsuccessful and the Second
Battalion immediately pushed through, with our Third Battalion still in
support, taking up a position on the northern edge of Bois de Donmartin.
The entire movement was completed about 5 P. M., November 10th. During
these hours, our Third Battalion suffered considerably at the hands of
the Germans. Heavy shelling seemed to be "the order of the day" but
we noticed, with satisfaction, that our own artillery was giving a good
account of itself - judging by the noise of the French and American
pieces! The writer is quite certain that his comrades will never forget that cold and foggy night of November 10th-11th - that dreadful
night of uncertainty for all!

Early on the morning of November 11th, around 4:10, word was sent to our Second Battalion that the advance, as previously planed, was not to be continued. This order, of course, soon reached the men of our Third Battalion and caused all to speculate what was "in the wind". What had happened? None seemed to know. It was about 9:30 on the morning of November 11th that we received our first intimation that all hostilities were to cease that day at eleven o'clock - that an armistice had been arranged. Little faith, however, was placed in this - "just another rumor" - by the men in our outfit. How could it be true? Were not both sides slaughtering men by the hundreds in that terrific firing which could be heard all along the entire front? Did that incessant booming speak of peace? Well, hardly, we thought! If any peace terms had been consummated, why didn't they give orders now to stop firing?

Our Third Battalion, lying in support, received orders to move up! We advanced through the woods and, at times, were compelled to march in single file - the undergrowth was so dense. We passed a small detachment of American artillerymen. They informed us that their outfit had also received word about an armistice. Was it really true after all? It was now nearly eleven o'clock and still there was no let-up in that terrific barrage! The writer recalls that some lieutenant in the outfit pulled out his watch and remarked: "Well, men, it is five minutes until eleven!" Just at that moment, it seemed that every piece of artillery on the American and French fronts opened up, accompanied by every available cannon the Germans could muster into action! The din was terrific! The very earth vibrated under our feet! The whining of shrapnel, the rapid firing of the hidden machine guns and, above all, that constant roar of the heavy artillery, we, of the 111th, shall remember to the end of our days! For the next five minutes this kept up with the toll of killed and wounded mounting! Suddenly the firing ceased! All was strangely quiet! The same lieutenant again pulled out his watch. ELEVEN O'CLOCK! What happened in the next few minutes seemed like awakening from some terrible nightmare! "Was it really over?", we asked ourselves again and again. "What next?" The survivors of our Third Battalion - now reduced greatly in numbers - just stood in their places and waited! We expected every passing second to hear again the first gun opening up another barrage! We expected to hear shortly that it was "only another rumor about an armistice" and that "this man's war" was not over yet! But that ominous silence persisted - ominous to us because we had long since learned that such a period generally was the forerunner to some real fighting! Soon, official word was received by our officers that an armistice had been arranged and that orders were momentarily expected whereby all troops would be moved to the rear! At that particular time, your writer happened to be a member of a rifle-grenade squad. I had on hand, as my "tools of trade" about a dozen grenades, the weight of which had been bothering me for a considerable time. Nearby, I saw a small shack built, no doubt, to shelter rations. What an ideal spot to deposit my burden! While my lieutenant, above referred to, wasn't looking my way, I quickly hid my grenades under the building. "If the war wasn't over after all, it would be just too bad for me," I thought! Anyway, I was too exhausted - mentally and physically - to think much about it one way or the other! This, dear comrades and friends, is the writer's recollection of that memorial day and hour in the history of the world, November 11th, 1918, at 11:00 A. M. with our Third Battalion, 111th In-

fantry, on the line!   Each man "up front" that day will have his own
particular story to tell.   All will agree, however, on one point, I
am sure.   It is with extreme sorrow that we recall to mind our comrades who lost their lives or were severely wounded during those last
terrible five minutes of the Great World War - men who had safely gone
through months of hell only to be "knocked off" at the last minute!

It was about six o'clock that evening, November 11th, before the
battalion received orders to start the long march back to its quarters
in the Bois de Nonsard.   Need the writer recall that march?   How
jubilant we all were - the songs we sang - forgetting for the time-
being those last fatiguing hours at the front!   The war was over!
It did not seem possible!   Suppose that there could be some mistake
about it?   Well, anyway, we were now marching "back" and that was
something at least to be truly thankful for!   One comrade had in his
possession a fairly recent edition of a newspaper and we saw in bold
headlines something about the Kaiser abdicating!   And, at the sight
of that, did we sing "Kaiser Bill" with vim and vigor?   I say we did-
and how!   Making the woods echo with our shouting and singing, the
usually long kilos seemed short on this, our last, hike from the front
lines!

Our Third Battalion, in high glee, reached the now familiar Bois
de Nonsard around 2 A. M. of the 12th.   We at once "turned in" for the
balance of the night, or rather morning, thoroughly exhausted after our
experiences of the last twenty-four hours.   Each man (who came back)
occupied his old quarters again.   A number of vacant bunks served as
grim reminders of war's bloody toll!   How inviting the filthy stables
seemed!   After mess that morning, the general conversation turned to,
"When do we go home?"   "What next?"   Questions of like nature flew
thick and fast but no satisfactory answers were forthcoming!   Some "wet
blanket" passed along the "encouraging" bit of news that our Division
had been assigned to the Army of Occupation and would probably receive
orders soon to march into Germany or into Russia, or somewhere - anywhere but that march to the boat which was to take us back to God's
Country - America!   (It was learned later that we really had been
designated a part of the Army of Occupation but had been relieved of
that duty!)

If we expected our last days at Nonsard to be days of leisure, now
that this man's war was over, we were doomed for a bitter disappointment!   No such luck!   At least the infantry part of the U. S. Army
must live up to its reputation!   My comrades, I am sure, will appreciate just what that reputation meant!   Rest?   Just lounge around,
reporting at mess calls, more rest and peaceful dreams night and day?
Well, not much!   Real hard work was the order of the day right after
mess on the morning of November 12th!   When not drilling - and let me
say here that we did plenty of it after the armistice over those muddy
fields around Nonsard - our Battalion joined the First and Second Battalions of our regiment in going on salvaging expeditions which took
us within the radius of some twelve kilometres all around the Bois de
Nonsard.   For the benefit of those of my readers not familiar with
the work required on these salvaging details, I will state that it
meant sending men out to search for and gather up all discarded war
material such as shells, pieces of shell, ammunition, equipment, etc.,

etc., -- in fact anything we found as a result of troop occupancy either by the Germans or the armies of the Allies. All this material we gathered up and dumped on designated salvage piles. If we found anything too heavy to handle, such as cannon and other large field pieces, the discovery was reported back to Headquarters and mules were later dispatched to do the necessary hauling. For days our Battalion literally combed the country for miles around. The men would form in long lines abreast, each man about five paces from his neighbor on his right and left. In this formation, we would march slowly forward, picking up what happened to be in our path and depositing it in bags carried for the purpose. It reminded many of "policing" the ground around tents at old Camp Hancock back in the States, only this time we were not required to gather up cigarette stumps! The work was particularly pleasing to all "souvenir-cranks" in the outfit! Many a German helmet, rifle, belt or similar equipment found its way into private American ownership! Some few American dead were found. The exact locations of the bodies were reported back to Headquarters and later these unfortunate soldiers received a decent burial. Colonel Martin writes of this work as follows: "The salvaging process was particularly hazardous, the ground being covered with unexploded shells and 'potato-mashers' but with good management, no accidents occurred." Salvaging work was continued every day, including Sundays!

Thanksgiving Day came but, by way of extra "Eats" for the men of our Third Battalion, it was "just another day" for us! The writer remembers sitting on the side of his bunk in Stall No. 3 of his stable abode eating a rather meager helping of that good old reliable army "stew" and washing the same down with some concoction styled "coffee"! It was on Thanksgiving Day that General Hay, the Division Commander, presented the coveted D. S. C.'s to deserving heroes of the 111th!

About the middle of December, due to the bad housing and heavy rains, several moves were made which, however, did not include our Third Battalion. The First Battalion was moved to Pannes to a better area. On December 20th, the Second Battalion was moved to Hatton-ville. On December 21st, the First Battalion moved to Creue. This move was for the bettering of billets for the men. On December 23rd, Regimental Headquarters and Headquarters Company were also moved to Creue.

At Christmas time, insofar as "eats" were concerned, our Third Battalion could not complain! The cook for Company I could not get his supply of turkeys in time to prepare them for Christmas Day but on the 26th, the men of my outfit had all the roast turkey they could possibly eat, together with the usual "trimmings" of dressing, gravy, etc., etc. The Knights of Columbus showered us with generous gifts of cigarettes, candy, chewing-gum, cigars, etc., so, altogether, we can look back to a rather pleasant Christmas in the Bois de Nonsard. Our Third Battalion gave a show in the old church at Nonsard, which was voted to be superior to anything ever seen on Broadway! (Due to the fact that the writer missed seeing this show, no lengthy description is given. This is regretted. Perhaps some comrade can elaborate on the story.) Many spent most of the holiday in answering letters received from the folks back home, acknowledging gifts, Christmas cards, etc., which arrived in time to be enjoyed on that day. Good old

American home-cooking, cakes, candy, etc., were in evidence everywhere but not for long!   When any comrade was caught opening his box,
all gathered around and, in most cases, shared in his Christmas cheer!
The men of our Third Battalion showed a generous spirit in this respect!   An amusing definition of a doughboy's Christmas box is given
in The Stars and Stripes, issue of Friday, February 15th, 1918.   It
reads: "Christmas Box - A broken-into parcel partly filled with
wristlets, mufflers, heavy sox, knit helmets, mittens, kidney pads and
tummy bands that arrives in France about the middle of July."   Good
fortune, however, favored us!   Our Christmas boxes arrived in plenty
of time!

New Year's rolled around but, outside of the holiday the day afforded, it passed without a great deal of extra celebration.   At midnight, however, many braved the cold night air and went outside to
fire off their rifles in honor of 1919.   For us, the New Year was
soon to bring its changes!   At this writing, I am sure that all of my
old comrades look back to those last days spent in the Bois de Nonsard
with mingled feelings of pleasure and regret - pleasure when recalling
old friendships, those long winter evenings made seemingly short by
gathering in little groups around our fires, telling yarns, swaping
jokes, singing, shooting craps, playing cards, etc., etc., - regret
when realizing that now those dear comrades, many of them good and true
pals, are separated - scattered all over the United States, perhaps
never to be together again, at least, in this life!

CHAPTER 26.

CHAMPOUGNY AND FORT de PAGNY DAYS.

Speculation was now rife as to how long it would be before we either advanced into German territory or would be taken out of the Army of Occupation and sent back home. Many excited discussions took place on these most important questions during our last days in the Bois de Nonsard. The answer came on January 6th, 1919! Bright and early on the morning of that day our entire Division started its march Southward. The direction, alone, assured every man in our Third Battalion that at last the Twenty-Eighth appeared to be homeward bound!

On Wednesday, January 8th, after a three days' march, the 111th reached its destination in the Colombey-les-Belle area. Regimental Headquarters were established at Maxey-sur-Vaise, First Battalion Headquarters at Maxey-sur-Vaise, Second Battalion Headquarters at Burey-en Vaux, and our Third Battalion Headquarters at Champougny. Companies A and B of the regiment were quartered at Maxey-sur-Vaise; Companies C and D at Taillancourt; Companies E and G at Sepvigny; Companies F and H at Burey-en-Vaux; Companies K and L at Champougny; and Companies I and M at Fort de Pagny. (At this point, the Machine Gun Company left the regiment for special training and did not rejoin the command until after it had reached Le Mans.)

How glad we all were after that fatiguing hike was over! The heavy packs were beginning to tell on us! Arriving at the little town of Champougny, Companies K, L and M dropped out of the column and I Company continued on its way up a long, steep and winding road which finally terminated at the entrance to an old French stronghold - Fort de Pagny. This fort, we later learned, was built by the French in 1879, and together with five or six similar fortifications nearby, served to protect a large area of adjacent territory. It is situated on the crest of a high elevation and affords a splendid command of the country for miles around. The fort itself was built partly underground and so nicely camouflaged that we had no idea of being anywhere near a large building until we arrived at its castle-like gates. Company I was immediately assigned to quarters in several of the hugh barrack rooms. These rooms were equipped with iron bunks in rows of two to a tier somewhat like an upper and lower berth on a Pullman. What strange surroundings after our weeks spent practically all the time in the open! We wondered if the place was infested with rats! Somehow, those long, damp and ill-lighted corridors seemed to suggest the presence of sewer rats! The entire building - outside and in - its large court-yards - its stone masonry - its moats with drawbridges all reminded us of pictures seen and stories read of ancient castles in foreign lands! Those bunks looked inviting enough, however, and it is

Fort de Pagny

Entrance

Fort de Pagny

Courtyard of the barracks

Fort de Pagny

Chamber on the floor of the
troop barracks

safe to bet every man in Company I slept sound during that first night spent in old Fort de Pagny! Company M joined us the next day, January 9th, and we were soon put on a regular drilling schedule again - "much too soon", all agreed! Company I occupied one-half of the fort and Company M had its quarters across a court in the other half of the building.

We shall endeavor here to relate, somewhat in detail, our experiences during the weeks our Third Battalion occupied the area in which Champougny and Fort de Pagny were located. What busy and eventful weeks they were! Drill, drill, drill every day, with numerous maneuvers thrown in for good measure! Now, a "maneuver" in the military sense of the word is very different from that of a close-order-drill, as we soon learned to our sorrow! We discovered, too, that it required considerable territory and called for plenty of "wind" and grit! To the uninitiated, I will state that a maneuver was, in fact, nothing more nor less than a good old-fashion sham-battle! Our entire Division at this time participated in these "battles", capturing and recapturing imaginative objectives; advancing for miles over rough ground, observing all the precautions necessary in real warfare! On several occasions, we actually employed the use of loaded rifles, trench-mortars, hand and rifle grenades, etc. Unfortunately, the latter practice resulted in several accidents, one of which, it was reported, proved fatal! All this drilling and maneuvering generally called for loaded packs which did not tend to make picnics of the affairs! It was while Companies I and M were stationed at Fort de Pagny that we had our first severe snow storm of the winter. That particular morning we were out on one of our maneuvers but the blinding snow-storm, accompanied by a high wind, won the battle! We were compelled to beat a hasty retreat back to the fort - much to the satisfaction of officers and men! Many times during these weeks we "captured" the smaller forts for miles around as well as old Fort de Pagny itself!

During these days matters took on a brighter aspect. Many of our men who had been wounded during the war and were sent back to hospitals for treatment now rejoined their comrades at the fort. Night after night in the old building the World War was fought over and over again, around our little wood stoves, that is, if we happened to be fortunate enough to have wood to burn in them! Fire wood was a very scarce luxury and toward the last of our stay at the fort we were obliged to send out daily details to the nearby forests (some not so "nearby") on "wood-chopping expeditions". We, of course, had our field kitchens with us and fared pretty well at this time insofar as "chow" was concerned. It goes without saying that we also had our old "bosom" friend, the playful cootie, with us! By this time, however, all had become accustomed to the tiny and evasive little creatures! They, at least, gave us something to occupy our spare time during the long winter evenings! In fact, one of the most popular sports at the old fort proved to be "shirt-reading" parties! The man who killed the most of these pests in a given time was declared the winner of the contest! Some of the men hit upon the scheme of burning Mr. Cootie to death with the aid of candles! Whole nests of them - Mr. and Mrs. Cootie, their children, cousins, aunts and uncles - discovered under a seam, could thus be quickly annihilated! This method, however, proved to be rather costly as evidenced by many a burned shirt! The general health of the men at this time was not so good. All underwent several innoculations at different periods. One man, if the writer has been correctly informed, died with pneumonia. He was buried just outside of the building. Mail was regularly received and many took advantage of the fairly comfortable quarters in writing long-delayed letters to relatives and friends back in the States.

The writer at this point is reminded of a rather amusing story in connection with nights spent in the old fort and, while the subject is somewhat delicate to approach, we shall endeavor to be as polite as possible in the telling thereof! Now, when some four or five hundred men are housed in a building to remain there for any length of time, certain provision must necessarily be made for the demands of nature, especially if said building lacked the proper toilet facilities. Fort de Pagny, being of French construction, naturally one could not hope to find even so much as a handy drain-pipe! Consequently, in lieu of toilets, our officers had installed at certain corners in the long corridors hugh cans which we were told, or rather commanded, to make use of during the nights, if occasion arose. These cans, it may be stated, were not stationed just outside of our sleeping quarters but were some distance away - generally down some long, dark and chilly hall! Here is where the point of our story comes in! Many of the men, after undressing and in their bunks for the night, seriously objected to "hiking a mile" through the cold corridors in order to reach the nearest can! Consequently, after two or three nights at the fort these corridors presented a sorry spectacle and afforded a terrible smell! We shall not dwell at length on the matter but will leave it to the reader's imagination! Suffice it to say, however, that after an inspection of quarters by our officers, the men were "hauled up on the carpet" and given a sound lecture on sanitation with accompanying threats of punishment, etc. Not satisfied with the lecture alone, guard-duty was called into play and, thereafter, details were organized to patrol the halls at nights. The guards were instructed to arrest any man caught "in the act" outside of bounds - the can! This guard-duty was not at all pleasant to perform and was imposed upon those caught disobeying some rule or regulation. Standing guard on a two-hour shift over a can in some dark and cold corridor at night in the dead of winter was, indeed, a severe penalty! This broke up the bad practice but not before many a buck private had his name written on the "black list"! The story seems amusing now that it is "mellow with age" but at the time "the escapade of the can" was anything but amusing, especially to those caught and punished!

In writing the above, brings to mind a mishap which befell one of our men when the Battalion was making preparations to evacuate the area. In policing the grounds around the fort, it seems the unfortunate soldier (probably after imbiding a little more of French champagne than was good for him) stumbled and fell into one of the latrines (trench variety) which had been dug and had been in daily use ever since our occupancy of the place! The writer is thankful to say that he was not an eye-witness to the catastrophe but can vouch for its truth by the statements of any number of comrades who actually saw the horrible spectacle. This may well be termed "trench warfare" with a vengeance!

It was while our Third Battalion occupied Fort de Pagny area, during the early part of February, that the entire regiment took a trip via hob-nails to Domremy, the birthplace of Jeanne de Arc. Outside of the long hike there and back, all enjoyed the day very much. Colonel E. C. Shannon, of our regiment, who was very much liked by all the men - "One Yard Shannon", they had nick-named him when on one occasion he led his men fearlessly through the thick of battle and he, himself, advanced to within a few yards of the German lines - thereby showing that he would not send his men into danger without being with them also - gave a short address of an appropriate historical nature. The regimental band then followed with the stirring music of The Marseillaise, at which we stood at "Present Arms!" facing the beautiful statue of Jeanne de Arc erected by the French in honor of their beloved heroine. We then filed into the little cottage and on into the very room where The Maid of Orleans was born in the year 1412! On coming out, we walked over to the magnificent church built on the spot where she had received her visions and where she had become inspired to lead the armies of France to victory over the English generations ago! Father Aristo V. Simoni, (awarded the D.S.C.), Chaplain of our Third Battalion and one of the noblest characters who ever wore the uniform, addressed us in the church building and accompanied the men through the large edifice on a tour of inspection. All particularly admired those wonderful oil paintings - each picture representing an important event in the life of Jeanne de Arc from the time she received her first inspiration or vision to her last moment on earth - bound to the burning stake. All were greatly impressed. We learned more in the space of a few minutes about the life of France's martyred saint than if we had spent hours over some history. In the Basilique numbers of French regiments have placed small bronze tablets, and once a year the priest in charge says mass for the souls of the departed members of the regiments represented by these tablets. The genial old Padre in charge of the Basilique requested that the 111th add its tablet to a place of honor on the walls, and any members of the regiment who may ever visit Domremy will there find a perpetual memorial to their departed comrades! Many of the boys brought back souvenirs from Domremy. It seemed that all the inhabitants of that small village were conducting souvenir shops! And they "soaked" the boys plenty, too! We did not get back to the fort until about eight o'clock that evening. We were about "all in" but, after a good meal and rest, agreed that the visit was really profitable.

Other privileges were granted which greatly helped to break the monotony of routine duties at the fort. The men were permitted to visit nearby towns - Maxey-sur-Vaise, Taillancourt, Sepvigny, Burey-en-Vaux and Champougny - providing they agreed to return by 10 P.M., at which time Taps were sounded. Some, of course, took advantage of this privilege and went on A.W.O.L., showing up, maybe, the next day or a day or two thereafter! There were always men who abused special favors granted and, sometimes, the innocent had to suffer for the guilty! These culprits were forced to perform extra duties, such as guards, kitchen police, etc., etc. Some of the worse offenders were confined in the "jug" to cool off, as it were! Take it from the writer, old Fort de Pagny boasted of some beautiful "lock-ups"! (This bit of information, however, was not gathered from any personal experience!) Several football games were played between the different battalions of the 111th. Boxing matches were also arranged, much to the amusement of the spectators. At times, these friendly bouts were anything but entertaining to at least one of the combatants! The writer recalls here a little story which may or may not be of special interest. Anyway, the tale will serve to show the general spirit of fun and mischief then prevailing at the Fort. One evening, I was busily engaged in writing a letter. From my bunk, I could hear the boxing matches going on down in one of the large mess rooms. Suddenly, to my despair, I heard a man with a pair of extra good lungs sing out: "Where's Compton?" "Let's go and get Compton!" Now, I never did pride myself on being a boxer - infact never had the gloves on in my life, so one can imagine my predicament! Immediately, I looked around for some place to hide! I didn't want to box anyway that night! I heard the boys coming pell-mell up the stairs after me! In desperation, I tried to conceal myself but several dear (?) comrades in the room took the situation in hand and promptly turned me over to the "boxing committee" which by that time had entered. I saw at a glance it was no use trying to resist! So, down the steps we went and before I knew it, I was in the center of the ring with gloves on, facing some tough bird who, in private life, had evidently been a coal miner or mayhap a brawny tiller of the soil! An ex-bank clerk vs an ex-laborer! Needless to add, that particular match created very little excitement for the "customers"! I believe I lasted one round of three minutes and was about half-way through the next when - well, it is just as well to draw the curtain at this point! Tonight, I am wondering whether I ever did go back and finish that letter I was writing when so rudely interrupted! I bet, if I did, I didn't say a word in it about my short pugilistic career! One night, around this time, we were visited by a travelling motion picture outfit and all thoroughly enjoyed the entertainment given in one of the mess halls. If the writer's memory serves him right, it was a picture in which Mary Pickford had the leading role. For many, it was the first movie seen since leaving the States. About this time, someone in I Company discovered real talent among our ranks in the person of Private William Curry! Thereafter, almost nightly, Curry entertained the boys with such recitations as "Gunga Din", "The Face on the Bar Room Floor", "Down in the Lehigh Valley", etc. Many will doubtless recall, with a smile, our gifted and accommodating buddy standing on top of a mess table while he recited line after line amid the generous applause of an appreciative audience! How we listened spell-bound as he generally started off with, "Twas a balmy summer's evening and a goodly crowd was there,**"! Good luck to you, Curry old comrade, wherever you are! Some of the more industrious wiled away the long winter evenings after mess by manufacturing finger rings out of French coins. This work necessitated a great amount of patience and skill combined with incessant hammering - much to the discomforture of those nearby who preferred to read or sleep! But, what could a man say if his buddy happened to be one of these ring fiends? (The writer hopes that a certain comrade, Roy E. Ostrander, reads and takes notice!) Pay day - a day of much rejoicing - finally rolled around and, to the familiar tune of:

> "All we do is sign the payroll,
> All we do is sign the payroll,
> All we do is sign the payroll,
> And we never get a gol-dern cent!"

the happy men formed in line to receive their "Thirty Per"! Many a bunk in the old fort was vacant that night! All who could possibly "make it" by hook or crook left the confines of barracks and, in singles, pairs and groups, hastened to the nearest village like so many sailors on shore-leave! Champagne flowed like so much water that night! What mattered if the following morning produced "big heads" and empty pockets? We had a glorious time while it lasted! So the days passed. Plenty of hard drilling, plenty of recreational exercises and time to devote to our own personal pursuits - all helped to dim, somewhat, the many horrible recollections of those terrible days and nights spent at the front!

Two events of major importance to the 28th Division took place during the time our Third Battalion was stationed in this area, namely, Divisional reviews by Lieut. General Robert L. Bullard, Commander of the Second Army, under whose leadership our Division had served, and by General Pershing. Both reviews took place at Colombey-les-Belles, the first around the middle of February and the second on March 10th, 1919. On the day - a cold one too - that we were reviewed by General Bullard, our battalion, as well as the balance of the regiment, hiked it over to the reviewing grounds. When General Pershing held his review, however, we were more fortunate, as the troops were conveyed to Colombey-les-Belles in trucks. Never will the men of our battalion forget the great preparations incident to these reviews! How we greased and polished our steel helmets (now stencilled with the red Keystone, the Division insignia) until they fairly glistened in the sunlight! The hard labor we put on uniforms, shoes and equipment - not forgetting that dreaded job of thoroughly cleaning the barrels of our rifles! How we cursed when a piece of rag lodged in the guns and delayed operations until we could remove it! Word was passed around - another "rumor" - that "Black Jack Pershing" (with all due respect to General Pershing) personally inspected each man's rifle and that he did so attired in white gloves! We were told, woe to the unfortunate doughboy if those white gloves got soiled by a greasy rifle! The reader can imagine how the men worked over their pieces! Just before the review by General Pershing, we were all amused by the antics of dozens of aeroplanes of all makes and sizes which flew over the field. It seemed each plane endeavored to outdo the others in hazardous and death-defying "stunts". More than once we thought a plane was surely falling when, suddenly, it righted itself and went sailing away just a few feet above our heads! Watching these air maneuvers, helped to pass away the time before the General put in appearance. The weather was none too good - rather damp and penetrating. The first signal we received announcing the arrival of our distinguished Commander was a blast upon some bugle at the far end of the field. Soon, the actual review was underway. General Pershing passed through the entire Division on foot. As he came to a battalion, that unit stood at "Attention!" and remained in this position until he reviewed it. Occasionally, he would stop and, it seemed to the writer, would question some doughboy. What passed between the General and Mr. Buck Private on these occasions remains to this day a dark secret! Following the review, General Pershing awarded additional D. S. C.'s to the men of the Division. The entire 28th then marched in review. All this occupied the greater part of the afternoon. We were pretty well fagged-out on our return to the fort, even though driven back in the trucks. And did the boys do justice to supper that night? After a good rest, however, we soon forgot how tired

we had been and the cares of the day.   All were truly thankful that
the review (which had been dreaded for days) was at last over! Later,
our Division was highly praised on the fine showing made! Apparently,
the white gloves were not soiled after all!   (For the reader's information, we might add that the General, except in one or two instances, did not take a man's rifle for inspection - much to the relief
of all!)

CHAPTER 27.

LE MANS.

During these latter days at Fort de Pagny, the question was frequently asked, "When do we go home?"   This query always brought forth
many a lively discussion.   No one, however, seemed to be able to give
any satisfactory answer to it!   If those "higher up" had any definite
knowledge on this subject, it was certainly kept "a State secret"!
Rumors came and went thick and fast!   Suddenly, (they did things like
that in the A. E. F.) the answer to this most important question of the
hour came in the command of, "Pack up!", which, needless to add, was
obeyed with alacrity!

On St. Patrick's Day, March 17th, 1919, we bade farewell to old
Fort de Pagny and rather enjoyed our last hike down that steep hill
leading into the town of Maxey-sur-Vaise, although every enlisted man
in the outfit was heavily burdened.   Upon reaching the railroad
station, there we saw a long train of box cars waiting to receive us.
After first partaking of a cup of hot chocolate and some cakes furnished by the Y. M. C. A., we soon forgot all about our heavy packs and
looked forward with pleasant anticipations to the journey ahead.   The
sky was cloudy and the day a rather chilly one, so the men thoroughly
appreciated that hot repast.   All were anxious now to "pull out"!
Some of the cars were equipped with small wood stoves.   The men who
were fortunate enough to be assigned to these cars, soon had fires going in them.   We left Maxey-sur-Vaise about noon, amid much rejoicing!

It is regretted that with the passing of so many years, our varied
experiences on this trip - humorous and otherwise - have become dim and
vague in the mind of the writer.   Looking back, it all seems like a
dream only partly remembered!   Therefore, in lieu of a story about our
train ride through France on this particular occasion, we can do no
better than to quote some verses published in The Stars and Stripes,
issue of October 11, 1918, which will, at least, give the reader some
idea of what we experienced.   The poem is appropriately named "Hommes
40, Chevaux 8" and is by Steuart M. Emery, A. E. F.

"Roll, roll, roll, over the rails of France,
  See the world and its map unfurled, five centimes in your pants.
  What a noble trip, jolt and jog and jar,
  Forty we, with Equipment C, in one flat-wheeled box-car.
      We are packed by hand,
        Shoved aboard in 'teens.
      Pour a little oil on us
        And we would be sardines.

Rations? Oo-La-la! and how we love the man
Who learned how to intern our chow in a cold and clammy can.
Beans and beef and beans, beef and beans and beef,
Willie raw, he will win the war, take in your belt a reef.
  Mess kits flown the coop,
   Cups gone up the spout;
  Use your thumbs for issue forks
  And pass the bull about.
Hit the floor for bunk, six hommes to one homme's place;
It's no fair to the bottom layer to kick 'em in the face.
Move the corp'ral's feet out of my left ear;
Lay off, sarge, you are much too large; I'm not a bedsack, dear.
  Lift my head up, please,
   From this bag of bread.
  Put it on somebody's chest,
   Then I'll sleep like the dead.
Roll, roll, roll, yammer and snore and fight,
Traveling zoo the whole day through and bedlam all the night.
Four days in the cage, going from hither hence,
Ain't it great to ride by freight at good old Unc's expense?

  We were not, however, "four days in the cage", for on the night of
March 19th, around eight or nine o'clock, we arrived at our destination,
Le Mans Embarkation Center. A light snow was falling as we detrained
at the railroad station. It was not long before we were ordered to
"Fall in!" and the march to camp began.

  The Le Mans area was a very large one. Barracks and squad tents
dotted the spacious fields. The Third Battalion was assigned to tents
and our life here was soon underway. Our time, for the most part, was
taken up in preparation for embarkation to the States and, consequently,
the companies had very little drilling to do, for which all were thankful! The purpose of this camp, we were advised, was to delouse, re-
equip the men, and prepare all paper work preparatory to sailing for
home. It developed, however, that the principal business there was to
furnish working parties for camp construction work! Upon the arrival
of the Commanding General of the Division, the details were reduced and
the work systematized.

  At Le Mans, we went through our first thorough and scientific de-
lousing in an effort to rid ourselves and our clothing of cooties. For
the benefit of those not initiated into the mysteries of the operation
of a delousing plant, - "mad houses" we called them - an attempt will
be made to briefly describe the method by which we parted company with
Mr. Cootie. Before going over to the delousing building, we wrapped
up all of our belongings, such as blankets, extra clothing, etc., - in
fact anything in which we thought a cootie might be hiding - in our
shelter-havles or pup tents. We even took along our steel helmets,
gas masks containers and rubber slickers. We then formed in long
lines at the entrance to the plant, after first depositing our helmets
and slickers in racks on the outside of the building. (These articles
were cleaned while we were inside getting our baths.) On entering,
each man was given a rack upon which he hung everything to be deloused,
including his clothes worn over to the building. We then carried

these loaded racks into a long boiler-like room, being careful to place them in the same numbered position corresponding to the number which was written on each man's rack. After these immense boilers were filled with clothing, etc., the doors were tightly closed and a high pressure of steam turned on. This hot steam was thoroughly charged with a powerful disinfectant. The fumigation lasted about forty-five minutes. While this was taking place, the naked men filed into another section of the building and there indulged in a hot shower bath, using a special brand of liquid soap which was guaranteed to put out of business the most healthy cootie! After our bath, (and they gave us time to take a good one), we were furnished with towels. Following a brisk "rubbing down", we felt like new men! We were then directed to another part of the plant where each man was given a new suit of underwear and a pair of socks. We then, again, lined up at the boilers, as about this time the steaming process was through. A great cloud of steam issued forth as the doors were opened and through this we marched to our respective racks. This was a warm job as the air inside of those boilers was none too cool and our belongings were steaming hot! The smell was none too pleasant, either! Any discomforture we might have felt, however, was dispelled upon realizing that, for the time-being at least, we were really rid of all cooties! We jumped into our clothes (now quite dry) and had the satisfaction of knowing that they were clean - the first time in many, many months! Everything was systematized down to the smallest detail at these delousing plants but in the handling of so many men at one time, there was bound to be more or less confusion - hence they were nick-named "mad houses" by the soldiers. (This name was also applied to the Discharge Units back in the States, of which more will be related herein.)

From April 1st to 6th, inclusive, the Regiment was on the Belgian camp target range, about 14 kilos northeast of the Forwarding Camp, on the Le Mans-Paris Road, shooting the instruction and record course, there being 200 targets in operation on the range. It is understood that several marksmanship badges were awarded to the men of our Third Battalion. The writer happened to be on his furlough at the time and missed this, consequently he is unable to go into details regarding this or the three days' field meet held in Le Mans during our stay, at which time about a hundred men from each company a day were given passes to attend.

On April 11th, a provisional company of seventy-five men, under command of Colonel Shannon, with similar companies from other units of the Division, was formed, the occasion being the presentation by the Division Commander of decorations to certain officers and enlisted men, and of major operations ribbons for the regimental colors. The operations ribbons awarded to the 111th at this ceremony were as follows:

Chateau-Thierry Sector.........July 7-14, 1918
The Champagne-Marne Defensive..July 15-18, 1918
The Aisne-Marne Offensive......July 18-Aug. 6, 1918
The Fismes Sector..............Aug. 7-Sept. 3, 1918
The Oise-Aisne Offensive.......Sept. 4-7, 1918
The Meuse-Argonne Offensive....Sept. 26-Oct. 9, 1918
The Thiaucourt Sector, Toul....Oct. 16-Nov. 11, 1918

About this time, as stated above, the writer received his long-anticipated furlough. A word or two at this point in our story regarding leaves granted the men while "Over There" will not, therefore, be out of place.

General Pershing, in his Final Report to the Secretary of War, written from General Headquarters American Expeditionary Forces, Sept. 1, 1919, states under the caption "Leaves and Leave Areas", as follows:

"22. A leave system announced in general orders provided for a leave of seven days every four months, but it was necessary to suspend the privilege during active operations. In the leave areas free board and lodging at first-class hotels were provided for the soldiers, and the Y. M. C. A. furnished recreational and amusement facilities. A number of new areas were opened by the Service of Supply immediately after the Armistice, improved transportation accommodations were eventually secured, and arrangements were made whereby men could visit England, Belgium and Italy.
"It was my desire that every man in the American Expeditionary Forces should be given an opportunity to visit Paris before returning to the United States, but the crowded condition of the city during the Peace Conference, transportation difficulties, and other reasons, made it necessary to limit the number of such leaves."

Leave areas were scattered all over France - some down near the Italian border and others up on the northern boundary and coast. In special and deserving cases, as stated in the General's Report, men were given leave to go over to England and other nearby countries. Many took this rare opportunity and visited relatives and friends living in the Old Country. The men, when on these furloughs, were given complete personal liberty, as long as they did not run afoul of the civil and military laws governing these leave areas. Each place had its quota of Military Police to take care of those who wanted to make trouble. It was the nearest approach to civilian life then obtainable by the soldiers of the A. E. F.!

The writer went on his furlough, with about eight others from his Company, to the St. Malo leave area. St. Malo (Brittany), a channel port and fortress and a frequented watering place, occupies a granite promontory at the mouth of the Rance, opposite Dinard, on the northern coast of France, off the English Channel. The town proper, a maze of quaint and narrow streets of seventeen and eighteen century houses, is enclosed by walls. The narrow isthmus, known as Le Sillon, joining it to the mainland is flanked by docks on one side and by the broad sandy beach on the other. Seaward, the view is varied by an archipelago of rocky islets.

Upon detraining at the railroad station, we were ordered to "Fall in!" We marched around to one side of the building where already the men on furlough were assembling. All wondered "what was coming off?" Pretty soon an army medico mounted the station platform and addressed the men. He gave us to understand that we had the liberty of the entire town; that the time was our own to use as we pleased - to thoroughly enjoy the privileges and amusements the area afforded, but at all times and under all circumstances to conduct ourselves like gentlemen and not, in any way, bring discredit upon our country and our flag. He then proceeded to warn us about making the acquaintance of undesirable companions, particularly the women, we were liable to meet while on leave. Then followed a long and plain-spoken discourse on the evils of venereal diseases, the steps to take if any man exposed himself to that disease, prophylactic treatments, where to obtain them, etc., etc. After that lecture, it was a brave man indeed who would dare stray "from the straight and narrow"!

After the lecture, the little group from I Company joined forces with a larger contingent and, under the guidance of area officers assigned for the purpose, we were escorted around the edge of the town and along a stretch of sea wall and sandy beach. Along the way, small groups were singled out and taken to their respective hotels, which dotted the beach. Most of my comrades and myself were billeted in a beautiful chateau which commanded a fine view of the water. This magnificent hotel, which had the appearance of a private residence rather than an inn, was managed by a genial and highly cultured French lady, assisted by numerous obliging native servants. Our hostess later informed us that at one time she had resided in New Orleans, La. She spoke English fluently. Each man had a bed to himself in a room that was scrupulously clean. And what a bed! Will the writer ever forget that high French bed with its downy mattress? What a contrast to Stall No. 3 at old Nonsard! We had but to press a button and a maid would quickly respond to wait on us! What service! Even breakfast in bed, if we desired it! For the first time since landing on foreign soil "to fight for something or other", we were treated like American gentlemen, and gentlemen of means at that! The cuisine was excellent! If, however, a more fastidious Doughboy called for something not on the menu, a nominal charge was made.

The Y. M. C. A. maintained an immense casino at St. Malo, where the men could go and read from a large and well stocked library; writing rooms were also at our disposal; a large theatre where every night a splendid show was put on for the entertainment of men on leave. Movies were exhibited every afternoon. In short, everything was conducted for the pleasure and comfort of the boys and one never spent a dull moment at this casino. In the evenings, dances were gotten up by the "Y" girls and other workers at the pavilion. The "Y" also operated shower baths in connection with the casino, which proved very popular with the men. It was so nice to be able to take a decent bath whenever one felt like it! Bands in the Place du Chateau during the days, concerts in the evenings; sea bathing; sailing boats for hire, etc., - all contributed to the amusement of Mr. Doughboy on leave! The attractions of Dinard and Parame' were also within easy reach! It all reminded the men of good old Atlantic City back in the States - minus the famous boardwalk, however!

Excursions were also conducted to nearby places of historical interest. One day, they took a party of us over to Mont St. Michel. The trip, thirty-four miles (55 km.) from St. Malo, was made by train (not the box car variety this time) and took about 2½ hours to get there. As we alighted from the cars, in front of us rose the famous abbey on the Rock of Mont St. Michel, an isolate cone of granite rising from an expanse of sand. One of the chief natural curiosities and ancient monuments of France consists of this granite islet 260 feet high, girt around at its base by a circlet of mediaeval walls and towers, above which rise the quaint irregular houses of the village, plastered as it were against the rock and piled one above another. The whole is crowned by the ancient abbey, with its lofty walls and immense buttresses flanking the side tower and spire. The historical associations of this shrine - of the archangel Michel - the saint of high places - are not inferior in interest to its outside aspect. It seems that in the year 708, an apparition of St. Michael appeared to St. Aubert, bishop of Avranches, and commanded the building of an oratory on the summit of the Mont. The abbey was the final culmination of this strange visitation!

We followed the steep and narrow lane of the Grande Rue, the sole thoroughfare of the town, with its gabled and over-hanging houses, mostly occupied by inns and shops where "souvenirs" were sold. The flagstones which covered the narrow sidewalks were worn smooth and slippery. The street terminated at the main entrance to the abbey. We were then met by guides who took us, in small parties, through the ancient structure - its long and winding corridors - its dark dungeons many feet under the foundation - its interesting museum - up in the lofty towers - through its immense banquet halls - altogether a tour not soon to be forgotten! The guides spoke excellent English and went out of their way to explain points of historical interest. Here, a certain dungeon had its story - a story of some cruel punishment inflicted centuries ago! There, a dismal tower held its secret - and so on through the gloomy pile!

After the tour of the abbey, we had plenty of time left in which to give the town "the once over". As stated, one street seemed to constitute the entire village. Like Domremy, the souvenir business seemed to be about the only occupation of the inhabitants. The native merchants made most of our short stay! A doughboy on leave, if he has money to spend, always spends it! Those French merchants seemed to sense this and, no doubt, reaped a harvest of francs during our visit! Before boarding the train for the return trip back to St. Malo, we filed into one of the numerous cafes' and there, by much pointing and bad French, managed to make a very comely mademoiselle understand what we wanted in the way of eats and drinks.

Just before our train pulled out, an incident occurred which may be of sufficient interest to herein record. All were aboard and in readiness to leave. Something was evidently holding us up, however! On looking out of the car windows, we saw a bunch of excited Frenchmen trying to converse with a small group of our men. After much palavering and shrugging of shoulders on the part of the "frogs", the little party finally broke up, the Frenchmen making for the abbey and the Americans boarding the train, which then steamed ahead. We learned later that a very precious exhibit - a sword or something - had been stolen from the museum in the abbey! Whether it was ever recovered or was carried back to St. Malo on that train, no one in our car knew!

In closing our brief remarks relative to furloughs, the writer holds a deep sense of gratitude toward the Y. M. C. A. for the good time he had while on his leave at St. Malo, with the assurance that this sentiment expresses the views of his comrades on this trip. Needless to say, all were extremely sorry when the time came to pack up and leave this "haven of rest and pleasure" to go back and live in squad tents again! The thought of leaving all this luxury behind for the old chow line and beans was not a very pleasant one! What a "come down"! Our one consolation, however, was the knowledge that when we did rejoin our outfits, we would find them engaged in peaceful pursuits and not holding down a front line expecting to be butchered any minute! And so, back to Le Mans after one week of heavenly bliss!

Considering everything, we rather enjoyed life at the Forwarding Camp. Most every night, the "Y" and Knights of Columbus staged a good show in one of the many huts. The men were never at a loss where and how to spend an enjoyable evening. As previously stated, very little drilling was done but our officers always managed to find something for Mr. Buck Private to do in the way of various "fatigue duties" in and around the camp grounds. At times, this assumed the proportions of hard manual labor with pick and shovel! All who could possibly escape this work considered themselves fortunate indeed! "Gold-bricking" - a lame back, sore feet, or some other physical disability, was much in evidence! Quite a number responded to "sick call" in the mornings! After being excused from all labor, it was remarkable how speedily the afflicted recovered!

About this time, the writer received a lucky "break" and, instead of shouldering a pick and shovel, he was detailed to the 111th Regimental Headquarters in a clerical capacity. One rainy afternoon, I was summoned to the tent of my Company's Commander, Lieut. Harry O. Clayberger. Wondering "what was up", I hastened over with some feeling of dread. (The day previous, I had indulged in a little "gold-bricking" myself in order to escape a mean detail! Naturally, I thought that I was being "hauled up on the carpet", to use a phrase familiar to every doughboy.) My anxiety was short-lived, however! The interview resulted in taking dictation from an officer who was then preparing a brief history of the activities in France of Company I of our Third Battalion. He had learned from my service record that in private life I had been a stenographer. (The data I obtained in this way was very helpful to me a number of years later when I undertook to enlarge on the story of my old outfit.) I took my notes over to the 111th Regimental Headquarters where I transcribed them on a typewriter. Subsequently, this led to being permanently detailed there to assist in the work of typing Sailing Lists - names and addresses of all officers and enlisted men of the 111th scheduled to soon leave for the United States. This "paper work" was more to my liking! While rather confining at times, it was better than being detailed to the "pick and shovel brigade"!

It was while our regiment occupied Le Mans that the representatives of Fletcher Photograph Company, a Washington, D. C. firm, took pictures of the various outfits at the Forwarding Camp. All who placed orders for these pictures received them soon after their return home. (My

Taken from Twenty-eighth Division: Pennsylvania's Guard in the World War Volume 2, 1924, By Colonel Edward Martin

framed photograph of old "I" Company, though rather faded with age, is one of my most cherished possessions and always occupies a place of prominence in my home.   Each face in that happy group, from smiling Lieut. Clayberger to the humblest "buck" private, brings back its particular memory!))

CHAPTER 28.

ST. NAZAIRE.

We shall open this chapter with some appropriate verses by Grantland Rice, which appeared in "The Stars and Stripes", issue of May 2, 1919. The poem is entitled "The Song of St. Nazaire", and reads as follows:

"Hurry on, you doughboys, with your rifle and your pack;
 Bring along your cooties, with your junk upon your back;
 We'll house you and delouse you and we'll douse you in a bath,
 And when the boat is ready, you can take the Western Path.
    For it's home, kid, home - when you slip away from here -
    No more slum or reveille, pounding in your ear;
    Back on clean, wide streets again,
    Back between the sheets again
    Where a guy can lay in bed and sleep for half a year.

"Hurry on, you lousy buck, for your last advance;
 You are on your final hike through the mud of France;
 Somewhere in the Good Old Town, you can shift the load.
 Where you'll never see again an M. P. down the road.
    For it's home, boy, home, with the old ship headed west;
    No more cooties wandering across your manly chest;
    No more M. P.'s grabbing you -
    No more majors crabbing you -
    Nothing for a guy to do except to eat and rest.

"Move along, you Army, while the tides are on the swell.
 Where a guy can get away and not the S. O. L.
 Where the gold fish passes and the last corned Willy's through,
 And no top sergeant's waiting with another job to do.
    For it's home, kid, home - when the breakers rise and fall -
    Where the khaki's hanging from a nail against the wall -
    Clean again and cheerful there -
    Handing out an ear full there -
    Where you never have to jump at the bugle's call."

At last, orders came to "pack up" and on Sunday, April 13th, our Third Battalion moved out of Le Mans. This time, all had a pretty good idea as to our destination - something we never knew before the signing of the armistice! We were leaving in the old reliable "Hommes 40, Chevaux 8" bound for St. Nazaire, a port of embarkation! What a merry lot of doughboys we were on this, our last, journey in France via box cars! The freight cars, this time, were of American construction

and were much larger than those of French manufacture, but we called
them "Hommes 40, Chevaux 8" just the same!   We were pleased to note
that these cars rode much easier than the French variety.   We pulled
out of Le Mans late in the afternoon.   It was between two and three
o'clock the next morning, April 14th, when we reached our journey's end -
St. Nazaire.

Rain was falling in torrents, which made it very disagreeable
while we were "falling in" preparatory to our hike through the town.
It was just getting light when we finally marched away from the station.
The heavy rain still persisted!   We discovered that the town of St.
Nazaire was quite a large place but on account of the very early hour
and the inclemency of the weather, its streets were comparatively deserted.   The entire morning was very stormy with high winds which blew
the cold rain against our faces.   By this time, however, we had become
hardened to French weather and were reconciled by the one thought of
"being this much nearer home"!   On the way to camp, we marched for
some distance along the sea coast and soon forgot our drenched condition
in the realization that it would only be a matter of a few days, perhaps,
when we would start our voyage across the big pond bound, at last, for
the good old United States and our loved ones waiting there for us!

Wet to the skin, we finally arrived at the section of the camp allotted to our Third Battalion (Embarkation Camp No. 2) and were soon
quartered in barracks.   We were told not to wander off and not to unpack, as orders were expected any minute transferring the new arrivals
over to Camp No. 1, about a mile away.   After breakfast, which was
served in an immense mess hall which accommodated a regiment at a time,
we made our way back to the barracks and soon had fires going in an attempt to dry our clothes.   About the middle of the afternoon, the expected order came around to "Fall in!" and we began our short march over
to Camp No. 1, which proved to be the Isolation Camp.   The two camps
covered quite an area and had facilities for handling thousands of in-
coming soldiers bound for the States.   (General Pershing, in his Final
Report, gives some interesting data relative to the return of troops to
the United States.   He writes: "Brest, St. Nazaire, and Bordeaux became
the principal embarkation ports, Marseilles and Le Havre being added
later to utilize Italian and French liners.   The construction of the
embarkation camps during unseasonable winter weather was the most trying
problem.   These, with the billeting facilities available, gave accom-
modation for 55,000 at Brest, 44,000 at St. Nazaire, and 130,000 at Bordeaux.   Unfortunately, the largest ships had to be handled at Brest,
where the least shelter was available.   To maintain a suitable reservoir
of men for Brest and St. Nazaire, an Embarkation Center was organized
around Le Mans, which eventually accommodated 230,000 men.")

About four or five o'clock found us in our new quarters.   We were
told to unpack and make ourselves comfortable for a few days' stay.   Nobody seemed to know definitely the exact day set for sailing, that is,
nobody "among the rank and file"!   Our time here, though only four
days, seemed to go by very slowly for two principal reasons.   First,
we had very little to do and, second, all were so impatient to embark -
to get out of that country which, for us, had been a country of blood-
shed, mud, filth, rats and cooties!   Our one desire now was to return

as quickly as possible to the "Land of the Free and the Home of the Brave"!

No drilling marked our brief stay at St. Nazaire. The men, however, were assigned to numerous duties in the camp - K. P., guard, policing the grounds, etc., etc. Some last minute changes had to be made on the Sailing Lists but your writer was not detailed for "paper work" at St. Nazaire. A day or two after we arrived, the Battalion marched over to Camp No. 2, where all underwent a thorough physical examination. This examination was chiefly for the purpose of ascertaining if any man in the outfit was suffering from a venereal disease. The initiated will understand that these "short arm" inspections at this time were greatly dreaded by the entire regiment. The men feared that if a disease was discovered, it might not only delay the unfortunate's return to the United States but might also delay an entire company! Needless to add, all breathed a sigh of relief when these inspections were over and every man pronounced physically sound. (Some of my readers may be curious to know what is meant by a "short arm" inspection! This is too delicate a subject to discuss at length in any but a medical work. The uninformed, however, will doubtless have no difficulty in guessing its true meaning. Leave it to a soldier to supply a "fitting" name!) Pretty much the same feeling existed among the men when we were examined at St. Nazaire to make sure that we would not carry Mr. Cootie to the States as a stowaway on board the boat! To illustrate how thorough this cootie examination was, we shall say a few words about it. We had not been in camp long - possibly twenty-four hours - before the Battalion filed through another delousing plant similar to that at Le Mans. This time, after being deloused, each man had to pass inspection at the hands of an officer seated at a table on which was thrown a brilliant electric light! The officer in question was armed with a powerful magnifying glass. As we filed by, we deposited on the table a shirt, blouse or piece of underwear which was then closely examined for any live cooties. If a cootie was discovered, the owner of the offending garments was compelled to make another trip through the plant. Word was passed around that if many men in any one company were found with cooties, that particular outfit could not sail until every sign of the pest was obliterated! Much spare time at St. Nazaire, therefore, was occupied by the old A. E. F. diversion, "reading shirts"! The only difference in the sport at this time was that if a man did happen to discover one of the things crawling under his neck-band of his shirt, he now kept his discovery a secret!

"His teeth are sharp and he's quick on his feet,
His office is just where your shirt and pants meet;
From the top of your head to the tip of your toes,
The tiny, elusive wanderer goes.

"You can duck a bullet, dodge a shell,
Race a shrapnel sent from hell,
But the wise Old Doc, is sure to find
Your speed won't leave the cooties behind."
(By James L. Roberge, U.S.M.C., from "The Stars and Stripes".)

On April 17th, our Third Battalion received official word that on the following day we would embark. (The first half of the regiment had boarded the U. S. S. Minnesotan on Wednesday afternoon, April 16th.) Our turn had come at last!

The writer is sure the memory of that last night in France is indelibly impressed upon the minds of all comrades! It was a night full of joyful anticipations and very few, if any, regrets over the fact that we were at last leaving the Old Country. As we lay in our bunks, what thoughts ran through our minds! I wonder how many of the boys offered up thanks to their Great Commander for seeing them safely through it all? I wonder how many good resolutions were made - to "turn over a new leaf" upon arriving home? Were not some of our thoughts centered around what sort of a reception awaited us in the States? Would we get our old jobs back? Would we find that "she" had remained true to us or would her affections be showered on another? What must we tell them if questioned about our experiences in the war? Would they believe us? The married men, no doubt, wondered how their wives had managed to keep the little home together during their absence - how much Junior had grown - would the little one remember his daddy? These and a thousand similar thoughts doubtless chased through our minds as we closed our eyelids in sleep on that very last night in France!

April 18th, 1919, was ushered in by a warm sunshine. It seemed that Mother Nature had concluded to say "Goodbye" with a smile - wanting us to know that even France could be sunny at times! How different now from those cold and dismal winter mornings up there on the front lines! After breakfast, we busied ourselves in making up packs, all thankful that this time we were really headed for home with the damn things!

USS KROONLAND full of troops returning from Europe,1919

CHAPTER 29.

THE VOYAGE HOME.

"A ship there sailed - my dreams return
　　To the days of yesteryear,
To the night of bliss - the parting kiss,
　　The ship that brought me here!

"A ship will sail - my visions turn
　　Once more to the bounding foam,
To love's sweet charms, the waiting arms,
　　To the ship that brings me home!"
　　　　　(By Arthur Morris, A. E. F.)

We had one more meal in camp and shortly after mess, around the
middle of the afternoon of April 18th, we responded to the command of
"Fall in!" and with smiling faces began our last hike upon the sod of
France. As we approached the docks, we could make out the graceful
outlines of the ship that was to take us across, the U. S. S. Kroonland. She was by far the largest vessel at anchor that day in the
little harbor and while not nearly the size of the ship which brought
us over, she had accommodations for about 4,000 troops.

The various companies lined up at the gang-plank in alphabetical
order, as on boarding the S. S. Olympic for England. As each man's
name was checked upon the Sailing List, he marched aboard. Here we
were quickly assigned to numbered bunks which were arranged in tiers of
two each, one bunk above the other. After depositing our belongings
in our respective quarters, we hastened up on deck to watch the remainder of the troops come aboard. Crowds of soldiers and sailors
(American and French), together with many civilians of St. Nazaire, had
gathered at the docks to see us off. We amused ourselves by pitching
pennies to the little French urchins and watching the general scramble
which ensued to obtain the coveted coins. About five o'clock, we had
our first mess aboard ship, to which we did full justice. (It may be
stated here that just before we reached the docks, each man was served
with a cup of hot chocolate, cakes, chewing gum and cigarettes by the
Y. M. C. A. workers in town. Our last memory of the "Y" in France,
therefore, is a pleasant one!)

Promptly at six o'clock, the good ship, Kroonland, weighed anchor
and commenced her long voyage back to the United States - and home!
Amid wild cheering, "Farewells" and "Bon Voyage" from those on shore
and to the sweet and plaintive strains of "Aloha Oe" played by the
sailor band aboard, the transport almost imperceptibly steamed away from

her dock and slowly made her way through the narrow channel and thence out into the open sea.   As Van Dyke so appropriately puts it:

"Oh, its homeward bound and homeward bound, America for me,
    I want a ship that's westward bound to plow the rolling sea,
To that blessed land of Room Enough, beyond the ocean bars,
    Where the air is full of sunlight and the flag is full of stars!"

The return voyage, destined to be of eleven days' duration, was well underway!   The majority of the men remained on deck (it was a pleasant evening) watching the shores of France gradually fade away on the horizon.   Thoughts of mingled character occupied the mind of the writer and he could see from the expressions of those around him that many of his comrades were, very likely, entertaining similar thoughts. I shall attempt, briefly, to describe my feelings as, at that hour, we were making our exit from the stage whereon all had played such prominent roles in that drama, or rather tragedy, The World War! My thoughts were of an entirely different nature than were my reflections when, nearly a year ago, I saw from the deck of the S. S. Olympic the shores of America vanish from sight! Now, our positions were just the reverse! And what a difference! We were leaving behind forever that life of warfare and hardship "Over There" to once more take up the threads of our lives back in America - to be again among our loved ones - to hear their voices again - to see their familiar faces - father - mother - brother - sister - sweetheart - all eagerly waiting for "their boy" to come home! From the living, my thoughts sadly turned to the men in my own outfit who had made the supreme sacrifice, some of whom I saw die up there on the front lines - men whom I had personally known and liked - Mason, Pepperman ("Pep of the 28th"), Arlicavage, and many others - comrades who had just lately shared so much in our daily lives, whose names were, this time, missing from the Sailing List - those brave boys of the Third who had given their all for the Cause and who now lay buried "somewhere in France"!   (It is regretted that, owing to almost insurmountable difficulties in obtaining the necessary data, the names of all these heroes are omitted in this work.) However, their names are now inscribed in a greater history! May the sacrifice they made for humanity's sake not be in vain and may the glory of their deaths in France live forever in the hearts of all!

"To you, our honored dead, who gave
    Your all that Freedom's banner,
Free from shame, might proudly wave
    Before the world forever.

"To you who lie in peaceful rest
    Beneath the silent crosses,
We pledge our all, our lives, our best,
    To 'Carry On' forever.

"The charge you left we gladly take,
    Nor ask for aught, but that
Worthily, for your dear sake
    We 'Carry On' forever."
                (Walker, 6th Marines.)
                    -

George W. Cooper, formerly Battalion Sergeant Major, in his book,
"Our Second Battalion", sums up, in one paragraph, our return voyage.
I shall take the liberty of quoting, as follows:

"During the voyage we wore blue denims to protect our
uniforms and our life preservers for about the first three
days, this for fear we might hit a floating mine. Men were
detailed to help fire the boilers of the Kroonland, because
there was a shortage of help. At about the middle of the
ocean, the ship sprang a leak and had ten feet of water in
it. The vessel was listed on one side for about a day, but
the water was pumped out and we finished the journey with no
further mishaps."

We were favored by good weather with the possible exception of one
day. On that day a slight squall blew up and some of the men who remained below had touches of sea-sickness. The writer was just beginning to congratulate himself upon escaping that dreaded malady when,
suddenly, the roll of the vessel won! However, on coming up on deck
into the fresh air, I soon revived. This sea-sickness among the
soldiers furnished plenty of amusement for the ship's crew, who offered
all kinds of "remedies" to the suffering doughboys!

The men were left pretty much to their own pursuits and passed
away the days reading, playing cards, strolling around the boat, etc.,
etc. Gambling in any form, that is, playing for money, was strictly
forbidden. However, more than one little game was "pulled off" on the
quiet almost under the very noses of the ship's officers. When the
sailors would let us alone, we simply enjoyed ourselves lounging around
on the decks in the sunshine - taking life easy. The crew of the
Kroonland were continually at work scrubbing decks, it seemed. More
than one doughboy on this voyage had his "day-dreaming" rudely interrupted by some gob armed with a scrubbing brush and hose! "You can't
stand there, soldier!" became a familiar phrase to the troops. The
poor soldier was thus forced to beat a hasty retreat or take the con-
sequences - a good wetting - only to be again disturbed in like manner
at some other part of the vessel. All this was taken good-naturedly,
though. Before the voyage was half over, we found the crew of the
Kroonland to be all good fellows and agreeable companions. We had
several "Abandon Ship" drills to prepare us in case of emergency but
were not compelled to continually wear our life preservers, as we did
on our voyage to England.

Radio messages were daily received and the news so obtained from
the United States was quickly printed in the form of a miniature newspaper and distributed among the troops for the sum of five cents per
copy. When the ship was within a thousand miles of America, we were
informed that we could send messages to our folks at home, if we so
desired. Several took advantage of this opportunity, paying a nominal
fee for the service.

Of course, various details were organized aboard, such as guard
duty, kitchen police, etc. No soldier's life would be complete without "detail" duties thrown in for good measure! Ask the doughboy!

Some of the soldiers voluntarily helped the stokers just to have something different to do - others were detailed for this rather hot job. The writer did not escape being "detailed" on this trip. Fortunately for him, however, he was not assigned to the furnaces! His work, for several days at least, was of an entirely different character. It consisted of "paper work" incident to the landing of the troops. I rather enjoyed this detail. I had the use of a fairly good type-writer and did my work in the officers' quarters - "far from the maddening crowd", as it were! "Some class!", I thought. Twice coming back we underwent physical examinations ("short-arm" inspections) con-ducted by the ship's doctors. Our meals were entirely satisfactory. While the food was rather coarse, we had plenty of it and never went hungry as we did aboard the S. S. Olympic. We also had more com-fortable sleeping quarters than on our first voyage across. It is believed that all preferred the iron bunks to hammocks swung between decks. On numerous occasions we were entertained at nights by motion pictures, which generally followed wrestling or boxing matches. Some hard fought battles were witnessed between picked men of the ship's crew and the soldiers aboard!

One particular event of importance and interest to all occurred during the voyage. We can do no better than to quote from a Phila-delphia newspaper which later told the whole story, as follows:

"The Kroonland brought home exactly 268 Philadelphians, four of whom wore Distinguished Service Crosses, and of the quartet, Sergeant Albert Schad, 6416 Saybrook Avenue, of Company I, 111th, had the unexpected honor of being decorated amid impressive ceremonies in mid-ocean.

"The presentation was made by Colonel Davis, chief of staff, assisted by Lieutenant Colonel Franklin P. Haller, Jr. of Folcroft, Delaware County, second in command of the regi-ment, and in charge of all the troops on the transport. Schad wears more than a D. S. C. for he has three separate and distinct citations, which entitle him to a cluster of ash leaves above the medal.

"The other men with the coveted crosses are: Captain Thomas Bailey, 5325 Lena Street, Germantown, commanding K Company, and also at present in charge of the Third Bat-talion of the 111th, and Privates Alfred R. Murphy, 1266 South Twenty-third Street, and William Nixon, 2234 Waverly Street, both of the medical detachment of the same regiment. All three were decorated before leaving France, but Ser-geant Schad's cross was evidently withheld for the purpose of establishing a unique record by such a mid-sea presenta-tion.

"The ceremony, attended by the entire ship's company, as well as every soldier who could crowd forward, took place on the promenade deck last Sunday afternoon. A plat-form had been erected on the promenade deck which produced a stage visible from the entire deck below. Upon this plat-form Sergeant Schad mounted, accompanied by Colonel Davis and Lieutenant Colonel Haller. The latter presented him to the chief of staff. After Colonel Davis had read the cita-

tion, 'For extraordinary heroism in action near Montblainville, France, September 30', he pinned the medal on the
sergeant's shirt, delivering at the same time a brief eulogy
of the non-com's splendid work.

"Today, Sergeant Schad told his own story of how he
happened to win the D. S. C.   He spoke first about his
earlier experiences in the war, relating a little incident
which he serves best of all to explain why he is a daring
soldier.   This incident came in no bragging style.   It was
just a little something that happened to him - nothing much -
interesting, though.

"'Up at Fismette on August 11, I had a funny experience',
he said.   'I was walking along through the village when -
spat - someone shot at me.   It sort of seemed to have come
from the direction of a certain house, and I went over and
searched the place.   Didn't find anything, though.   I sort of
forgot about it and started away when - spat - comes another
bullet.   Pretty close, too.   Well, I went back and made a more
thorough search and found a boche hiding in a fireplace.'

"Yes, well, what did you do to him?"

"Fed him with his own iron rations."

"And now about that citation, there wasn't anything much
to that, honest there wasn't.   They've been making a whole
lot of unnecessary fuss over that.   It was up around Mont-
Blainville, on September 30 and about three o'clock in the
afternoon a machine gun was getting rather troublesome.   I
took fifteen men armed with rifles and hand grenades and we
started out to see what we could do.   I thought it wouldn't
be a bad plan to move carefully, so I told the men to hug
the ground while I did a little reconnoitering.   The first
darn thing I did was to run right into the machine gun, with
four boches manning it.   I got two of them and the others
beat it.   I called my men and we started in pursuit and
bumped smack into about 150 Huns.   There was some scrap.   We
lost two men killed and four wounded, and we killed an awful
bunch of them and the rest fled.   It happened over in the
77th Division's sector, so we could not count the dead.

"Then, on October 4, when we were trying to take La
Chene Tondu, I took another platoon of men out and we
captured a little hill.   Right away the Huns started counter-
attacking.   They kept it up all night, wounding two of our
men, but we hung on, and the next morning I counted between
sixty and eighty dead Germans out in front of us.'

"And this brilliant non-com, with such achievements as
these to his credit, started out in life to be a carpenter,
and may go back to the old job at the Brill Car Works, in
West Philadelphia."

The ceremony was probably the first of its kind ever conducted on
the high seas and it created a great deal of interest, especially among
the sailors.   It served, too, to break the monotony of our daily
routine and, for a time, helped us to forget just how impatient we were
to land.   Taking everything into consideration, though, our return
voyage was an enjoyable one.   Compared with the voyage over to England,
it seemed like a pleasure jaunt!   -

Evening Public Ledger

NIGHT EXTRA FINANCIAL

THE WEATHER
Washington, April 30.—Rain tonight and tomorrow.

VOL. V.—NO. 195

PHILADELPHIA, WEDNESDAY, APRIL 30, 1919

PRICE TWO CENTS

IRON DIVISION BOYS HOME AND CITY WILD WITH JOY; PORT OF FIUME MUST BE FREE, PRESIDENT'S STAND

POCAHONTAS IN WITH MEN OF 28TH DIVISION

Wild Welcome Accorded Pennsylvania Soldiers Safely Landed From Troopship

TRANSPORT MERCURY ALSO HERE, READY TO UNLOAD

Overseas Veterans Immediately Sent to Camp Dix to Await Demobilization

"WAR BRIDES" WERE ABOARD

Welcome Boats Carrying Mothers, Wives and Sweethearts Acted as Escort

RELATIVES AND DELEGATIONS TO GREET TROOPS

SAMUEL H. ASHBRIDGE

ORLANDO WINS SUPPORT VOTE IN PARLIAMENT

Deputies Indorse Peace Action, 382 to 40—Socialists Withhold Their Aid

UNANIMOUS SENATE BACKS UP ENVOYS

Premier Assails France and England Do Not Concur in Fiume Claim

PORT EXCLUDED BY TREATY

Declares "Cries of Suffering Brothers" Impel Nation to Demand East Coast

Powers Discover Solution of the Kiao-Chau Problem

Prepare Answer to Oriental Riddle They Hope Will Be Acceptable to Both China and Japan

WILSON HOLDS TO DANZIG PLAN TO SOLVE ISSUE

Text of Memorandum Given to Italian Delegates April 14 Now Made Public

AUTONOMY FOR FIUME, EXECUTIVE INSISTS

Port Should Be Included in Customs System of Jugo-Slavic State

OUTLET FOR NEW NATIONS

President Bases His Conclusions on 14 Points—Explains Previous Statement

HAPPY KIN DEPART TO MEET SOLDIERS

Fathers, Mothers and Wives Carried on Pocahontas to Greet Troops

BAND FURNISHES MUSIC

CHARTER TO PASS, PENROSE OPINION

Looks for Final Action by Senate on Measure Next Week

REGISTRATION BILL, TOO

EXTRA

17 INFERNAL MACHINES FOUND IN MAIL FOR PROMINENT MEN

GIRL HELD FOR THEFT; ACCUSER CALLED SON OF LATE U. G. I. HEAD

SOLDIERS AT DIX NOT FOR PARADE

Partial Vote of 111th Infantry Men Shows Sentiment Against Plan

CONFERENCE TO DECIDE

FOES' PEACE TRAIN STONED EN ROUTE

Windows Smashed Before Teutonic Foreign Minister and Others Reach Versailles

TROUBLE NOT SERIOUS

FORMER JUDGE REED NAMED BY GOVERNOR TO SERVICE BOARD

Clearfield Jurist Appointed to Fill Vacancy Caused by H. M. McClure's Death

CHAPTER 30

HELLO, STATES!

(To tune of "Goodbye, Broadway, Hello, France.")

"Goodbye, trenches, hello, States,
We're coming back to stay!
Goodbye, whizz-bangs, Huns and cooties,
We don't like your way;
Bully beef, we're full of you;
We want no more hard-tack,
So goodbye, trenches, hello, States!
Your soldier boys are coming back."
(Hugh J. Schuck, Sgt., Co. C, 4th Engrs.)

Around midnight, April 28th-29th, we were awakened by cries of "Shore lights ahead!" from the men on watch. Shortly afterward the engines of the Kroonland stopped and we dropped anchor to wait until daylight before docking. (On leaving France, so Dame Rumor had it, we were bound for Norfolk, Virginia. We had been at sea only a few days when our course was changed by a wireless message which ordered the transport to New York. As stated, this information is based solely on a rumor and whether it is authentic or not, the writer has no way of telling.) We were now at anchor in New York harbor.

At daybreak on April 29th, we were greeted by that sight so many, many times longed for - the shores of America! To say that the Statue of Liberty and New York City's famous sky-line looked good to us, would be putting it mildly! Nothing ever appeared so welcome! By the confusion and excitement among the soldiers who packed the decks, it was very evident that not a single man regretted being back in "God's Country" again! As if to especially welcome us home, the morning was a beautiful one! It was indeed a merry lot of doughboys aboard the good ship Kroonland that wonderful Spring day of April 29th, 1919! Our band aboard played some lively airs. The music was soon mingled with the continual blasts of numerous whistles from the many steamboats at anchor in New York harbor. Even factory whistles ashore joined in the general welcome! Presently, a large river steamer, bearing a hugh sign which read "The Mayor's Welcome Committee", circled around our boat. The steamer was packed and jammed with hundreds of passengers. Some of these passengers, we later discovered, were relatives and friends of the returning soldiers. All waved flags and handkerchiefs! It was indeed the thrill of a lifetime for every doughboy aboard - the knowledge that at last we were among our own people again - folks who spoke our language - citizens engaged in peaceful pursuits and not every man wearing a uniform!   We were sick and tired of uniforms!

After breakfast (all were too excited to eat much) the Kroonland slowly steamed up the Hudson.   By this time, the men had their packs made up and had gathered all their equipment preparatory to debarking as soon as the vessel made her dock.   The transport finally reached her berth on the north side of Pier No. 2, Hoboken.   The various army officers comprising the Debarkation Staff first came aboard.   They were soon followed by a flock of photographers, newspaper reporters, messenger boys, etc., etc., all adding to the general noise and confusion! Finally, all necessary preliminaries were over and the first troops marched down the gangway to the pier.   No one but a doughboy who has been through it can describe our feelings as we at last set foot on American soil!

The troops were lined up on the pier and, once more, we answered "Here!" as our names were checked off the Sailing List.   Cries of "When do we eat?" next filled the air!   That important question was not long in being answered!   A pleasant surprise was in store for us! We marched up some steps into a portion of the pier building which had been made into a hugh mess hall.   There, the ladies of the American Red Cross showered us with a barrage of sourkraut, smoked-linked sausage, rolls, butter, cocoa, candy, cigarettes and chewing gum!   Our very first meal in America after those dreary months in France will not be soon forgotten by the men who landed that day!

The writer at this point in his history of The Third Battalion will take the liberty to quote at length from a newspaper article written by William Bell Clark, Staff Correspondent of "The Philadelphia Press", which gives a rather good and accurate story relative to the docking of the Kroonland.   The article is dated New York, April 29th, 1919, a section of which relating to Sergeant Sohad having already been herein quoted.   The entire account, leaving out the story of the D. S. C. ceremony aboard ship, reads as follows:

"145 Philadelphia survivors of K, L, M Units among 2800 Pennsylvania men back.   Handful of heroic West Philadelphia men all that is left of old 6th Regiment.   Troops sent direct to Camp Dix after docking at Hoboken.   Kroonland brings rest of 111th.   Transport laden to decks with 28th Division men. 111th at maximum war strength, but with less than 40 per cent. of original personnel.
"All that is left of K, L and M Companies of West Philadelphia Battalion of the old 6th Regiment, N. G. P., came back from France today - a little handful of 145 men.
"Twenty survivors of E Company had arrived the day before, making a battalion total of 165.   That 165 represents what remains of the 600 who in August, 1917, went down to Camp Hancock to ultimately become a part of the 111th Infantry of the 28th (Keystone) Division.
"The transport Kroonland, laden almost entirely with lads of the 28th Division, brought the balance of the 111th up the Hudson to Hoboken piers today.   The regiment is com-

plete at Camp Dix tonight, at full war strength, but with less than forty per cent. of its original complement on the muster rolls. On the Kroonland also was the 109th Machine Gun Battalion, formed more than a year ago from two companies of the old 4th National Guard Regiment, leavened with nearly 100 Philadelphia lads from the old 3rd Regiment. There were forty-six of the 100 Philadelphians with the unit at the end of the war; the other fifty-odd being casualties. Those forty-six were on the transport.

"The big liner also carried two other 28th Division units, one, the Pittsburgh Company of the Divisional Military Police, with a sprinkling of Philadelphians; the other a detachment of Divisional Headquarters, including ten staff officers, headed by Colonel David J. Davis, of Scranton, General Muir's Chief-of-Staff, and the only National Guard officer in the entire American Army to hold the position he does.

"The port of debarkation's 'Memo. 560', announced approximately 2800 men of the 28th Division on the Kroonland. About 50 per cent. of that total of 2800 were replacements in the eight companies of the 111th Infantry the replacement percentage was far higher - there being scarcely more than eighty of the original 250 men per company remaining. Even these eighty do not mean that units emerged on November 11th with that many survivors. Dozens of men in each company have recovered from wounds and gas and rejoined the old crowd since the first of the year.

"Scarcely less severely has the 109th Machine Gun Battalion been struck. In the continual fighting between July 14th and November 11th, it lost thirty-seven men killed and 404 wounded. Its complement is 750. Some of the wounded have rejoined, but the replacements yet average between fifty and sixty per cent. It consisted in the beginning of 650 boys from Lancaster and Columbia and Allentown, and 100 Philadelphians, of the old 3rd. Today, on the Kroonland, it was found that its men hailed from almost as many States as the replacements of the 111th.

"The Pittsburgh Military Police Company reported many cases of gas, but the nature of its work rendered it less liable to the major casualties. It has been thought that the Philadelphia Company would also be on board, but instead some seventy Philadelphia lads are with the Third American Army in Coblenz, the order recalling them to the division arriving too late for them to embark with their companions from the western part of the State. ***

"To return to the great Kroonland, which can carry nearly 4,000 troops, and which was signally honored upon this passage by conveying men of one of the most gallant divisions in the American army, she came up the Hudson shortly before 9 o'clock today with a great red Keystone on a field of white displayed suspended from the yard-arm of her forward mast. From the base of her bowsprit to the curving rail of the after-cabin, she was covered with a

swaying khaki mass, the majority of which acted most de-
leriously happy.

"Once more there was no body of home-town folks to
welcome these returning Pennsylvania heroes, and, as in the
case of the Minnesotan yesterday, the reception, such as it
was, was tendered by the New York Red Cross women and the
debarkation band.

"As the big liner rounded gracefully to her berth on
the north side of Pier No. 2, Hoboken, the khaki mass dissolved into individual figures and almost every figure bore
the little red keystone, replica of the big standard forward, on its shoulder. A navy band on the Kroonland was
playing something which was lost in the wild cheering of
the returning men, but the army band on the pier had better
luck.

"It chose a familiar air to those home-hungry lads, a
welcome melody which was suddenly switched to that rousing
chorus, 'Hail, Hail, the gang's all here!' The Kroonland
began to sing in unison, when the provoking band changed
the tune again. The lads on the liner listened and then
broke into a great roar of appreciative laughter. The new
air was 'How dry I am.'

"Every time a transport comes into New York Harbor,
the Army band does that, and every time it goes a little
better than the time before. It made a big hit with the
28th Division men, who roared with laughter as the entire
length of the liner had slid close to the pier and the bulk
of the wharf-house cut off a view of the musicians and the
sound of their playing.

"Then came the boarding, first by the numerous army officers who comprised the debarkation staff and then by the
newspaper men, who in the majority were Philadelphians and
Pittsburghers seeking men of their own home town. While
the army men prepared the men for debarkation, the cor-
respondents sought out their prey.

"It was in that work that one really realizes how ter-
ribly the 28th Division infantry regiments and machine gun
battalions have suffered. Take this incident.

"A group of doughboys, with 111 on their collars and
crossed rifles below were lined along the rail. The little
initial under their rifle announced they were members of M
Company, and M Company, in the days of Camp Hancock, had
125 or more Philadelphians in its ranks.

"Anybody here from Philadelphia?" was the question.

"The group looked up. "I'm from Minnesota", said one,
"and I'm from St. Louis", said another.

"A third broke in: "There's some Philadelphia boys in
the company I know, you ask that chap over there. He's been
with the company a long time."

"That chap" said he came from New York, but he volunteered to find some Philadelphians. He brought back one,

who advanced the information that there were about forty-five of the old crowd still with the company. Forty-five out of 125!

"A 109th Machine Gun Battalion man came along.

"You looking for Philadelphians?", he asked.

"Well, I'm one. I'm Corporal Joseph A. Foley, of B Company, 109th Machine Gun Battalion, and I live at 5638 Boyer Street."

"Many Philadelphians in the battalion?" was the question, because it is generally understood that the 109th Battalion was made up chiefly of Central Pennsylvanians of the Fourth National Guard Regiment.

"Not so many now", said Foley, "but originally there were about 100 in the four companies. You see we are all old Third Regiment boys, most of the gang coming from South Philadelphia, and when they merged the Third and the Tenth down at Hancock to form the 110th Infantry, they picked out the best of us as machine gunners."

"A modest lad, this Foley.

"Come here, you fellows", he broke off, addressing some of his comrades. "This chap wants the names of Philadelphians." He turned to "this chap". "They're all B Company men", he explained.

"I'm from Philadelphia", announced the first in the group to arrive. He gave his name. All of them have the army habit of giving their last name first, and then their first name. To one not used to it, it is rather trying and it took several attempts before the newcomer finally established his identity as Newton Alexander, 605 North Thirty-third Street, instead of "Alexander Newton", as he gave it.

"Then the rest came along. There was Sergeant Joseph A. Coady, of 936 Chelten Avenue, Germantown, and Sergeant Francis Grugan, of 3025 Gray's Ferry Road, and Sergeant Nicholas Clauser, of 1336 South 18th Street, and a number of others, all of whom will be found in the list published elsewhere.

"Coady acted as spokesman of the company. He said that the 109th Machine Gun Battalion had been in the fighting with the 56th Infantry, brigaded with the 111th and 112th Infantry, from July 14th, when it went into reserve with the brigade behind the 39th French Corps at the Marne, until the whistle blew in the Thiaucourt sector facing Metz at 11-11-18.

"As for B Company alone, it had eight killed and forty wounded in the vicinity of Fismes, and three killed and seven wounded in the Argonne, and one killed and fifteen wounded in the Thiaucourt sector,

"We've had 80 per cent. replacements in B Company", Coady explained. "Our original strength was 172 and there are less than 80 of the old men left."

"Several of the men broke in to tell Coady not to forget to give the major a boost.

"You bet", he agreed. "He's a Philadelphian, you know, Major John W. Foos."

"Which was not quite a correct statement, as Major Foos comes from West Chester. However, he is almost a Philadelphian. "Major Foos commanded us at Hancock and he took us over and commanded us over there, and he's brought us back", Coady continued. "And I'm telling you, he's some man. He's some bird of a soldier, and we are all for him, every man of us."

"Yeah, Bo, that's telling it", agreed "the gang".

The Philadelphia boys have known Major Foos long before the war, as back in the old National Guard days he commanded the Third Battalion of the old Third Regiment.

"By this time the troops were beginning to move toward the pier and the machine gunners were called back to their trench helmets and packs with their eulogies of their major unsung.

"A little further along another major was encountered, but this one was from the 111th - Major W. W. Gill, of Pittsburgh, commanding the second battalion of the regiment.

"He gave us some interesting statistics regarding the 111th. A little further indication of what the men went through.

"Our regimental war strength is 3,800 men", Major Gill said, "and we had a total of 2,800 replacements, which means that about three-fourths of the Regiment is gone. The replacements were largest before we started into the Argonne when we received 1,200 men, bringing us up to full war strength - 250 men and even more to a company. When we were relieved in the Argonne on October 8th, we averaged just about forty men to a company."

"Then take Courlandon up in the Aisne sector. Sept. 6th, when we advanced from the Vesle up the heights to the ridge overlooking the Aisne, we lost 400 men in three hours. We were the only American division engaged there, fighting with the French on either side of us. Our casualties in the 111th came when we were drawn out of Fismes, sent around to the rear and brought up to fill a gap between the 55th Brigade and the French."

"Coming over in the boat, we were looking at a book which contains the pictures of the 114 officers who went overseas with the regiment last May. There are just thirteen of us coming back. We had twelve officers of the 114 killed and fifty wounded and then we lost other officers, replacements, whom we would see today and learn that they were dead tomorrow."

"General Pershing's report fails to give our division credit for two fights."

"The first, when we relieved the 3rd American Division at Crezancy, at the Marne, on July 16th, and the second, in the advance north of Fismes on September 6th. All told we've run into some mighty fine scraps. One of the best was on July 24th, at Le Croix-Rouge Farm, north of Epieds, on the way to the Fort de Fere. "

"Some of the boys speak of it as 'our lost battalion'. What happened was that the end of our line got hung up by machine gunners and four companies, E, H, I and K, with Colonel Shannon in the middle, pushed ahead like a V. There was an hour or more of pretty desperate work before we got it worked out all right. I reckon the four companies were pretty nearly surrounded at one time."

"Colonel Shannon is a wonder. You know he and Col. George C. Rickards, commander of the 112th Infantry, are the only two National Guard colonels who managed to maintain their commands in the division. That is going some."

"Major Gill was asked about the final offensive.

"Well, we really never got started on the big offensive for that was to be a whole Second Army matter and was scheduled to begin on November 14th. After the war had ended, we got the general idea that it was to have been an enveloping movement, with the 28th Division plugging straight at Metz, while other divisions started to circle. I don't believe they would have expected us to gain Metz ground, but we'd have gone through the Germans just the same. I suppose there'd have been a lot of us, though, who wouldn't have come back."

"The 111th was in the region of Dommartin, about fifteen or sixteen kilometers from Metz when the armistice became effective. We had started a little straightening out process on the afternoon and night of November 10th, just preparatory work to the big stuff which was to have come, had the war continued."

"Speaking of the spoils of the regiment, the major said that in the Chateau-Diable Woods, just west of Fismette, they captured thirty German machine guns and turned them on the boche the very next day. Other hauls included several six-inch cannon and a whole battery of 77's which the Germans had left behind in their haste to evacuate certain portions of the Argonne ahead of the American advance.

"Two of the company commanders of the 111th, Captain Carroll Missimer, 2055 South Fifty-seventh Street, of M Company, and Captain Joseph B. Ralston, of 1810 South Adler Street, of L Company, were but recently promoted from lieutenants. Both were wounded in action, but returned in time to participate in further fighting. Captain Ralston carries with him a fragment of helmet. It is all that remains of the one he wore when a German shell burst nearby and carried most of it away.

"Captain Thomas Bailey, of K Company, who is also acting battalion commander, refused to tell anything about the D. S. C. award, but did tell how he happened to be in charge of the Third Battalion. He said that Major Rattleman, of Pittsburgh, had been the commander up until just one hour of sailing time, when he was transferred to the 6th Regular Division. The captain explained that the major had "put in" for a transfer, but when it failed to materialize decided he was glad of it and was anxious to get home. Then the provoking transfer came through at the last moment and spoiled his plans.

"There are two other officers of the 111th beside Captain Bailey with the D. S. C.; one is Lieutenant Thomas J. Cavanaugh, of Pittsburgh, and the other Lieutenant Frank Batta, of Chillicothe, Mo. A replacement who won the honor while with the 28th and is still with them as an officer of K Company, Cavanaugh's heroism consisted in taking command of a platoon while still a non-com and extracting it from a perilous position, the result being both a war cross and promotion. Batta's performance was somewhat similar.

"With Colonel Davis, chief of staff of the division, were several Philadelphia officers. One of them was Major W. Butler Windle, of 7708 Navajoe Street, Chestnut Hill, a nephew of President Judge Butler, of the Chester County courts, and who himself in pre-war days practiced law in Chester County.

"Major Windle was assistant judge advocate general of the division, and he paid quite a tribute to his superior, Lieutenant Colonel C. Leon B. Berntheisel, of Columbia, the divisional judge advocate general. Major Windle said that Colonel Berntheisel acted as divisional liason officer when in action, and had won great praise from General Muir for his work. The major was asked what his work was when in action and he insisted that he had nothing dangerous to perform.

"He spoke highly also of General Muir, whom he termed 'a strict disciplinarian, but a splendid soldier, admired by all his men.' Of Colonel Davis, the chief of staff, he could not say enough.

"Colonel Davis, however, was extremely reticent about himself. He was City Solicitor of the City of Scranton for twenty years, and in the old National Guard divisional staff for almost the same period. It was learned that he had been recommended for the D. S. C. for his work with the division. Colonel Davis and all the staff members were much interested in the prospect of a divisional parade in Philadelphia, the colonel expressing his surprise when he learned that there were hitches in parading the entire division.

"Why, I thought it was all settled that we were to parade", he said.

"By some peculiar circumstances the ten men of divisional headquarters were carried on the Kroonland as casual officers which enabled them to take the balance of the day after their arrival and go where they pleased, having to turn up in Camp Dix tomorrow morning. Major Windle met his wife, who had come on to New York, and several of the others announced their intention of striking right for home.

"Lieutenant Harold Butts, of Allentown, who commanded the 28th Divisional Military Police, told how the Philadelphia company was left behind in Coblenz with the Army of Occupation. He said that the company under Captain Henry Crofut, former police drillmaster at Philadelphia, had been transferred to the Third French Army Corps around Verdun on

September 25th, and after the armistice was sent to the
Third Army, Captain Crofut, in the meantime, being transferred to the 89th Division.

"At that there were a number of Philadelphians with
the company on the Kroonland, among them being Sergeant
George F. Nick, 1418 Thompson Street, a former motorcycle
patrolman attached to the Tenth and Thompson Street Police
Station, and Private William F. Bradley, 2248 Sears Street,
a former mounted patrolman.

"Bradley said that the police were kept mighty busy
directing traffic behind the lines and handling prisoners.
The 28th Division police alone had handled 15,000 prisoners
during the war. The company had seven men wounded in the
Argonne and ten gassed at Fismes. He told of one experience in a church steeple, during the advance toward the
Vesle, when infantry men reported mysterious flashes coming
from the belfry. Two of the M. P. - he could not remember
the names - went up to investigate, traveling like real
sleuths, and nabbed two Huns who were about to open fire
with a machine gun on some doughboys below. The prisoners
were taken back to headquarters. What became of them
Bradley could not tell.

"The Pennsylvania officers, aside from the divisional
headquarters man on the Kroonland, were these:

Military Police
Lieutenant Harold A. Butz, Allentown.
Field and Staff, 111th
Lieutenant Colonel Franklin P. Haller, Jr.,
   Folcroft.
Second Battalion
Major William W. Gill, Burgettstown, Pa.,
Lieutenant Walter Trainer, Doylestown.
Third Battalion
Captain William Bailey, Germantown;
Lieutenant William L. Cosel, New Castle.
Medical Detachment
Captain Clifford H. Arnold, Ardmore;
Captain Alvin E. Bueger, Pittsburgh.
Machine Gun Company
Captain Edwey Z. Wainwright, Pittsburgh.
Company G
Captain Richard H. O'Brien, Scranton.
Company M
Captain Carrell Missimer, 2055 S. 57th St.
Company L
Captain J. B. Roulston, 1810 S. Adler St.
Company H
Captain Phelps L. Gill, Erie, Pa.
Company I
Lieutenant F. W. Davis, 5896 Washington Ave.
Company K
Captain Thos. H. Bailey, 5325 Lena Street;
Lieutenant Clyde M. Dain, Clarion; Lieutenant
James E. Renshaw, Thorndale.

<u>109th Machine Gun</u>
Major John W. Foos, West Chester, Pa.
<u>Company A</u>
Captain W. C. Rehm, Lancaster, Pa.
<u>Company D</u>
First Lieutenant Joseph R. Eisenlsoun,
Reading, Pa.

"These officers and men of the 111th Infantry, who returned on the Kroonland, have received the Distinguished Service Cross for extraordinary heroism in action:

Captain Thomas Bailey, 5325 Lena Street,
Germantown, Company K.
Lieutenant Thos. J. Cavanaugh, Pittsburgh,
Pa., Company K.
Lieutenant Frank Batta, Chillicothe, Mo.,
Company K.
Sergeant Albert P. Schad, 6416 Saybrook
Avenue, Philadelphia, Company L.
Corporal William Shore, Pittsburgh, Pa.,
Company L.
Private Alfred R. Murphy, Philadelphia,
Medical Detachment.
Private William Nixon, Philadelphia,
Medical Detachment."

The Philadelphia Public Ledger, dated New York, April 29, 1919, tells the following story incident to the docking of the Kroonland:

"One question, and one only, seemed uppermost in the minds of the officers and men of the second half of the 111th Infantry, which arrived at the debarkation pier in Hoboken this morning. That was: "Did Two-Yard-Shannon beat us?" 'Old Two Yards', officially known as Colonel E. C. Shannon, commander of the 111th, had beaten them in by more than 24 hours. He brought the first half of the contingent in on the Minnesotan yesterday.

"Sporting blood in the A. E. F. was not limited to victories against the Germans. The Minnesotan left St. Nazaire two days before the Kroonland but those who came on the second ship were sure that they would overtake the Minnesotan and get back to God's Country - doughboys' own term - before the Colonel. The Kroonland is one of the fastest ships of the transport fleet and it seems that several wagers were made between the two contingents.

"As the big transport steamed up the North River this morning, the most conspicuous thing in sight was a red Keystone 10 feet high, swung between two masts in the forward part of the boat. The brilliant red gleamed in the morning sunlight and threw into relief the big white '28' painted on the emblem. The Keystone was made of wood and was manufactured by the soldiers on board ship. It was hoisted into position last night.

"No transport is complete without mascots, and 'Armistice', an orphan puppy of France, was the favorite on the Kroonland. Company M brought Armistice over. November 11th, while the company was going through its last fight, the little dog, then a blind little puppy only a few hours old, was found huddled in a hole in the Nonsard Woods. It was picked up and brought home.

"On board the Kroonland with the 111th, was the 109th Machine Gun Battalion, the members of which are from Lebanon, Lancaster, Columbia and other towns in the same territory. There was also the 28th Military Police Company of the 28th Division. This was commanded by Lieutenant Harold A. Butz of Allentown.

"A half hour before the Kroonland sailed, Major Wm. A. Rattleman of Pittsburgh, commander of the Third Battalion, was transferred to the 6th Division, a regular army unit.

"The Machine Gun officers were: Major John W. Foos, West Chester, Pa., commanding; Captain George W. Daley, Auburn, N. Y., Headquarters Company; Captain Wm. C. Rehm, Lancaster, Pa., Company A; Captain Fred J. Sullivan, Buffalo, Company B; Lieutenant Walter Clark, Ogdensburg, N.J., commanding Company C; Captain John R. Murphy, Oda Grove, Iowa, Company D.

"The following officers of the field staff of the 111th came in on the Kroonland: Lieutenant Colonel Franklin P. Haller, Jr., Folcroft, Delaware County; Captain Richard J. H. Spurr, Lexington, Kentucky; Lieutenant John S. Anderson, Blairsville; Lieutenant Harry Geltz, Alliance, Ohio; Major William W. Gill, Burgettstown, Pa., commanding the Second Battalion; and Captain William Bailey of Germantown, acting major of the Third Battalion.

"The following company commanders were aboard: Medical Detachment, Captain Clifford H. Arnold, Ardmore, Captain Alvin E. Bulger, Pittsburgh, and Captain Claude A. L. Lyon, Tiffin, Ohio; Machine Gun Company, Captain Edwey Z. Wainwright, Pittsburgh; Company F, Captain William W. Harper, Natchez, Mississippi; Company G, Captain Richard H. O'Brien, Scranton; Company H, Captain Philip L. Gill, Erie, Pa.; Company I, Lieutenant Harry O. Clayberger, Washington, D.C.; Company K, Captain Thomas Bailey, Philadelphia, Pa.; Company L, Captain Joseph B. Roulston, Philadelphia, Pa.; and Company M, Captain Carroll Missimer, Philadelphia, Pa.

"It was announced upon the landing of the Kroonland that the officers and men had subscribed $20,000.00 to the Victory Loan during the voyage home.

"The men, after answering roll-call on the pier, were taken on ferry-boats to trains that carried them to Camp Dix."

The Pittsburgh Dispatch gives the following interesting account:

"Heroism feats, under galling fire, are told by 111th veterans, sheltered again in home Camp.
"Last of great regiment's members, cited for bravery

in France's major battles in 1918, step off Kroonland to
get rousing welcome back to America! Quickly entrain for
Camp Dix.

"The remainder of the 111th Regiment of the Keystone
Division, with a small division headquarters detachment,
the division's Military Police, and the 109th Machine Gun
Battalion Headquarters, Medical Detachment, and Companies
A to D, inclusive, totaling 88 officers and 2,600 men,
stepped ashore at Hoboken today from the transport Kroonland, happy to be home and rest awhile before marching in
review before their home folks.

"A few hours after arriving at Hoboken, the 111th men
were entrained for Camp Dix, New Jersey, near Trenton, where
they joined the others of the regiment who arrived there
yesterday, after having landed from the transport Minnesotan
at Brooklyn. All the famous 111th Regiment is now safely
housed tonight on home soil.

"As the Kroonland came up the harbor this morning, it
flew a flag decorated with a big red Keystone and the figures
'28' in white in the center. The transport had been met
down the Bay early in the morning by members of the Pittsburgh Mayor's Reception Committee, who again commandeered
the naval mine-sweeper 'Sea Gull' and Lieutenant Colonel
Bertram L. Succop headed the party and he was roundly cheered
when he megaphoned a message to the ship telling the returning heroes that Pittsburgh 'welcomes you with all its heart!'
At the Hoboken pier the welcoming committee had opportunity
to take the boys by the hand and cry and smile unaffected
greetings.

"The Kroonland, bearing the last contingent of the
famous 111th Regiment, came up through the smoky haze of the
harbor with a hugh Keystone in red suspended between her fore
and main masts, so that no one a mile away could miss seeing
the symbol of the State, and in big white figures '28' stood
out, painted on the Keystone, so that no one should fail to
understand that on board was the pride of Pittsburgh and the
pride of the State as well. They should have had a legend
beneath: 'By this sign we conquer' for, shattered in its
ranks but glorious in its victories, the regiment comes back
sadly depleted in numbers.

"Like the reception the day before to the companies of
the regiment which returned on the Minnesotan, every well-
fare worker was present to give something to the boys to
show that America, regardless of locality, welcomed them
home. The Red Cross women canteen workers were at the pier
waving their flags of individuality and the American standard, and before the gang-plank was down, they had lowered
flags to stand by the hot coffee wagons and the baskets of
buns that were served as soon as the men were in line on the
pier. The Salvation Army lasses, near to the heart of the
doughboys, were there with chocolates and free postal cards
and telegraph blanks which could be filled in and sent to
relatives and friends without cost to the returning soldiers,
and when the Salvation Army were not looking out for the mes-

sages, they were giving out bars of chocolate. The men
from the Knights of Columbus were busy with their cigarettes,
chocolates and cared for mailing of missives home as well.

"On the army pier, the debarkation band played popular
airs and when 'Hail, Hail, the Gang's All Here' blared out,
there was an answering roar from the men on board.

"As the checking off progressed, the men were given a
hot meal served by the Red Cross but furnished by the great
army kitchen at the port of debarkation, and within a short
time, they were on their way to Camp Dix.

"When it went into the grand offensive at Chateau
Thierry to halt the 5th German offensive, there were 3,300
officers and men, mostly Pennsylvanians, largely Pittsburghers. Nearly one-third have joined the great silent
army beyond the line. The regiment's fatalities, as well
as those of the entire 28th Division, are hardly equalled
by another military contingent from America who fought the
Hun.

"Lieutenant Colonel Haller was in command of all the
troops on board the Kroonland. Major William W. Gill of
Pittsburgh, in command of the Second Battalion, returned
brushing aside the question: 'Were you wounded?' with 'Yes,
gassed twice, but don't mention it'. He gave some light
on the fighting history of the old 18th and its losses. At
first he wished, he said, to correct an impression that the
replacements that were given the regiment at the last of the
war, because of its tremendous losses, were of no great use,
because they were 'green' troops. 'Don't say that of them',
he said. 'It is true that they were lacking somewhat in
training and many times had to be shown just what to do, but
never was there a question as to their willingness, their
bravery, nor did they ever complain when called on. They
were as good soldiers as they knew how to be and they ac-
quitted themselves well wherever they were placed. The
regiment had 3,800 men before it entered the front lines.
We have had 2,800 replacements, that is, three-quarters of
our original number have gone. Not all dead, by any means,
but outside of the losses in killed and wounded, the others
have been scattered along the entire front. We have had
117 non-commissioned officers sent to us, and when we went
into the fighting in the Argonne, we had to have 1,200 men.
Those new men of whom I have before spoken were recently
trained but they were men willing to do or die.'"

The Pittsburgh Post tells the story, as follows:

"Smiles and wound stripes were the universal insignia
worn by the 1,888 men of the old 18th Regiment who came into port this morning on board the Kroonland from France.
They were the most exuberant organization of Pittsburgh
soldiers which has docked in New York harbor and the Service
Records, locked away in the field trunks of the company ad-
jutants on board, showed that they are also among the most
valiant soldiers who have landed.

"An army band was blaring forth a musical welcome from the docks at Hoboken when the big steamer touched the pier, but the soldiers soon matched this with a band of their own, which blared down from the topmost deck.

"When they had done with their musical revelry and had jostled and shoved each other down the two gangplanks on to the pier, the entire 111th Infantry was back in America again. At noon, they started away for Camp Dix, N. J., there to rejoin the rest of the regiment who landed Monday. The Machine Gun Company and Companies F to M, inclusive, of the infantry, composed the 111th men who came on the Kroonland, totaling 62 officers and 1,888 men. Their boat came into quarantine during the night and tied up off the station until this morning.

"Before the day had fairly dawned, a whistle shrieked, a signal up the bay, and soon the Government mine-sweeper, Sea Gull, with a score of Pittsburghers aboard drew up, wheeled around out of the channel and began slowly to encircle the big ocean liner.

"A number of former 18th Regiment officers were on board the Sea Gull, and they greeted the men of the regiment in the name of the Pittsburgh authorities. When the liner lifted her anchor at 9 o'clock and swung out into the stream with her nose toward New York, the boat with the Pittsburghers 'frisked' along the side as an escort.

"Two score nurses from the Red Cross, each with a big white banner with a red cross waving wildly over her head, was one of the official reception committees that stood on the end of the Hoboken pier and greeted the soldiers. The boat of the Pittsburgh committee had dropped astern as the transport came into her berth, and the only Pittsburghers on the dock were newspaper men. But outside, pressed solidly against the iron fence surrounding the docks and administration buildings at Hoboken piers, more than 100 residents of Pittsburgh were waiting a glimpse of the returning soldiers.

"The men were led off the steamer and marched out into the yard beyond the docks before being lined up for inspection and checking up, and the ones who waited outside the fence were able to see, to shout to, and, in the end, to converse with their relatives among the soldiers, for the company formations were broken up after a time and the soldiers allowed to approach the iron pickets.

"This was a concession that many Pittsburghers were denied when they came here to greet the other half of the 18th regiment and the 15th regiment. Those units were docked at the Brooklyn piers, which are so surrounded with warehouses and fences and stern guards that relatives were not allowed within three city squares of the soldiers.

"Hundreds of stories of individual heroism were told as the Keystone men sunned themselves in the great yard in front of the army piers, but the throngs of nice girls gathered outside the iron fence heard most of them. The young women had come to Hoboken to welcome some detachments of the 77th, but they showed their impartiality by extending cordial greetings to the Pennsylvanians, and it was not long before the high picket fence for blocks was lined on one side by rows and rows of youths in olive drab and on the other by attractive young girls in Spring frocks of gay colors. And so the doughboys who were not lucky enough to be welcomed by their own relatives and friends did not have to stand aside and be envious of the good fortune of their comrades.

"The soldiers could not be blamed for striking up acquaintances with the fair welcomers, and they might be excused for stretching the truth a little in telling of their year's experiences overseas, for they had to entertain their audience, and it was so refreshing to talk to American girls again. One really did not care what he said just as long as they appeared interested and laughed and joked and said they would like to meet one where there weren't so many others around. Oh, it was great! It was something the first of the regiment missed, because it landed in Brooklyn, where the crowds are kept blocks and blocks away. The throngs became so great before the Keystone men got ready to entrain for camp that the police and army authorities had to stretch ropes along the curb and keep the New Yorkers away from the fence that the sidewalk might be used for those who kept moving. While the young women heard yarns from 'over there' which were not 'all wool', officers of the regiment told of exploits where the facts formed the themes of the stories."

We shall conclude the newspaper stories about the docking of the Kroonland by quoting from The Philadelphia Inquirer, issue of April 30, 1919, the account being dated New York, April 29th. The item reads as follows:

"Defeated by a day in a race across the Atlantic, the transport Kroonland, bearing the second half of the 111th Infantry Regiment, arrived here among blaring bands and hooting whistles early today. The Kroonland, though technically defeated in her race against the Minnesotan, which brought in the first half of the 111th yesterday, achieved a 'moral victory' as she started two days later.

"On board the Kroonland, which is a fairly large ship, were 63 officers and 1,888 men of the 111th, under Lieut. Colonel Franklin P. Haller, Jr., of Folcroft; Machine Gun battalion under Major John W. Foos, of West Chester; 10 officers and 10 men of the 28th Division Headquarters Company, and 186 men of the 103rd Military Police.

"Unlike the Minnesotan's load of returning heroes, the Kroonland's contingent was an uproarous one. For one thing, they had a larger ship, and for another, there were more of them. They howled greetings to everything and everybody, they sang, 'How Dry I am' in tones which startled even Hoboken, a place accustomed to many soldiers and much howling. They howled for the Red Cross, they howled for the

Salvation Army, and they appeared ready to fall upon the necks of the first visitors from home.

"The Kroonland's men were proud of their red Keystone. They made a Keystone 20 feet high and 15 feet wide out of good strong fence boards; they painted it a brilliant red, and they hung it up on the forward deck of the ship. In a good light, it could be seen almost as far as the vessel itself. It bore in white the figures '28'.

"The men on coming into the slip, set up the familiar slogan: 'When do we eat?' and even beyond their own hunger, they were concerned for the feeding of their mascots, of which they had several.   One of the dogs and the favorite was a Belgian police named 'Armistice' and which had been found as a blind pup shortly after the death of its mother at the front.

"The Iron Division had an extraordinary typhoid fever record in France - extraordinary that it did not have a single case. The influenza cases also were kept low. Col. Wm. J. Crookston, the Division Surgeon, attributed this to the men's own hygienic training at Camp Hancock.

"The Military Police on board were divided into two companies, one from Philadelphia and vicinity, the other from Pittsburgh.

"All the men went to Camp Dix, to be distributed later among other camps for demobilization, some of the men coming from points as far away as the Pacific Coast. Few of them wanted to parade, their great desire being to get back home.

"The 111th failed in any particular to over-shadow the superb record of the Machine Gun Battery, which had a record for subtle and deadly fighting. It lost no less than 37 officers and men killed and 404 wounded. Most of the men replacing the casualties were from the West.

"Major Foos said yesterday: 'We had a fearless battalion of men.' His words were re-echoed by Sgt. Harold J. Graves, of 5934 Summer Street. 'You can talk about your doughboys', said he, 'but the machine gun men are the men to go over the top. We had to advance with the first waves and establish our positions, and our battalions didn't have the easy job that people supposed.'

"Capt. Carroll Missimer, of 2055 South 52nd Street, had a remarkable escape from death when a piece of shell tore away half of his trench helmet and a portion of his pack. A fragment of the shell lodged in his skull, where it still remains.

"Capt. Missimer and First Lieutenant Joseph Rees, of 6215 Walnut Street, shared their escapes unequally. Though Capt. Missimer was wounded, Lieut. Rees had so many escapes, from even a scratch, that he became known throughout the Division as 'Barrel of Luck'. Officers of the Division declared he had missed death, or long periods in hospitals, more than any man they had seen. On one occasion, his pack was shot away, but he was unwounded.

"Sgt. Walter Leitch, of 137 S. 59th Street, was another who was fortunate. A bursting shell left him blind for two months, and even now only his right eye is perfect. His face bears the marks of his wounds, though he is not disfigured. Pvt. John H. Randolph and Pvt. Chas. H. Bonner, were two out of the twenty men aboard the ship who had gone through the war without receiving a wound. Pvt. Nathan Margolis, of 1637 S. 52nd Street, was forced to cook when a Hun shell found the kitchen of Company L, of the 111th, and killed off the cook and two assistants. With shells falling all around the place, Margolis went in and cooked dinner.

"The suggestion that Philadelphia and Pittsburgh each have a parade of its own men raised the question yesterday as to which city should be given the regimental colors. The fact that the regiment will probably appear in history as representing one or the other city is expected to figure in a series of claims which will come before State and Federal officials for disposition of the colors. The worst of it is, the 111th is the only regiment of the division whose colors are permitted to carry the 'Chateau Thierry band'. At present the regimental colors have seven streamers attached, each representing an engagement in which it took part. These, however, are but temporary, and will be replaced by silver bands around the staff. The streamers represent Chateau Thierry, the Champagne-Marne defensive, the Aisne-Marne offensive, the Fismes sector, the Oise-Aisne offensive, the Meuse-Argonne offensive, and the Thiaucourt-Toul sector."

Mention is made in the above newspaper articles about the docking of the Minnesotan, the transport which carried the first contingent of the 111th Regiment back to America. As this ship brought over the commanding officer of our regiment, Colonel E. C. Shannon, it may be of special interest to quote the following story taken from the Philadelphia Public Ledger, issue of April 29th, the item being dated New York, April 28th. While it is true that the account has no direct bearing on the fortunes of our Third Battalion, our beloved commander is rather prominently mentioned therein, and the story of our home-coming would not be complete without a word or two concerning "Two Yard Shannon".

"We cut the hell out of them!"
"It took only those seven words for Colonel E. C. Shannon, of the 111th Infantry, to describe the work of the 28th (Iron) Division in France.

"With 1,174 of his men, he arrived on the transport Minnesotan at Pier 7 in Bush Terminal, South Brooklyn, this morning. The rest of the command will arrive in Hoboken tomorrow morning on the Kroonland. Lieut. Colonel F. P. Haller, Jr. is in command of them.

"And it didn't take much of an observer to find the truth of Colonel Shannon's remark. On every side as the men debarked were to be seen D.S.C.e, Croix de Guerre and other war decorations. It was truly a gathering of heroes. There was not a man in the whole outfit who had not his little tale, if he would only tell it. But the majority were silent, and it was only by mingling among their 'buddies' that any thing at all could be gathered of their exploits. And even then the informant was regarded as a 'tattle-tale' by his fellows.

"But Colonel Shannon could not say too much about his men. He isn't 'Colonel Shannon' to them, however, except on dress parade. 'Old Two Yards' is his pet name. And why? Ask any of his doughboys! Here's what they will tell you: 'Why, simply because he was always within two yards of every front of the line! The rear guard never saw much of 'Two Yard Shannon'. He was always too far in advance for that. He was a fighting Colonel! There was no regimental headquarters in the rear of the line that would hold him when the battle was on! He was with us, every man! And there is not a man among us that wouldn't go to hell and back for 'Old Two Yards''.

"And for all this whole-hearted praise, he is the mildest mannered and quietest that could be met. Col. Shannon stood at the end of the gangplank looking out over the dock, where half of his command – all that had come with him – stood in company formation waiting for the ferries to carry them to the trains that were to take them to Camp Dix.

"The Colonel's pride in his men showed in every word and every gesture. And why shouldn't he be proud of them? 75 men of the regiment have been decorated with the D.S.C. and all the citations for bravery and awards of croix de Guerre would take columns to tell!

"But the contingent that Colonel Shannon is bringing home on the Minnesotan and the Kroonland is a mere skeleton of the original that he led in that first battle at Hill 204, at Chateau Thierry on July 1st, 1918. Then he had practically the entire personnel of the old 6th and 18th Regiments, National Guard of Pennsylvania. There were some 1500 in the original quota of the units that returned today. But in the ranks today in these units, there were only 116 men from the 6th and 140 men from the 18th.

"And here are the official casualty figures of the first battalion alone:

Officers killed...............	20
Officers wounded.............	33
Officers missing.............	None
Men killed...................	496
Men wounded..................	2,077
Men missing..................	482

It was no wonder 'Old Two Yards' was proud! And here is what he said about them: 'They are the finest lot of two-fisted fighting men in the world! The whole Pennsylvania National Guard was that and more, but my men were the best! We showed some of our taunters of olden days that we were not the 'tin soldiers' as they called us when we went up to Mt. Gretna for our annual encampments. I would lead those men to the end of the world and consider myself privileged. Should they parade? Why, it would be an insult not to allow them, but all those plans are up to the War Department.

There could not be a prouder man in the United States than
I if I were only allowed to lead those men in a parade both
in Philadelphia and Pittsburgh."

From the above, it is believed the story of the home-coming of
our Third Battalion has been fully covered. Of course, each man will,
no doubt, recall his individual experiences of that eventful morning.
The newspaper articles have been quoted verbatim and due allowance should
be made for any errors therein reported.

First of Twenty-eighth at Dix

The first batch of those who arrived on the Kroonland are expected to reach camp at half past 5 o'clock this afternoon. Other sections will follow soon after with the remainder of the regiment. Those coming include 888 men and sixty-three officers of the 111th; 186 men and three officers of the Twenty-eighth Company military police, and fifteen officers and 702 men of the 109th Machine Gun Battalion.

By the time they arrive virtually all the units already here will have gone through the disinfecting process and the newcomers will take the places of comrades vacated in the quarantine area.

Veterans of the 111th Infantry, the first big contingent of the Twenty-eighth Division to arrive home from overseas, are receiving a real "welcome home" at Camp Dix today.

Hundreds of visitors from Philadelphia and other sections of the state are at the big cantonment seeking loved ones, renewing old acquaintances and listening eagerly as the Pennsylvania guardsmen relate experiences under fire.

Absolute freedom of intercourse between the veterans and their visitors is allowed, and as a result the barracks to which the 111th men have been assigned are crowded to capacity with friends and relatives of the overseas men and the soldiers themselves, each eager to hear all about what happened to the other while the guard was abroad.

In all 1765 officers and men of the famous Iron Division arrived in New York on board the transport Minnesotan yesterday and were sent to Camp Dix. The men had been sounded on the idea of a divisional parade in Philadelphia and were eager to participate in such a review if it does not keep them away from their homes too long. But their main thought is to get home again and to take up the thread of their lives where they dropped it to enter the fight against kaiserism.

The camp began to assume a festal air early this morning. The men had hardly finished the morning mess when visitors began to arrive in automobiles. From that time on there was a continuous stream of visitors flocking toward that section of the camp set apart for the Pennsylvanians.

The companies of the 111th now at the camp are Companies A, B, C, D and E, and headquarters company, the medical detachment and the supply company of the same regiment. But 282 of the men come from east of the Susquehanna, most of them hailing from the Pittsburgh region.

Camp Dix, NJ, 1918 (Photo Courtesy of Library of Congress)

CHAPTER 31

CAMP DIX, N. J.

"I will be the gladdest thing under the sun;
I will touch a hundred flowers, and not pick one.
I will look at cliffs and clouds with quiet eyes;
Watch the wind bow down the grass,
And the grass rise.
And when lights begin to show up from the town,
I will mark which must be mine,
And then start down.
("The Hill Back Home," Pvt. C. W. Gaugler, Q.M.C.)

At last, every man in our Third Battalion who came over on the Kroonland was accounted for and all names were duly checked off the Sailing List. After being taken care of by the American Red Cross, we next boarded special trains bound for Camp Dix, Wrightstown, New Jersey.

Before boarding the coaches, we were supplied with postal cards to mail to relatives and friends, acquainting them of our safe arrival in the United States. Some of the boys sent telegrams, blanks being given out for that purpose. Then came the happy boarding of the train - this time what we termed "a regular train of cars" - the good old U.S.A. make! No "Hommes 40, Chevaux 8" this trip! No more were we treated like so many sheep being shipped to market! Up-to-the-minute passenger coaches awaited the returning heroes of the 28th! The ladies of the American Red Cross saw us off with baskets loaded down with big red apples and chocolate candy bars. Not a man was overlooked! Needless to add, the boys soon lightened the load of the ladies! And didn't those fair American girls look good to us! The train sped on carrying its khaki-clad passengers nearer and nearer camp and "home sweet home"!

The afternoon of April 29th was pretty nearly spent when we reached our destination. We found Camp Dix built along the usual lines of army cantonments at that time scattered throughout the United States - the same old sandy soil, the familiar barn-like barrack buildings, with here and there a little tent city to vary the monotony. The place seemed barren of trees. On the short hike from the camp railroad station to our barracks, we noticed a number of soldiers strolling leisurely around wearing red chevrons attached to their sleeves. We wondered, "why the red chevrons?" We were informed, upon inquiry, that these men had been mustered out of the service - honorably discharged - and were merely remaining in camp for perhaps a few hours longer before their departure for their home towns. Reaching our section of the hugh camp, the Third Battalion was soon "under roof" in one of the large barrack buildings.

That night, after a day full of excitement and pleasant anticipations, the men slept like tops under an American starlit sky - on American soil - Americans among Americans once more!

Our few remaining days as soldiers of Uncle Sam were very, very busy ones indeed! We had not been in camp many hours before we got our final cootie bath and issued new clothing. As this is the last we'll hear of Mr. Cootie, it may be appropriate to quote the following lines from The Stars and Stripes, issue of Friday, May 30, 1919. The poem is entitled "The Passing of the Cootie" and was written by Howard J. Green, American Military Supply Depot, Rotterdam, Holland.

> "The cooties got together
> And held a big convention
> To discuss the question whether
> They should call the world's attention
> To a matter quite neglected
> In the Conference of Nations:
> For the cootie had suspected
> He was going to lose his rations.
>
> For, with armies all dissembled,
> 'Twould be ultimate starvation;
> So the cooties all assembled
> To work out a good salvation,
> 'The question is alarming!'
> The cootie-king agreed;
> 'Why, with all the world disarming,
> How are we going to feed?'
>
> For weeks the cooties wrangled
> Upon how to exist,
> When the complications tangled
> With a new and sudden twist;
> A bad and faithless cootie
> Had wandered from the rest,
> Neglected his real duty
> For a major's sweater-vest.
>
> Now, the major was commanding
> A corps of sanitation
> And was constantly demanding
> A clean extermination
> Of all the cootie-hatches
> 'Till there was ne'er a trace,
> But-look!-the major scratches!
> See the anger on his face!
>
> A cootie! Without losing
> A precious moment's time
> His men were roused from musing
> And acquainted with the crime.
> 'No cootie shall be living
> When this day's sun has set!'
> Swears the major, unforgiving,
> 'My leaf is on that bet!'

> He got his scouts to find them,
> And then filled the place with steam;
> His machine was there to grind 'em;
> You could hear the cooties scream.
> Now the cootie-curse is over,
> 'Cause one cootie left the rest
> To be a truant rover
> On a major's sweater-vest."

It is safe to say that no "truant rover" could be found on the person of any Buck Private in our entire outfit after we had gone through that de-lousing process at the camp. Some of the men had fairly decent uniforms but wanted entirely new outfits to wear home. These "wise" ones de-liberately went to work with knives, bayonets, nails or pieces of glass and in short order had their "ODs" ready for the scrap pile! This bit of "Strategy", however, turned out rather disastrously for a number of the would-be dudes! After ripping and otherwise disfiguring their uni-forms, many of these unfortunates were unable to procure the right size again - much to their chagrin! All rifles and ammunition, along with other equipment, we "turned in" at Camp Dix. This applied only to the men who were scheduled to be discharged at the camp and go from there directly to their homes without participating in any parades. The men were granted permission to keep, as souvenirs, their gas masks, steel helmets, slickers and overcoats. Of course, the uniforms we wore were also given us by our grateful uncle! Many of the boys had become passionately fond of their rifles and wanted to keep these also - some even offering to buy them from the Government. This was not permitted, however. As far as it is known every man, sooner or later, was obliged to part company with his beloved "piece" - a word the men had for their army rifles. However, we are getting a little ahead of our story. The 111th had its last review before Colonel Shannon at Camp Dix. It was there, too, that we said goodbye to many of our comrades - those who were going on to other camps for demobilization.

From this point, the writer can only relate some of the events at Camp Dix in which he personally participated and recalls - happenings which may or may not agree with accounts and dates given by other com-rades. At about this time, our Third Battalion was beginning to split up into various groups - some of the men remaining at Dix for parades, some going on to other camps for demobilization and others going direct-ly to their homes after being discharged at Camp Dix - so that it is im-possible to say whether the following applies to every man of our Third Battalion or not.

The writer now tells of his experiences as a former member of Com-pany I, Third Battalion, 111th Infantry. I had signified my intentions about not parading. As I resided in the eastern part of the United States, I was scheduled to be honorably discharged from the service at Camp Dix and was supposed to go directly home from there.

On May 3rd, our group underwent a final physical examination before being mustered out of the army. For this examination, we were paraded in nature's garments through a long building with doctors, seemingly, at every turn. One medico examined the men for "flat feet", another gave us that old "short-arm" inspection again, another applied a stethoscope to our chests and dentists were on the job to examine teeth – not overlooking optometrists, otologists, etc., etc. Oh! we were all thoroughly gone over that day! A slap on the back accompanied by curt, "You're alright! Next!" was the general procedure. The writer recalls that long line of naked men slowly moving forward. None were called aside or taken out of the line. Apparently, no one in our group had suffered any ill-effects from experiences "Over There" – at least they did not show up in that particular examination at Camp Dix!

During the afternoon of May 4th, 1919, the writer was officially mustered out of the army and became a civilian again. I will attempt here to describe the process as performed in Discharge Unit No. 3, (the "mad house", as the men called it) at Camp Dix, N. J. As each man's name was called from his Service Record, he entered the building and was given his papers at the door by one of the officers attached to the Unit. Following each other in single file, the men were then interviewed, in turn, by numerous officers seated at desks arranged in a row. Each officer asked certain questions which had to be satisfactorily answered. Notations were made on our Service Records. Finally, we came to the clerk whose duty it was to fill out our discharge certificates. Every ex-service man (honorably discharged) is familiar with the wording on these certificates. For the information of any of my readers interested, I shall endeavor to quote a certificate, using mine for the purpose. On its face, appears the following:

"Honorable Discharge from the United States Army. (The seal of the United States Government.) To all whom it may concern: This is to certify, That Paul L. Compton, No. 1,781,128, Private Company I, 111th Infantry, The United States Army, as a testimonial of honest and faithful service, is hereby Honorably Discharged from the military service of the United States by reason of Circular 106 W.D., 1918. Said Paul L. Compton was born in Fredericksburg, in the State of Virginia. When enlisted he was 28 years of age and by occupation a Stenographer. He had blue eyes, light brown hair, light complexion, and was 5 feet, $7\frac{1}{2}$ inches in height. Given under my hand at Camp Dix, N. J., this 4th day of May, one thousand nine hundred and nineteen. (Signed) J. G. Knight, Major, Infantry, U.S.A., Commanding."

On the reverse side of the certificate is the following:

"Enlistment Record. Name: Paul L. Compton. Grade: Private. Inducted: Nov. 21, 1917, at Upper Marlboro, Maryland. Serving in first enlistment period at date of discharge. Prior service: None. Noncommissioned officer: Never. Marksmanship, gunner qualification or rating: Not qualified. Horsemanship: Not qualified. Battles, engagements, skirmishes, expeditions: 5 German offensives, July 14 to 27, 1918; Ourcq Vesle, July 28 to Sept. 7, 1918; Meuse Argonne, Sept. 26, Oct. 7, 1918; Thiaucourt sector, Oct. 16, to Nov. 11, 1918. Knowledge of any vocation: Stenographer. Wounds received in service: None. Physical condition when discharged: Good. Typhoid prophylaxis completed: Dec. 7, 1917. Paratyphoid prophylaxis completed: Dec. 7, 1917. Married or single: Single. Character: Excellent. Remarks: Served with A.E.F. Left U.S. May 5, 1918. Arrived U. S. Apr. 28, 1919, with Company I, 313th Inf. to Company I, 111th Inf. to date of discharge. Signature of soldier:

(Signed) Paul L. Compton. (Signed) J. G. Knight, Major, Infantry, U. S. A., Commanding Discharge Unit No. 3."

After going through the "mill", we issued forth from the other end of the building civilians again- just plain misters now - privates, corporals and sergeants no longer! The little red chevrons were handed each man along with that all important piece of paper - our Discharge Certificates, bearing in bold black lettering: "Honorable Discharge from the United States Army"! Each man received his "bonus" of Sixty Dollars together with any "back pay" due. A railroad ticket office was conveniently located nearby and many of the men at once bought tickets for their respective home towns. The writer left Camp Dix late on the afternoon of May 4th for Washington, D. C. - and home!

In concluding our chapter on Camp Dix experiences, we shall now quote items of interest appearing in various newspapers at that time. These articles give, in concise form, something of our daily life while there and from them it is believed that all comrades can easily reconstruct the entire story as they remember it.

Philadelphia Public Ledger,
Camp Dix, N. J., April 29th:

"There is not a pediculous person left among the 1750 officers and men of the First and Second battalions of the 111th Infantry which were debarked at Hoboken yesterday morning. Upon their arrival here last night, every man jack of the two units was placed in the quarantine area, where all were passed through the disinfecting process this morning.

"The business of disinfecting the men from overseas was attended to with dispatch in order that the area might be cleared to make way for the influx of more Keystone men tonight. The process, which is regidly applied by the Government to all contingents returning from overseas, to prevent any possible spread of contamination, includes a complete renovation of cleaning in the mamouth steam drums at Camp Dix Sanitary Station. The men, spick and span in cleansed or new uniforms, were moved this afternoon to quarters of the depot brigade, at the extreme southern end of New York Avenue.

"All the men also were sent to the surplus property building. There they turned back to Uncle Sam the rifles that many of them had carried all over Europe. Many of the men seemed loath to part with these weapons. They pointed to the notches on the stocks of their guns and many took the numbers of their old rifles, hoping to purchase them later from the Government. Mess kits they had used through European camps also were turned in to the Quartermaster. In turn, however, the men were given the complete outfits of uniforms and clothing that is now supplied to every soldier leaving the service and were allowed to retain their trench helmets and gas masks."

Philadelphia Inquirer,
Camp Dix, N. J., May 1st:

"Approximately 8,000 members of the 28th Division at Camp Dix are anxiously awaiting the day that will see them in their homes. Rain and strange surroundings once again, as well as the discomfortures of the delousing process, combined today to keep them pretty busy. So busy, in fact, that two members missed important foreign decorations at the hands of Major General Charles H. Muir, the divisional commander.

"But busy as they were and harassed by the weather, they eagerly inquired about plans for their demobilization. In every one of the barracks, even over to the newly arrived Pennsylvanians, that was the sole topic of conversation.

"Only the men of the 111th Infantry, commanded by Col. E. C. Shannon, are really happy. The War Department has ordered, inasmuch as the majority of the men are from the western part of the State, that about 900 be sent to Camp Sherman in Ohio for demobilization. They will leave Camp Dix tomorrow or Saturday. They will parade in Pittsburgh before going to the point of demobilization. The 111th Infantry was made up largely of the old 18th Infantry of the Pennsylvania National Guard.

"The uncertainty as to the arrival of all of the units of the Division is a factor in the problem brought up about the proposed parade to be held in Philadelphia. It will be as big as can be given. But higher military authorities feel that the men from distant parts of Pennsylvania and from other sections should not be kept waiting at Camp Dix until the Division is assembled.

"From early morning until late tonight, soldiers of the Iron Division went through the delousing process. The capacity of the machines at Camp Dix is very great, but the troops from the Keystone State have arrived in such numbers, and are still coming, that it is being tested to the limit.

"It was the delousing process that prevented the bestowal on one soldier today of a French decoration. And it made another one late for that very important moment in the life of a soldier. But, "Uncle Charlie" Muir, as the commander of the Division is known, comprehended and went through the program twice."

The Pittsburgh Post,
Camp Dix, N. J., May 2nd:

"Transportation officers at the camp notified Col. E. C. Shannon at 6 o'clock tonight that it would be impossible to get transportation for the 111th Regiment for Pittsburgh until May 6th. An hour before, they had announced from the transportation office that the date would be May 9th. Earlier in the day, Col. Shannon had been promised trains for his regiment at 7 o'clock tonight, and all the preparations had been made for the departure this evening for a parade Saturday.

"The men are in despair. There had been such glowing promise of the original plan of a Saturday parade being carried out, that all the packs had been made up, and every other preparation had been completed for the departure.

"At 5 o'clock tonight, Col. Shannon had said that it would still be possible to put out tonight, if the trains were ready. Now everyone has given up hope of starting before Tuesday.

"Almost every man in the regiment had wired relatives or friends that he would be in Pittsburgh Saturday, and some of them are so intent upon keeping their promises that they dashed over to the recruiting office when it became plain that the regiment could not get away tonight. Under the re-enlisting plan of the army at this time, a man is given a thirty-day furlough, beginning immediately, if he enlists for a period of one year.

"It was estimated tonight that at least one out of every 100 men in the organization were re-enlisting to get an immediate furlough. No one relishes a four-day stay here, now that they are so near home, and they dislike it even more than they dislike another year in the service, although they dislike that enough!

"The orders for transportation were received by the camp transportation officers from the district representative of the railroad administration at Hoboken, now Hoboken claims it has received orders from Washington to hold the Pittsburgh regiment.

"The regiment will have to travel in day coaches when it does go out, for the final order received today said it 'could move May 6th if it chose to go in day coaches.' Day coaches do not greatly alarm the men, for they have been used to travelling in box cars in France.

"The regiment will take 1,319 to Pittsburgh for the parade, it was announced tonight. Of these, 1,264 are enlisted men and 56 officers. Probably not more than three-fourths of these men are men from Western Pennsylvania, the rest being soldiers from Western states who have volunteered to parade in Pittsburgh and be discharged at Camp Sherman.

"There will be three trains for the organization. The first will be in charge of Col. Shannon, the second in charge of Major W. W. Gill and the third in command of Lieut. Col. Franklin P. Haller, Jr.

"At a meeting of the company officers this afternoon, called to notify them to be ready to move on an hour's notice, Col. Shannon gave orders that each man who goes to Pittsburgh must have an overseas cap. The caps must be worn when they get off the train and they must carry their helmets and gas masks. When they enter the parade, they will put on their helmets and carry light packs."

The Pittsburgh Post,
Camp Dix, N. J., May 1st:

"Col. Shannon, commander of the 111th Infantry, today

gave out the official list of officers of the regiment who
were killed, wounded or gassed while in action, together
with the company to which they were attached, the date of
their casualty and cause.   In all, 22 officers were killed
or died of wounds or gas; 51 were wounded or gassed and none
was reported missing.   Of the enlisted men in the regiment,
396 were killed or died of wounds or gas; 2,097 were wounded
or gassed, and 182 were reported missing.   The table showing the officers losses follows:

Killed

Louis Fielding, Capt., Co. E, 9/9/18, died in hospital of
        wounds.
John M. Clark, Capt., Co. F, 8/11/18, shellfire.
Edmund Lynch, Capt., Co. B, 8/12/18, shellfire.
Arthur Schlosser, Capt., Co. G, 9/27/18, gun shot wounds.
Orville Thompson, Capt., Co. M, 8/11/18, hand grenade.
Ralph Busch, 1st Lieut., Co. E, 8/11/18, shrapnel.
Walter Ettinger, 1st Lieut., Co. A, 9/8/18, machine gun fire.
Lee C. Fletcher, 1st Lieut., Co. K, 9/8/18, concussion high
        explosive shell.
Michael W. Keith, 1st Lieut., Co. M, 9/9/18, died in
        hospital, gassed.
Geo. Poffenberger, 1st Lieut., Hdq., unknown, died in
        hospital, gun shot wounds.
Wilhelmus Rice, 1st Lieut., Co. M, 10/2/18, died in
        hospital of wounds.
Robt. Woodbury, 1st Lieut., Co. A, 8/12/18, shellfire.
Daniel W. Brooks, 2nd Lieut., M.G., 9/6/18, machine gun fire.
Chas. H. Fisk, 2nd Lieut., Co. A, 8/24/18, machine gun fire.
Frank Glendening, 2nd Lieut., Co. B, 8/12/18, shellfire.
Henry W. Gunlach, 2nd Lieut., Co. L, 8/11/18, machine gun.
Frank Kirke, 2nd Lieut., Co. C, 11/4/18, shellfire.
Leland G. Larner, 2nd Lieut., Co. B, 8/12/18, shellfire.
Harold W. Painter, 2nd Lieut., Co. K, 10/2/18, gun shot
        wounds.
John W. Quinn, 2nd Lieut., Co. B, 7/18/18, shellfire.
Richard Vaughan, 2nd Lieut., Co. A, 9/18/18, machine gun.
Marcel Von Beroghy, 2nd Lieut., Co. F, 9/6/18, machine gun.

Wounded

Alan G. Donnelly, Major, 9/8/18, shell shock.
Clifford Arnold, Capt., M.C., 7/19/18, gassed.
Clifford Arnold, Capt., M.C., 9/8/18, gassed.
West E. Blain, Capt., Co. I, 8/22/18, shrapnel.
Jas. A. Groff, Capt., Co. K, 10/2/18, gun shot wound.
Chas. Johnson, Capt., H.Q., 8/12/18, shellfire.
Robt. Pollock, Capt., M.G., 9/6/18, machine gun fire.
Jas. A. Williams, Capt., Co. A, 8/9/18, machine gun fire.
Wm. Allen, 1st Lieut., Co. B, 8/12/18, gassed.
Thos. Bailey, 1st Lieut., Co. K, 9/8/18, gassed.
Arthur Burnett, 1st Lieut., Co. I, 11/5/18, shrapnel.
Frank C. Horner, 1st Lieut., Co. C, 8/12/18, bursting shell.

Henry Keller, 1st Lieut., Co. D, 8/12/18, shellfire.
Howard Mellinger, 1st Lieut., Co. F, 8/14/18, gassed.
Howard Mellinger, 1st Lieut., Co. F, 8/23/18, gassed.
Albert Miller, 1st Lieut., M.G., 8/11/18, shellfire.
Carroll Missimer, 1st Lieut., Co. L, 10/2/18, shellfire.
Earl L. Reese, 1st Lieut., Co. L, 10/4/18, gun shot wounds.
Jos. Roulston, 1st Lieut., Co. L, 8/11/18, shellfire.
Wm. Shaal, 1st Lieut., Co. E, 8/12/18, gassed.
Anthony Wausnock, 1st Lieut., Co. A, 11/10/18, gun shot
        wounds.
Richard Arnold, 2nd Lieut., Co. I, 9/26/18, gun shot wounds.
Thos. Bailey, 2nd Lieut., Co. K, 7/19/18, gassed.
Frank Batta, 2nd Lieut., Co. G, 8/13/18, shellfire.
Horace P. Conrad, 2nd Lieut., H.C., 8/17/18, shellfire.
John H. Earl, 2nd Lieut., Co. G, 9/28/18, gassed.
Wm. Ewing, 2nd Lieut., Co. F, 10/2/18, machine gun fire.
Thos. Gallagher, 2nd Lieut., Co. L, 8/11/18, shellfire.
Paul W. Harrell, 2nd Lieut., H.Q., 10/4/18, gassed.
Meyer Kestinbaum, 2nd Lieut., Co. C, 8/11/18, machine gun
        fire.
Fred Klingsmith, 2nd Lieut., Co. F, 9/6/18, machine gun fire.
Chas. E. Krey, 2nd Lieut., Co. E, 10/2/18, gun shot wound.
Harry J. Kulp, 2nd Lieut., Co. G, 7/18/18, machine gun fire.
Harry A. Kurtz, 2nd Lieut., Co. H, 9/30/18, gun shot wound.
Walter Lehman, 2nd Lieut., Co. M, 10/1/18, shellfire.
Jos. A. Logan, 2nd Lieut., Co. D, 10/2/18, gun shot wound.
Frank W. Mehrten, 2nd Lieut., Co. E, 8/12/18, gassed.
Thos. Merryweather, 2nd Lieut., Co. F, 9/6/18, machine gun
        fire.
John S. O'Brien, 2nd Lieut., Co. B, 10/7/18, gun shot wound.
Richard O'Brien, 2nd Lieut., Co. F, 7/17/18, gassed.
Leonard Radtke, 2nd Lieut., Co. H, 9/27/18, gun shot wound.
Thos. Robertson, 2nd Lieut., Co. G, 9/28/18, gun shot wound.
Gerald Robinson, 2nd Lieut., Co. G, 7/17/18, gassed.
Gerald Robinson, 2nd Lieut., Co. G, 9/30/18, gun shot wound.
Alfred N. Rohr, 2nd Lieut., Co. G, 8/11/18, machine gun fire.
Robt. Sears, 2nd Lieut., Co. A, 9/7/18, shellfire.
Chas. Simpson, 2nd Lieut., Co. D, 7/17/18, shellfire.
Wingate Smith, 2nd Lieut., Co. E, 9/6/18, machine gun fire.
Otto G. Vadakin, 2nd Lieut., Co. H, 9/30/18, gun shot wound.
Jas. B. Wharton, 2nd Lieut., Co. C, 8/9/18, machine gun fire.
Donald R. White, 2nd Lieut., Co. A, 7/15/18, gassed.
Elmer Wilbur, 2nd Lieut., Co. D, 8/10/18, machine gun fire.
Francis Welton, 2nd Lieut., Co. B, 8/12/18, machine gun fire."

The Pittsburgh Post,
Camp Dix, N. J., May 3rd:

        "Practically the entire Allegheny company membership
of the 18th regiment will be home tomorrow.
        "More than 1,200 members of the 111th Regiment were
swarming out of camp at 10 o'clock tonight.   All the roads
were filled with 'Red Keystone' men and almost every bus in
the district had been requisitioned for runs to

Philadelphia, where the men have to make connections for
Pittsburgh. Between the passes and the discharges, almost
the entire regiment had left Camp Dix tonight.

"The regiment has not entrained - as a regiment - but
in his capacity as an individual soldier, nearly every one
of the men from the Pittsburgh district has entrained. By
noon today, the streets should be filled with them. '64-
hour passes' is the answer. Late yesterday afternoon, when
it became certain there was no longer any chance of the 18th
getting away from here before Tuesday at the earliest, it
was announced at Regimental Headquarters that every man due
to parade in Pittsburgh whenever the regiment goes there,
was eligible for a pass good until Tuesday morning.

"The time of departure of the train that will carry the
regiment from Camp Dix Tuesday on its 'official' journey to
Pittsburgh was announced by the railroad administration this
afternoon. The first will leave at 2:45, the second at 3:15
and the third at 3:45. The first train will arrive in Pittsburgh at 7 o'clock Wednesday morning, if it is not delayed.

"But, in the meantime, the flying visit will be made.
The announcement about passes started a rush on Regimental
Headquarters. Within 15 minutes, the place looked like a
box office at a World's series game. A line of hundreds of
soldiers trailed off from the building in which Col. Shannon's
office is established. Passes were given out with a free
hand and all afternoon time-tables were at a premium in this
camp. Everywhere, the little groups bent over schedules,
figuring out how they could make Philadelphia in time to
catch the earliest 'rattler' for home.

"The situation is paradoxical, or at least it will be
if the men who have received passes manage to find accommodations on the Pennsylvania Railroad to get them home.

"For several days, the regiment has been held up here
because there are no cars available to get it to Pittsburgh
and this cannot be done until Tuesday at the earliest.

"Yet, Regimental Headquarters conceives that these men,
turned loose, upon their own initiative, can do what all of
Uncle Sam's Generals and all of his Colonels have not been
able to do so far - getting transportation facilities to get
themselves home. However, no one is questioning the procedure. All of the Western Pennsylvanians seem to consider
themselves perfectly competent to arrange the matter. Some
of them may enter Pittsburgh by way of the 'rods' and the
'blind baggage' but everyone is happy.

"The passes require the men to be back in Camp Dix
Tuesday morning, when, as now expected, they may turn right
around and get on another train to leave this place for good.
This will enable them to stay in Pittsburgh until Monday night.

"Some of the men express doubt as to their ability to
do much marching in Pittsburgh whenever the regiment gets
there as a unit. Transportation in day coaches is expected,
and an overnight ride in a day coach, immediately after a
rush trip from camp to Pittsburgh and back, is not calculated
to put a man in the best physical condition for much hiking

over hard, paved streets.   However, they are not particularly concerned over that.

"An inrush of civilian visitors is expected here tomorrow.   The camp is kept open from 8 in the morning to 8
at night, and at least 20,000 relatives of the men detained
here are expected to take advantage of the fact.   Some of
the Pittsburghers are a little uncertain as to whether they
ought to take advantage of the pass offer or not, fearing
they might pass the home folks en route here.

"Sunday passes for men other than those who will parade
in Pittsburgh are good only until Monday morning.

"Mustering out is a slow process here.   1,200 Philadelphians were sent to the mustering out office this afternoon, but only a few got through.   The pay office will be
kept open tomorrow to hurry things along."

The Pittsburgh Post,
Camp Dix, N. J., May 4th:

"Go home clean!", Chaplains' general order to the 111th
men!   Ever since the first order to move toward home came
to the 111th Regiment a couple of months ago, the men have
been going through one course after another of instructions
preparatory to going home.   They had come to feel that going home required almost as much training as going to the
battle line, and their memory of the length of time they
spent at Camp Hancock was making them fearful.   And today
they started upon a new and most unexpected course.   It was
the course in 'cleaning mouths'.   Not with the tooth brush
and dentifrice, you understand.   This cleaning had to be
done with the aid of a bridle (to be put upon all rash
tongues) and a strong will.   The receipt was given out this
morning by almost every Chaplain of the Iron Division to the
men who came to religious services in the camp.

"The Chaplains warned them that they are going home and
they must not shock their families by 'cussing'.   And the
Chaplains mostly thought it would be a good idea to go into
training right now.   The men of the Cross admit it is going
to be a hard matter, since soldiers swear as a matter of
course, and swearing is the great indoor sport of the army.

"But the Chaplains put it right up to the men.   'What
would your people think if they heard you use the phrase
that made the Virginian so mas in the book of that name?'
And the soldiers being in chapel answered not, even though
they might have wanted to swear at that, too.

"All the men in the 111th Regiment succeeded as soldiers
and Col. E. C. Shannon, their commander, believes they are
going to succeed in private life.   That's why he's hoping
to get group photographs of all the men in all the companies
of his organization.   He wants to be able to confront pan-
handlers with the proof of their duplicity when they come
begging of him in the future in the guise of members of his
old regiment.

"The Colonel received a group photograph of Company A

this afternoon and packed it carefully away in his field
desk. 'I want to have one picture like that of every company to hang up in my office,' said the Colonel. 'Then
when the tellers of tales of woe come up to Columbia, Pa.,
they will have to pick themselves out on the picture before
they will get away with any tale about being with the 111th!'"

The Pittsburgh Post,
Camp Dix, N. J., May 4th:

"Orders came down this afternoon from Regimental Headquarters that mean the dismemberment in real earnest of the
111th Infantry Regiment. These orders instructed the company commanders to send all Western troops in their organizations to the regular camp transfer units, beginning tomorrow morning. The men will be sent from these units to
the camp nearest their homes for discharge.
"It is estimated that the order takes almost 40% of
the members away from the regiment.
"For the Western Pennsylvania men of the unit at Camp
Dix, the day brought no change. They are still booked to
entrain for Pittsburgh Tuesday afternoon and parade in
Pittsburgh Wednesday, and railroad administration officials
said the order will not be changed.
"The regiment as represented in camp today was a mere
skeleton. Col. E. C. Shannon and many of his line and staff
officers remained here, but the enlisted men streamed away
Saturday night until the passes ran out.
"Issuance of passes at the last minute is reported to
have disrupted plans for a number of men in the old 18th
Regiment. Men got passes and rushed homeward, and this
morning found their relatives down at camp hunting for them,
having passed each other in the night. The camp has been
packed with visitors all day. The weather is gracious,
much of the most pleasant day since the first of the Pennsylvania men reached Camp Dix, and every train from Trenton
or Philadelphia came to the camp station with two locomotives
tugging at its long line of coaches. Autos and jitneys also
brought load after load from nearby cities.
"There was no work done in camp and for the Pennsylvania
men there is little or no work to do. At the paymaster's
office, some of the Eastern members of the 111th Regiment
who were started through the demobilization machine Saturday
were being paid off and receiving their red chevrons."

The Pittsburgh Dispatch,
Camp Dix, N. J., May 4th:

"Part of 111th Regiment is discharged. Over 1,000
men reviewed by Colonel for last time. Leave for parades.
"Their fighting days over, their fame immortally written in history, 1,183 veterans of the 111th Infantry were
discharged here today amid scenes of romance, pathos and
patriotism marking the beginning of the disintegration of

the 28th Division.   Under orders of Major General Scott,
the Pennsylvania men were discharged as nearly as possible
in groups, according to home localities and camp headquarters,
in order that their home towns and cities may as far as possible carry out their plans for welcoming celebrations.

"For the last time, the famous regiment, made up
originally of the old 18th of Pittsburgh and the old 6th of
Philadelphia, passed in review before its beloved commander,
'Old Two-Yard" Shannon.   Ten minutes before the parting,
while waiting for the discharges, the men were not over
enthusiastic about parades, but, once out of the army, seeing their comrades marching away in delegations behind bands
from home and with the old colors flying, the jubilee bacilli
began to work.   'See you in Pittsburgh at the big shine',
was the parting greeting of many groups of discharged lads.
The Pittsburgh contingent of the 111th is scheduled to leave
on Tuesday."

The Pittsburgh Dispatch,
Camp Dix, N. J., May 6th:

"After a delay in waiting for transportation, the
Western Pennsylvania members of the 111th, being transferred
to Camp Sherman for discharge, got away this afternoon.
There are 1,200 men in the detachment which, in charge of its
old commander, Colonel E. C. Shannon ("Old Two-Yard" Shannon),
will stop in Pittsburgh for participation in a welcome home
celebration and parade.   The remainder of the 111th Infantry was discharged here Sunday.   Men from eastern counties
of Pennsylvania who remain for the divisional celebration
in Philadelphia are to be allowed to carry their complete
equipment in the parade, the War Department has announced."

We shall bring our Camp Dix story to a close by quoting two more
newspaper items - the first from The Pittsburgh Dispatch, issue of May
8th, 1919, which should be of interest to all comrades of our Third
Battalion, especially to former members of Company I of that unit.   The
article in question pays a splendid but deserved tribute to I Company's
old commander, Captain Yates D. Fetterman, and reads as follows:

"Capt. Fetterman's heroism is cited by members of the 18th.
"Discussion as to the bravest man in the army naturally
is of interest.   For the members of the 111th Infantry in
general and those from Company I in particular, there is only
one answer - Capt. Yates D. Fetterman of Mt. Lebanon.
"Not only do members of the old 18th maintain that Capt.
Fetterman is the bravest man in the army, but they also as-
sert he is the coolest and most beloved officer in the regiment.   Although the captain is a disciplinarian, all the
boys united in saying yesterday that there is no officer
under whom they would rather serve.
"Young in years, Capt. Fetterman endeared himself to
the boys by extraordinary bravery in action, while serving
as the commanding officer of Company I.   Many brave deeds

performed by this officer were told yesterday, and probably the most noteworthy is one he performed while in battle about Fismes.

"During the battle, it became necessary to carry back wounded men over a bridge across the Vesle. Every time such an attempt was made, German machine guns would open fire on the stretcher bearers. As he was an expert sharpshooter, Capt. Fetterman went to the river and single-handed kept up a rifle barrage upon the machine gun nest which enabled the wounded to be transported safely across the river. Locating the boche nest, which was situated between two poles, he would signal to the stretcher bearers and then open a fire which prevented the Huns firing on the wounded. He kept this up all day."

The second item, appearing in The Philadelphia Public Ledger, issue of May 15th, 1919, tells of the troop movement from Camp Dix preparatory to participating in the parade held in Philadelphia on the same date, and reads as follows:

"Camp Dix, N. J., May 14th - 12,000 men moved from Dix in six hours.

"Transportation of 28th here is made in record-breaking time.

"In one of the most successful troop movements in the history of Camp Dix, and the largest since the signing of the Armistice, 12,000 officers and men of the 28th Division were moved out of camp by train in less than six hours. 17 trains were needed to convey the Iron Division veterans to Camden, where they were ferried to Philadelphia. The first train left at 8 o'clock and the last at 2 o'clock. So smoothly did the military and railroad management co-operate that at no point was there a hitch or a delay in the schedule.

"An idea of the problem faced by H. E. Person, general agent of the U. S. Railroad Administration, who planned the transportation end, is shown by conditions on the single-track line from the camp. During the interim between the dispatching the 17 Iron Division trains, it was necessary to handle 18 trains in the regular traffic schedule and prepare the terminal for the reception of another big assignment of returning overseas men this afternoon. The movement of the troops from the camp to the trains was checked by Major J. J. Firestone, of the 28th Division Military Police, in co-operation with the office of Col. Harker, camp demobilization officer. Mr. Person believes it will be possible to bring the Division back to camp in the same order and in the same time. 18 trains will be used in the return movement, the returning organizations entraining at the 15th Street yards of the Pennsylvania Railroad in Philadelphia. They will be routed back over the Delaware River bridge."

CHAPTER 32.

THE TWENTY-EIGHTH PARADES:

"Today the Twenty-eighth parades -
I cannot see them through the trees.

"The trees who lift their arms in thanks
That those they love have wandered back,
And call a benediction down
Upon the ones who stayed behind
To guard the trees of France.

"The trees who through the winter days
Unbendingly present their arms,
The trees who stand so firmly there,
The thin line of eternity.
Not snow nor rain can wash from them
Their certain immortality.

"The Twenty-eighth parades today -
I cannot see them through the trees."
(H. J. M.)

To those of our comrades whose good fortune it was to have participated in parades and "welcome home" celebrations, this chapter, it is
hoped, will bring back vivid memories of two notable dates in the history
of our Third Battalion, namely, May 7th, 1919 and May 15th, 1919, on
which days the 28th Division paraded in the cities of Pittsburgh and
Philadelphia, respectively.

To those of our comrades whose bad fortune it was to have missed
these parades and celebrations, this chapter, it is likewise hoped, will
be even more appreciated and enjoyed.

While it is again necessary to resort to newspaper items in the
telling of our story, it is believed these articles can be generally
relied upon as to accuracy on facts and descriptions.   Being handicapped in obtaining data from other sources, the writer therefore feels
that in quoting the following he has truly endeavored to make the best
use of all available material and will be pardoned if the accounts lack
originality.

Complete newspaper stories   will be quoted on each of the two
parades, then account to be supplemented by items of interest pertaining,
directly or indirectly, to the celebration on the day of each review.

The Pittsburgh Post,
Wednesday Morning, May 7th, 1919;

"Both regiments will arrive here within two hours;
separate parades to be held by units this afternoon before
entraining for Camp Sherman for discharge. Whistles will
announce to eager Pittsburghers the arrival of the veterans
at East Liberty. Big reception arranged."

"Schedule of Arrivals: The two regiments will arrive
at the East Liberty Station in sections as follows:
15th Engineers
First Section.....................7:30 A.M.
Second Section...................8:00 A.M.
111th Infantry
First Section....................6:00 A.M.
Second Section...................6:30 A.M.
Third Section....................7:00 A.M."

"Mayor Declares Half-Holiday to Welcome Pittsburgh's
Heroes.

"A half-holiday in the schools and industrial and manufacturing plants was declared yesterday by Mayor E. V. Babcock, in honor of the return of the 15th Engineers and the
111th Infantry. In his Proclamation, the Mayor bids the
city be joyful and impress upon the returning soldiers the
genuineness of their reception.

"The Proclamation follows: 'The long-awaited day when
Pittsburgh would have an opportunity to welcome and honor in
large numbers her returning heroes has at last arrived.

'Back home from the fields of battle, where they covered themselves with lasting glory, tomorrow come the boys of
the 111th Infantry and the 15th Engineers, every mother's
son of them a 100% hero. Under another name, our old 18th
regiment has lived up to its glorious reputation. The 15th
Engineers also is essentially our own and represents the free
will offering of Pittsburgh and Western Pennsylvania to the
sacred cause of liberty and freedom.

'Let our welcome be enthusiastic, sincere, whole-souled
and boundless. These heroes on the field of battle, making
possible the victories achieved by the allied armies, have
been proudly acclaimed Nation-wide and have contributed much
to final victory. Tomorrow they return home in triumph.
Let us make the welkin ring with our plaudits. Let us show
by the very volume of our greetings that to them we owe a
bigger debt of gratitude than we can ever repay.

'Detailed announcement of the plans for welcoming and
honoring the soldiers of both the above units will be made
by the Mayor's Committee of Welcome to homecoming troops.
The original plans of the Committee will be carried out as
nearly as possible and the two regiments will parade separate-
ly. The first parade will leave the Mosque about 4 P. M.
and the second about an hour later, depending upon the time
of arrival of the second unit at East Liberty Station. The

regiment arriving first will be the first to parade. The
headquarters of the 111th Infantry will be maintained at
Forbes Field during the day, where relatives and friends of
the men will have full opportunity to see them immediately
after breakfast. The headquarters for the 15th Engineers
will be maintained all day at the Mosque.

'The companies will be located partly in the Mosque
and partly in Memorial Hall, according to a schedule which
will be on display. Here also an opportunity will be given
for the friends and relatives of the boys to meet them immediately after breakfast.

'Wherefore, I, E. V. Babcock, Mayor of the City of
Pittsburgh, requests that all merchants of East Liberty
close their stores during the morning hours, at which time
the units are expected to arrive; that all down town stores
close not later than 4:30 P. M., tomorrow, Wednesday, May
7th, 1919; that all schools, public, parochial and private,
close at 12 o'clock, noon, in order that our children may
have an opportunity to see these soldiers fresh from the
battle fields of France; and that so far as practicable all
employers grant their employees at least a half-holiday to
extend triumphal greetings to these returning heroes. I
urge that all residences and places of business along the
route of both the morning and afternoon parades be fittingly
decorated and that our National flag be displayed wherever
possible.

'Ticket holders for the first parade must vacate immediately after the parade passes the reviewing stand to
make room for the ticket holders for the second parade.

'Given under my hand and seal of the City of Pittsburgh this 6th day of May, 1919.'"

The Pittsburgh Post,
May 7th, 1919:

"Program for Today's Reception of Troops Fixed by
Committee.

"All difficulties in the program for the reception of
Pittsburgh's two veteran regiments were straightened out
late last night. After a conference between members of
the Mayor's Welcome Committee and officials of the Pennsylvania Railroad and telegraphic communication with Lieut.
Colonel Theo. H. Schoeff, commanding the 15th Engineers,
the final official program for the reception was announced
as follows:

6 to 7 A. M. - Arrival of the 111th Infantry at East Liberty
                Station.

7:30 to 8 A. M. - Arrival of the 15th Engineers at East
                Liberty Station.

7:30 to 9 A. M. - Both regiments march to Syria Mosque,
                where breakfast will be served.

9:00 A. M. - The 111th Infantry proceeds to Forbes Field
                for reception.

9:00 A. M. to 12 noon - Relatives and friends received by

the 15th Engineers in Syria Mosque and
Memorial Hall. The members of the 111th
Infantry will meet friends and relatives
in the grandstand at Forbes Field.

Noon - Presentation of banners and service flags to both
regiments by Mayor E. V. Babcock.

12:30 P. M. - Presentation of banner to the 15th Engineers
by the Mothers' Association, by Rev. Dr. Hugh
T. Kerr.

1 P. M. - Luncheon for both regiments at Syria Mosque.

2 to 3 P. M. - Resumption of reception by both regiments.

3 P. M. - The 111th Infantry forms in Fifth Avenue for parade
down town, passing reviewing stand in Liberty Ave.
at 4 o'clock.

4 P. M. - The 15th Engineers form in Bigelow Blvd. for parade
down town, passing reviewing stand at 5 o'clock.

6 to 7:30 P. M. - Entrainment of both regiments at Fort Wayne
Station for Camp Sherman."

The Pittsburgh Post,
May 7th, 1919:

"Route of Veterans' March Through City to Entrainment
Point;

"The Route to be followed by both the 15th Engineers
and the 111th Infantry Regiment during the parades this
morning and this afternoon will be as follows:

"Detrainment at East Liberty Station. March over the
following route during morning from the East Liberty Station
to Syria Mosque for breakfast: Penn Avenue to Whitfield
Street, Whitfield Street to Baum Blvd., to Morewood Avenue,
to Wallingford Avenue, to Neville Street, to Bayard Street,
to Bigelow Blvd. to Syria Mosque. March over the following route during the afternoon from Syria Mosque and Forbes
Field to Fort Wayne Station; Fifth Avenue to Liberty Avenue, to Water Street, to Penn Avenue, to Federal Street and
Sixth Street bridge, to Federal Street, to Ohio Street, to
Madison Avenue, and return to Fort Wayne Station for entrainment to Camp Sherman."

The Pittsburgh Post,
May 7th, 1919:

"Rain all day" gloomy prospect for celebration.
"It is difficult to understand why Kansas should interfer with the reception Pittsburgh has planned for the soldiers of her two veteran regiments, which return from overseas today.
"But Weather Forecaster, Henry Pennywitt, declares it
has. For a storm broke in Kansas yesterday and after
travelling rapidly in a Northeasterly direction, is due to
drench Pittsburgh this morning. If it does, it is not impossible that the parades will have to be called off. The
weather will have nothing to do with the receptions planned

THE PITTSBURG PRESS
FINAL EDITION

CROWDS CHEER HEROES

PITTSBURG'S VETERANS WHO HAD BIG PART IN WINNING WAR—THE OLD 18TH

CITY JOYOUSLY GREETS OLD 18TH AND 15TH ENGINEERS

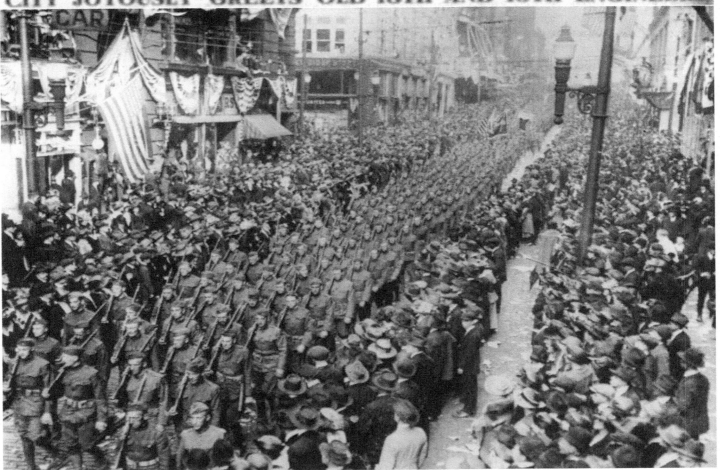

Bottom Image from The Pittsburgh Post May 7, 1919

for either regiment, however, for the 15th is to be fed and quartered within the safe retreat of Syria Mosque and Memorial Hall, and the 111th will greet its friends and relatives in the grandstands of Forbes Field, 'whence no angry downpour may reach them.'

"Little prospect is held out by the Weather Bureau for anything but rain all day today."

The Pittsburgh Post,
May 8th, 1919:

"National Guard Vindicated: Record Betters Regulars. Seven major activities bring pride to veterans. Feeling shown in flashing eyes. Only real fighters of unit parade before admirers. Vindication! Vindication and the consciousness of it - that was the motivating emotion in the heart of every man who came back yesterday with the old 18th regiment.

"It was the feeling that made them sportive and gay, certain all the while that they wouldn't lose stature in gaiety. It was the feeling that sent them tramping like the great, grim veterans they are down the streets of the city in the parade with which they blazed the trail yesterday afternoon. It was the feeling that made their eyes flash and that gave their steps spring, and that made them erect and stern when they weren't relaxed into their real boyishness. It was a feeling that seemed to give them an air of saying defiantly: "Yes***we're National Guard troops", secure in the knowledge that those regimental colors with their seven major activities inscribed are a treasure that no regulars possesses.

"They came home vindicated and they knew it. They were proud of many things, but proudest of all that they are National Guard troops.

"And Pittsburgh gave them a reception that must have torn many hearts, for it was a reception that brought out hundreds of the relatives of men who went away with the 18th and who have not come back. No one had contemplated that. It had been rather tacitly agreed that those who grieve would spend the day behind closed shutters. But they must have felt the urge of the occasion; they must have felt it a meed of honor that they must do their men, for they were there. The black bands and gold stars identified them, even if it had not been for the all-revealing abashed manner in which surviving members of the old regiment went up to these black-banded women with murmured messages and words of condolence.

"It is, above all else, a fighting regiment, and Pittsburgh yesterday saw the quintessence of its fighters. It was a kind of refined - one might say, a sifted, hand-picked - regiment that displayed itself here. Much of the chaff of replacements had been separated from the wheat of all-the-way-through fighters at Camp Dix, and almost without exception, the men who came here were the men who saw all the battles, and not those who came in at the end to 'fill up'.

"There were exactly 1,309 persons in the organization when its train pulled up into the East Liberty Station in the morning, and just about half of those were from Pittsburgh and vicinity. The others were men from the West and far West, replacements mostly, but replacements who got into the battle early and who are securely welded into the traditions of the organization. So securely welded, indeed, that they were with the old 18th because they wanted to see the home of the regiment with which they fought, and which will perpetuate their deeds.

"Those meals in the wide expanses of the Syria Mosque's dining-room; those tramps through the streets out in Oakland, and the more formal, more soldierly march through the down town and Northside sections, represent all they will carry into the future of Pittsburgh - and it is a fevered, noisy, enthusiastic and above all hospitable Pittsburgh they glimpsed. They saw more of Pittsburgh probably - at least they saw more of Pittsburgh's people - in one day than any other unit of men have ever been privileged to see in a similar period, for hundreds of thousands swarmed about them in the little more than 12 hours they were in the city limits.

"It was just a few minutes before 6 o'clock in the morning when the first train of the three sections bearing the old 18th pulled into the East Liberty Station, and the soldiers descended into a city all dripping as with a heavy dew. It was a little rain, but it was only little and the infantrymen didn't mind it. They gobbled up a hasty lunch from the hands of the women at the station, and, their second and third trains puffing in, the men lined up and started away through the shiny asphalt streets, tree-lined and wet, toward the Syria Mosque.

"Colonel Shannon and his staff was first, the band just behind them, and the fighting men back of it. The battalions and the companies were lined up by seniority of officers, and not by alphabetic succession, and the arrangement puzzled many persons who looked on. Just behind the band was the Second Battalion, in command of Major William W. Gill, the only major left in the regiment. Behind Major Gill and his staff were the member companies of this Second Battalion, with F Company first, in command of Capt. R. C. Harper; E, in command of Capt. Yates D. Fetterman; H, in command of Capt. Phelps L. Gill, and G, in charge of Capt. Richard H. O'Brien. The First Battalion, which came next, was in command of Capt. Merle A. Weissinger, and in its line were Company B, commanded by Capt. Claude Cubberly; Company C, in command of Capt. Frank C. Horner; Company D, commanded by Lieut. Ledbeater, and Capt. Weissinger's Company A. The Third Battalion brought up the rear, and was led by Capt. Thomas Bailey. At its head was Company K, commanded by Capt. Thomas Bailey; Company L, in command of Capt. Joseph Roulston; M, in command of Capt. Carroll Missimer, and I, commanded by Lieut. Harry O. Clayberger.

"In such a manner, they marched past the big automobile plant at Baum Blvd. and Morewood, where hundreds of workmen woke the neighborhood with their shouts of welcome and the shrill of their donkey engine's whistle, down the quiet leafy-laced stretch of Wallingford Street, where residents were out in bathrobes and cloth clippers to wave them welcome, and along past the institute for the blind, where a band was playing them a reception, and where hundreds of white-clad, sightless boys and girls shouted words of welcome.

"From this spot, the roof of their regimental home, the 18th Regiment Armory, was first visible again to their hopeful eyes. A little further on and they had turned sharply and were tramping down Bigelow Blvd., past the Syria Mosque. At the steps of that structure, Colonel Shannon and his staff swung out of line, the band took up its position on the grass behind, and the regiment tramped on past in informal review. Just short of Fifth Avenue, the line wheeled, the formation changed, and the men were strung out along the curbstone by platoons. With the whole regiment in place, thus, came the order to stack arms, and the men were sliding out of the 'harness', being their helmets, gas masks and ammunition belts. All these they piled upon their rifle stacks and into the Mosque they marched, by columns of twos. Parents and relatives swamped them on the street and the air was merry with the clatter of arm stacks that had been tripped up and sent sprawling. But they extricated themselves finally and made their way into the basement of the Mosque where hundreds of co-eds from Pitt were waiting to serve them.

"Breakfast out of the way, they trooped out into the street again, and stood about for a time. Then the order to march came again, and they went over Fifth Avenue and up to the rear of the old armory. Into the drill grounds they filed, and at a signal, hundreds made dives for the lone wooden bench, which stretched several hundred feet along one fence, with a shiny tin water basin, up-turned, at every foot.

"And they were home! As a regiment, they were in their regimental home, but there were hundreds of them who were eyeing it for the first time, and for whom it had no pleasant memories.

"After the washing-up ceremony, they were on the march again, this time to Forbes Field. They filed through the gateway and onto the diamond, and in an instant every man, woman and child in the stands rose as one with a glad yell on every lip. The men swung smartly down it to the home plate, swung out the path past first base, around in front of the right field bleachers, across 'the back of the field, and when the head of the line pulled up, it was down near third base again. Lined up thus, the regiment was strung out all the way around the ball park.

"They stacked guns there, and were dismissed, and ran whooping to their relatives, who stood in the grand stands, carefully sorted out by companies. The rain broke again, just then, and added to the scurry toward the grand stand. But everyone was safely tucked away out of the rain's reach, after a time, and things went on as they were supposed to have gone.

"In the stands, little family groups clustered about individual soldiers. A mother silently rubbing the wrists of her strapping big son; a father on the other side smug because smugness was all that could repress tears; and about them boisterous brothers and sisters hardly alive to the solemnity their parents sensed in the scene. Sisters and brothers, you know, can't admire silently.

"And here and there were knots of men who had no friends or relatives there - men from the Pacific coast, perhaps - who couldn't see half the jollity in the occasion, and who showed it. Its trying to be glum when everyone's joyful and all they had to do was to be glum.

"And more family groups. But they were acting like family groups. There was repression everywhere. Everyone was ill at ease. When they were talking, it was mostly about the trouble mother had getting to the right stand, and what the policeman said to father, and the wrong routes taken by this person and that. All nervousness and anxiety, and tongue-tiedness. And yet the hour was speeding nearer at which the soldiers would have to line up again and cease being sons and brothers. Besides, almost everyone was holding back tears at that session in Forbes Field, and tears held back are not conducive to jollity.

"Very near first base, the formalities started with the presentation of a khaki banner to the men of the Machine Gun Company. It had been made by Mrs. Anna Scott Massick, of 5849 Ellsworth Avenue, mother of one of the men in the regiment, James Massick, and was presented to the company by Major R. Gardener, a member of the G. A. R., after an address from the stands. The banner was received for the company by Sgt. Lewis Herron.

"A little later, a more imposing and more general presentation took place in the outfield, when a flag was presented by the city to the regiment in honor of the 518 men of the regiment who died in the service. It had a great gold star, and the figures '518' above. The entire regiment was lined up for the ceremony. Mayor Babcock, facing Colonel Shannon and his staff, told the men how proud the city is of them and their deeds and how mindful it is, withal, of the men who fell. 'I am just a soldier", said Col. Shannon, taking the banner, 'and soldiers aren't supposed to say much. But this is one of the proudest moments of my life. It is a proud moment because I am able to bring back to you these of the men who were entrusted to my care. I did not belong to the regiment originally; I came to it a stranger, and I was told that I had been given a lemon. But it wasn't a lemon, gentlemen. It proved up in the only test a soldier is expected to measure up in - the test of the battlefield. The battlefield brings out the man or the coward, and there weren't any cowards in the old 18th. They can fight - these men. And the boche knows it. Our's was one of the four divisions the boche did fear.' As he ceased speaking, the band started 'The Star Spangled Banner', and the regiment began to move out of the grounds and over again to Syria Mosque for dinner. As they went, Colonel Shannon promised that this new flag would remain with the standard of regimental colors in the possession of Pittsburgh.

"From the Mosque, the men came back as they could, one by one, to Forbes Field, where they talked for a time with their relatives. They were scheduled to move out for parade at 4 o'clock, and they moved, although it was raining harder than it had at any time during the day. And so they started upon their parade."

The Pittsburgh Post,
Thursday Morning, May 8th, 1919:

"Pittsburgh heroes get homage of thousands as they parade through streets to cheer of welcome; dead not forgotten. 15th and 18th Regiments' brief stop in city day of historic events. Happy relatives surround happier veterans until parade starts, then line streets from curb to buildings. Soldiers entrain for final camp.

"War came home to Pittsburgh yesterday - but it came in a glorified, exalted manner, highly idealized. Both the regiments which had sucked so much of the life blood of this city in their going were back, and in their coming they lifted Pittsburgh magically from the sack-cloth-and-ashes kind of patriotism to the flag-waving, cheering sort which is so typical American and so soul-satisfying to Americans. With the old 18th regiment men tramping through the city and with the 15th Engineers marching gallantly after them, Pittsburgh yesterday really learned how to wave flags - and why. In a sense, Pittsburgh really came into its inheritance; in a sense, it stood up and was among men.

"Two regiments, each with a name, 2,400 men and more, each with a record - these and all about them hundreds of thousands of humans, cheering, shouting, tearing at one another in the very madness of happiness' pinnacle, made it a day hectic with emotions. At a moment, Pittsburgh was all hands that would be clasped; again in a moment, it was all lips that would be kissed, and in the end it was all a voice that would be heard - and was!

"At 7 o'clock last night both regiments were gone, the day was but a dream, and Pittsburgh had wilted into normality again. And then, the essential characteristic of the day began to take its proper place in the minds of folks - they began to see that half its verve, half its enthusiastic madness was due to that feeling mothers and fathers had that their men really were not with them yet, that they still were going away; that the era of farewells had not passed for them, after all; that their men were still slipping away, even though they were only slipping away to real freedom and the grand re-union. They began to see that last night.

"And then the heavens, too, contributed to that atmosphere on real war that hung over the celebration. There was war in the heavens all day. Sunshine - blazing, uncomfortable sunshine - was constantly vanquishing and constantly being

vanquished by rain that was fitful and gusty and that had a
way of wafting down sometimes as if it were really regret-
ful that it had to disturb the fete. That rain really "made"
the old 18th's reception, though. There aren't a great number of men back who went away with the regiment, but there
are some, and no one of them could forget that it rained just
like that - only perhaps a little harder and a little madder -
when the regiment tramped away in August of 1917. And they
had a way of ejaculating: 'Oh, is it still raining here?'
that was very droll. They are a droll bunch now; they say
they get that from the 'Frogs'. That was all a Frenchman
was good for, you know, being droll.

"There were two other days in Pittsburgh that measured
a little up to yesterday in the wildness and unconventional
aspect of things. One was armistice day and the other was
pseudo-armistice day. Nothing else could at all compare,
and even those shouldn't be compared, for they were highly
centralized celebrations for the most part, while the excitement of yesterday ran from East Liberty in through the resi-
dent sections to Oakland, down through the heart of the
municipality, into the business section, out of it into the
warehouse district and then away over through the Northside.

"But the down town section reproduced in some measure
the fervor and noise - and the waste paper - of those other
two days. The skyscrapers were layers of human beings as
they had been at no other time except on those days last
November. The crowds were ungovernable to an extent equalled
only at that time. And, since the armistice days borrowed
their thunder from Halloween, there was a Halloween tinge to
yesterday's fete - although it was too broad daylight to be
anything like a real Halloween in anything except noise.

"And two regiments in one day had Pittsburgh buffeted
hopelessly from one extreme of emotion to the other. It
didn't have time for a reaction between the first regiment
and the second, and it was only when it was all over that it
found the manner in which piled up feelings do react when
they can. There was a pause for an hour or so between the
two great parades through the city, but an hour is insuf-
ficient and no one had lost the hoarseness of the shouting
for the 18th when the 15th swung along.

"The men - well, the men were blase, mostly. They felt
it to be their role and they filled it. Army life had a way
of making one fill one's role. They hadn't many eyes for
the sidelines and they hadn't any ears for them at all, for
it is nearly impossible to use ears for useful purposes when
folks shout as they shouted yesterday. Even bands were
idiotic luxuries that waisted breath and had no effect. All
one heard, aside from frenzied shouts, was the steady thump,
thump of hobnailed boots on cobbles.

"Such a pageant as the parade Pittsburgh never before
witnessed. It was one which brought into play many emotions,
sent newly-found sensations coursing through strong men and
weak; through sweet-faced, sobbing mothers, and through gray-
haired "dads". People clinched their jaws as the depleted

ranks of some of the companies made the mind's eye see battle-
scarred, but glorious France, where, under peaceful skies now,
the sacred dead of the sacred cause lie - 'gone west'. There
were tears and sobs mingled with the deafening cheers of welcome. There were husky voices and tear-dimmed eyes turned
toward these remaining heroes as they stepped along Liberty
Avenue before the massive reviewing stand, to the martial air
of their own 'fighting bands'. This 'ace of aces' of infantry regiments and the pioneer unit of engineers elicited
the greatest ovation the city has ever given.

"After many months of patient waiting and longing,
Pittsburgh's cup of joy at last had overflown, and the pentup feelings of thousands were spent in a wild delirium of joy,
of welcome, from these sincerely thankful and God-fearing
'folks at home'. Nor were missing soldiers of both units
forgotten. 'Don't forget a line or two for the ones who
ain't here', called a sergeant trailing behind the men of
Company D, 111th Infantry. The words were addressed to two
score men in the press box opposite the reviewing stand. Few
outside of them heard it. It was just a plain, earnest appeal from a plain and earnest soldier.

"The first parade was the 18th's. The regiment had been
lolling around out at Forbes Field and at the old armory of
the regiment all day, awaiting the command to 'march'. And
when it came, they marched, although it was raining more
fiercely at that moment than it had at any time during the
day. With Colonel E. C. Shannon marching at their head and
his staff immediately behind, they stepped out through the
driveway between the grand stand and bleachers and onto the
street, their helmets coursing with water and their uniforms
rapidly becoming soaked. And through all the down-pour,
with their women folk standing there in sorry, bedraggled
finery, they marched on, up Bigelow Blvd., past the Schenley
Hotel and then sharp left into Fifth Avenue.

"The 15th's men were at ease on the green of the Memorial
Hall and along Bigelow Blvd. near the Mosque as the infantrymen went past and they presented a more critical lot of re-
viewers than any others along the line. From the beginning,
both sides of the street were lined. There were men and
women three or four deep at every spot and the condition was
the same all down through Oakland and into Soho. That big
swing in Fifth Avenue, near Robinson Street, has a reputation
of being a certain, last-record kind of vantage point for
parades; one can always find room there on the curbstone during a parade. But yesterday the condition didn't hold.
Three or four deep was the rule all the way through there,
too, and the grass balconies about St. Agnes' Catholic Church
were crowded with humans. Behind them, and all around on
every open space there were automobiles parked and St. Agnes'
bell was swinging fiercely, in welcome.

"All the Southside seemed to have disgorged itself into
the narrow streets in Soho, and the precipitous side streets
intercepting it. And then, further down toward town, the
parade got into that intimate, gossipy stretch of Fifth Ave.

that always presents such a homey, family appearance at a
parade.   There are always little pickaninnies sitting on
the curbstones, and children usually grade up from them in
size.   And the houses are always so filled there - filled
until they seem to overflowing, with humans hanging out of
every window, and perched precariously on the ledges of the
roof.   Oh, its worth a world to parade through that section
of Fifth Avenue!

"And then the men got down into the real Fifth Avenue -
the two or three squares which are Fifth Avenue in dead
earnest.   There they lost all this intimate side of things
and came into a down town section which is just one high, impersonal voice - impersonal, although it is a hundred thous-
and personalities bundled into one.   And the voice shouted
down from the skyscrapers, and up from the curbs, and back
and forth from one building's sheer sides to the other, until
that narrow canyon was bedlam.

"Half a dozen police motorcycles, their mufflers wide
open, and burning gas in an uproarious, hair-raising abandon
of noise, came first, and everyone seemed forced to make as
much noise as the motors, and the tumult was on.   The crowds,
impatient of police ropes and chary of restraint, were bulg-
ing out into the streets.   The motorcycles rushed down and
the crowds swung back onto the pavements.   But the motors were
gone then, and the crowds were out again, out so impetuously
and in such great numbers that the men had hardly room to march.

"And the whole scene was bathed in confetti and shredded
paper.   Up in the office buildings they emptied the paper
baskets just as they did in the mad affairs of last November,
and it 'rained' - or 'snowed' paper, as you will.   On the
ledges of the roofs of some smaller buildings ambitious persons had carried great bundles of paper up, piled it carefully, just at the edge, and then with a great shove, sent
it tumbling into the street below, all at once.   And the
wind caught it and whirled it about and took it up and down
the street, to drop softly at last for blocks.

"Shouting was a rather vain performance, down there, but
they shouted.   They shouted until they found that whistling
was much better, and that cat-calls of the old gallery days
was better.   And with 20,000 men whistling cat-calls, bands
could play without their bandmasters hearing them.   They are
courageous musicians, though, and they played on through it
all.

"Diamond Street and Oliver Avenue - the two "backways"
to which all foot-traffic goes when Fifth Avenue is clogged
with a parade - were like refugee-filled roads near the front.
Everyone who had tried Fifth Avenue and had despaired of getting down there was struggling down Diamond or Oliver; and
everyone who had been down and thought they should be up
nearer Grant hill, took the same streets.   For periods
during both parades, both the streets were impassable.

"The subterfuge of taking the reviewing stands away down
to the Point to drag out the line of march and entice the
mobs away from the crowded sections of Fifth Avenue - it

succeeded alright in getting thousands away from the crowded
sections, but there were thousands more to be accommodated
than ever before, and Liberty Avenue just supplied a spot
for those extras.

"One or two office buildings along that end of Liberty
Avenue and the two railroad bridges over the street a little
further down, were just reproductions of Fifth Avenue at its
most crowded moments. And just beyond them, its thousands
of flags and banners gleaming in the sun that was getting
well down by this time, were the long stretches of grand
stands that had been erected for the veterans of other wars
and the parents of the soldiers. With its multitude of
banners and standards, it looked for all the world like a
scene into which the armored cavaliers were about to ride -
and into it the cavaliers did come.

"With thousands of people, including relatives of the
soldiers, filling the spacious reviewing stand which stretched along Liberty Avenue from Third to Water Street, the arrival of the "old 18th" was awaited. Three-quarters of an
hour before the parade came, rain fell from the overcast sky.
Instantly, a canopy of umbrellas appeared where before there
was a riot of flags, service emblems and gaily colored para-
sols. For fifteen minutes the rain fell, then, from behind
a cloud blacker than the rest, the sun reappeared, the rain
stopped, and, in the distance was heard the blare of the infantry band.

"There was scarcely a dry eye in the great crowd as the
regiment, headed by Col. E. C. Shannon ("Two-Yard-Shannon"),
passed the center of the stand where Mayor E. V. Babcock, his
welcoming committee and scores of city, county, state and
Federal Government officials were seated. Col. Shannon
raised his hand to a sharp salute. The Mayor returned the
salute and the depleted files of Pershing's 'men of iron'
passed by amid a tumult of applause.

"After passing the reviewing stand and crossing the
Federal Street bridge, the two regiments marched up Federal
Street to East Ohio Street, to Madison Avenue, to North Canal
Street, where they boarded special trains on the Fort Wayne
Railroad for Camp Sherman, Ohio. Cheers of thousands greet-
ed the soldiers on their march to the Northside.

"The 111th Infantry was the first to entrain, leaving in
three trains, at 6:17, 6:24 and 6:43 o'clock. Each train
was made up of 11 coaches. The 15th Engineers left in two
trains of 13 coaches each. The Engineers departed at 7:12
and 7:33 o'clock.

"The infantrymen, marching at first eight abreast, then
four abreast, stepped by as sprightly as they did nearly two
years ago, when they paraded from their armory in Oakland on
the first lap of their great journey.

"Numerous were the wound stripes on the fighters'
sleeves. Gold chevrons, mute evidence of some Hun weapon
or gas, shimmered in the bright sunshine of the late afternoon. Many bared their heads as company after company,
their ranks thinned - too much thinned - passed rhythmically by.

"The Engineers' regiment, Col. Theo. Schoepf in the lead, followed the "old 18th" after an interval of almost an hour. With Major Morganroth in command of the first battalion and Major E. E. Archibald leading the second, the men marched past the stand, the regiment band playing a lively march. Deafening cheers greeted them. There were calls of 'Hello, Dan!', 'Old pal George!', shrill, high-pitched voices of little girls calling 'Uncle Frank', or 'Brother', and frantic calling and waving of flags from every section.

"The men in khaki smiled broadly. They chanced an occasional glance in the direction of a familiar voice, but the straight line of men and rifles was never broken. Here and there a sister or sweetheart, braver than the rest, ran the gauntlet of jibes and calls from two solid walls of humanity to march, arm in arm, with their heroes. The scene was one that will live forever. Pittsburgh soldiers had done their share - to the fullest extent - and Pittsburgh welcomed them back in a manner that the soldiers will never forget.

"Sections were reserved in the reviewing stand for members of the Grand Army of the Republic. Three score of these veterans of the dark days of '61 - '65, watched the triumphant procession of the soldiers of today. And they cried, these veterans. They made no effort to conceal their feelings by blowing noses or concealing their bronzed, furrowed faces behind handkerchiefs. They cried outwardly, and cared not who saw them. Besides the G. A. R., there were reservations for Veterans of Foreign Wars, Boy Scouts and other military organizations.

"Nor was this event of events devoid of humor. Walking with military tread past 100 wounded soldiers from the Government hospital at Parkview, Frederick Collier, a 14-year-old Boy Scout, his breast fairly covered with Scout medals and Scout honor emblems, set the wounded heroes to cheering. They yelled lustily. They cried out, in good humor, 'Croix de Guerre', 'D.S.C.', 'Order of the Bath' and followed this by demands for a speech. The lad, turning sharply on his heel in true military fashion, saluted rigidly, smiled and marched on. While the thousands in the stand awaited the arrival of the first soldiers, a 'flivver', propelled by a dozen boys, with a very stout man at the steering wheel, made its uncertain way from Third Avenue, past the entire reviewing space to Water Street. Cheers greeted this funny entourage the whole way, and if the stout gentleman tries all the suggestions on how to fix the 'flivver' that were hurled at him from a thousand throats, he will have a lifetime job ahead of him.

"The popularity of the Salvation Army with doughboys returning from overseas was attested by the warm reception given Salvationists everywhere along the line of march by the returned heroes. Everywhere the blue poke bonnet, the peacetime headgear of the Salvation Army lassie, or the overseas cap of the Salvationists was seen, the soldiers cheered or waved their hands at the Salvationists. Everywhere before,

during and after the parade, the Salvationists were conspicuous by their ministrations to the soldiers. 10,000
chocolate bars, 10,000 doughnuts, and thousands of sandwiches and tobies were given away to the marching soldiers,
other soldiers who watched the marchers and relatives and
policemen. "

The Pittsburgh Post,
May 8th, 1919:

"Three colonels grace regiment. Only one of honors
18th brings home. Ever see a three-colonel regiment?
They're rarities, alright, but that was one of the honors
the old 18th brought to Pittsburgh yesterday. It was a
three-colonel regiment in the parade. Ordinarily, there
was just the colonel and the lieutenant colonel in a regiment. But in the 18th, there was a colonel and two lieutenant colonels yesterday. At the head of the line marched
Colonel E. C. Shannon. Behind and a little to the right
of him walked Lieut. Col. Franklin P. Haller, Jr., second
in command. And besides him, just the same chunky kind of
a man, who might have passed for his ruddy, robust twin,
was Lieut. Col. Bertram L. Succop of the Southside, who
went away from here as second in command of the regiment
and who occupied that position until almost the end of the
war. He is home now, but was down in New York at the return of the regiment, and Col. Shannon there invited him to
march with the organization."

The Pittsburgh Dispatch,
May 8th, 1919:

"Bronzed warriors of 111th and 15th take city by storm.
Conquering soldiers who fought through war's heaviest battles and brave boys who made it possible for front line men
to win are shown fitting reception here. Crowds thrill,
cheer and weep as men march by.
"May 7th, 1919, will go down on the pages of municipal
history as Pittsburgh's greatest day!
"For in all their bronzed glory, the conquering heroes
of the 111th Infantry, the "old 18th", and the 15th Engineers,
yesterday came marching home.
"While Pittsburgh did not throw itself into the wild
delirum that marked the day of the signing of the armistice,
there was a deeper and greater joy in the hearts of the
thousands at the realization of the promise of that day in
November - the promise that once more their loved ones
would be their's.
"All Pittsburgh thrilled, cheered and wept with joy
at the sight of the straight, dauntless youths who not quite
two years ago had quit the shop, the store and the office,
as Hannibal had the plow, to save the world, and had returned the greatest military men on earth.
"Shower after shower descended throughout the day on

happy Pittsburgh, but failed to dampen the ardor and joy of the homecomers or of the welcomers.

"Through the somber gray of the wet dawn, the first train of eleven day coaches of the three trains bearing the 'old 18th' crept into the freight yards of the East Liberty Station at 5:30 o'clock. The many men who were sleeping were aroused by the cries of the ones awake: 'East Liberty once more!' 'Oh, boy, home again!' 'This is the stuff!' Soon the long train was a babble of happy voices. What mattered the rain - the fatigue of a night on stiff seats - the - anything? For here was home!

"Immediately upon the arrival of the train, the whistles, bells and other means of noise of East Liberty attempted to drown out the sound vibrations of each other.

"Mayor Babcock, leading his welcome committee, greeted Col. E. C. Shannon, in charge of the regiment, who was one of the first to alight from the train. Soon the platform around the train was swarming with uniformed men, anxious to get as near the soil of their beloved town as possible.

"Brig. Gen. Albert J. Logan, who was in charge of the 'old 18th' was on hand but recognized only a few of the men as those who had left Camp Hancock two years ago.

"The second section of the train arrived at 6:00, and the third at 6:15. Came the cry from one soldier, 'Say, fellows, its raining, we won't have to wash this morning!'

"At 7:30, the great throngs that were waiting outside the depot - and had been waiting since long before dawn - for a sight of their heroes, were greeted by the never-forgettable vision of the first line of olive-drab clad men marching with quick, steady step out into Penn Avenue. A great roar of welcome arose from the thousands of throats.

"Ten minutes after the infantrymen had started their march to Syria Mosque, the first train carrying the 15th Engineers pulled into the station. Twenty minutes later, the second section arrived with Col. Theo. M. Schoepf in command. They were welcomed by the Mayor's committee, given sandwiches and coffee and in an hour had followed the 111th to the Mosque.

"East Liberty, despite the early hour, had turned out in its entirety, it seemed. From the depot to the Mosque, the roped-off sidewalks were lined with cheering, waving thousands. At Penn and Highland Avenues, girls in white dresses scattered roses before the marchers. Hundreds of school children lined the streets. The parade was led by motorcycle and mounted police. The first soldiers in line were members of Company F, the greatest losers in the regiment. Everywhere from East Liberty to East Ohio Street, Northside, the streets were ablaze with color - American flags, service flags, bunting and the gold and black of Pittsburgh.

"At Syria Mosque, the men were served with a breakfast, according to their testimony, reminded them not at all of trench 'chow'. The meal was served by co-eds of the University of Pittsburgh.

"Following breakfast, the Engineers visited with relatives and friends in the Mosque, while the lllth marched
to Forbes Field, where they were given a great ovation.
Shortly after their arrival on the field, one of the day's
spasmodic rains began and continued for thirty minutes,
driving most of the men under the grandstand.

"When the rain ceased, Mayor Babcock made the official
speech of welcome and presented the regiment with its service flag from the city. A short time later, he presented
a service flag to the Engineers.

"Mrs. S. E. Maxwell, president of the Mothers of the
15th Engineers, presented the Engineers with the colors and
a banner from the mothers. Following luncheon in Syria
Mosque, there were further receptions by relatives of the
soldiers.

"The sun came out during the middle of the afternoon
and added to the monster crowds that lined the path of the
two parades. The infantrymen began their march at 4 o'clock
and the Engineers at 5. Never have such throngs - wild with
joy - witnessed a parade in Pittsburgh.

"But the showers continued to run true to form and
shortly before the infantrymen reached the down town district,
a quick, snappy rain brought tens of thousands of umbrellas
into play. The great reviewing stand, with the raising of
the protections against the storm, seemed to suddenly become
transformed from a background of many colors into a black
sheet.

"The line of march was Fifth Avenue, to Federal Street,
to Madison Avenue, where the men were entrained for Camp
Sherman, where they will be discharged.

"Long before the hour appointed for the lllth to leave
Syria Mosque for the parade down town, the reviewing stand
at the foot of Liberty Avenue was filled with relatives of
the boys and members of military organizations. A cordon
of police was thrown about the huge bleachers which extended for nearly three squares along Liberty Avenue, and no one
was admitted who could not show the white card which was
distributed among the near relatives of Pittsburgh soldiers.

"And a happy, good-natured crowd it was. Surely, there
were a few clashes and now and then Evelyn told Grace that
she might at least take off her hat, or quit punching her in
the ribs with that swagger stick that Henry sent from Paris.
And so if things didn't go just the way they should, if the
parade was a little late coming and if it did rain a little
now and then, it failed to put a damper on the crowd.
Everybody who wore any kind of a uniform was cheered.

"About a half hour before the parade was due, wounded
men from Parkview Military Hospital took their places in the
stand. As they marched past, cheer after cheer swept the
crowd. Here were the men who had given their greatest
possession - health - for their country. They returned the
ovation with salutes and smiles, although some of them were
scarcely able to walk.

"Salvation Army lasses passed doughnuts to soldiers and

sailors in the stands and were given a great hand.

"At 4:45, the official reviewing party, headed by motor-cycle policemen, drew up in front of the official box and were escorted to their seats in front of the Mayor's welcoming committee. Included in the official party were: Gen. Albert J. Logan, former commander of the 56th Brigade and also former colonel of the old 18th; Mayor and Mrs. Babcock, L. H. Burnett and other executive officers of the welcoming committee; the nine Councilmen; Mrs. B. L. Succop, chairman of the 18th Regiment Auxiliary Association; Mrs. S. E. Maxwell, chairman of the Mothers of the 15th, and E. A. Hess, chairman of the Fathers of the 15th.

"When it became known through the crowd that the boys were on the way, there was a rush for vacant seats in the stand. A locomotive pushed two passenger cars onto the trestle running parallel to Liberty Avenue and these were soon filled. An enterprising Negro, whose home fronted on the line of march, hung out a sign which read: 'Window Space - 50 Cents'.

"At 5:05, the cry went up: 'Here they come!' and a min-ute later the mounted policemen who formed the vanguard of the procession arrived opposite the stands. Closely following them came Col. E. C. Shannon and his staff, followed by the regiment's famous band, more than half of its members bearing wound stripes. Then came the men, as fine a body of troops as Pittsburgh as ever seen. They plainly showed the effects of travel and loss of sleep, but determined to look their best before the home folk. They marched with snappy step and heads erect.

"As company after company passed, the joy of the crowd knew no bounds. Men and women laughed and cried at the same time. Emotions such as they had never experienced swept over them. As some of the companies appeared, people clinched their jaws tightly, for it could be plainly seen that there were many missing from the ranks. And it brought to mind the long lists of casualties.

"Here and there a sad-eyed mother or father could not keep back the tears. Their son had marched away with the regiment which was before them but had been left behind on some shell-torn field of glory and would never march beside his comrades again. But the joy of the occasion could not be forgotten and they smiled and cheered through their tears.

"During the intermission between the parades of the 111th and the 15th Engineers, Loyds' band entertained the crowd and a singers' club armed with megaphones sang popular airs. Ap-peals also were made in behalf of the Victory Loan.

"When the Engineers appeared, a little after 6 o'clock, the stirring scenes of an hour before were repeated. It would be hard to say which regiment made the best appearance or received the greatest welcome. Both of them are Pa Pitt's own boys and he was just as glad to see one as the other. The 15th marched in column of squads and wore their overseas caps instead of the steel helmets which the men of the 18th wore.

"As each regiment came abreast the part of the stand oc-cupied by veterans of the Civil War, the officers came to

salute and the men were given the command, 'Eyes Right!'
The boys of '61 returned each salute and one of them called
out, 'I'd a-been with you, boys, if it wasn't for this
rheumatiz!'.

"At the end of each parade were automobiles driven by
members of the Women's Motor Corps and filled with wounded
members of the regiments. They were received with wild acclaim and were showered with candy and cigarettes from the
crowd. They all seemed mighty glad to be able to appear with
their own organization even if they were not able to march
beside their pals.

"Organizations represented in the reviewing stand were:
The Army & Navy Union; Veterans of the Spanish-American War;
Veterans of Foreign Wars; Mayor's Welcoming Committee; returned veterans and wounded men, relatives of the 15th and
18th regiments and Civil War veterans.

"Employees in the Imperial Power Building, just back of
the stand, kept up a continual shower of paper which blew over
the crowd and into the ranks of the men as they passed.

"Down town hotels were filled yesterday and last night
with out-of-town people who had come to welcome the boys.

"The Chestnut Street Pennsylvania Railroad yards, where
the two units entrained last night after the parade, was the
scene of merry leave-takings - merry because all the boys
were sure 'We'll be back, discharged, by Sunday.' The first
section of the "old 18th" pulled out for Camp Sherman at
6:30 o'clock; the others followed at intervals of 10 minutes.
The first Engineers' train left at 7:07, and the second, 10
minutes later."

The Pittsburgh Dispatch,
May 8th, 1919:

"Greet heroes of 18th. Dense masses throng line of
march as old guard parades. Ovation tremendous. Wild enthusiasm shown all along route. Men leave for camp.

"Here they come!" The cry flashed up the path of march,
heralding to unnumbered thousands the approach of Pittsburgh's
legionnaires of the former Pennsylvania National Guards, who
yesterday were blessed and wept over in one of the most
tremendous demonstrations ever accorded a victorious army
home from the wars. As the majestic, measured march of the
glorious 'old 18th' swept over the streets of Pittsburgh
yesterday, the emotion of the city's soul was wrenched from
the hearts of its citizenry.

"From the moment the boys arrived yesterday morning at
the East Liberty station, until they departed last night from
the Federal Street station, the chord struck was invariably
intense. Never before has Pittsburgh seen the like of the
procession yesterday afternoon down Fifth Avenue. Shortly
before 4 o'clock, the city was waiting, while in Forbes
Field the bayonets of a 'red' regiment of infantry were
glinting. The command to move was given and the troops
marched off in a shower. The bands struck up and the old

18th marched down Fifth Avenue with rain beating on tin
hats. Then the shower ceased, the sun came out on a happy group of soldiers, their kin and their multitude of welcomers.

"At Fifth Avenue and Lothrop Street, an overseas in-
valid was waiting. A mother murmured over a tear on her
boy's face as he jerked a shattered arm to proud salute, as
the regimental colors passed. From that point down to the
reviewing stand, countless individual welcomes were extended to the men.

"These individual occurrences were the bright spots in
the ovation. Pathos entered when Gen. Albert J. Logan, with
tears in his eyes, hurried to find Col. E. C. Shannon, commanding the regiment, as the first train drew in. Major
J. L. Weldin and Capt. Cain, invalided officers of the regiment, were at the station and Capt. Cain was the first man
to alight, having journeyed in with the men.

"At 9:55, assembly was sounded. The regiment, led by
its own band of 32 pieces, moved from the grounds. The
musicians, 30 of whom were wounded or gassed in action as
litter bearers at Courlanda, confined themselves to light
selections. The only time The Star Spangled Banner was
played was when the regimental service flag was presented
to Col. Shannon.

"The next halt was made in the enclosure of Forbes
Field, where the previously packed stands roared out a
greeting of good will. After deploying about the field,
the command was permitted the freedom of the field until
luncheon. They threw their packs to the ground and ran to
the stands, becoming immediately the centers of family reunions.

"The men of the regiment, not natives of Western Pennsylvania, and who had been added as replacements to the
111th, betook themselves to the players benches and some
stretched on the grass to rest.

"The continued their visit with relatives until 1:15
o'clock, when recall was again sounded and the men scamper-
ed out upon the ball field to their location of their
respective companies, for the flag presentation.

"A few minutes later assembly was sounded. The companies were arranged facing Mayor Babcock and his welcoming
committee. Col. Shannon and his staff stood in front of
the troops.

"With the Mayor when the presentation was made were
Gen. Logan; former Mayor Joseph G. Armstrong; Murray Liv-
ingston; L. H. Burnett, chairman and members of the Mayor's
committee.

"The Mayor was introduced by Chairman Burnett, who extended to the soldiers the 'glad hand of welcome' and told
them jow proud the city was to welcome them. 'Actions
speak louder than words', he said, 'and the people of Pittsburgh have already shown you what they think of you and will
show their appreciation further in the parade which will be
held this afternoon.' Carrying the flag of red and white

silk, upon which was inscribed the numerals '518' and a single gold star, to represent that number of men who had died while in the service of the old 18th, Mayor Babcock said: 'My heart is full of patriotism and appreciation for what you and your brave men did in France and I hardly know where to begin or end. It has been a long time since Pittsburgh has had a jollification that can be compared with the return of you soldiers. Today, Pittsburgh is in the midst of her glory. We welcome you with outstretched hands and we are grateful to you for what you have done for us in the World War. Pittsburgh today bids you welcome. We know no creed, color or nationality. You have been fighters in every sense of the word, and you soldiers, all brave and strong, are welcome home.'

"The Mayor then stepped forward and placed the flag in Col. Shannon's hands, saying: 'There are 518 gold stars represented on this flag - 518 brave Pittsburgh and Pennsylvania men who made the supreme sacrifice somewhere in France. Somewhere in France are 518 little white crosses. These boys cannot be here, but we reverence them and will thank them forever. Mr. Commander, I present you with this service flag. Let me congratulate you very cordially and present you with this flag in behalf of Pittsburgh - one of the greatest cities in the world!'

"With moistened eyes, Col. Shannon accepted the flag and said: 'I am just a soldier - one of the boys. Today is the proudest moment of my life. Today, Mr. Mayor, I bring back to you what remains of the old 18th regiment, heroes and soldiers, every one of them. When I took this regiment over, prior to leaving for France, I was a stranger and was told that I was getting a "lemon". But today, I can say, there was no more formidable fighting machine in the army - in France - than the old 18th. War is the crucial test which brings out whether a man is a coward or a hero. These boys went through this war and there was not a coward among them. They were all soldiers and all men.' Col. Shannon then turned the flag over to acting Color Sergeant Jack Laudny, who carried it on parade.

"Following the flag presentation, the men were marched in formation to Syria Mosque, where they had their second great meal of the day. As the men finished their lunch, they were permitted to leave, and returned to Forbes Field singly and in groups. There they visited their relatives for about half an hour and said their goodbyes - until they return from Camp Sherman.

"At 3:30 o'clock, assembly again was sounded and the men fell in wearing their trench helmets and with fixed bayonets.

"And then came the down-pour. Despite the seeming obstacle on the part of nature, the parade of the 18th was one the like of which never before was seen in the streets of Pittsburgh. Along the route from Syria Mosque to the reviewing stand, the streets were packed with people who cheered and yelled and laughed and cried as the remnant of the old 18th passed. The crowds stood on both sides of the streets, completely filling both sidewalks.   Along the route, the noise from the welcoming throngs was deafening and at times was so great as to drown out the music of the regimental band.

"At the head of the column was a cordon of mounted police, and a short distance behind them, marched Colonel Shannon and the members of his staff. Following these came the 111th band, and behind this were the soldiers of the First Battalion, the Second Battalion, the Third Battalion, and the Medical Company.

"Oakland's reception to the parading heroes was the noisiest which they had yet encountered. Men, women and children crowded the streets, and their shouts and yells, together with the horns, whistles and other noise making apparatus, made a volume of sound which had never been been heard there.

"As the troops passed by McKee Place, a woman rushed to the street and strewed American Beauty roses and other flowers in their path.   The hill leading to Mt. St. Mary's Academy was crowded with school children, nuns and others who witnessed the parade from the heights. As the head of the column passed by St. Agnes' Church, and entered Soho, the bells in the church were rung, and continued to ring until the last man in the parade had passed. Soho's reception to the boys was characteristic. The crowds grew thicker, and the noise increased. Youngsters, perched high on the many bill-boards, created terrific din by kicking their heels against the signs. Individual shouts of, 'Hurray for Mickey!' and 'Go to it, long boy!' and many other like phrases were numerous. Jitney Park attracted the attention of all the soldiers in the regiment who lived in Soho, for there they beheld the service flag erected in honor of the men of the district in the service, and read their own names inscribed on the honor roll.

"The crowds in lower Soho, in and about Brady Street, were rivaled only by those in the down town section of the city. They over-flowed both sidewalks to the street, and all the side streets were packed.

"A wonderful scene was presented as the men swung past Brady Street and up the hill to Miltenberger Street.   By this time the sun was shining, and the reflection of its rays upon the rain-moistened bayonets and steel hats made them glisten like diamonds.

"The marchers received their first baptism of confetti as they passed Washington Street, where girls from the upper windows of the Washington Trust Company threw down to the street bushels of small pieces of paper which drifted about through the air like falling snow flakes and lingered upon the hats and shoulders of the men.

"A bit of realism was added as the troops passed Grant Street. A machine gun, mounted upon a Victory Loan float, spat forth its deadly rattle with blank cartridges as Col. Shannon and his staff went by, and the firing continued until the termination of the parade.

_____ "The greatest crowds lined both sides of the street from Grant down Fifth Avenue to Liberty Avenue.   Every window, in stores, hotels and business houses was filled with girls, who dropped confetti upon the soldiers in such quantities that a veritable paper storm raged.

"The band played as it marched down to Liberty Avenue but it was impossible to hear any of the instruments save the bass drum because of the pandemonium which reigned. Although Col. Shannon marched with military dignity over the entire route, he could not prevent a smile as he passed Smithfield Street.   Many of the other officers also wore grins as they swung in Liberty Avenue, so that it was quite evident that Pittsburgh had been successful in its attempt to provide a fitting welcome for the old 18th.

"After they had passed to Liberty Avenue, the men were marched in platoon formation.   This was continued until the men arrived in front of the reviewing stand, when the command of 'Right, by squads' reverted them to squad formation.

"After passing the reviewing stand, the parade continued to the Northside, where the old 18th bade au revoir to Pittsburgh until it returns, no longer a military unit, but a body of civilians."

The Pittsburgh Dispatch,
May 8th, 1919:

"The command of the 111th as it arrived here yesterday is as follows:
          Colonel E. C. Shannon
          Lieut. Col. Franklin P. Haller, Jr.
          Major W. W. Gill
          Capt. M. A. Weisinger, Company A
          Capt. Claude Cubberly, Company B
          Capt. Frank Horner, Company C
          Lieut. Leadbeater, Company D
          Capt. Yates D. Fetterman, Company E
          Capt. Wm. W. Harper, Company F
          Capt. Richard H. O'Brien, Company G
          Capt. Phelps L. Gill, Company H
          Lieut. Harry O. Clayberger, Company I
          Capt. Thos. Bailey, Company K
          Capt. Jos. Roulston, Company L
          Capt. Carroll Missimer, Company M
          Capt. Wm. P. Snow, Headquarters Company.
          Capt. R. Wainwright, Machine Gun Company
          Lieut. John Braun, Supply Company
          Capt. Bulger, Sanitary Detachment
          Capt. Henderson, Regimental Supply
          Lieut. J. S. Anderson, Gas Operations
          Capt. Richard Spurr, Personnel Adjutant.
          Capt. J. A. Dickson."

The Pittsburgh Dispatch,
May 8th, 1919:

"Commander of the 111th gives Shannonisms -
"The boys we left in the soil of Northern France will
never be forgotten! How we love them!
"These lads I bring to you are wonderful; they con-
quered death by their audacity, and life by their heroism.
I offer an appeal to honor. These boys will soon be among
you, and they will need that job. He is a scoundel who
fails the chance to 'stand by' such men as these. We've
soldiered hard; our only regret is for our comrades who
passed. What have I been thinking of in France? - of this
day!"

It is believed that the above-quoted newspaper articles cover, generally, the parades of the 111th Infantry and the Engineers held in the
City of Pittsburgh on May 7th, 1919. From them, it is believed that all
comrades who participated can very easily reconstruct the stories to con-
form to individual experiences of that day.

We shall now proceed, in like manner, to cover the Divisional parade held in the City of Philadelphia on May 15th, 1919.

Before quoting stories of the parade itself, it may be interesting
to glance over some of the many headlines and short news items appearing
in the Philadelphia papers at the time.

The Philadelphia Public Ledger,
Tuesday Morning, May 13th, 1919:

"City in readiness for last parade of Iron Division.
Plans complete in each detail. Muir and staff arrive tomorrow morning. Trains from Camp Dix leave every 20 minutes.
Arrangements include breakfast for men, baseball game and
freedom of city."

The Philadelphia Public Ledger,
Tuesday Morning, May 13th, 1919:

"Losses of the Iron Division, 17,771 officers and men.
Lieut. Col. Clement, assistant chief of staff of the Iron
Division, yesterday announced the official casualty figures
on the entire division. They were sent to him from Washington. The figures are as follows:

Killed in action...............	62 officers;	1,761 men
Died of wounds.................	36 officers;	671 men
Died of disease................	6 officers;	200 men
Deaths from other causes.......	5 officers;	110 men
Total loss by death............	109 officers;	2,742 men
Missing and prisoners..........	1,174 officers; and men	
Severely wounded...............	114 officers;	3,704 men
Slightly wounded...............	190 officers;	5,861 men

Wounded, degree undetermined...   92 officers; 3,785 men
Total wounded...................   396 officers; 13,350 men
Grand Total, dead and wounded..   505 officers; 16,092 men
Grand Total, all casualties....17,771 officers and men."

The Philadelphia Public Ledger,
Wednesday Morning, May 14th, 1919:

"City in gala attire for 28th's welcome. Peerless is
delayed. First units arrive this morning headed by General
Muir and staff. Day of freedom here precedes great parade.
State pours its throngs into city to honor its warriors to
morrow."

"Probably fair for parade. Probably fair Thursday is
the forecast of the Weather Bureau for the day of the parade.
It will be fair today, according to the forecast issued at
Washington last night."

"28th to cross river on special ferry. Trip from Camp
Dix to be made on 23 trains, each carrying 750 soldiers."

"Don't throw souvenirs during the Iron parade! Major
General Muir, commander of the Iron Division, requests that
no souvenirs or food be thrown to the men while they are
marching tomorrow. The parade will be conducted along
strictly military lines. The men will march at attention.
The General says that under these conditions nothing thrown
could be picked up by the men. The showering of the men
with flowers, however, will not interfer with the marchers.
General Muir also requests that the men be unmolested by relatives as they march. All those who watch the parade are
asked to keep within the lines and not to rush to any of
their loved ones as they pass."

"Women preparing for Iron parade. Various organizations
will care for marchers from start to finish. Few will be in
line. War workers have completed plans to care for men who
made history."

"Paraders will hear own songs as they march. Bands and
thousands of voices to help them keep step while they pass in
review."

"Official Time Schedule of Iron Division Parade. The
official schedule of tomorrow's parade, as compiled by Lieut.
Col. Chas. Clement, assistant chief of the 28th Division
staff, is as follows:
        10:00 A.M. - Leave Broad & Wharton Streets.
        10:20 A.M. - Broad & Chestnut Streets.
        10:35 A.M. - Independence Hall.
        10:50 A.M. - City Hall.
        11:20 A.M. - Parkway and Spring Garden Street.
        11:36 A.M. - Spring Garden and Broad Streets.

12:10 P.M. - Broad and Diamond Streets
12:30 P.M. - Shibe Park.

"This schedule is based strictly upon the hope that the parade will move with precision and allows for no delays. Col. Clement estimates it will take the soldiers an hour and three-quarters to pass a given point."

The Philadelphia Inquirer,
Wednesday Morning, May 14th, 1919:

"Gov. Sproul declares holiday for great parade. City tense with excitement as hour for pageant draws near. Fear expressed that 108th Artillery may arrive too late to participate."

The Philadelphia Inquirer,
Thursday Morning, May 15th, 1919:

"No rain to mar parade, weatherman's promise. Cloudy, but no rain. This is the prediction that the weatherman had on tap last night for parade weather today. He said we were going to get rain, but like a cheerful soul he also added that it would hold off until after the parade anyway. 'Its raining now', he concludes, 'as far north as Norfolk and as far east as Chicago. We are going to get it tomorrow sometime, but not until somewhere around night-fall.'"

"Route of Keystone Division Review. The route of today's great parade follows: Starts Broad & Wharton Streets, North on Broad to Chestnut; East on Chestnut to Third; North on Third to Market; West on Market to City Hall; out Parkway to Spring Garden; East on Spring Garden to Broad; North on Broad to Lehigh; West on Lehigh to Shibe Park."

"Philadelphia A-Thrill with Excitement. Opens its gates to heroic sons who await their triumphant march. 18,000 men of Iron Division to march in parade. Heroes to pass shrine of liberty which they fought to maintain in lands across the sea. Memorial wreath for every county in State to commemorate those who died."

"All parts of State send visitors here for today's parade. Many thousands of pilgrims arrive to honor Keystone fighters. Prominent officials head home town delegations; many reunions. Iron Division units arrive in city for their final review."

"Horrors of ghastly conflicts on blood-stained fields of France forgotten as smiling heroes march through applauding throngs preparatory to receiving homage of Philadelphia today. Coming trains crowded with thousands of up-State folk bent on witnessing greatest military demonstration ever staged in this city; program opens with dinner to Gen. Muir."

Evening Public Ledger

VOL. V.—NO. 208.   Published Daily Except Sunday.   PHILADELPHIA, THURSDAY, MAY 15, 1919   Entered as Second Class Matter at the Post-office at Philadelphia, Pa.   PRICE TWO CENTS

IRON DIVISION MARCHES IN WELCOME-HOME PARADE
THROUGH DENSE HUMAN LANES EIGHT MILES LONG

Hilarious Crowd Numbers 2,750,000, Says Mills; Thousands Jam Central Part of Town

Throng in City Streets Largest in Its History

Climb to Roof Tops and Windows to Greet Boys; Blaze of Color Waved on Every Hand

Philadelphia became a joyous, hysterical, seething mass of men, women and children today when hundreds of thousands strong the people voiced a hearty "welcome home" to heroes of Pennsylvania's own Twenty-eighth Division.

It was the largest body of persons ever assembled in this city to view a parade, according to William B. Mills, assistant superintendent of police, who estimated their number to be 2,750,000.

Under the guidance of song leaders, they sang and cheered as the khaki-clad fighters strode by. From pure happiness they wept and with tear-dimmed eyes, they stood with bared heads as the draped casket, drawn by six white horses, saddled and with the stirrup guards turned backward, passed in the rear of the procession.

Then they "fell in" behind the soldiers and marched to Independence Hall, singing and cheering, and passed reverently before the Liberty Bell, jamming the streets and holding up traffic, but venting their praise in no uncertain manner.

Every nook and corner along the line of march, balconies and windows in the big office buildings, grandstands and roofs of houses, were crowded with the happy faces of a grateful people.

They came from every section of the city, the state and from New Jersey. They pushed and shoved each other on the streets and tried the patience of the police, home guards and military police, but no one seemed to care about personal discomforts—not even those who were drenched through the carelessness of the driver of an automatic sprinkler-cleaner. To see, to hear, to cheer, were their only objective.

Fully 100,000 persons massed the central section of the city around the City Hall and its approaches and down

Chestnut and Market streets, when the signal to clear the traffic from the streets was given at 9 o'clock. They had been assembling singly, in pairs and groups along the ropes since early morning. They clung to their places like glue and it was only after much arguing and gentle persuasion that those who gripped the ropes at the street corners relinquished their holds long enough to permit others to pass through.

Nearly 150,000 persons came from New Jersey, ferry and railroad officials estimated. Camden ferryboats were jammed to capacity throughout the morning hours. A steady stream of men, women and children poured into the ferry house at Market street, and the Camden police formed them in long lines, which extended back more than a square.

As soon as a ferryboat was loaded to capacity the sale of tickets was stopped until another boat came in. Every extra boat on both the Pennsylvania and Reading ferries was in use to handle the crowds.

Size of the Crowds You Were Jammed In

Total of Spectators

2,750,000—Estimate of Assistant Superintendent of Police Mills.
1,000,000—Estimate of Governor Sproul.
100,000,000—What it seemed like to some of us.

Where Crowds Were Thickest

Broad and Wharton streets, 8000.
Broad and Chestnut streets, 10,000.
Sixth and Chestnut streets, 2000.
Broad and Market streets, 10,000.
Broad and Spring Garden streets, 9000.
Broad and Diamond streets, 8000.
Broad street and Lehigh avenue, 7000.

GENERAL MUIR IN FINAL REVIEW OF HIS FIGHTING DIVISION

At Broad and Diamond streets General Muir left his place at the head of the line and watched his boys go by in farewell review.

"Mayor and Governor extend greetings of city to Gen.
Muir. Families of soldiers will be cared for. 'The City
is your's", Mayor tells Gen. Muir as men cross river."

"Units in Parade - Order of March. The units in the
parade, the order in which they will march and their strength
follows:

Unit	Strength
Major Gen. Chas. H. Muir, with the 28th Division Headquarters, the Headquarters Troop,	300
55th Brigade	
Headquarters Troop, Capt. Paul E. St. Clair, commanding,	23
110th Infantry, commanded by Col. Jos. H. Thompson,	3,630
109th Infantry, commanded by Col. Wm. R. Dunlap,	700
56th Brigade	
112th Infantry, commanded by Col. Geo. C. Richards,	
111th Infantry, commanded by Col. Edw. C. Shannon,	
109th Machine Gun Battalion, commanded by Major John W. Foos,	
108th Machine Gun Battalion, commanded by Major Louis Waters,	775
107th Machine Gun Battalion, commanded by Major C. M. Smith,	500
53rd Field Artillery	
Brig. Gen. Wm. G. Price and Headquarters Company,	64
108th Field Artillery, commanded by Col. Frank Lecocq,	1,676
109th Field Artillery, commanded by Col. E. St. John Greble, Jr.,	1,605
107th Field Artillery, commanded by Lieut. Col. A. V. Crookston,	1,542
103rd Field Signal Battalion, commanded by Capt. Ralph W. Knowles,	
Auxiliary & Supply Units	
103rd Engineers, commanded by Col. Frederick A. Snyder,	1,764
103rd Field Signal Battalion, commanded by Major Thos. P. Rose,	467
103rd Train Headquarters, commanded by Col. M. E. Finney,	34
103rd Ammunition Train, commanded by Col. H. A. Williams,	1,194
103rd Sanitary Train, commanded by Lieut. Col. Wm. E. Keller,	871
103rd Supply Train, commanded by Major Jas. B. Wheeler,	479
28th Division Military Police, commanded by Lieut. H. A. Butz,	165
Casuals and demobilized men,	2,000"

The Philadelphia Public Ledger,
Thursday Morning, May 15th, 1919:

"Iron Division will parade today, reviewed by loved ones amid cheers for their gallant deeds. Men who whipped Germans in many battles throng streets after welcome by Mayor and admiring thousands of Pennsylvanians. Troops from all over nation in line of march; citizens of all sections here for welcome. Procession moves promptly at 10 o'clock from Broad and Wharton Streets. General Muir to head troops. Everything in readiness for event. Joyous crowds welcome the 28th. Festive spirit pervades city as thousands pay homage to Iron Men. A great big welcome greets the arriving heroes of the Iron Division. Tremendous crowds welcome the 28th. Cots untouched as 28th's friends keep them busy until 'wee sma' hours'."

"Partly cloudy today, forecaster predicts. Clouds may overhang the Iron Division parade today, according to the official weather predictions from Washington. But it probably will not rain. The reports say that it will be partly cloudy today and tomorrow, without much change in temperature. Geo. S. Bliss, local weather forecaster, predicts, however, that the parade probably will not be marred by rain."

"The Gist of the Parade:
Starts from Broad and Wharton Streets at 10 o'clock.
Ends at Shibe Park about 12:30 P. M.
19,000 men, the majority of whom were former Pennsylvania National Guards, will march.
Street traffic in parade streets and nearby suspended from 9 A. M. to 4 P. M.
All street cars re-routed during the parade hours which ordinarily would touch parade streets.
18 First-aid stations at convenient points.
Persons holding grandstand tickets should be in their places as early as possible because of the crowds.
400 cheer and song leaders will keep the crowds in good spirits while waiting.
20 bands and 40 string orchestras will be stationed at various points.
Gov. Sproul will pass the crowds lining the streets, starting from Broad & Huntingdon Streets at 9 o'clock.
The Governor and Mayor Smith will review the parade from a stand erected in front of Independence Hall.
Major General Chas. H. Muir will hold his final review of the division as it passes Broad & Diamond Streets."

"Dinner honors Muir. Price to head Guards. Invitation to lead State troops extended by Gov. Sproul at Banquet to commander of the Iron Division."

"Police mobilized to guard throngs. Officials enroll 5,500 men to handle great rush of parade visitors. Will divert trolley cars. Other traffic to be halted along route. Emergency stations provided."

"Women preparing parade details. Additional comfort stations to be opened to accommodate review crowds. Lodgings are in demand. Red Cross Canteen Bureau orders provender to feed Iron Division troops. Rigid traffic rules during today's parade."

"$2. for each Iron man. City to distribute money to soldiers for meals today."

"Old home sights warm hearts of native sons in 'night of joy'. Minute-late friends fail to meet boys billeted on City Piers."

"Old Liberty Bell moved out to greet State's heroes. Late yesterday afternoon, the great symbol of American freedom was placed in front of Independence Hall, where it may be seen this morning by the marching men of the Iron Division as they pass the cradle of the liberty for which they fought in France."

"Chief of Staff says all Americans are proud of the 28th.
"To the Editor of the Public Ledger:
"The parade of the 28th Division in Philadelphia on May 15th, calls to mind the unusual service of this splendid body of men. The Iron Division was preeminently a fighting division, having spent 80 days in line, and 49 of these, or considerably more than half, in active sectors. It suffered heavier casualties than any other division of the army drawn from the original National Guard, and among the divisions that served in France its casualties were fourth in number, being only surpassed by the First, Second and Third Divisions of regulars. 58 of its members were awarded the D. S. C. for exceptional gallantry. It was one of the four National Guard divisions selected for the First Army of Occupation; and the divisions chosen for this purpose were from the most effective.
"The 28th Division returns to its native state with a record which has caused its numerical designation, 28, to be retained as one of the numerical designations of the permanent divisions which it is hoped to establish for the regular army. Its record is not only a matter of pride to Pennsylvanians - all Americans are proud of it.
"(Signed) P. E. March, General, Chief of Staff."

"28th Division's valiant sacrifices upheld best traditions of the Keystone State in fighting on the Marne, Ourcq, Vesle and in the Argonne Forest in four months battling. Smashed to pieces time after time, Pennsylvania's sons never faltered until victory rested upon their banners. Heavy losses exceeded only by regulars of first three divisions."

"Nearly three score of Keystone officers and privates have been decorated with the D. S. C. or medals from the U. S. - French, English and Belgium also have decorated these gallant soldiers for their valor against great odds. Infantry, artillery, ambulance corps and staff officers are included among those so honored. Many of 28th given medals for bravery. Soldiers of the 28th Division, men who came from every section of Pennsylvania, won some of their honors by fighting their way through a hail of shrapnel or bombardment of shells to rescue comrades or obtain objectives. The official citations of these men show heroic deeds which write glorious history for the State."

The Philadelphia Press,
Thursday Morning, May 15th, 1919:

"Heroes of 28th who have won the D. S. C. Iron Division men to get award for valor - 111th Infantry:

Capt. Chas. C. Conaghty, Taunton, Mass., for going out into 'no man's land' with a rescue party and saving four wounded men in the vicinity of Crezancy, July 17, 1918.
Capt. Robt. S. Cain, Pittsburgh, armed with revolver, led an attack on the enemy in the woods near Fismes.
Capt. Edmond W. Lynch, deceased, Sharon Hill, went to the rescue of two platoons which he saved but lost his life.
Capt. Thos. Bailey, 5325 Lena Street, Germantown, made a hazardous reconnoissance under terrific firing near Fismes, September 4, 1918.
Sgt. Thos. Cavanaugh, Pittsburgh, for remaining in action after being wounded at Fismes, August 11th and 12th, 1918.
Corp. Robt. R. Riley, Chester, for extraordinary heroism at Fismette on August 10, 1918.
Corp. Raymond Peacock, Norristown, handled machine gun with wounded arm in volunteer action, taking Fismette, August 10.
Corp. Jay Dunlap, Company L, for rescuing wounded comrade, East Pittsburgh.
Pvt. Harry F. Carnahan, Company M, for carrying wounded comrades over a shelled bridge, Birdville.
Pvt. Jos. A. Dunn, Company K, for capturing four machine gun men, 2721 George Street, Philadelphia.
Pvt. Wilson H. Leiter, Company M, for rescuing wounded under fire, Harrisburg.
Sgt. Elmer I. Eppiheimer, Company I, although thrown from a bridge into river, delivered message to battery telling them that barrage was falling short. West Chester.
Pvt. Wm. J. Nixon, sanitary detachment, rescued wounded at Fismette under fire, 2324 Waverly Street, Philadelphia.
Corp. Edw. J. Jordan, Company M, rescued wounded under fire and was slightly injured, 4511 Merion Ave., Philadelphia.
Sgt. Elmer F. Woomer, deceased, Company M, led attack long in advance of men and was killed. Myerstown.
First Sgt. Thos. Gaddis, Company K, killed two machine gun crews with grenades. Oil City.
First Sgt. Albert Schad, Company L, oak leaf to be worn with D. S. C. for several heroic actions in exposing himself to fire to save men in Argonne, 6416 Saybrook Ave., Phila.

Sgt. Alfred Stevenson, deceased, Company C, carried messages through fire and went to rescue of comrades and was
Killed. Linwood.
Sgt. Edwin Macbeth, Company C, rescued two soldiers under
fire. Pittsburgh.
Corp. Wm. Shane, Company I, for dragging wounded officer to
safety under fire. Pittsburgh.

"It is believed that there are a number of others not
yet mentioned, as regimental commanders have 'put in' for
numerous other heroic acts on the part of their men."

The Philadelphia Press,
Thursday Morning, May 15th, 1919:

"17,000 men of 28th take city by storm for parade today. Paeans of cheers greet first regiment and 109th Infantry in preliminary march. Mayor greets Muir. Tells
General soldiers own city. Troops to have dinner at Shibe
Park, then leave for Camp Dix. Surging mass of humanity
packed streets in central part of city until midnight.
Great congestion along Broad Street from Chestnut to Spruce,
where merrymakers formed in endless procession, all intent
on maintaining the carnival spirit. Reception to city's
boys delight to General Muir. Major General Chas. H. Muir
went to the Union League and sat down to rest after he and
his division had been welcomed and been given not only the
freedom of the city but the city itself yesterday morning.
'Our welcome was all that we could have expected', he said.
'I am immensely pleased with it.' An expectant look came
into his eyes as he mentally looked forward to today. You
could see that what was in his mind was that his boys would
go through their peace-time parade with the same eclat with
which they went through their wartime fighting. 'I hope
it don't rain', he said. His 'statements' are notoriously
far from voluminous. 'The Division has done some of its
best work in the rain', interjected Major Edward Hoopes,
the General's aide. 'Of course, we'll parade if it rains',
the General said. 'Its now or never. But it will be so
much better if it doesn't rain!' General Muir re-empha-
sized his caution to the public not to push in on the parade, or to throw food, gifts or souvenirs to the soldiers.
They must march at attention.

The Philadelphia Press,
Thursday Morning, May 15th, 1919:

"Order of March of Today's Parade:

        Police Escort
        Cortege in Honor of Dead Division
             (15 min. interval)
        Police Escort
             (50 yds.)

The Commanding General
        (20 yds.)
Division Staff
        (10 yds.)
Enlisted Personnel
        (10 yds.)
Headquarters Troops
        (50 yds.)
55th Infantry Brigade
        (30 yds.)
110th Infantry Regiment
        (30 yds.)
109th Infantry Regiment
        (50 yds.)
56 Infantry Brigade
        (30 yds.)
112th Infantry Regiment
        (30 yds.)
111th Infantry Regiment
        (30 yds.)
107th Machine Gun Battalion
        (30 yds.)
109th Machine Gun Battalion
        (20 yds.)
108th Machine Gun Battalion
        (30 yds.)
53rd Field Artillery Brigade
        (30 yds.)
108th Artillery
        (30 yds.)
109th Field Artillery Regiment
        (30 yds.)
107th Field Artillery Regiment
        (20 yds.)
103rd Trench Motor Battery
        (30 yds.)
103rd Engineer Regiment & Engineer Train
        (30 yds.)
103rd Field Signal Battalion
        (30 yds.)
103rd Train Headquarters
        (20 yds.)
103rd Ammunition Train
        (30 yds.)
103rd Sanitary Train
        (20 yds.)
103rd Supply Train
        (20 yds.)
28th Military Police Company
        (50 yds.)
Wounded Division in automobiles
        (50 yds.)
Nurses - Base Hospitals Nos. 10, 20, 34 & :
        Navy Base No. 5.

```
            Ambulance Corps
              (30 yds.)
          Platoon of Mounted Police."
```

The Philadelphia Inquirer,
Friday Morning, May 16th, 1919:

"All Philadelphia pays tribute to its soldier sons.
Great wave of patriotism overwhelms city as residents vie
with one another in rendering homage to men who won im-
perishable fame on Europe's battle fields.   Enthusiasm of
spectators tempered by undertone of solemnity as tragic sacrifices of great war are recalled.   Gen. Muir, with misty
eyes and husky voice, bids boys goodbye.

"Berry-brown and stalwart, and every inch the fighting
men from overseas caps to hobnailed shoes, the heroes of the
28th Division marched in review here yesterday before two
millions in the glory and tumult of a demonstration that
seemed to shame Niagara to an echo and beat Vesuvius to a
whisper.   Eight miles long stretched this great multitude
into whose hearts swept these khakied legions with the same
irresistible force that had carried them victorious through
the lines of old Hindenburg.

"Anguish-laden months and the year-long vigil by the
homes and firesides of the Keystone State had harnessed this
tornado of acclaim against the day when the serried ranks of
veterans would come marching home to the homage of those in
mufti who had fought their fight as well.   So, when this
majestic, supreme moment arrived yesterday, the great heart
of this wonderful throng turned to pour out a diapason of
welcome that rolled down upon the tramping hosts, a vast,
torrential flood.

"Even this great jubilee in honor of the achievement of
the victorious legions which filed past in sprightly style
and military precision could not mask entirely a deeper note
of solemnity.   Many in the stands and along the sidewalks
realized the supreme sacrifice that had been made by men of
this division, and recalled, with poignant sorrow and grief,
the 4,025 who are sleeping now under the soil of France,
martyrs to liberty.

"The memories of this tragic sacrifice tempered the enthusiasm of these spectators, and even restrained their
shouts as the memorial float came along in the wake of these
dun-brown ranks, symbolizing the thoughts that permeated many
of those who witnessed the wonderful occasion.

"So, while the cheering and the tumult multiplied in
many places, in others it was chained by a somber realization
that silence could best pay tribute to the immortal dead.
Especially was this true of the crowds that circled about
Independence Hall, where the Liberty Bell stood, silently
watching over these men who had carried her message to a
higher and a greater purpose since it first proclaimed the
birth of the Nation.

"The crescendo of this ovation, however, was reached in

the Parkway, where many of the relatives of the boys in line assembled and where the wounded heroes of other divisions added their voices to the affection and the enthusiasm that were lavished on these serried legions. Bands blared their music, cheer leaders awakened the stands to fresher and more frequent tumult, while sounds and music burst upon the air, like some festival prepared for a Roman general back from his journey of conquest into other lands.

"Along Spring Garden Street, too, there was no diminuation of this massive, magnificent outpouring. The Girls' High School, at 17th Street, had mobilized its fair students into a singing host robed in white, surrounded by a beautiful tableau of 'Peace and Victory'. Miss Edith Brandt was America, Miss Katheryn Alexander was Brittania, and the other nations of the Allies were represented as follows: Italy, Miss Esther Sideman; Belgium, Miss Helen Crowley; Serbia, Anna Manley; France, Helen Snyder; and Victory, Miss Dorothy Yockel. The Misses Katherine Toy and Margaret Coyle appeared as the Keystone girls.

"Broad Street, from Spring Garden to Lehigh Avenue, was a continual babel in which shrieking whistles and ringing bells blended with the human agencies that were voicing their homage and love in a perpetual din. From Broad Street to Shibe Park, where the parade was dismissed, the same roar of acclaim was fostered, every throat seemingly united in the business of pushing out all the noise of which it was capable.

"Major General Charles H. Muir, a fine upstanding warrior, had ridden his charger at the head of the men he had led to glorious achievement and undying fame, prouder than any centurion of ancient Rome. As division commander, however, he found the dying minutes of the review the hardest he has experienced in all his splendid career. For, at Broad and Diamond Streets, this grizzled warrior, a Michigan soldier by birth but a Pennsylvanian by adoption now, said farewell to the boys who had emblazened the fame of the Keystone fighters in the shot heard around the world at Chateau Thierry, Fismes, and other memorable battles. With eyes a trifle moisty and voice a bit husky, he uttered his valedictory in the silent salutes he gave to the marching hosts that passed.

"The tremendous throng marshalled here, like some wondrous army of Pilgrims marching toward a sacred shrine, descended yesterday upon the city from every nook and cranny in the Commonwealth. Pennsylvania had declared a holiday for her people to voice the jubilation and thanksgiving that permeated the state because the boys were home from the war; back from the world's mightest conflict with their deeds written in the history of a nation to the everlasting glory of their home state, and with their courage and bravery and fortitude stamped indelibly on the annals of time.

"The Governor of the State came down to witness the legions march past him in stately review. Mayors of the various cities appeared in the grandstands to view this triumph of the sons of their municipalities. Churchly dignitaries and civic fathers dotted these places of prominence to see the splendid spectacle, while the mothers and the fathers and the sisters and the brothers came down to show the world how proud they were of every son and brother in the ranks. Plain patriots, with no kin carrying tin hats in this parade, came out, too, inspired with zeal, to split their throats and rack their nerves telling the martial pilgrims that the people who stayed behind were mighty proud of the crusaders from over seas.

"Over this multitude, too, bristled the pride that the millions all felt in these splendid, brawny lads in khaki. They could recall the time, not many years back, when such a spectacle would have fostered the ribald jest or the covert sneer about the 'tin soldiers'. They could recall, with some sorrow, some with shame, and others with anger, a time not so distant when the National Guard on parade could provoke only the compliments of their kinsmen, rather than the whole-souled approval of the City and State.

"But all that was forgotten, obliterated in the triumphs won by the magnificent fighting men who marched along under slanting gray bayonets, as unconcerned as if they had never helped to humble the Hun or had played little part in the great task of making the world safe for democracy. Under the thunders of the mighty ovation, too, the minds of the multitude harked back to months before.

"They could remember how these battalions had departed as boys, sailing away on transports under the cover of night, with no cheers for their god-speed or no maternal kiss for a blessing. These proud mothers and fathers remembered, too, how their lads, mere boys, had gone on that great adventure with a smile on their lips, the spirit of bravado with which youth always welcomes trouble or embraces the chance for a scrap.

"Thus they had left their homes, their firesides, their shops and factories, farms and mills. They had departed on their pilgrimage to dedicate their bodies and their lives to the principles which were proclaimed at Independence Hall nearly a century and a half ago, and had left, sublime in their courage and brave in their faith. They had gone ready to suffer, to fight and to die for the precious heritage of carrying the torch of liberty overseas, and to hold high the banner of freedom from the ruthless hands of tyrant or autocrat who would snatch these precious symbols of democracy from the pedestals to which they had been raised. But, despite the splendid motive which had called them over the seas, they had been simply boys to those who stayed behind. Boys, whose mothers still regarded them as children and whose fathers might still have a lurking suspicion that the sons could still be amenable to the paternal strap.

"Now they were back and they were MEN. Iron men, the grateful French called these Pennsylvanians as they saw the dash and the courage with which these mere striplings taunted death in the hell of Chateau Thierry or the inferno along the Vesle. They bore back, too, the emblems of their bat-. tle scars in the wound stripes emblazoned on the sleeves of their tunics. Boys they had gone and veterans they had re- turned. They had won their laurels against the pick of the flower of the German army, and, as the vast multitude realized this historic spectacle in the light of the suffer- ing and the sacrifice their lads had endured, a mighty sob welled up in its throat to choke back for an instant the cheers that leaped to its lips.

"None of this sentimental and emotional urge that swept the stands and the sidewalks was pictured, however, on the faces of these serried legions that plodded along the route. They seemed to stand invulnerable against the roar of the cheers that broke against their ears like the bombing of the surf. Their eyes usually were carried to the front and were not tempted to stray by the rustling of the gigantic forest of flags that danced and nodded from every window, every hand and every available spot along the eight miles of par- ade.

"If their eyes revealed anything, it was the frank dis- play of feeling that, after the sufferings they had endured, the wonderful roles they had played, this march of peace was an anti-climax. They were glad to pass in dun-brown ranks before the idolatrous gaze of the boy, the worshipful ad- miration of girls, the tears of mothers and the smiles of fathers, but for the martial heroes this day held no person- al meed of military glory.

"However, if the millions caught a glimpse of these innermost thoughts that swayed the doughboys, it was sub- merged and lost in the tumult evoked by the spectacle. No mortal agency could still this acclaim, but a mute symbol that passed on its sorrowful way could instantly bring these millions to a hushed and reverent silence.

"At the end of the column, its approach heralded by a dirge from naval buglers, was the cortege to the memory of the immortal dead who had laid their lives on their country's altar and made the supreme sacrifice for liberty. Six milk- white horses, riderless and led by six doughboys, drew the caisson, still bearing its sign of battlefield days in the gaudy and incongruous camouflage on its body and wheels.

"Wreaths had been laid upon a great silken banner that swathed the harsh body of the gun-carriage, and beside the float strode the escort of honor, eight heroes whose breasts were adorned with the D. S. C. Behind this little pro- cession marched a flag-bearer and two aids, bearing aloft a service flag of blue silk, circled with tiny gold stars. Near the pole were the numerals '4025' to designate the heroes who gave their lives while fighting with the division. As soon as the plaintive, mournful notes of the bugle floated to the throngs, women wept and men instantly bared their heads in tribute to the gallant boys who are keeping the eternal bivouac of the dead, 'somewhere in France'.

"This note of sadness, however, was the single thread of sorrow that worked into the warp and woof of the jubilee.

To the city at large, it was the occasion for general thanksgiving, the day when all the dammed fervor stored all these months of wearied waiting was to flow at flood-tide. The center of the city was buried in bunting and peopled by such a tremendous throng that the spectators were lined one row upon the other from the curbing to the edge of the structures that bulwark the end of the sidewalks.

"Few spectacles staged in this cradle of the Nation have attracted such a magnificent throng. There were hundreds who maintained a vigil all through the night in order that they might keep their right of squatter sovereignty intact over some precious spot on Broad or another desirable street. Some of these were girls, dressed in their Sunday best, who spread newspapers on the sidewalks and sat upon them.

"Mothers trundled babies in arms or in go-carts through the vast crowds until they reached some place where they could see these heroes on the march. The main thoroughfares were simply black with the crowds, but the magnificent spectacle was the Parkway. Here the great stands, erected to house the mothers and fathers of the soldiers and the notables of the civic world, were densely packed. Flags of the Allies fluttered in the breeze and stood like great, trembling pickets against the rear of the wooden structures. The old reservoir looked like some great bare mountain crag which had suddenly bloomed and blossomed into a great human garden. Thousands upon thousands of spectators stood or sat on this bluff at the Parkway, gazing down the magnificent vista that stretches before the eye to City Hall.

"This dense crowd packed dozens deep was mottled here and there by the khakied uniforms of soldiers or scouts, while the adjacent buildings were packed in every window and on every roof with its denizens. Amateur steeplejacks climbed to the tops of little towers or tanks, there to enjoy in solitary grandeur the splendid spectacle as it was unfolded to their vision.

"Even the air held its vantage point for several fortunate individuals. A great captive baloon was sent toward the skies, so constructed that it looked like a huge pachyderm trying to stand on its head. Beneath floated a wreath encircling a red keystone with '28' inscribed in white numerals upon the crimson field.

"Young America thrilled to the sight of real soldiers, heroes of battle and conquerors of the Hun, on the hike. The idolatrous youngsters crowded to the ropes, and in some cases the boys, and often the little girls who came with them, were barely more than two or three years old. One of these virtual babies had his toes tramped upon when a Park guard, with more energy than ability as a horseman, rode upon the child's foot in pushing back the throng.

"However, the real envy of all the school boys who saw Johnny come marching home was Ernest Nolan, 12 years old, of 1750 Water Street. He became a member of Battery F of the 107th Field Artillery yesterday, although he wasn't enrolled and he was not included in the original personnel. But

Ernest marched, just as he told his ma he would several
weeks ago. 'I thought I would turn out with the boys',
said this shaver, 'so ma bought me this uniform and I sewed
on the red keystone. Don't keep me any longer as I have to
stick with these fellows.' Luckily for the paraders,
Ernest was the only pioneer of this sort among the small
boys, or else the line of march would have been augmented by
every kid in the city.

"Picturesque in their faded suits of blue and the caps
of '61, were numbers of Grand Army men who camped in their
chairs at City Hall, watching with filling eyes these stalwart young soldiers march back in triumph as they had done
in the wonderful days after they had saved the Union.

"One veteran, however, refused to sit on the plaza, so
he hiked to the Parkway where the wounded heroes were seated
before the grandstands. He was David Gower, of 1425 North
Marston Street. As bugler of Troop F of the 7th Pennsylvania Cavalry, he had marched with Sherman to the sea, and
hap collapsed while marching in the triumphal procession
fifty odd years ago at 7th and Walnut Streets. He has two
grandsons with the A. E. F. and in their honor he informally
adopted all the maimed boys gathered about him.

"These wounded, too, as they rolled along at the rear
of the cavalcade in automobiles, received a handsomer
ovation than their buddies who were trudging along on foot.
The sight of these wounded heroes seemed to stir every
patriotic impulse to even stronger emotions, and as they
came along, the stands rose to their seats in one vast
mighty welcome.

"The weather man proved his veracity by keeping the
day free from drizzle, and even the sunshine came out the
barrage which a cloudy day laid down in the heavens. The
millions were orderly and made no attempt to violate the
instructions of General Muir and the police, and, because
of this orderliness, there was no trouble. And this had
no small part in making the review the greatest and most
noteworthy spectacle of a military nature ever held in the
city."

The Philadelphia Public Ledger,
Friday Morning, May 16th, 1919:

"Joy fill hearts of 2 million spectators as 19,000 men
of Iron Division pass in review. People from every corner
of State swell mighty chorus of cheers as greetings to greatest parade ever seen here. Scores of motors carry wounded
showered with flowers along the line. Perilous service of
Keystone Division is shown by wound stripes on arms of
brilliant fighting men. Dogs of war, too, wear wound bars.
Eight in march wear D. S. C. Well and disabled meet first
time since battle. Pupils of Girls High School at 17th and
Spring Garden Streets stage Victory tableau while parade
passes. General Muir reviews troops for last time. 'Best
reception ever', is General Muir's verdict.

"Proudly, the old commonwealth of Pennsylvania yesterday took into her arms the boys of the 28th Division and furtively brushed away her tears. If there was sorrow, it was hidden. Instead, there was a great welling up of joy that quite filled the hearts of the 2,000,000 spectators along the eight and one-half miles of march from Broad and Wharton Streets, up Broad, down Chestnut, up Market and out through the magnificent Parkway, and then up Broad Street and out to Shibe Park on Lehigh Avenue.

"Hello, Johnny", "Yea, Bill", "Oh, Frank" and "there goes Freddy" echoed and re-echoed in a great paean of delight from thousands of voices in every square, from the throats of all sorts and conditions of people from every corner of Pennsylvania, swelled in a mighty chorus that left no doubt in the minds of the marching men that their folk were indeed happy beyond all reckoning to see them.

"The ominous black silk band with the gold star was missing. There were those who said that the mothers, the fathers and the widows had left the emblem of sorrow at home that they might not lessen the happiness of those whose sons had been spared. But undoubtedly there were many bereaved parents who lacked the courage to look upon the mates of their sons, remaining away from the scene of joy that might have rasped their wounded spirits.

"And in the long line that took nearly two hours to pass any point, there was only a single somber note - an impressive one, to be sure, but only one. This was the cortege at the very end of the procession, a cortege made up of an ammunition wagon drawn by six milk-white stallions saddled in bright new leather, empty, and flanked by eight heroes, who each wore the D. S. C.

"Immediately preceding them, however, were four score automobiles that carried the wounded. They were the life of the party, as one spectator remarked, and the broad grins that spread over their faces told the crowds that the disabled wanted no sympathy.

"Roses and carnations and flowers of many hues were pinned to the khaki and the soldiers were as happy as a child with a new toy. These boyish veterans were not used to wearing flowers and many a quip passed along the line as they pinned them on their coats.

"It was a reunion, too, between the well and the disabled as the motor cars passed along, for the wounded had not seen their old messmates since the fighting abroad. Pvt. Smith had been wounded in the Argonne, say, and had gone back to a casualty clearing station and hospital, while his fellows had pressed on to Varennes. Yesterday they met again and the encounters were touching.

"The main body of the marchers comprised rank after rank of infantrymen and artillerymen, the old National Guard of Pennsylvania. In the line were the 110th Infantry, made up of the old 10th, of Greensburg, and the 3rd, of Philadelphia; the 109th, including the old 1st of Philadelphia, and the old 13th, of Scranton, large detachments of the 111th and the 112th, taking in, respectively, the old 18th, of Pittsburgh, and the old 6th, of Philadelphia; and the 16th of Oil City, and the 8th, of Harrisburg. Following them came the 107th Artillery, the 109th Artillery, the 103rd Engineers, the 103rd Sanitary Train, the 103rd Signal Corps and the various ammunition and supply trains.

"All these had seen real service in France and the wound stripes - one, two and even three - on the right forearm showed that the service had been perilous. On the left arm an unusually large number of single gold stripes, each for six months' service, signified that the division had gained many replacements, men who had taken the place of Pennsylvanians who had been put out of action.

"Another sign that the 28th Division bore less resemblance to the old National Guard that had taken part in the Mexican affair, was signified by the scarcity of Mexican campaign medals - bronze with a blue ribbon. There were many, of course, who had taken part in that expedition, but the absence of a large number was full of meaning.

"The well-remembered jaunty step that always marked the Keystone National Guard was not there either. To the military experts this must have been a disappointment. To the people who lined the streets and filled the grandstands, however, there was no disappointment, for every one knew that parade marching is not learned on the battlefield, and these soldiers had spent their time in fighting and not in parading fancy evolutions. It was a sturdy step, a strong step and one that had shown itself quite competent enough to catch goose-stepping Germans.

"Each soldier wore his overseas cap, set at a rakish angle. There was jauntiness in this that spelled defiance and a devil-may-care spirit fully in keeping with what the 28th Division did. On the back of each man was the trench helmet, each marked with the scarlet keystone that the general staff said the division should wear to mark out for all these Pennsylvanians' bravery.

"The first ovation for the khaki clad came from the South Philadelphians. They were particularly interested in the old 3rd Regiment. Every man, woman and child in that section seemed to be there and those who were not were in the big grandstands along the Parkway. But of that more later. The crowd down town was cosmopolitan and the greetings were directed more especially to Tony and Isadore and Stanislaus.

"Then as the troops moved northward, the character of the crowds changed. People from other sections had taken up places of vantage, obeying the suggestion of Police Superintendent Robinson that people should avoid Chestnut Street as far as possible.

"At Washington Avenue, girls employed by A. B. Kirschbaum occupied the windows, and their enthusiasm found an answer in quick glances from the soldiers, who tried hard to be soldierly and friendly at the same time.

"With Spruce Street passed at a rapid march, the spectators became more numerous, and as the marchers swung into Chestnut Street, they walked between solid walls of people ten and twelve ranks deep. Some spectators had spent the night here, sitting on newspapers on the sidewalks. Many had brought their breakfasts, and discarded paper lunch boxes littered the pavements.

"Light marching order had been prescribed, the soldiers wearing the canteen, an emergency kit and a poncho. Each infantryman carried a rifle, as did the Engineers and the members of the trains.

"Of music there was little in the procession itself. The military bands played stirring marches, but the greater part of the melody came from the bands stationed in and under the grandstands. Sometimes these well-meaning musicians threw the marchers out of step and there was considerable merriment then.

"Ten minutes after 10 o'clock, Major General Charles H. Muir, astride Minstrel, the blooded horse loaned for the occasion by Miss Constance Vauclain, raised his hand. Sharply the word of command passed down the ranks from Colonel to Major to Captain to Lieutenant to Sergeant, and the parade was under way. Broad and Wharton Streets was the starting point. A slight mist hung over the marching men as they moved forward. This was dispelled within a few minutes, however, and perfect weather conditions marked the parade until the last of the men were filing into Shibe Park at the finish, when the clouds again gathered. But, no rain fell.

"Through a veritable babel of songs and shouts that echoed through the canyon formed by the high buildings, the division advanced rapidly to Independence Hall, turned into Third Street and then into Market to the City Hall.

"At the northeast corner of the Municipal Building was a group of Civil War veterans, men who marched in 1865, when the glorious Pennsylvania regiments came back. They were old men, to be sure, but the sight of their sons and grandsons brought back the memory to them, and these veterans, looking through spectacles that recalled the past vividly, stood up and cheered. The khaki-clad lads looked to the left, half saluted and smiled. The veterans of the old and the veterans of the new had established a bond of comradeship.

"Then the regiments turned into Arch Street and out the Parkway. Here a stage had been set for the most dramatic scenes of the day. High in the air reared the big grandstands where sat the relatives of the young men marching below them in the street.

"Cheer leaders raised their megaphones. There was a scream of delight from the stands that magnified into a tremendous roar as the first lines of the old 3rd Regiment came opposite. The up-state regiment, the old 10th, of Greensburg, passed with a scattering round of applause. These soldiers naturely were not interested in the Philadelphia stands and the Philadelphia stands were not interested in them - that is, not as a mother is interested in her son.

"But when the 3rd came, there was a shout and the lads under the jaunty caps looked up. Eager eyes from the stands scanned the faces of the soldiers. Eager eyes from the ranks scanned the faces of parents, wives and sweethearts. Then from the stands came the cries of recognition. From the ranks came an answering nod - nothing more for had not the General ordered that this be a military parade?

"Then came the Scranton contingent. No interest on either side of the high walls of the stands was displayed. But when the old 1st appeared, there came a repetition of the scenes that had marked the appearance of the 3rd. And so as each Philadelphia unit came into sight, there followed the same rejoicing. It was a great day for those in the stands, it was a great day for those who marched on the pavement.

"By this time, however, the rigors of the march began to tell. Here and there a man dropped out and stretched himself out on the earth in front of the grandstands.

"A great observation balloon of the army began to rise as the first of the line appeared on the Parkway and remained in the air the whole time of the parade, commencing the descent as the last of the parade, the cortege, passed into Spring Garden Street from the Parkway.

"So the men marched and marched. It was getting to be more and more difficult for them, and as they passed the combined stands of the Southeastern Pennsylvania Chapter of the American Red Cross, the Emergency Aid and the National League for Women Service, there were audible remarks from the women that the men looked real tired.

"Occasionally, an up-state soldier would ask a Philadelphian how far it was to this place called Shibe Park. But men stuck and the withdrawals were few.

"At 17th and Spring Garden Streets, the pupils of the Girls' High School had arranged a striking tableau which they called 'Peace and Victory'. Winsome school girls posed on the steps. Miss Edith Brandt was America, Miss Katheryn Alexander was Brittania, and the other nations of the Allies were represented as follows: Italy, Miss Esther Sideman; Belgium, Miss Helen Crowley; Serbia, Anna Manley; France, Helen Snyder; and Victory, Miss Dorothy Yockel. The Misses Katherine Toy and Margaret Coyle appeared as the Keystone girls.

"Up Broad Street the division proceeded and the joy of the South Philadelphians as revealed by the citizens of the lower part of that thoroughfare was repeated by those living on the northern section of the street. Many small grandstands had been erected in front of residences and other structures. The smallest grandstand in the city was in front of the Central High School, where two women had an observation platform all to themselves.

"Some of the fore-handed Electrical Bureau men, who were posted on little platforms on poles, had invited their wives, and from these observations had an excellent view.

"The dogs of war, the various and varied pups that acted as proud mascots for the soldiers, began to show signs of
fatigue as the parade approached Columbia Avenue and the
soldiers lifted them up in their arms. Each dog wore a
khaki blanket and one of them bore two wound stripes.

"But as Diamond Street came nearer, the dogs were made
to shift for themselves onntheir own feet, for it was here
that General Muir reviewed the troops. The fine old commander watched his men pass before him for the last time and
the General, once credited with being an inflexible martinet,
wept!

"Spread across the street was a banner, 'Welcome, Second
Artillery', but the old 2nd was still at sea on the transport
Peerless.

"Then came the long last mile to Lehigh Avenue and then
west to 22nd Street to Shibe Park, where the welcome dinner
had been prepared.

"With exclamations that clearly indicated approval that
the last lap of the parade was in sight, the doughboys rushed
for their meal. It was a perfect end to their parade.

"Captain William B. Mills, assistant police Superintendent, who is an excellent judge of the size of crowds, estimated that 2,000,000 spectators viewed the parade. He had
2,240 policemen to guard their safety, and, aided by the
military police, the Home Defense Reserve and the Fairmount
Park guards, the captain kept perfect order.

"As the crowds walked homeward and the parade was over,
one thought came to the minds of all - seconded by the
19,000 men who had just marched - and that thought was -
'Thank God, we're all home again!'"

"Major General Charles H. Muir, in response to questions,
made the following farewell statement to Philadelphia last
night: 'It was the most enthusiastic, unanimous, direct-
from-the-heart reception of fighting men I have ever seen
given or ever expect to see given. I do not expect to retire until I am compelled to do so - by old age or otherwise.
My orders take me to the port of embarkation at Hoboken for
duty in command of Camp Merritt.'"

The Philadelphia Press,
May 16th, 1919:

"Mighty 'Iron' Men Hailed by Populace as Valiant Heroes.
State Guardsmen went to war with little acclaim, but receive
high honor on return. Multitude pays tribute.

"They drifted into the armories of Pennsylvania before
the great mass of the public realized the United States was
in war; before a word was breathed about conscription; even
before there was much talk of pro-Germans and pacifists.
They entrained for a southern camp in the presence of small
gatherings of weeping relatives. They were gone - Pennsylvania's volunteers - and almost unknown, almost unremembered
by all except those under their own rooftrees, they drilled,

they froze, they became hardened soldiers.

"Later still, when the people of the United States had
commenced to apprehend that there were a couple of million
boys in France, there came back from the European battle-
fronts meager news of the dauntless, unrelenting feats of
the 'Iron Division', the 28th Division, the Keystone Volunteers, Pennsylvania's National Guard, and the men who joined
it promptly and instinctively because they were the most
genuine sort of patriotic Americans.

"The war came to an end soon after that.   It was said
that it came to an end because the Prussians could not stop
the 'mad Americans' who dashed back their vaunted Prussian
Guards, who ignorantly took 'impregnable' fortifications,
who threw themselves recklessly into withering tempests of
fire and steel where the Germans thought no man could live,
and therefore no man could come there to conquer them.

"The casualties were published and the public of Pennsylvania - not those who bowed their heads in sadness for
kinfolk dead - but those who hardly knew there was a 28th
Division - raised their heads with pride because it was
learned that a Pennsylvania division had so distinguished
itself that none but the regular army divisions, who had
been in France a longer time than any, could approach the
total of men who had given their lives to whip the Hun.

"Then the men who had drifted to the armories, and who
had been virtually smuggled from the cities of Pennsylvania
to their southern training camp, commenced to return to this
country.   Casuals with red keystones on their shoulders
came off transports in groups of 25 or 50, and people in
Philadelphia actually asked what the red keystone meant.
They were told very proudly and very emphatically.   It was
noised about that these lads with the red keystone were the
men of the Iron Division.   They were the men who, individually, had captured or killed scores, hundreds of boches.
They were the Pennsylvania Keystone Volunteers.

"And so yesterday, when those who had arranged that the
division, or what remained of it, filled out here and there
with replacements from Oregon to the Philippines, should be
assembled at Broad and Wharton Streets, there turned out into the streets of Philadelphia an army almost as large, perhaps larger, than the army of Americans which was in France
when these Keystone men arrived there.

"The very skies seemed filled with people, who came
from all parts of Philadelphia and from hundreds of cities
and villages throughout the State, to tell the Keystone
volunteers that at last all Pennsylvania knows them, that
all hats are off and all hands are raised in salute to the
worthiest men and boys in the whole great Commonwealth.

"At about 7 o'clock the multitude commenced to range
itself over the eight miles of parade route from Broad and
Wharton Streets to Shibe Park.   By 9 o'clock, people were
standing in lines two and three deep over this entire line,
although it was to be after 1 o'clock when the first soldier

should reach the end of the distance. By 10 o'clock, over the major portion of the route the throngs were so dense that only slow progress could be made along any of the side-walks. And when the parade actually had started, those who were away from their front doors, if these doors fronted any-where along the route, might as well have given up any hope of seeing the interior of their homes until some time after noon. They could not reach the doors.

"It was noticeable that the police advice to spread as much as possible over the entire distance and not to con-centrate too much at particular points was followed generous-ly. There could not have been a more amenable or patient or better behaved multitude.

"Not all requests were complied with, however. An ef-fort had been made to keep people off of fire-escapes, roofs and ornamental balconies. Apparently, no one had heard of this request, or if they had heard of it, they did not give it any attention. The sky was the limit of the vantage points which were attained by the eager sight-seers. And even the sky was not immune from invasion. The hugh captive balloon on the Parkway, looking like a weird, ungainly beast of prehistoric age, rose into the ether with several sight-seers in its basket and wreaths and banners centered by huge '28s' pendant from its rigging. An airplane or two flew overhead. They, too, must have been for sight-seeing pur-poses, for hardly any noticed them in the presence of the marching soldiers, though some of the flowers which drifted from the planes found their way into the soldiers' hands.

"There were narrow canyons of people and wide-spreading coliseums jammed with them. In Broad Street, Chestnut Street and Market, music and song, yells and cheers rever-berated between highwalls of humanity. Out along the Park-way and beyond to the old reservoir near the turn into Spring Garden Street, there was a wide sweep densely crowded, a vast, tumbled anthill with people crawling about on the skyline, which consisted of the reservoir hill and of many abandoned and decrepit houses and factories. The huge stands, crowd-ed with mothers and wives and fathers and children of the volunteers stretched through it all, the broad parade ground in between.

"The wounded and incapacitated, merrily singing songs and kidding themselves and everyone else, occupied camp chairs on the grass before the stands; at the cross streets tots and aged stood for hours jammed hopelessly against the restraining ropes. Thousands of flags, a clear blue sky, the hazy outline of buildings toward the center of the city, dancing, foolish-looking cheer leaders who did a worthy job at furnishing an outlet for the pentup emotions of the blood kin of the division in this wide, inspiring prospect, added the rest of the superficial scenery. It all was covered by an impalpable, imponderable atmosphere, a deep under current of tense, thrilling consciousness of the day's meaning that could not have been equalled anywhere else.

"And up at Lehigh Avenue, where early in the morning

there were crowds, though they were sparser then than far-
ther south in the city, there was another touch not duplicated anywhere else. It is a street of humble homes, with
humble, homemade decorations which typified in their rudely
cut card-board keystones, stringy, vari-colored festoons,
and homely, well-meant festivity just that little place on
which the minds of most of the marchers who later were to
traverse this avenue of praise and adoration probably dwelt
more than on anything else - Home.

"This was the vista of humanity at 9 o'clock when the
Headquarters Troop on horses came to attention before the
Union League while Major General Charles H. Muir mounted
The Minstrel, the thoroughbred prize winner of Miss Constance
Vauclain. Continual increments were added from the side
avenues when the General clattered down Broad Street to
Broad and Wharton, the hoof-beats of his escort echoing be-
tween the files of people.

"At 10 o'clock, it was learned that the memorial caisson, which was to precede the parade by fifteen minutes, accompanied by a guard of D. S. C. winners, and drawn by eight
milk-white horses, was not quite ready. General Muir decided it must come at the rear of the parade, for the orders
covering every minute of the demonstration must be carried
out. At 10:02, the mobilized warriors began to march up
Broad Street, the parade straightening out automatically
from the units who stood ready in the side streets all
through the neighborhood.

"Word was flashed by telephone over the entire expanse
of the route that the men had started, and the roars which
went up from Broad and Wharton Streets at the actual sight
of the start were duplicated by the cheers which greeted the
information of the start which was given out by men with
megaphones.

"Small and modest grandstands which were filled with
people, and beneath which and on whose cross-pieces were
those who looked out, cranning their necks from contorted
positions; factory buildings decorated with scores of flags
and with holidaying employees filling the windows with merry,
laughing faces; the Washington Avenue Railroad Terminal over-
run with people; the steps of the library further down the
street crowded and its yard filled; shouting, grinning
families looking from dingy third floor homes, which yesterday they would not have exchanged for mansions - all these
were along the first few blocks of the parade; and they
thought they had the cream of the day, for there the inhabitants had the honor of first greeting with raucous yells,
and screeched inarticulate cries for the heroes the State
delighted to honor.

"Further down the Avenue, just as most of the marchers
noticed the tall apparition of William Penn hazily in view,
with a triumphant American flag fluttering from his hat brim,
which looms over City Hall, there was the School of Industrial Art, entirely obscured by a grandstand, the City Club
with its stand loaded down, and so propped up underneath by

intimately packed humanity that it might have collapsed and
still not have budged an inch until the parade was over.
Then came the hotels, and the situation became more tense.

"From the tenth floor of one of them, where apparently
were families who had engaged rooms simply in order to see
the parade, there started one of the first of the showers
of various things which came down on the heads of the soldiers. Some enthusiastic youngster apparently had made
use of a penknife to rip open a pillow, or several pillows,
for a cloud of feathers came drifting down over everyone,
and the din of cries was increased by loud laughter and
merry calls.

"A more sober and restrained tribute, but one no less
sincere than any of the rest, was given by a gathering of
dignified gentlemen at the Union League, just beyond the
gayly decorated stand of the Manufacturers' Club. The
Victory Statue near City Hall seemed to beckon to the
swinging ranks to approach for a benediction, but they
wheeled, their bayonets an apparent forest of spears crossing in view, because of the evolution, like an abattis which
covered the column, and proceeded down Chestnut Street.
The ranks of 12 stretched from curb to curb. The ranks of
spectators stretched from curb to cornice. In between and
around-about were pounds on pounds of fluttering paper frag-
ments, a veritable 'snow-storm' of them. They seemed swept
by the gusts of cheers, and the swirling currents of music
which eddied constantly to an undertone of regulated pound-
ing hob-nailed marching shoes.

"The backs of the marching soldiery seemed to stiffen
as they marched down this street, made deafening by the
closely walled space overhead, for they knew what was before
them. They knew they were approaching the very heart of
America, and of the American tradition which they had per-
petuated by the mighty valor of their own service. The
musicians tried their instruments. The squads straightened
out. Guns were brought more nearly in alignment - for these
men are primarily fighters, not paraders, and if a West
Pointer should lay a string along any line they made it
would be found not much, but a little, off the shortest
distance between two points.

"Suddenly, with the burst of the brass instruments and
the low, reverbrating roll of drums, the music struck into
the ruffles and the flourishes, which showed the Liberty
Bell was reached. The officers gave a sharp command as
they saluted. All eyes came to the right with a certain
smartness. The Sons of the American Revolution, who formed a color guard, holding the standards of the Revolution-
ary War which were taken from their cases in Independence
Hall, were visible, and the historic relic itself stood
revealed - by its side a figure which at first seemed a
little incongruous, but which represented a great deal of
the meaning of the whole parade.

"It was that of a mother whose son went to France, and
who was found by a guard weeping her eyes out back of the

Hall because she could not get through to see the parade of her son's comrades. She was brought to the central point of honor of the whole day's celebration, and sat waving a white handkerchief as constantly as an automaton but with the smile of smiles on her face, until the entire column passed.

"The salute was kept until the reviewing stand just below was passed. Here were Mayor Smith and Governor Sproul and Adjutant General Beary. The latter two had gone over the entire route of the parade a short time before in a victoria, surrounded by an escort of cavalry from the Pennsylvania Military College at Chester.

"As each succeeding regimental band passed the Bell, through the narrow defile made by the artistically designed stands with their colors and their reminders of battles fought and won, the ruffles and flourishes were repeated. All was noise, increasing in volume until the parade had passed to the point at which the wounded men in automobiles, and the nurses appeared.

"Then noise surpassed itself, making more effective the sudden silence which fell shortly afterward when the funeral cortege arrived, and all who happened to be seated arose to stand in a throbbing silence, to fight still harder the emotions which thrilling through all hearts had made tears come and faces twist over wrought up emotions the day long.

"Slowly, drawn by the white horses, and led by those who had received the highest honors for fighting with no care for their own lives came the draped caisson with the wreaths of bay leaves, symbols of victory and mourning. A huge keystone, symbol too of victory and death, was on the catafalque of dead dreams but living vision. In a silence almost oppressive, overwhelming in its immense meaning of lives sacrificed, a wreath was laid at the base of the Liberty Bell, the altar on which individual liberty and life were laid that freedom might live for humanity.

"While this ceremony was being enacted, the column had passed the Custom House which was virtually covered with sightseers down to Third and over that street to Market into another avenue of overpowering noise and light and decoration. The most elaborate effort had been made by the department stores to deck themselves fittingly for the procession. A golden eagle spread itself over the face of Strawbridge & Clothier's store, made golden by electric light. Gilded vessels full of palms decked the corners of the building. The National colors, and the emblems of the 28th Division and its various units were painted over the front of the building in large figures. A huge legend of welcome was at the center of it all.

"Benches and chairs were brought out on available levels at the Post Office building. Faces appeared at every point over the Reading Terminal and silver coin was rained down into the streets. Many of the soldiers remained at attention, almost, but gave various signs which showed how strong the temptation to pick up some of the fallen wealth was. One bold spirit did stoop to retrieve a silver dollar; some boys ran out and handed some of the rest to the men, and then several squads stooped of themselves and gathered in the rest. Some food which was handed to them was also received - thankfully received.

"Before this point was reached a number of men too exhausted by their trying experience in getting into their billets yesterday, some of them after sleepless nights, or nights spent in efforts to sleep on hard floors at some of the armories, had given up the gruelling effort of the eight miles hike and had left the line. A few separated themselves from the parade all along the remainder of the line of march, incapable of going another step. Some of these bore wound stripes on their sleeves, as did, it seemed, the majority of the marchers.

"Large signs with the insignia of both the 28th and 79th Divisions hung before the impressive front of the Wanamaker store, where crowds of excited mothers and wives of Wanamaker's employees who served overseas occupied a specially constructed grandstand. Immediately after passing this place, where one of the most enthusiastic ovations of the line of march up to that point was given, the column started to swing into the most inspiring stretch of all the terrain it traversed.

"Columns bearing flapping keystone banners and streamers with the buff and blue of Philadelphia made the northeast and north plazas of City Hall festive and resplendent. Enthusiastic crowds were in the two grandstands at that point. But in chairs near the northeast stand were nearly 200 old men in blue uniforms wearing medals just as the khaki-clad paraders wore medals.

"They were the veterans of the Civil War and proudly they stood to salute their younger brothers, and smartly they saluted the standard of a union they fought to preserve.

"The sounds and sights of the first part of the march were repeated as the column rounded into Broad Street for the short block to Arch, and out Arch to the Parkway, where was the central arena of the sublime spectacle. As a column of soldiery the procession was immensely impressive, making the wheel about Logan Square into the broad, fresh thoroughfare lined by the municipal stands, but once the thousands set foot in that space there were hundreds of faces which ceased to be simply the more or less impersonal visages of grim, self-restrained warriors, sternly prosecuting a military duty. They became the faces of boys from Scranton and Pottsville and West Philadelphia and from a score of other places.

"Old men and old women, the latter of whom had sat looking in a sort of uncomprehending way at the huge spectacle as though taking in but little of what it all meant, and younger men and women, holding children by the hand called names out loud, shouting with joy. From the ranks of men whose attention was less perfect here than at any point except toward the very end of the parade, there came the won-

-derful answers: 'Hello, Pap!', 'Oh, Mame!', 'Oh, you, Potts-ville!' Even the row of pigeons on the ridge pole of a nearby Catholic church, who seemed to watch the parade under-standingly, gave further symptoms of intelligence. They fluttered their wings and placed their bills close together as they saw the home folks greet the homing folks.

"Throughout the entire expanse of the Parkway, where there were more than 17,000 people in stands, and nearly that many covering the old reservoir hill, where there were urchins in the holes of buildings in the process of demoli tion, and youngsters sitting on the tops of water towers; where there were tens of thousands simply jammed together in cross streets and where, just around the corner were the large stands of the Emergency Aid, the Colonial Dames and the Philadelphia Red Cross Chapters, there was a heightened frenzy when the end of the parade again drew into view.

"The wounded men in automobiles; not sorry, sad wounded men, but jubilant, appreciative wounded men, sitting on the mud-guards of trucks, sitting in the folded tops of limous-ines, wearing their war crosses, their D. S. C. medals, wav-ing flags from the tips of crutches, were there. All stood up to receive and all waved their flags with a little more abandon. The overseas nurses with one, two, three service chevrons followed after and got the same sort of reception. Many cheers were still to be expended when the Ambulance and Base Hospital units appeared.

"Along North Broad Street, where there were impassable jams, there were many who crowded toward the point where General Muir saw his division pass for the last time, and where an ironical sign before the 2nd Regiment Armory gave warm greeting to the 108th Field Artillery, which is com-posed of the former 2nd Regiment, N. G. P. - and which is not yet home, the columns passed to Shibe Park, and passed gladly. There they were fed in plenty, but several blocks before they reached there they seized with a starvation clutch the sand-wiches and other food which was given them by spectators, who decided it was more blessed to give away the food they had brought with them than to eat in the face of doughboys and other fighters who were so evidently faint and exhausted as many of them were.

"By 3 o'clock, the first detachment of men was getting onto the trains at North Philadelphia and the last detachment of spectators were struggling desperately together, some in the crush of people which resulted when the orderly crowds, restrained by the police and by hemp rope, broke up in just plain citizens, filled with the memory of a great and historic occasion which perhaps they never will see duplicated.

"There were surprisingly few accidents and unfortunate happenings, due to the elaborate police preparations, and the good humored and public spirited manner in which the public gave its cooperation. So far as known, none who tried to see the parade failed, either."

Philadelphia Public Ledger,
Friday Morning, May 16th, 1919:

"Banners bring memories of battles to the 28th.

"Chestnut Street yesterday was a vivid reminder to the boys of the Iron Division of their work in France.

"From beyond Broad Street to Third Street every trolley pole was decorated with banners and wreaths. The banners of sky-blue have emblazoned upon them in gold the names of the battles in which the Iron men were the principals. These were the donation to the celebration of the Chestnut Street Business Men's Association. The banners and wreaths were designed by them, worded by them and paid for by them. Every principal battle was represented, and as the boys marched they read of Fismes and Hill 204, of Fismette and Chateau Thierry and of the other score and more places that will remain in their recollection for the rest of their lives."

The Philadelphia Press,
May 16th, 1919:

"Greatest day Philadelphia ever witnessed," declares Gov. Sproul.

"Gov. Sproul and Mayor Smith speaking of the review of the 28th Division troops yesterday were in unison in declaring the event to be the greatest in the history of the Municipality or the Commonwealth. Gov. Sproul said, 'It is the greatest day Philadelphia or the State ever had. It far exceeds the Peace Jubilee celebration held in this city in 1898. It is a wonderful tribute of the city to these gallant boys.' Mayor Smith said, 'Philadelphia is mighty proud to be able to greet the wonderful lads of the Iron Division. It was marvelous and I am thoroughly pleased with the wonderful success of the reception.' The Governor and the Mayor announced that the crowd far exceeded a million. Gov. Sproul also estimated that more than 500,000 persons from various parts of the State saw the parade."

The Philadelphia Inquirer,
May 16th, 1919:

"Major General Charles H. Muir reviewed the men of the Iron Division yesterday at Broad and Diamond Streets. Before him passed the men who returned to the United States with the Division. These paid him the strict military compliment prescribed as the honors to a divisional commander reviewing his men. There passed also the hundreds of wounded casuals from the division. Then came the solemn cortege in honor of the dead of the division, who numbered 4,025. General Muir bared his head, holding his overseas cap in his right hand tightly clinched. 'It is the last time,' he replied to a query as to the review. 'And those figures are right — they did not flinch and they paid the price.'"

City Turns Out in Mighty Home Tribute to Pennsylvania's Iron Division Veterans

CHAPTER 33

"You're Out the Army Now!"

No more do the terrors of "First Call"
    Awake our Johnnie now,
No more to stand at "Reveille"
    Or fall in line for "chow".

No more does a sergeant's whistle
    Shriek the call for drill,
No more can Johnnie "gold brick"
    And say he has a "chill".

No more does a "shave tail's" ugly look
    Or a "skipper's" word that's sharp,
Disturb him in his quarters
    While he plays upon his harp.

No more to stand like a statue
    While the starry flag's hauled down,
No more to have to beg a "pass"
    To see the sights of town.

No more to walk a lonely stretch
    Upon his turn at guard,
No more to answer the sound of "Taps"
    "Lights out!" Oh, thank God!

For Johnnie's out the Army now
    And dolled in his Sunday's best,
He calls around to see his girl –
    The khaki is "at rest"!
             (Paul L. Compton.)

Philadelphia's rousing celebration – the wild cheers and shouts from exhilarated millions, the blare of bands, the rhythmical tread of marching soldiers, the smiles, laughter and tears – was truly, and appropriately too, the "swan song" of the dying 28th – Pennsylvania's famous Keystone Division.   For, hardly had the last echo died away down the canyons of the city's streets before the khaki-clad hosts were speeding on their way to camp to receive their discharges from the United States Army.

The locale of our story again shifts to Camp Dix, New Jersey, where the majority of soldiers of the 28th residing in the eastern part of the United States received their discharges.

However, before going to New Jersey with the boys, we wish to quote at this point a telegram sent by the Mayor of Augusta, Georgia, to the 28th Division, upon the occasion of the parade held in Philadelphia. The article appears in The Philadelphia Press, issue of May 16th, 1919, and reads as follows:

"Augusta's Mayor sends best wishes to 28th.

"In addition to sending to this city a delegation of men and women of Augusta, Georgia, to pay tribute to the men of the 28th who trained at that place before going to France, the Mayor of Augusta, A. D. Tobin, yesterday sent this congratulatory wire to 'The Press': 'Augusta, Ga., May 15th, Editor, The Press: Best wishes and everything good for the boys of the 28th Division. All Augusta proud of them.'"

The following, quoted from The Press, issue of May 16th, tells briefly something of what transpired upon departure of the troops bound for Camp Dix, N. J. for discharge:

"Marchers bid City cherry farewells. Speeded on way to camp with plentiful 'chow'. Used to long hikes. 'So Long, Philly!, you certainly showed us a great time!'

"This was chorused over and over again by the 15,000 soldiers of the 28th Division as they left for Camp Dix after the parade yesterday. The soldiers marched from Shibe Park, where they were given lunch, at 22nd and Lehigh Avenue, on Lehigh Avenue to 18th Street, where they turned down Sedgely Avenue to the railroad station.

"Thousands of friends and relatives of the departing men were on hand to say a brief goodbye. The streets were jammed with men, women and children who lined the road by which the soldiers proceeded to the station. There was many a mother at the gates, waiting for some khaki-clad boy maybe to merely get a last glimpse of him before he went back to camp.

"Goodbye, Jim!", said one woman standing on the curbstone. "I hope to see you home soon." "I'll be home Saturday night, Aunt Maggie", shouted back Jim. "Save something good to eat!" Another soldier, bidding his mother goodbye, said: "I'll be home to dinner Sunday, Mom. Whatever you do, have some pie!"

"More than 15,000 men returned to camp after the parade yesterday. Not all the men who paraded went to Dix, because many have already received their discharges from the service. As fast as they can be issued, discharges from the army will be given to the men, and they will be free to return to their homes in this city.

"Many of the men who took part in the parade were replacements who came from other States. These had nothing but praise for Philadelphia and its hospitality. "You've got some town here", said one. "But, gosh, how I wish I was in Denver!"

"The men were not very fatigued after yesterday's march. They did not carry their full packs, and this made the marching easier. The route was only 8 miles long, much shorter than many of the night marches the 28th Division made in France.

"At the railroad yards, a corps of Knights of Columbus wel-
fare workers supervised the distribution of 'chow' and cigarettes. Sandwiches and cake, and steaming hot coffee prepared
on the field stoves by the K. of C. workers, were given to the
men, who immediately 'fell to'. Each man also received a
package of cigarettes before going on board the trains."

Camp Dix, New Jersey, during these last hours of the dying 28th,
was a hive of busy activity from dawn to the wee small hours of the
morning. We may gain some idea of this by here quoting from The
Philadelphia Press, issue of May 17th, 1919, which reads as follows:

"Camp Dix, N. J., May 16th - Rushing discharges of
Pennsylvania Iron Men. Camp Dix sets new record by releasing 3,500 soldiers in one day.
"All daily records for discharges at a single post
since demobilization began were shattered here today when,
between 9 A. M. and 10 P. M., 3,500 soldiers were paid off.
The departing soldiers came chiefly from four divisions -
28th, 29th, 78th and 82nd, with a sprinkling of casuals
from every division in the army.
"The Discharge Center was the hub about which the interest of thousands of soldiers and other thousands of
civilians awaiting to greet them reveled during the day.
Two great throngs of soldiers besieged the long, low building. From one crowd passed a continuous line that filed
in through the east gate and out at the north. They were
the men making out their final papers and will be discharged tomorrow. The other fed an unbroken line into
the south gate, where the men passed rapidly before a rapid-
fire paymaster, and five minutes later emerged as civilians
from the west gate, to be rushed to waiting automobiles or
trains by friends.
"Nearly the entire 114th Infantry, the first and second
battalions of which were discharged this afternoon, were
rushed home in automobiles. Paterson and other Passaic
County communities, with 125 cars, took home more than 300
veterans of the old second New Jersey.
"Every place of importance in South Jersey that had men
of the old Third listed for discharge today had sent automobiles to carry home these heroes.
"Iron Division engineers were among the first discharged
this morning, when the entire 103rd Regiment of Engineers was
demobilized.
"Major General Muir will decorate, either at Camp Dix or
at some public ceremonial in their home state, two more boys
of the 28th Division, citations for whom, with awards of
D.S.C.s arrived today from General Pershing's headquarters.
Announcement was also made by Col. Davis, Chief of Staff, of
the award of a D.S.C. to Sgt. Albert P. Schad of Philadelphia,
a member of the 111th Infantry. The young Philadelphian is
probably the first American soldier to be decorated on ship
board.
"Fiction is stale compared with the facts of Sgt. Schad's

bravery", says Col. Davis. It was during the fighting in the Argonne. Schad, who was a "Top" Sergeant and didn't have to be there, was leading a squad in a charge when a German machine gun nest fired upon them. Schad told his men to lie low, while he alone crept forward and with hand grenades cleaned out the nest, killing some of the Huns and capturing the others.

"Later, during the same fight, his lieutenant having been killed, Schad was leading an entire platoon, when again his men ran into hot machine gun fire. Refusing to risk his men needlessly, he filled his blouse with grenades and, under fire all the time, worked into a position from which he could hurl them at the Huns. He killed the 16 men in the nest and rushed in to get the gun. Before he could summon his platoon, another German line attacked him from the rear. He swung the German machine gun about, mowed down the first line of fresh assailants and during the evening and night, crouched among the 16 dead Huns, and single-handed, continued to hold off repeated German raids."

"The 109th Field Artillery of Pennsylvania signed their final papers this morning and will be ready for discharge tomorrow."

About this time, during the height of busy scenes at old Camp Dix, came a message - a farewell message - from Major General Charles H. Muir, the division's beloved commander. His final words should be of ever-lasting memory to all comrades who served under him. Again, we are indebted to The Philadelphia Press, issue of Saturday, May 17th, 1919, for the following interesting item:

"General Muir gives Farewell Message to Immortal 28th. "Uncle Charley" asks boys to carry soldierly qualities into civilian life. Division now dissolved. Entire personnel is expected to be mustered out by next Wednesday.

"Although Major General Charles H. Muir reviewed his men for the last time at Broad and Diamond Streets on Thursday, his official connection with the Iron Division did not end until yesterday morning. Then from Division Headquarters he issued the following statement and with it the 28th, famous sons of the staunch old Keystone State, ceased to be an A.E.F. unit:

"The existence of the 28th Division now ends. Each member has every right to be proud of its deeds during the great drama in which it took part.

"It now becomes the duty of the surviving members of the division to take up their normal duties. The call of camp, field or barracks may take some of you back 'to the colors', but the great majority will return to the professions, the sciences, the arts and the labor that constitute the life of a people.

"In saying farewell, the commander under whom you served expresses the hope that the gratitude that marks your return may in no way unfit any for further and increased usefulness; that each will bring to his new task that in-

MAJOR GENERAL CHARLES H. MUIR

Major General Muir, known to every doughboy of the Twenty-eighth Division as "Uncle Charley" because of care and consideration of his men, commanded the Division when it went to France and until just before the armistice was declared. When the Iron Division returned to this country, General Muir again took command.

Image from Citizen's Reception to the Soldiers, Sailors, Marines and Nurses of Chester, Pennsylvania and Vicinity
June 20-21, 1919 On their return from The World War 1914-1919

dustry, courage and fidelity that mark the true soldier."

One of the final newspaper stories of the day concerning the 28th Division's last hours at Camp Dix, New Jersey, appears in The Press, under date of May 17th, 1919.   The item reads as follows:

"There was an air of lethargy about Camp Dix yesterday. Groups of soldiers from the 28th lolled about outside head-quarters.   It seemed strange to them to be without a com-mander. 'Uncle Charlie' ruled his men with a rod of iron, but the love he had for them shone out in every action. While the thought of discharge was a glowing one, they all wished that they could have been kept under his command until they were actually booked to leave camp.   This hang-ing around without any definite thing to do, and no real head, was something new to them and caused a sort of un-comfortable, lost feeling.   In order that there might be some one to report to, the Headquarters Troop, composed of about 200 men, was left in charge of the division.

"At General Headquarters, the order of discharge has been arranged in this manner: The first to arrive in camp will be the first dismissed, and accordingly the 103rd Engineers were released today.   Following will come the 109th Infantry, 109th Field Artillery, 103rd Field Signal Battalion, Headquarters detachment, Headquarters Troop, 28th Company Military Police, 103rd Train Headquarters and the 55th Infantry Brigade Headquarters.

"The order issued by Major General Hugh L. Scott, com-mander of Camp Dix, as to the equipment each man is en-titled to take with him includes: (1) cap or (1) hat and cord; (1) O.D. shirt (woolen); (1) service coat (woolen); (1) pair breeches (woolen); (1) pair shoes; (1) pair of leggings or spirals; (1) belt; (1) slicker; (1) overcoat; (2) suits underwear; (4) pair stockings; (1) pair gloves; (1) gas mask and helmet (if issued); (1) set toilet arti-cles; (1) barrack bag; (3) scarlet chevrons.

"One unit of the 112th Field Hospital Ambulance was expected to get out today, and they will be sent to the camp nearest Pittsburgh to wait final discharge.   The 28th Division is expected to be discharged by May 21st.

"At present, the only units besides those in the 28th Division which are at Camp Dix are the 147th Field Artil-lery, consisting of 1,200 men; 303rd Field Signal Battalion, 331 men; 307th Field Artillery, 1,688 men; 308th Field Artillery, 1,514 men.   The last two are parts of the 78th, or Lightning Division, which trained at Camp Dix, and con-sists of men from New York, New Jersey and Delaware."

CHAPTER 34.

IN MEMORIAM.

"When the Men of Iron have passed,
  In triumphal array;
When they have heard the homage
  That our joyous cheers shall pay;
Eyes Right! Salute that silent host,
  On Glory's page enrolled,
Who gave their iron in measure full
  And proved their Souls of Gold!"

Philadelphia Public Ledger,
May 15th, 1919:

"Glory Guards Bivouac of Dead under Lilies of France.
First complete list of those who died for the right. Major
General Muir authorizes the publication of Roster compiled
by Personnel Officer from many thousands of reports gathered
by battle-field observers in every campaign.

"The Public Ledger publishes here for the first time
complete list of 28th Division warriors who were killed in
action or who died of disease or other causes abroad. Record shows Keystone dead from every part of Pennsylvania,
with scarcely a regiment that failed to give a man that
Democracy might live as long as the world endures.

"Blue Stars change to Golden Hue in every County of the
Commonwealth, from the Eastern border to the Western - some
towns lose many lads - all nationalities represented in
Honor Roll.

"In this list of the dead, the immortal dead of the 28th
Division who sleep the long sleep under the lilies of France,
the Public Ledger is enabled to publish for the first time
and exclusively the name of every man who met death from
whatever cause while serving across the seas. This com-
pilation began with the arrival of the Division abroad and
concludes at the time when the main embarkation back to
America began in April. This roll is presented here through
the courtesy and by the authority of Major General Chas. H.
Muir, who led the Division through its campaigns. The com-
piler was Major Chas. E. Sohl, of Elkins Park, the Divisional
Personnel Officer, who made up the list from many thousands
of reports written by his subordinates - another illustration
of the magnificent way in which the army officers did all
they could to relieve the anxiety of relatives of the fighting men in this country."

IRON DIVISION'S BATTLE LOSSES GREATEST AMONG GUARD UNITS

Lieutenant Colonel Clement, assistant chief of staff of the Iron Division, furnishes the latest official casualty figures on the entire division.

The figures are as follows:

Killed in action—Sixty-two officers, 1761 men.

Died of wounds—Thirty-six officers, 671 men.

Died of disease—Six officers, 200 men.

Died of other causes—Five officers, 110 men.

Total loss by death—109 officers, 2742 men.

Missing and prisoners—1174 officers and men.

Severely wounded—114 officers and 3704 men.

Slightly wounded—190 officers, 5861 men.

Wounded, degree undetermined—Ninety-two officers, 3785 men.

Total wounded—396 officers, 13,350 men.

Grand total, dead and wounded—505 officers, 16,092 men.

Grand total, all casualties—17,771 officers and men.

This was a greater number of casualties than suffered by any divisions except the First, Second and Third Divisions, made up of regular army men and marines.

(Casualties by units as prepared by the War Department three months ago. Latest figures will swell casualty list of each organization.)

The casualties of this division, not including wounded, were:

Units	Killed in action	Died of wounds	Missing in action	Prisoners	Total
109th Infantry Regiment.....	349	136	376	251	1112
110th Infantry Regiment.....	436	134	373	119	1142
111th Infantry Regiment.....	362	114	214	24	714
112th Infantry Regiment.....	272	93	153	143	661
107th Machine-Gun Battalion..	4	3	1	0	8
108th Machine-Gun Battalion..	22	21	7	1	51
109th Machine-Gun Battalion..	0	0	0	0	0
107th Artillery Regiment.....	21	11	3	0	35
108th Artillery Regiment.....	19	9	3	1	32
109th Artillery Regiment.....	17	15	8	0	40
103d Trench Mortar Battery..	5	0	1	0	6
103d Engineers Regiment....	37	17	35	0	89
Totals.....................	1544	553	1174	612	3890

More than two million American soldiers served in WWI, 50,000 of whom died in battle.

Image from Evening Public Ledger-Philadelphia May 15, 1919

THE 28TH DIVISION MEMORIAL SHRINE
(Boalsburg, Pennsylvania)

- By -

PAUL L. COMPTON
(Formerly Pvt., Co. I, 111th Inf.,
28th Division, A.E.F.)

P R E F A C E

The 28th Division was organized in August 1917 from National
Guard units of the State of Pennsylvania. In September, the
Division moved to Camp Hancock, Augusta, Georgia, and after establishing themselves in squad tents pitched picturesquely along
"Company Streets", began an extensive training program under
competent military instructors in modern warfare, destined to be
of some seven months' duration. In March 1918, the division was
brought to full strength by the assignment of selective service
men from Camps Lee, Virginia; Meade, Maryland; and Travis, Texas.
In April, it moved to Camp Upton, Mineola, Long Island, New York,
preparatory to embarking for France.

Summary of Operations in the World War:

Chateau-Thierry Sector.....................June 28 - July 14
Champagne-Marne Defensive..................July 15-18
Aisne-Marne Offensive......................July 18 - August 6
Fismes Sector..............................August 7-17
Oisne-Aisne Offensive......................August 18 - September 7
Clermont Sector............................September 19-25
Meuse-Argonne Offensive....................September 26 - October 10
Thiaucourt Sector & Woevre Plain
    Operation..............................October 16 - November 11
Subsequent Service.........................November 12 - May 1919

The writer of these verses was inducted into the Service on
November 21, 1917, at Upper Marlboro, Maryland. He received his first
military training at Camp Meade (Company I, 313th Infantry) and joined
the 28th Division (Company I, 111th Infantry) at its quarters in Camp
Hancock, Augusta, Georgia, in the early Spring of 1918. He was honorably discharged from the Service at Camp Dix, New Jersey, on May 4, 1919.
The verses are based on personal experiences and are affectionately
dedicated to the memory of his fallen comrades

"***who wore the Keystone red

Proudly in camp and under fire,***"

THE 28TH DIVISION MEMORIAL SHRINE
(Boalsburg, Pennsylvania)

The 28th Division Memorial Shrine at Boalsburg, Pennsylvania, was first conceived by Colonel Theodore Davis Boal, now deceased, son of the founder of the village of Boalsburg. Near the end of World War 1, Colonel Boal, while serving with the 28th Division, conceived the idea of a Shrine to the memory of the Officers of the Division who had made the supreme sacrifice.

In the early 1920's, Colonel Boal erected on his estate at Boalsburg, a crescent wall of mountain stone to those Officers who had died or were killed in action with the 28th Division during World War 1. The center of the memorial wall contains an altar with a statue of the Madonna which was brought from Mexico by Pierre de L. Boal, sone of the founder and then Secretary of the United States Legation in Mexico City.

Appropriately, the Shrine is located in the Centre County community which is credited with being the birth place of Memorial Day. The Shrine tract borders on Spring Creek, which has been re-named the Vesle River as a reminder of the grim days which the Division faced in Europe in World War 1. The Shrine area is approached by passing a large well kept area that lies between State Highway Route 322 and Spring Creek. To reach the Shrine area, one passes over a stone bridge which has been erected over the stream. As indicated above, the altar is the center of the memorial wall which stretches for a considerable distance on each side of the altar. In this wall memorial plaques have been placed and dedicated to the Officers of the Division who lost their lives during World War 1. Also in the Shrine area many of the Division Units have erected memorials to the memory of their fallen comrades. The altar, above referred to, looks out upon other memorial monuments to 28th Division units scattered over a tree shaded lawn falling away to a tiny stream, the whole setting providing a quiet space for the memorializing of the honored dead.

(Note: The above description of The 28th Division Memorial Shrine at Boalsburg, Pennsylvania, is copied from a letter dated August 13, 1954, from Lt. General F. A. Weber, Department of Military Affairs, Adjutant General'd Office, Commonwealth of Pennsylvania, Annville R.D. 2, Penna.)

28th Division Memorial Shrine, Pennsylvania Military Museum.
(Images from https://www.pamilmuseum.org)

THE 28TH DIVISION MEMORIAL SHRINE
(Boalsburg, Pennsylvania)

The "Iron Division" has come home
    And men of iron you are,
The "Iron Division" has come home
    With honors from afar!

Far removed from war's black night
    And from the battle's din,
'Round yon altar at Boalsburg's site
    Our boys are "falling in"!

Our boys who wore the Keystone red
    Proudly in camp and under fire,
Our boys of whom it can be said
    Aroused the Kaiser's ire!

Gently wafted by a summer's breeze,
    A band of music greets their ears,
Softly issuing from a grove of trees -
    Nothing here to arouse their fears!

No harsh command is their's to hear,
    All's serene along Spring Creek's banks,
No foe awaits who may be near
    To engage, in combat, those silent ranks!

Upon a crescent wall of stone,
    Above an altar erected there,
Madonna welcomes Her sons home -
    Peace in answer to Her prayer!

They hear no more the cannon's roar
    Nor the machine-gun's rapid fire,
They see no more that human gore
    Hanging on bob-wire!

They sense, no more, that sickening smell
    Which reaches everywhere
When bodies, dead, turn black and swell
    When long exposed to air!

They crawl no more through brier and brush
    'Neath bullets over head,
They dread no more that awful hush
    Before attack is made!

They feel no more the cootie's bite
    While sweating in the mud,
They crouch no more with nerves drawn tight -
    That shell! Thank God! A dud!

They lug no more those heavy packs
   Through mire, trench and rain,
They suffer not with aching backs
   A kilometer to gain!

They hear no more with head bowed low
   The deadly shrapnel's whine,
They fear no more than an unseen foe
   May creep across their line!

They are burned no more by mustard gas
   Which permeated the air;
Nor wonder as they adjust their masks
   What day it is - and where?

No more is heard that cry "to arms"!
   In the stillness of the night,
No more is heard the gas alarms,
   Harbingers of a fight!

No miserable hunk of flesh they see
   In a shell-shocked foe or friend,
No pain-racked wounded on bended knee,
   Begging God his life to end!

No more of that waiting to go "over the top",
   Timed by an officer's watch;
No more of patrolling an out-post spot
   Alone on your first watch!

The sky, no more, o'er a distant hill
   Is lighted up tonight,
Big guns, no more, blast forth their fill
   To maim, destroy, to fright!

Your last fox-hole has been dug
   Out there in "no man's land",
No "iron rations" you laboriously lug
   Through woods, up hill, and sand!

Your litter-bearers haul no more
   The wounded to the rear,
Detail calls are heard no more
   To fall upon your ear!

Your dead you reverently buried
   Near the spot where first they fell -
A duty both grim and hurried
   As your Chaplain can tell!

No patrol is on a raid tonight,
   All's quiet along the Marne,
No gun is poised - no Hun in sight
   And no attack at dawn!

The Hun is routed from Argonne's Wood,
    His machine-guns now forever stilled;
'Twas there our boys so valiantly stood
    While a grateful nation heard and thrilled!

Chateau-Thierry, Champagne-Marne
    And that avenue of stately trees,
Oise-Aisne, Fismes and Aisne-Marne
    Lie peaceful, kissed by a summer's breeze!

The Vesle flows quietly on its way,
    Its waters pure and fresh -
Nor stained as on that day
    By human blood and flesh!

Thiaucourt, too, lies dreaming
    Of days that it could tell
When tons of shell came screaming
    Like messengers from Hell!

"No man's land" is your's tonight,
    The foe long since has fled,
Your job is done - a wrong to right,
    For which you nobly bled!

Yes, home again is that silent host
    And here we read each name
Who for democracy gave their most
    Without a thought of fame!

Here, reverently we salute you -
    You of our soldier dead;
Here, feebly we honor you
    For the sacrifice you made!

Madonna, Mother of all,
    Our dead are in Your keeping -
They who answered to the call
    Are home again here sleeping!

The "Iron Division" has come home -
    (It was headed for the Rhine!)
The "Iron Division" has come home -
    Their Memorial - this Shrine!

- By -

PAUL L. COMPTON
(Formerly Pvt., Co. I, 111th Infantry,
28th Division, A.E.F.)

Dedication of the District of Columbia War Memorial.
Photo includes John Philip Sousa and President Herbert Hoover.
(Image courtesy Library of Congress)

"THE DISTRICT OF COLUMBIA WORLD WAR MEMORIAL"

- BY -

PAUL L. COMPTON

<u>P R E F A C E</u>

By an act of Congress approved June 7, 1924, a Commission composed of eleven prominent citizens of Washington, D. C., was appointed for the purpose of erecting in Potomac Park in the District of Columbia a memorial to those members of the military and naval forces of the United States from the District of Columbia who served their country in the great war. (First World War). The Act provided, in part, that "such memorial shall be of artistic design suitable for military music; shall take the place of the present wooden band stand in Potomac Park, and that no part of the cost of the erection shall be borne by the United States."

- o -

The District of Columbia World War Memorial, a circular bandstand of Doric type, is located in West Potomac Park, south of the Lincoln Memorial Reflecting Pool on a line with 19th Street. The memorial, which is of Vermont marble, is 47 feet high, 44 feet in diameter, with 12 fluted columns supporting the dome. Around the top is the following inscription:

"A Memorial to the armed forces from the District of Columbia who served their country in the World War."

On the north side (east of the steps - cornerstone):

"This memorial was erected through voluntary subscriptions of the people of Washington. It was dedicated on Armistice Day Nineteen Hundred and Thirty-One by Herbert Hoover, President of the United States. Within this corner-stone are recorded the names of the twenty-six thousand Washingtonians who when the United States entered the World War answered the call to arms and served in the Army Navy Marine Corps and Coast Guard."

On the north side (west of the steps):

"The names of the men and women from the District of Columbia who gave their lives in the World War are here inscribed as a perpetual record of their patriotic service to their country. Those who fell and those who survived have given to this and to future generations an example of high idealism courageous sacrifice and gallant achievement."

Other appropriate inscriptions appear elsewhere on the memorial. Around the base are carved the names of the dead from the District of Columbia. The memorial accommodates a band of 80 pieces and is lighted by indirect lights. It was erected by the District of Columbia Memorial Commission at cost of $169,122.00 without expense to the United States.

I attended the formal dedication ceremony at the memorial on November 11, 1931. John Philip Sousa was in attendance and graciously conducted a band of music through a number - his own composition, "Stars and Stripes Forever" - during the exercises. This was shortly before his death in Reading, Pennsylvania, on March 6, 1932. The verses, however, were just recently written in memory of my deceased comrades and are based on personal experiences in the First World War while serving as a private in a combat regiment, the 111th Infantry of the 28th (Keystone) Division, A.E.F., composed, until the arrival of additional troops from other states and the District of Columbia, entirely of regiments from the Pennsylvania National Guard. The names of several of my fallen comrades are carved around the base of the memorial.

The photograph of the memorial was obtained from the department of the interior, National Capital Parks.

PAUL L. COMPTON

District of Columbia Memorial Commission - For the purpose of erecting in Potomac Park in the District of Columbia a memorial to those members of the military and naval forces of the United States from the District of Columbia who served their country in the great war.

Commission members:

Chas. A Baker

Edw. F. Calladay

John Joy Edson

Mrs. Wm. Corcoran Eustis

Isaac Gans
E. Lester Jones

Arthur D. Marks

Frank B. Noyes

Anton Stephan

J. R. McDonald

Gist Blair

Left to right, from 2nd person: Edith Wilson, Charles F. Adams, Helen Taft, and Patrick J. Hurley; Lou and President Herbert Hoover 3rd and 2nd from right
(Images courtesy Library of Congress)

THE DISTRICT OF COLUMBIA WORLD WAR MEMORIAL

Far removed from war's black night
    And from the battle's din,
'Round yon columns, marble white,
    Our boys are "falling in"!

Gently wafted by an autumn's breeze,
    A band of music greets their ears;
Softly issuing from a grove of trees -
    Nothing here to arouse their fears!

No sharp command is their's to hear,
    All's peaceful along the Potomac's banks,
No foe awaits who may be near
    To engage, in combat, those silent ranks!

No blast from a "Top Kick's" whistle
    Awakens them from their sleep -
"Outside! Side-arms and rifles!"
    (Recall how it made you leap?)

Packed as sardines in a can,
    No more they travel like cattle freight
In box cars known to every man -
    "Hommes Forty - Chevaux Eight!"

Nor are they herded into an Army truck
  To be driven - God knows where
In freezing weather, they trust to luck
  That warmth awaits them there!

They hear no more the cannon's roar
  Nor the machine-gun's rapid fire,
They see no more that human gore
  Hanging on bob-wire!

They sense, no more, that sickening smell
  Which reaches everywhere
When bodies, dead, turn black and swell
  When long exposed to air!

They crawl no more through brier and brush
  'Neath bullets over head,
They dread no more that awful hush
  Before attack is made!

They feel no more the cootie's bite
  While sweating in the mud,
They crouch no more with nerves drawn tight -
  That shell! Thank God! A dud!

They lug no more those heavy packs
  Through mire, trench and rain,
They suffer not with aching backs,
  A kilometer to gain!

They bear no more with head bowed low
  The deadly shrapnel's whine,
They fear no more that an unseen foe
  May creep across their line!

They are burned no more by mustard gas
  Which permeated the air;
Nor wonder as they adjust their masks:
  What day it is - and where?

No more is heard that cry "to arms!"
  In the stillness of the night,
No more is heard the gas alarms,
  Harbingers of a fight!

No miserable hunk of flesh they see
  In a shell-shocked foe or friend,
No pain-racked wounded on bended knee,
  Begging God his life to end!

No more of that waiting to go "over the top",
  Timed by an officer's watch;
No more of patrolling an out-post spot
  Alone on your first watch!

The sky, no more, o'er a distant hill
  Is lighted up tonight,
Big guns, no more, blast forth their fill
  To maim, destroy, to fright!

Your last fox-hole has been dug
  Out there in "no man's land",
No "iron-rations" you laboriously lug
  Through woods, up hill, and sand!

Your litter-bearers haul no more
  The wounded to the rear,
Detail calls are heard no more
  To fall upon your ear!

Your dead you reverently buried
  Near the spot where first they fell -
A duty both grim and hurried
  As your Chaplain can tell!

Dover lies tranquil in the morning's sun,
  Its white cliffs welcomed you
When first you stalked the cunning Hun
  And war, to you, was new!

Peace reigns supreme in Calais town
  Where once you trod its streets,
Nor do the bombs come whistling down
  To bid you make retreat!

The little French town and Mademoiselle,
  Just where the road made a bend,
The barn and the chickens you knew so well -
  All reminders of a departed friend!

That stall in a stable - your "home" while you trained,
  The pigs and the geese quartered nearby,
The long, dreary hours, indoors, when it rained,
  No letter from home - "Mail Call" passed you by!

The shell-torn church where once you prayed
  On a quiet Sabbath morn,
The village green where once you played
  Ere hate of foe was born!

The friendly villagers and bar-maids too,
  With whom you fain would chat
In language known but to a few of you -
  Your signs made up for that!

No "MP" now bars your way
   To visit a certain town,
No "KP" is your's to stay
   Your plans or keep you "down"!

No patrol is on a raid tonight,
   All's quiet along the Marne,
No gun is poised - no Hun in sight
   And no attack at dawn!

The Hun is routed from Argonne's Wood,
   His machine-guns now forever stilled;
'Twas there our boys so valiantly stood
   While a grateful nation heard and thrilled!

Chateau-Thierry, Champagne-Marne
   And that avenue of stately trees,
Oise-Aisne, Fismes, and Aisne-Marne
   Lie peaceful, kissed by a summer's breeze!

The Vesle flows quietly on its way,
   Its waters pure and fresh -
Nor stained as on that day
   By human blood and flesh!

Thiaucourt, too, lies dreaming
   Of days that it could tell
When tons of shell came screaming
   Like messengers from Hell!

"No man's land" is your's tonight,
   The foe long since has fled,
Your job is done - a wrong to right,
   For which you nobly bled!

Yes, home again is that silent host
   And here we read each name
Who for democracy gave their most
   Without a thought of fame!

Here, reverently we salute you -
   You of our soldier dead;
Here, feebly we honor you
   For the sacrifice you made!

Long may this Memorial stand
   To District men who gave their all
At home and in a foreign land
   In answer to their country's call!

- By -
PAUL L. COMPTON
(Formerly Pvt., Co. I, 111th Infantry,
28th Division, A.E.F.)

Part 2

Reflections

and

Ponderings

My definition of love:

LOVE IS THE HAND OF GOD

PLAYING A DIVINE SYMPHONY

UPON THE HEART-STRINGS OF

HUMANITY!

B y

PAUL L. COMPTON

The following verses were written prior to the enactment of the First World War bonus law and were accepted for publication in the Washington Times-Herald during the latter part of 1923 or the first half of 1924:

THE BONUS - YES OR NO!

The bonus or not the bonus, is the question of the day;
  To fight or not to fight was answered in one way!

To be or not to be crippled in the cause,-
  It was not their's to hesitate in the greatest of all wars!

To die or not to die, it was not their's to say,
  But face that Hell o'er there on Thirty Dollars pay!

To have, to hold, and keep for you and me,
  That priceless gift for all - our country's liberty!

To give or not to give what is rightly our's,
  Will, no doubt, be settled with the passing of the hours!

But what, old pal, will be verdict be? -
  They wait and watch, the boys who crossed the sea!

So, up!, awake!, ye men who make our laws
  And let all nations see that soldiers' bonus clause!

- By -

PAUL L. COMPTON
(Formerly Pvt., Co. I, 111th Inf.)
(28th Division, AEF)

The following verses were witten during 1923-1924,
and were accepted for publication in the Washington
Times-Herald:

BLIND JUSTICE!

Two men faced the judgment bar,
    One was rich and the other poor;
One arrived in his motor car,
    One was brought from a prison door!

For the rich, his money furnished bail
    And with gold his lawyers bought;
While the poor awaited trial in jail -
    All in vain a friend he sought!

Now these two men - the rich and poor -
    Were up before the honored Court;
The rich had stolen thousands or more,
    The poor, a winter's overcoat!

Our man of wealth, his trial was heard
    And after expert legal aid,
The Court declared the charge absurd:
    "Case dismissed!", the wise judge said!

Then he who stole the overcoat
    Was called to answer for his crime;
His trial was brief, suffice to note
    For the deed he's serving time!

                    - By -

            PAUL L. COMPTON

JUST A DOG

When the hours at the office are over
   And the grind is through for the day,
I know that she'll be waiting
   As homeward I wend my way!

I know that she'll be listening
   For my steps upon the walk
And will be at the door to greet me —
   (What a shame she cannot talk!)

I know she'll be glad to see me —
   This little pal of mine,
For that joyful bark assures me
   That she is feeling fine!

I know that she really means it
   As she greets me in her way,
For that wagging tail expresses
   Everything she cannot say!

Folks may forsake and shun you,
   But write this in your log:
There's a friend who'll stick forever —
   You guessed it — its your dog!

And when life's journey is over,
   In that land beyond the veil,
I hope that I'll be greeted
   By that little wagging tail!

—By—

Paul L. Compton
9/6/33

(Written in fond memory of my little
Pekinese pet, "MING TOY".)   PLC

A VISIT WITH MY FORMER SCHOOL TEACHER

(Affectionately dedicated to the memory of the late Miss Adelaide Davis, formerly an 8th
Grade teacher and Principal of the Emery Public School, Lincoln Road and "S" Street, N.E.,
Washington, D. C., and later a school division Supervisor. The Adelaide Davis Public
School, 44th Place and "H" Streets, S. E., Washington, D. C. is so named in her honor.
Mi   Davis was born in Lynn, Massachusetts, in 1861. After years of outstanding service
in the District public school system, during which she was eventually appointed a school
division supervisor, Miss Davis retired on August 31, 1929. She died here on Dec.24,1940.)

The years had been many, the years had been long
    Since last she bade me "Farewell!"
And wished me "good luck" as I left her class
    And that schoolroom I remember so well!

Yes, Time in its flight and a busy life
    Had kept us apart, though quite near,
Until one day I thought how fine it would be
    To visit with her this year!

With this thought in mind, I wended my way
    To her home on a quiet street;
For she had retired but the latch-string was out
    To old pupils she loved to greet!

How the minutes flew by as we chatted awhile
    Reminiscing o'er school days long past –
Events that transpired, names we recalled
    Of those who were in my class!

How the years rolled back to happier days
    Of mother, father, home and school,
As sitting there in the twilight hours
    I lived again through her gentle rule!

How I made her laugh as I recalled
    That day when marching out of step,
She screamed my name for all to hear:
    "Leon!" I can hear that warning yet!

"The sun that brief December day *** ",
    We both recalled with smiles
Whittier's "Snow-Bound" which was memorized
    In parts, at least, by lines!

Though her hair had turned to silver
    (For the years had left their mark),
This dear, little old lady
    Was young, in spirit, at heart!

For as we talked of those by-gone days,
    I saw before me there
Not just a tired old lady,
    But my teacher, young and fair!

Yes, I'm glad today I visited her
    At that particular time
For now she is His pupil,
    That old schoolmarm of mine!

PAUL L. COMPTON
(Class of 1904)

FANCY SPEAKS!

"My mistress calls me Fancy
  And fancy I am that
For I'm a Maltese Terrier
  (In case you want the fact!)

"With eyes concealed
  'neath my veil of spotless white,
They say that I'm shy of strangers
  But isn't that alright?

"For strangers may abuse me,
  May make my life a fright,
But I dearly love my mistress
  And, with her, I'm alright!

"I jump and dance when I hear her steps
  As homeward she wends her way,
And she knows I am thus expressing
  Every joy that I cannot say!

"On days when I am bathed
  And my long, white coat is snowy white,
I dread to dwell upon tomorrow
  And toss upon my bed all night!

"For Fancy, bathed, is a dear to all
  And all give me a hug;
They say that I then resemble
  A beautiful white fur rug!

"But Fancy, soiled, oh me! oh my!
  It is then that I take a flop,
For all declare in unison
  That I look like an old rag mop!

"But life, to me, is very sweet,
  Long, white hair and all,
And I hope that I'll live for many a year
  To answer my mistress's call!"

                 – By –

             Paul L. Compton

             10/15/51

JOHN DRAINEY, RAILROAD MAN

We will miss his words of wisdom
    And his cracks at the Carhart hat,
For we have all learned to love him and his
    "Well, I'll tell you about that!"

We will miss his home-spun stories
    As he told 'em "right off the bat",
But most of all we will miss his
    "Well, I'll tell you about that!"

No more will we see and hear him
    As third from the left he sat -
This senior member of the panel and his
    "Well, I'll tell you about that!"

The Master called John Drainey -
    His train arrived on time;
No schedules now to bother him,
    And no worries about a fine!

We'll miss this grand old railroad man,
    It certainly is a fact,
But most of all we will miss his
    "Well, I'll tell you about that!"

Somewhere on a peaceful siding,
    There's, unattended, a train upon the track,
Somewhere a voice has answered,
    "Well, I'll tell you about that!"

— By —

Paul L. Compton

7/12/51

John Drainey, a retired railroad engineer, at frequent times in the past and until his death in 1951, appeared as a panel member on the television program "Life Begins at 80". He quite often made remarks about hat creations worn by a fellow-member of the panel, a Mrs. Carhart. His favorite expression upon being asked a question by the Master of Ceremonies, Jack Barry, was "Well, I'll tell you about that!"

Shortly after his death, the above verses were written and a copy sent to his sister who gratefully acknowledged the same.

INVENTIONS'

We have our horseless carriages no longer limited to the rich,
  We light our homes and heat them by the turning of a switch,
We ride the air and the ocean's waves at marveleous rates of speed,
  While reclining aboard luxurious liners that supply our every need;
We talk to friends in distant lands without leaving the old arm-chair,
  We even shop from floor to floor without climbing up a stair;
We send a written message a thousand miles or more
  And its received and answered in minutes at our door!
We enjoy the greatest operas by the turning of a knob,
  Or hear the villian's nasty laugh and the heroine's pitiful sob;
We sit in comfort in our living rooms before a little box
  And see and hear the world go by or a steamer as she docks;
We are entertained for hours by pictures that move and talk,
  But to hear a lengthy speaker, we sometimes naturally balk!
We have the fireless cooker - the dream of every wife,
  And stainless steel you'll find employed in almost every knife!
We live and work in buildings that literally pierce the sky,
  We use a little gadget that detects your every lie;
We toss our soiled linen in a tub of whirling soaps
  And in a flash our laundry's cleaned beyond our fondest hopes;
We drop a nickel in a slot when dining out for tea
  To hear the latest hit tunes for just that little fee;
Doors are opened without our touch by breaking a beam of light,
  Books are read by the blind who have never had their sight!
Food is kept fresh indefinitely - stored in a big white chest,
  Rooms are cooled in Summer and flies no longer pest;
The ladies now get permanents to make their crowning beauty last,
  The men, with electric razors, shave in comfort and fast;
We can hear the voices of those who long since have departed from this sphere
  And can even see through solids - Is the millennium drawing near?
They say, with 3-dimensions, the moves will please pap
  To have some bathing beauty sit practically on his lap!
And, if you are tired and all run down and feeling - oh! so ill,
  All this can be corrected by swallowing a little pill!
And, when you are yourself again, and an enemy you would kill,
  Just press a little botton - electricity needs no skill!
We have a camera now - just load and give a little snap
  And in a jiffy you'll get the developed picture back;
We use in business and on the farm machines that almost think,
  (In fact this is being written with a ribbon and some ink!)
We explore the deepest ocean and work the deepest mine,
  Or conquer the highest mountain by inventions of our time;
We even reach beyond the blue to study some distant star,
  Or delve into the atom to learn just what we are! -
Inventions - some old, some new - we use from day to day,
  But, thank God, we get our children in the same old-fashion way!

By

Paul L. Compton

(Revised- Sept. 4, 1953)

ODE TO A POSTAGE STAMP

Little scrap of paper,
   With picture on one side,
To some - just a postage stamp,
   To me - you rank ace high!

Little scrap of paper,
   With glue upon your back,
You're given quite a licking!
   (Our apologies for that!)

Little scrap of paper,
   Your cost is very low
For the services you render
   To millions you don't know!

Little scrap of paper,
   Your cost is very high,
When you are a rarity
   Philatelists want to buy!

Little scrap of paper,
   Mounted on an album page,
There you become more valuable
   As year on year you age!

Little scrap of paper
   You look so very smart
On a "first day" cover
   You're a work of art!

Little scrap of paper
   You commemorate so well
Important dates in history -
   Events that each could tell!

Little scrap of paper,
   Quite a traveler you,
Bringing, sending messages
   Old, yet ever new!

Little scrap of paper,
   Via air and land and sea,
You surely do get around
   Tomwhich we all agree!

Little scrap of paper,
   Dressed in a block-of-four,
Collectors save and cherish you
   Because they love you so!

Little scrap of paper,
   Friend of kings and the common man,
All seek to possess and know you
   And save you if they possibly can!

```
        Little scrap of paper,
            When printed up-side-down,
        You surely cause a commodation
            As you become renown!

        Little scrap of paper,
            Known in every camp,
        Foreign and domestic,
            ALL HAIL THE POSTAGE STAMP!


                        - By -

                    PAUL L. COMPTON

                        2/22/54
```

Newspaper clipping: LINN'S WEEKLY STAMP NEWS — Ode To A Postage Stamp, By Paul L. Compton

Added verses: 2-24-54

```
        Little scrap of paper,
            Via air and land and sea,
        You surely do get around
            To which we all agree!

        Little scrap of paper
            Dressed in a block-of-four,
        Collectors save and cherish you
            Because they love you so!

        Little scrap of paper,
            Friend of kings and the common man,
        All seek to possess and know you
            And save you if they possibly can!

        Little scrap of paper,
            When printed up-side-down,
        You surely cause a commotion
        And you become renown!
        or
```

IF THEY COULD SPEAK!
(Thoughts on passing a cemetery)

No more planning,
  No more schemes,
No more moving
  To other scenes!

No more parting
  No more tears,
No more weeping,
  No more fears!

No more laughter,
  No more smiles,
No more trudging
  Weary miles!

No more sorrow,
  No more pain,
No more sunshine,
  No more rain!

No more fretting
  No more sad,
No more seeking
  More to add!

No more borrowing,
  No more regrets,
No more lending,
  Likewise regrets!

No more mother,
  No more dad,
No more children
  That you had!

No more husband,
  No more wife,
No more in-laws
  To run your life!

No more nagging
  No more praise,
No more wishing
  Hell to raise!

No more singing
  Songs you love,
No more praying
  To Him above!

No more warring,
  No more peace,
No more seeking
  Wars to cease!

No more going
  By the clock,
No more doors
  For me to lock!

No more seeking
  An office high,
No more telling
  One "white" lie!

No more sowing
  For me to reap,
No more aching,
  Tired feet!

No more saving
  For a rainy day,
No more doling
  Out my pay!

No more smoking
  My favorite brand,
No more drinking,
  (Not so grand!)

No more Winter,
  No more Fall,
No more Summer,
  Spring at all!

No more flowers,
  No more birds,
No more seasons
  To observe!

No more going
  On a date,
No more scolding
  When I'm late!

No more courting
  To get a wife,
No more keeping
  Her for life!

No more running
  Into debt,
No more worrying:
  "They'll get me yet!"

No more pretending
  What I am not,
No more coveting
  A certain spot!

No more working,
  No more rest,
No more being
  "At my best!"

No more having
  Chores to do,
No more envying
  The fortunate few!

No more reading
  What others wrote,
No more writing
  Or go broke!

No more studies,
  No more books,
No more teacher's
  Ugly looks!

No more sickness,
  No more health,
No more poverty,
  No more wealth!

No more losses,
  No more gain,
No more bosses,
  No more blame!

No more loving,
  No more hate,
No more guessing,
  "What's my fate?"

No more selling,
  No more buying,
No more trading,
  No more dying!

No more taxes,
  No more dues,
No more clothes,
  No more shoes!

No more fighting
  To get ahead,
No more for us,
  FOR WE ARE DEAD!

No more family,
  Home or friend,
No more! No more!
  THIS IS THE END!

-By-
PAUL L. COMPTON
4-1-54

On Getting Gray!

They say I'm getting gray,

    That silver among the gold

Is sad to see, and add:

    That I am getting old!

My friends, how wrong you are

    To judge me by my hair!

For don't you know my spirit

    Is still aa young and fair!

----By----

PAUL L. COMPTON

4/16/54

LIFE IS A GAME OF WAITING!

Waiting on the stork
  To bring you on this Earth –
Life is a game of waiting
  From your day of birth!

Waiting for your mother
  To supply each little need,
Waiting for your teacher
  To plant her precious seed!

Waiting, ever waiting
  In long lines at school,
Waiting, ever waiting –
  (You must observe the rule!)

Waiting until you're twenty-one
  To do just what you please
  nly to learn with much regret
  You cannot live at ease!

Waiting, ever waiting
  For a little word of praise,
Waiting for the boss
  To give you a little raise!

Waiting when you court your girl
  For just that proper minute
To pop the question upmost in mind –
  To get your spirit in it!

Waiting for the preacher
  To pronounce you man and wife,
Waiting for that blessed event –
  The greatest in your life!

Waiting on the corner
  For your little wife;
Awaiting lines await you
  For the balance of your life!

Waiting in the barber-shop
  For a haircut or a shave,
Waiting at the teller's cage
  To bank what you have saved!

Waiting for the elevator
  To take you up or down,
Waiting for the traffic lights
  As you saunter through the town!

Waiting in the Army
  For everything you need,
Waiting to sign the pay-roll,
  In lines to get your feed!

Waiting for the street car,
  Waiting for the bus;
Waiting for the mailman –
  Don't it make you cuss?

Waiting for your neighbor
  To return a borrowed book;
Waiting for your waiter
  To give him a dirty look!

Waiting for the Summer,
  Waiting for the Fall;
Waiting for the Winter
  And the seasons all!

Waiting for retirement
  From worldly cares and strife,
Waiting for tomorrow
  (Which never comes in life!)

Waiting for the doctor,
  Waiting for the nurse;
At last the game is over
  After waiting for the hearse!

– By –
PAUL L. COMPTON
12-8/54

-311-

THE OLD FAMILY ALBUM

Tucked away in the attic
  For many a year,
Lay the old family album
  With its pictures so dear!

What thoughts were awakened
  As I turned each worn page,
Now wrinkled and torn
  And yellow with age!

The old family album
  All covered with dust;
My grandma's old album,
  Its hinges in rust!

There's grandma and grandpa
  On the day they were wed,
Her hand on his shoulder -
  (He followed - she led!)

A picture of mother
  When she was a girl -
A cute little miss
  In gingham and curl!

A picture of father,
  High collared and tall,
In a quaint derby hat,
  Watch - fob and all!

There's the old farm house
  Where, they said, I was born
And the old meeting-house
  With its grave—marked lawn!

A photo quite old
  Of our dear Uncle Jim,
Who traveled afar -
  There was no holding him!

Another - all faded
  Of our fond Uncle Paul
Who used to read stories
  To us children all!

This bearded face
  Is of our Uncle Gene -
A master of verses
  And Biblical theme!

Near him, Aunt Julia,
  So stately and tall -
Her favorite expression:
  "I know it all!"

And here's Uncle Harry
  Whose family tree
Grew 'til it numbered
  A proud twenty-three!

Beside him, Aunt Sally,
  His good, faithful wife
And a wonderful mother
  All through her life!

Next, my great Uncle Jack
  Whom, they said, lost his mind
Delving in perpetual motion
  And machines of liked kind!

And here's great Aunt Mary
   Dressed in crinoline and lace;
They said she was a beauty
   And led "Old Jack" a chase!

And there's Cousin Bill
   In his Sunday's best -
"Black Sheep", they called him -
   (You can guess the rest!)

This old colored mamy -
   "Aunt Dolly", her name,
Was one of the family
   And loved just the same!

And, old "Uncle Tom"
   Her husband, so gray,
Who talked about times
   When he was a slave!

A faded daguerreotype
   Next met my view
Of some unknown soldier
   In the uniform of Blue !

My thoughts sped back years
   As at the old well
There stood brother and sister
   And dear Cousin Mell!

The little red school-house
   Where daily we'd trek
To learn the three R's
   And play by the creek!

The old swimming hole
   Where we'd oft break the law
By diving and swimming
   While clad in the raw!

And "Old Sailor Dan",
   Whiskers and all,
Known far and wide
   By his stories, tall!

Here, seated in a buggy
   On the way from town,
Are mother and dad
   With bundles loaded down!

Gathered 'round a Christmas tree,
   Toys scattered on the floor,
Dear home faces smile at me -
   All gone on before!

And, last but not least
   In his birth-day suit,
Here is year's truly
   In the days he was cute!

Memories, good memories
   From out of the past;
Faces, dear faces
   I'll miss 'til the last !

The old family album
   I tenderly closed -
My grandma's old album -
   God bless her soul!

- By -
PAUL L. COMPTON
July 31, 1955

"O TIME AND CHANGE!"

Time had left its changes
    In the town where I was born,
For many things could happen
    Since that August morn!

The rough country road and buggy rides -
    My mind traveled back to it all:
A State Highway now and speeding cars,
    Gas stations, restaurants, and all!

Time had left its changes
    In everything I saw,
In people, streets, and houses
    And the corner bar!

The old wayside inn at the fork of the road,
    No more greeted the eye:
A swank motel nowstands in its place
    As, with traffic, I speeded by!

Time had left its changes -
    Streets once quiet and dark
Were now ablaze with neon lights
    And hardly a place to park!

The little barefoot boy I knew next door -
    A grandfather now was he!
The cute little miss I knew down the street -
    A grandmother now was she!

Time had left its changes -
    The town was not the same,
Well remembered Main Street
    Was known by another name!

The pasture I knew in bygone days -
    Green there no more was the grass:
A parking lot, full, now met my gaze -
    My nostrils - fumes.... from the gas!

Yes, Time had left its changes
    In everything to see
And, in looking at a mirror,
    Had left its change in me!

- By -
PAUL L. COMPTON
(after a visit to Fredericksburg, Va. and
vicinity on December 30, 1955.)

"O TIME AND CHANGE!"

Time had left its changes
    In the town where I was born,
For many things could happen
    Since that August morn!

The rough country road,
    I can recall -
A State Highway now,
    Motels and all!

Time had left its changes
    In everything I saw,
In people, streets, and houses
    And the corner bar!

The old wayside inn
    I knew as a child -
A honky-tonk now
    With booze running wild!

Time had left its changes -
    Streets once quiet and dark
Were now ablaze with neon lights
    And hardly a place to park!

The little barefoot boy
    I knew next door -
A grandfather now -
    Children galore!

Time had left its changes -
    The town was not the same,
Well remembered Main Street
    Was known by another name!

The pasture I knew
    In bygone days -
A parking lot there
    Now met my gaze!

Yes, time had left its changes
    In everything to see
And, in looking at a mirror,
    Had left its change in me!

- By -
PAUL L. COMPTON

(after a visit to Fredericksburg, Va.,
December 30, 1955.)

"MERRY CHRISTMAS" INDEED!

Don't "Merry Christmas" me, you bloke,
For I tell you now that I am broke:
  With money gone
  And wife forlorn,
"Merry Christmas" - What a joke!

Don't "Merry Christmas" me, my friend,
But hear this tale unto its end:
  I may seem hard,
  But, please, no card
This year to my domicile send!

Don't "Merry Christmas" me, my dear
But rather, for me, just drop a tear:
  Er day was done
  With an air gun
Boys broke my window, do you hear?

Don't "Merry Christmas" me, dear Miss
And strike my name off your mailing list,
  For no card, please,
  My wife to tease -
To cast a shadow o'er our wedded bliss!

Don't "Merry Christmas" me, you all
And, please, no visitors come to call:
  Our doors are locked,
  Our goods are hocked,
The entrance's dark and you may fall!

Don't "Merry Christmas" me - not now -
(And with this verse I'll make my bow):
  My spouse is mad
  And I feel sad -
We both feel as "low" as we know how!

   - By -
  PAUL L. COMPTON
   12-25-55

T A P S

Taps - Afar and near I heard it
  As in my tent I lay,
    Go to sleep,
    Go to sleep,
  The bugles seemed to say!

Taps - Far from home I heard it
  At the close of that first day,
    Soldier rest,
    Soldier rest,
  The bugles seemed to say!

Taps - I was in the Army then
  Preparing for the fray,
    All is well,
    All is well,
  The bugles seemed to say!

Taps - O'er a lonely grave in France
  I heard a corporal play:
    Day is done,
    Gone the sun,
  His bugle seemed to say!

Taps - O'er the body of the Unknown
  On that ne'er forgotten day:
    Safely rest,
    Safely rest,
  The bugle seemed to say!

- o -

Taps - Many times have I heard it
  Sounded here and over sea,
    But, Taps, to me
    When first I heard it
  Will ever haunt my memory!

- By -
PAUL L. COMPTON
(Revised Christmas, 1955)

TAPS

Taps—Afar and near I heard it
  Amid my tent I lay;
    Go to sleep,
    Go to sleep,
  The bugles seemed to say!
Taps—Far from home I heard it
  At the close of that first day;
    Soldiers rest,
    Soldiers rest,
  The bugles seemed to say!
Taps—I was in the Army then
  Preparing for the fray:
    All is well,
    All is well,
  The bugles seemed to say!
Taps—O'er a lonely grave in France
  I heard a corporal play:
    Day is done,
    Gone is the sun,
  His bugle seemed to say!
Taps—O'er the body of the Unkown
  On that ne'er forgotten day:
    Safely rest,
    Safely rest,
  The bugle seemed to say!
Taps—Many times have I heard it
  Sounded here and over sea,
    But, taps to me
    When first I heard it
  Will ever haunt my memory!
        —By—
    PAUL L. COMPTON
(Formerly, Pvt., Company I, 111th
  Inf., 28th Division, A.E.F.)

Published in "The Red Keystone"
Issue of Mar.1956

MY OTHER MOTHER!

Down the lane of memory
  As through this world I roam,
My thoughts return anon
  To my Old Virginia home!

Ruins now mark the spot
  Where once the mansion stood,
And old familiar sights and sounds
  Are gone - I know for good!

The old well no longer stands
  Nor the spring-house close by -
All are gone but memories -
  My Virginia home, Goodbye!

Gone, too, to her reward
  Is one we held most dear,
One who cared for us as infants,
  And, when needed, was ever near!

One who saw me grow to man's estate,
  Nor shirked her duties never,
One who labored until the end -
  Until the cord was severed!

The "Old Black Mammy" and her bandanna red
  Are gone these many years:
God bless her soul and may she have
  Well earned rest - no more tears!

(Affectionately dedicated to the memory of
        Aunt Dolly,
     our old family servant.)

            -By-
        PAUL L. COMPTON
          12-14-55

AT TWILIGHT

In the quiet of the evening
  At twilight's restful hours,
I returned again in memory
  To that old home of our's!

In the quiet of the evening,
  I could see her sitting there
A-rocking and a-knitting
  In her favorite rocking chair!

In the quiet of the evening
  When shadows longer grow,
I could hear her softly humming
  In voice so sweet and low!

In the quiet of the evening,
  I could see her smiling through -
That same sweet smile she gave me
  And to everyone she knew!

In the quiet of that evening,
  Had the veil been parted
To reveal to me again
  One who had departed?

- By -

PAUL L. COMPTON

12-13-55

WHERE ARE OUR DEAD?

Where are our dead?
   Yesterday they were with us,
Sharing in our joys and woes,
   Today, "No voice is heard, no sign is made,
"No step is on the conscious floor!"

Where are our dead?
   Are they sleeping in their graves,
Waiting for that resurrection morn
   When the dead, in Christ, shall rise
At the break of millennium's dawn?

Where are our dead?
   Are they now in Heaven happy,
Knowing all - supremely wise?
   Or are they now in purgatory
There to rebuild blighted lives?

Where are our dead?
   Are they, in spirit, near us,
Ready at our beck and call?
   Or have they lost all memory
And do not return at all?

Where are our dead?
   Are they reincarnated in the flesh?
Do they again tread old familiar ways?
   Or are they cast into a lake of fire
To there atone for their sinful days?

Where are our dead?
   Is there a life hereafter?
Or is the grave, indeed, the end?
   No one really KNOWS the answer -
No mortal ever will, my friend!

Where are our dead?
   What awaits me after death -
After I leave this earthly sphere,
   Does not in the least concern me
BUT LIVING RIGHT WHILE I AM HERE!

- By -

PAUL L. COMPTON
12-7-55

ON HIS BIRTHDAY

(December 25, 1955)

We'll give grandma some slippers,
  Junior gets a bike,
We'll give grandpa a muffler,
  Brother gets a pipe!

We'll give mother silverware,
  Sister gets a roaster,
We'll give father a shaving-set,
  Auntie gets a toaster!

We'll give our next-door neighbor
  Probably just a card,
We'll give and give until it hits
  Our bankroll rather hard!

Gifts galore on His birthday
  Which we will gather in
To bestow upon our loved ones,
  But what will we give Him?

-By-

PAUL L. COMPTON
11-21-55

THE HAUNTED HOUSE

Alone and forsaken – deserted – it stood,
The house people feared near the edge of the wood;
Not a soul would live in it,
Not a child would go near it,
The place was shunned by the whole neighborhood!

Grim and aloof, a tragedy it told
Of a man who was murdered protecting his gold
And though long since the time
Of the night of the crime,
'Twas said that the dead stood guard as of old!

'Twas told in the village, at the stroke of ten,
Each night the ghost of "Old Miser Ben"
Returned to his gold,
Determined to hold
His secret, close, from the world of men!

Hearing this story and in for a lark,
O'er night in the house I decided to park,
So armed with ambition
But without ammunition,
I entered, alone, it was just after dark!

The March winds were sighing,
Through the trees dying,
A full moon's weird glow served me for light,
The night birds were crying,
All nature seemed vying –
Forces united to put me to flight!

After brousing around,
I laid myself down
In the room they had said was most haunted;
The whispering breeze
Seemed to put me at ease,
I then closed my eyes – undaunted!

Then a strange feeling
O'er me came a-stealing,
A feeling that eyes were upon me;
I looked all around,
I heard not a sound,
Still feeling that someone was near me!

The hours slowly passed
Until, yes!, at last
I faintly heard the clock in the village strike ten;
"Now's the time", I thought
(As courage I sought)
To meet face to face the ghost of "Old Miser Ben"!

Did I imagine a step on the stair?
Or was that caused by a current of air?
As a door slammed above me,
I hastened to see
Up a long stair - but no one was there!

From cellar to garret I explored the house,
Was that strange noise caused by a mouse?
On raising a latch
And striking a match,
I found in a closet an old bloody blouse!

What caused that rapping,
A ghostly-like tapping
In one room, alone, I could hear?
From whence came that sighing,
Like the breath of the dying?
Could the spirit of "Ben" be near?

I returned to my post -
The room of my "host",
The fatal hour alas had passed
And so far no "Ben"
On the stroke of ten,
Had I broken the spell at last?

Then a cold chill
The room did fill,
A fog seemed to settle about me;
The hoot of an owl,
A dog's distant howl -
All seemed combined against me!

There before my startled eyes
A shadowy form materialized -
First the shoulders, then the head,
A ghastly light,
A ghostly sight -
It was the spirit of the dead!

Then, through the haze
There met my gaze
A little old man with a beard;
It surely was he,
Who else could it be
But the ghost of "Ben" who was feared!

Down through the ages
On history's pages
Apparitions to men have appeared -
I could not but feel
That none were so real
As the one who now at me leered!

It bade me not linger -
That long, bony finger
As it pointed to a door in the wall,
To the exit I went
On an escape bent,
But stopped in my tracks at a call!

A call or a scream?
I awoke - from a dream?
And found myself peacefully lying
In that room where I thought
The spook certainly ought
Make himself known without trying!

- o -

Long into the night I waited
For the ghost again to "walk",
Long upon the thing debated
But my vigil proved for naught!

- o -

Years have passed
Since I last
Visited the house near the edge of the wood,
And sometimes I wonder
As o'er it I ponder
Did "Old Ben" return as they had said he would?

-By-
PAUL L. COMPTON
(Revised Nov., 1955)

MY BELIEF

(If it matters much)

When I explore the atom

And grasp its wonders there,

When I gaze into a microscope

And see what it unfolds,

When I look through a telescope

And marvel at what it reveals,

Or read an encyclopedia on the origin of man;

When I do all these things

(And read my Bible, too),

I cannot but believe

That Evolution is true!

- By -

PAUL L. COMPTON
11/2/55

A fire-mist and a planet,
  A crystal and a cell,
A jelly-fish and a saurian,
  And caves where the cave-men dwell;
Then a sense of law and beauty
  And a face turned from the clod -
Some call it Evolution,
  And others call it God!

(First verse of "Each in his own tongue")
By
William Herbert Carruth
(1859 - 1924)

DIFFERENT PATHS!

I have listened to the Catholics
  Talk about their Pope,
I have listened to the Protestants
  Dealing out their dope!

I have listened to the Baptists
  With their water and their fire,
I have listened to the Methodists
  With their punishments as dire!

I have listened to the Presbyterians
  And all they have to say,
I have listened to the Spiritualists
  Who return to earth, they say!

I have listened to the Christian Scientists
  (Who never do get sick),
I have listened to the Adventists
  Spread it on good and thick!

I have listened to the Episcopalians
  And worshipped in their way,
I have listened to the Lutherans
  Look for that brighter day!

I have listened to the Jews
  With their Messiah yet to come,
I have listened to the Congregationalists
  And enjoyed their sermons - some!

I have listened to Buddhism
  And smelled the incense burning,
I have listened to Mohammedanism -
  Their faces toward Mecca turning!

I have listened to Confucianism
  And found it very wise,
I have listened to Bahaism
  (Cut down to my size)!

I have listened to the theosophists
  And the doctrine of reincarnation,
I have listened to Calvinism
  And the theory of predestination!

I have even sat in silence
  At a Quaker Meet
And I've watched the Holy Rollers
  Wash each other's feet!

I have seen the Amish Mennonites
  With their beards and garb,
I have seen the "saved" go frantic
  With their wails and sob!

I have listened to the Disciples of Christ -
  Their beliefs in Heaven and Hell,
I have listened to the Latter-Day Saints -
  Need more I add to tell?

- o -

To tell you, dear reader,
  That all are but paths
Upon this lowly sod,
  That all are good and, when followed,
Will lead you home to God!

"You go to your church
  And I'll go to mine,
But let's walk along together!"
            Phillips H. Lord
            "Seth Parker"

- By -

PAUL L. COMPTON

10/27/55

THE PAST, THE PRESENT & THE FUTURE

Yesterday is gone forever -
   Buried in the archives of the past -
Are you proud of how you lived it -
   Every moment until the last?

Today is your's - the hour now -
   Every precious minute -
Its up to you and you alone
   What you may put in it!

Tomorrow may never come,
   That is, my friend, for you -
So make the most of the now -
   Follow the Golden Rule!

- By -

PAUL L. COMPTON

1/17/56

ON LOVE AND HATE!

Hate destroys that which nourishes it -

A cancerous growth - its roots in gloom,

So let love surplant its ugliness -

Let its flower within you bloom!

- By -

PAUL L. COMPTON

1-27-56

THE CHAMPION SHAKER

From early morn to late at night,
    You'll find her standing there,
Shaking everything in sight -
    A-giving 'em "the air"!

From early morn to late at night
    The bath-tub is the spot,
For there she does her shaking
    Right around the clock!

Pillow-cases, towels, and sheets,
    Slip-covers, rags, and shoes,
Paper bags, newspapers and such -
    About everything we use!

Ash-trays, brooms, and pans,
    Cigarette-holders, hose, and socks,
Underwear, dresses, and old tin cans,
    As well as an empty box!

Sheet music, books, and pads,
    Pencils, erasers - you'll get a kick
When you see her bending over
    A-shaking a lone tooth-pick!

Dollar bills fresh from the bank,
    Combs, brushes, and postage stamps,
Electric fixtures, bulbs, and cords,
    And, of course, electric lamps!

Everything gets a shaking,
    Everything, short or tall!
The kitchen clock is spared -
    (It's fastened to the wall!)

Birthday cards just newly bought,
    As clean as clean can be;
One morn I will awaken
    To find she's shaking me!

Yes, everything gets a shaking,
    Everything is a "must",
Yet, why is it, I ask you,
    That everything is in dust?

And, when she enters those Pearly Gates
    And is handed her crown of gold,
I bet that gets a shaking
    Before its very old!

- By -

PAUL L. COMPTON
4-4-56

CHANCELLORSVILLE!

(May 2-3, 1863)

My steps led back to Old Virginia
   And to her National Parks
In County Spottsylvania
   Where the Civil War she marks!

My thoughts turned back to Sixty-three
   And to those early days in May,
To the battlefields at Chancellorsville
   Where fought the Blue and boys in Gray!

'Twas here that General Hooker
   Engaged the armies of General Lee;
'Twas here that "Stonewall" Jackson
   Fell wounded - mortally!

A tablet now marks the spot
   Where Chancellor House once stood -
General Hooker's Headquarters
   Amidst historic wood!

I visited Jackson's Monument
   Near the spot where the General fell
Which told the story of those fatal shots
   And I knew that war is Hell!

The cannonading long has ceased
   On Rappahannock's banks,
The North and South as one united -
   To God we give our thanks!

The boys in Blue and the boys in Gray
   Clasp hands, as smiling through,
They roam again familiar camps
   In Sixty-three they knew!

— BY —

PAUL L. COMPTON

/22/56

ON STAMP COLLECTING

A stamp collector once I knew
Whose stamp collection grew and grew:
    With blocks-of-four
    And sheets galore -
Just what he had no one knew!

Now this stamp collector, I am told,
Loved his collection more than gold:
    But he made no Will
    His wants to fill
And the time had come when he was old!

Our stamp collector, as all men must,
Has passed away and returned to dust:
    (Now wipe your "lamps")
    What of his stamps?
They, too, lie buried, safe we trust!

Lie buried? - but not for long,
Someone sold 'em for a song:
    Someone who did not know,
    Someone who loved the dough -
All of which seems very wrong!

So, er I leave this mortal life,
I will all my stamps unto my wife:
    But, wifie, dear,
    Please listen here:
Consult a dealer who will treat you right!

- By -

PAUL L. COMPTON
4-26-56

WHEN ITS TIME TO RETIRE!

When your steps begin to falter
  And your sight begins to fail;
When your hair begins to fall out
  And around your gills you're pale!

When your hands begin to shaking
  And your plates no longer stick;
When your bones begin to aching
  And your "Annual" turns to "Sick"!

When your supervisor speaks
  In voice nice and loud and clear,
But the words on you are wasted -
  What is said you cannot hear!

When your thinking is a little slower,
  Your memory not so clear;
When your vitality is lower
  As seventy years you near!

When your joints begin to popping
  And you lose that vim and fire:
I'll tell you, brother, sister --
  It is time, then, to retire!

- By -

PAUL L. COMPTON
5/22/56

JUNE!

June is the month of roses,
    Graduations and brides;
Soft, fleecy clouds in the heavens,
    The Great Outdoors and rides!

June and the birth of Summer,
    Cradled in her bed of flowers;
Sunny days and starry nights
    Lull away her lazy hours!

In June all nature is smiling
    As blossoms galore unfurl,
Spreading their fragrance around us -
    Peace! All is right with the world!

June is the month of parting,
    But happiness is the rule
When teacher and scholar say Goodbye
    And are free, three months, from school!

- By -

PAUL L. COMPTON
6-7-56

THE LEE MANSION

In the Arlington National Cemetery,
   Near crosses row on row,
The old Lee Mansion is today
   Enshrined forevermore!

The old mansion in grandeur stands,
   A symbol of other days and times,
When gay young blades and their ladies fair
   Brought laughter there among the pines!

Where once gracious ladies entertained
   And danced the minuet in its halls,
No more its rooms resound with merriment -
   Silence reigns within its walls!

Old Mansion, if you could speak,
   What stories you could tell
Of the Civil War and General Lee
   And of the Southern belle!

- By -

PAUL L. COMPTON
2-16-56

-336-

U. S. BUREAU OF ENGRAVING AND PRINTING

Little scrap of paper,
   Printer's ink and skill,
Here's where you become
   A postage stamp and bill!

Little scrap of paper,
   Of you we are fond
When here you are fashioned
   Into a Government bond!

For here's where they are printed,
   Those elusive dollar bills,
Here's where they start their journey
   To ease the Nation's ills!

And here's where they are printed,
   The familar postage stamp,
Here's where they start a journey
   To end in some distant camp!

- B y -

PAUL L. COMPTON
2/21/56

UNITED STATES SUPREME COURT

In this magnificent temple on Capitol Hill
 The nation's "nine old men" are found,
For here momentous decisions are made and framed
 And by the highest tribunal are handed down!

Here sit in solemn dignity
 The Supreme Court justices of our land,
Here they make their deliberations
 Based on the Constitution of our land!

- By -

PAUL L. COMPTON

2/27/56

UNITED STATES CAPITOL

In a landscaped setting on Capitol Hill
   The halls of Congress are,
Here members of our Congress meet –
   They come from near and far!

Here laws are passed by those we trust
   To steer our Ship of State,
Here tourists by the thousands come
   To view at any rate!

Its dome rises majestically to the sky,
   Its Rotunda an inspiring sight,
Its President's Room, its Statuary Hall
   Where echoes rebound just right!

- o -

To that landscaped setting on Capitol Hill
   Eyes of the world are turning
To a nation that rules not alone by might
   But keeps her home fires burning!

- by -

PAUL L. COMPTON
10/20/55

MT. VERNON

Overlooking the broad Potomac
 As it flows to the bay,
Stand the pillars of Mt. Vernon
 As in Washington's day!

'Twas here the father of his country
 Once trod his beloved land,
'Twas here that Martha Washington
 Lent her ever helping hand!

The old mansion stands today
 As a memorial to the past,
Within its walls now silence reigns,
 Hats off as you pass!

For this is sacred ground you tread,
 Our Washington is buried here,
The father of our country,
 With Martha sleeping near!

Roll on, old Potomac,
 Roll thou on down to the bay,
You are, indeed, endeared
 For Washington passed your way!

   - By -

  PAUL L. COMPTON
   10/19/55

THE WHITE HOUSE

Presidents John Adams to Eisenhower
　Within these walls have walked,
Shaping the destiny of our nation
　By decisions – words they talked!

They say that Abigail Adams
　Hung her wash to dry
In the East Room of the house where
　Tourists now would pry!

They say that Andrew Jackson
　Strolled from its doors one day,
Stuck his cane into the ground
　Where his Treasury stands today!

They say that the ghost of Lincoln
　Prowls its halls at night,
That mysterious raps on doors are heard –
　No one is in sight!

They say that Theodore Roosevelt
　With his family of lively boys,
Turned the mansion inside out
　With their shouting, games, and toys!

We know that Woodrow Wilson
　Was fond of vaudeville
And that Harry Truman
　With his piano thrilled!

They say that F. D. R.
　With his knickknacks and his stamps,
Enjoyed a round of poker,
　As did Harding, Hoover, Grant!

We know that Mrs. Roosevelt
　Is always "taking off"
And that President Eisenhower
　Loves his game of golf!

Yes! Within these sacred walls have lived
　Our Presidents in their turn,
And, ever, the famous mansion waits
　For the next to serve his term!

THE JEFFERSON MEMORIAL

Son of old Virginia,
   The Presidential state,
The name of Thomas Jefferson –
   One of our nation's great!

Musician, stateman, President,
   He early lent his name
To the Cause of Democracy
   And everlasting fame!

The Declaration of Independence
   He drafted with great skill
Which eventually gave us freedom
   From England's dominate will!

The Louisiana Purchase
   He engineered with tact
And saw its completion
   When Congress passed the Act!

Son of old Virginia,
   Farmer, architect, friend,
This Memorial we raise to thee –
   Our thanks unto the end!

– By –

PAUL L. COMPTON
10/18/55

THE WASHINGTON MONUMENT

Like a sentinel on guard
   You rigidly stand –
A silent symbol
   Of a beloved man!

A man whose spirit
   Pierced the sky;
A man whose name
   Will never die!

A man whose patriotism
   Never faltered,
Whose love for truth
   Never altered!

A man whose wisdom
   Guided a nation,
Young in age, with
   Determination!

A man beloved
   By his countrymen:
All hail his name –
   George Washington!

– By –
PAUL L. COMPTON
10/13/55

IWO JIMA – FEBRUARY 23, 1945!

On the little isle of Iwo Jima,
   Looking toward the sea,
Mt. Suribachi raised its head
   In calm solemnity!

On the little isle of Iwo Jima,
   Advancing under fire,
A small detail of heroes
   Had but one desire!

On the little isle of Iwo Jima,
   Where heroes died and bled,
They would hoist the Flag of Victory
   Ere the foe had fled!

On the little isle of Iwo Jima,
   Nippon's cruelest lair,
The 28th Marines stormed the heights
   And raised Old Glory there!

On the little isle of Iwo Jima,
   Upon Mt. Suribachi's crest,
Proudly waves the Stars and Stripes –
   The 28th is "at rest"!

– By –
PAUL L. COMPTON
10/5/55

THE LINCOLN MEMORIAL

A greater Memorial he has built
  By his patience, tact, and skill -
A country united in strength and peace
  Nor divided against his will!

No North,
No South.

The North and The South united - one nation great and strong!

A greater Memorial he has built
  By his tolerance, faith, and heart -
A nation wherein no slavery
  Has a place or is a part!

No Master,
No Slave.

The Emancipation Proclamation - Lincoln rights a wrong!

A greater Memorial he has built
  To grace Eternity's pages -
The words he uttered at Gettysburg
  Will live down through the ages!

- By -
PAUL L. COMPTON
9/29/55

ANOTHER UNKNOWN SOLDIER?

On the green slopes of Arlington,
   By old Potomac's banks,
There sleeps in honored glory
   A soldier from the ranks!

Unknown by name but known to God -
   A soldier home - back from the wars;
Unknown by name yet mourned by all
   Who gave their sons for Freedom's Cause!

What matters his race, his color or creed,
   Or where he fell and when?
Suffice to say he represents
   Thousands of such - our fighting men!

Men have, since this country's birth,
   Given their all for Liberty's Cause -
The sacrifice supreme to make
   In ALL our nation's wars!

Need he be joined by another
   Unknown, his place to share?
On the green slopes of Arlington,
   Is not the Symbol there?

- By -
PAUL L. COMPTON
9-14-55

Original newspaper clipping published in
The Evening Star, Washington, D. C.
Friday, September 23, 1955

THE EVENING STAR, Washington, D. C.
FRIDAY, SEPTEMBER 23, 1955

Another Unknown?

On the green slopes of Arling-
      ton
    By old Potomac's banks,
There sleeps in honored glory
    A soldier from the ranks!

Unknown by name yet known
      to God—
    A soldier home—back from
      the wars!
Unknown by name yet known
      by all
    Who gave their sons for
      Freedom's Cause.

What matters his race, his
    color or creed,
    Or where he fell and when?
Suffice to say he represents
    Thousands of such—our
      fighting men:

Men who since their country's
    birth
    Gave their all for Liberty's
      Cause,
Men yet to make the supreme
      sacrifice
    In all our Nation's wars!

Need he be joined by another
    Unknown, his place to share?
On the green slopes of Arling-
      ton,
    Is not the Symbol there?

                    Ex-Service.

ANOTHER UNKNOWN SOLDIER?

On the green slopes of Arlington,
    By old Potomac's banks,
There sleeps in honored glory
    A soldier from the ranks!

Unknown by name but, known to God -
    A soldier home - back from the wars;
Unknown by name yet mourned by all
    Who gave their sons for Freedom's Cause!

What matters his race, his color or creed,
    Or where he fell and when?
Suffice to say he represents
    Thousands of such - our fighting men!

Men have, since this country's birth,
    Given their all for Liberty's Cause -
The sacrifice supreme to make
    In ALL our nation's wars!

Need he be joined by another
    Unknown, his place to share?
On the green slopes of Arlington,
    Is not the Symbol there?

-By-
PAUL L. COMPTON
9-14-55

APRIL 15, 1957
or
(Don't let this happen to you!)

"Mom, what is daddy doing
   With papers scattered 'round,
A pencil behind each ear
   And on his face a frown? "

"Mom, what is daddy doing
   Sitting over there,
His face buried in his hands,
   Pulling at his hair? "

"Mom, what is daddy doing
   Talking to himself,
Reaching for every book in sight
   That's piled upon the shelf? "

"Mom, what is daddy doing,
   Those figures adding up,
And when I went to speak to him,
   He barked like an angry pup? "

"Mom, what is daddy doing,
   Pacing up and down,
Reaching for the telephone,
   Calling all in town? "

"Mom, what is daddy doing
   That's getting up his ire,
Sitting there and typing
   Like a house afire? "

"Mom, what is daddy doing,
   Racing 'gainst the time?
A dozen times he has pulled his watch,
   I bet my bottom dime! "

" Son, what is your daddy doing?
   Be brave and hear the facts:
Your daddy forgot this year
   To file his income tax! "

" For 'tis the fifteenth of April,
   Nineteen fifty-seven
And the hour is getting late -
   Yes, way past eleven! "
            -o-
"Mom, what is daddy doing
   In that uniform of gray,
With numbers black upon his back,
   Form Ten Forty, did you say? "

- By -

PAUL L. COMPTON

AT A FAKE SPIRITUALISTIC SEANCE!

In a darkened room we gathered,
    Formed a circle, holding hands,
With our "medium" in a cabinet,
    Nearby, trumpets with phosphorous bands!

A hymn was sung, a prayer was offered,
    And like wind sighing through the trees,
From the cabinet there seemed to issue
    A moan followed by a chill-like breeze!

Another song of a livlier nature
    And soon before our startled eyes,
Near the cabinet but within our circle
    A form began to materialize!

First appeared the shade of Bernhardt,
    Sarah - the Divine -
Then the protruding chin of Roosevelt
    Which all pronounced as very fine!

Then, favoring us with a visit -
    "Honest Abe", beard and tall,
"Stonewall" Jackson, Lee and others
    Answered to our "medium's" call!

Then, by aid of ectoplasm,
    From that land beyond the veil,
There appeared the forms of Sheridan,
    Grant, and Sherman without fail!

Each "spirit" was soon identified
    By a "regular" in our midst -
Each "voice" was likewise recognized
    And none at all were missed!

A trumpet appeared to leave the floor
    As we watched its phosphorous band,
Then o'er our heads it gently floated,
    Held aloft by a spirit hand?

A voice - at first a whisper,
    Growing louder as it said,
From the trumpet, we heard distinctly:
    "Grieving friends, I am not dead!"

"I'm your guide, an Indian maiden,
    "At your bidding, have no fear,
"Minnie-Ha-Ha - 'Laughing Waters'
    "In your circle I will be near!"

Then voices of the "dear departed"
    Mingled with the loved of earth
As "messages" sent and answered
    Brought comfort, advice and mirth!

(But this I clearly noted
 And feel that I must tell -
Our "medium" for that seance
 Had met each sitter and knew some well!)

Then there followed table-tilting,
 "Spirit" raps and music queer;
Through it all and there to "guide" us
 "Laughing Waters" ever near!

Suddenly, from out the silence
 Thundered a voice loud and strong:
"Sitting Bull begs forgiveness
 "Of General Custer for that wrong!"

Laughing Waters - her voice grows weaker
 As the seance nears its end -
Brings the warriors once more together,
 Not as foes but friend to friend!

In that darkened room I waited
 For a message which never came -
Will that silence n'er be broken?
 Have my loved ones forgot my name?

Messages from the great and near-great
 Seemed to come at our "medium's" call;
But for these I'd give and gladly
 For just a word from my all in all!

Long into the night I waited
 But I waited all in vain -
No familiar form nor voice approached me
 With a message from the Spirit Plane!

Are only the spirits of the famous
 Allowed to leave their Heavenly home?
I'd trade them all for a personal message
 Which I could call my very own!

Laughing Waters, "Goodnight" whispered
 As a bluish light seemed to dance
Around our "medium", who came from under
 The spell of a first-class "trance"!

In that room, now lighted, we crowded,
 Trumpets scattered o'er the floor -
The Faithful around our "medium" gathered -
 The gate? Fifty Dollars at the door!

Please, Washington, Grant, and Lincoln,
 Be good boys and remain at home
And give the lesser spirits a chance to enter
 When to a seance again I roam!

       -By-
      PAUL L. COMPTON

THE GREATEST BLESSING!

The pink-tinted dawn is dispelled by the sun,
   A glorious day through its course must run,
The most inspiring sun-set soon fades from our sight
   And the wonders of night pass with morn's early light!

The blossoms of Spring soon fall from the tree,
   The months of the Summer are numbered but three,
The beauty of Autumn is soon of the past
   And Winter's white mantle, the snow, does not last!

A freshly plucked flower but withers and dies,
   A book, once enjoyed, on the shelf lies,
A Heavenly symphony, alas, reaches its end
   And distance oftimes loses a very dear friend!

The song of the bird is hushed by a shot,
   Our pets are soon buried on some vacant lot,
A beautiful dream - but its only a dream,
   A wonderful love that is flashed on a screen!

A sumptuous repast has its last course,
   The joy of the moment may die at its source,
For the gladness of now, tomorrow may fade -
   Fond hopes, aspirations may well face the grave!

These blessings God sent us in numberless lot,
   They pass - again our's - and we lose them not;
But the greatest of all - you'll not have another,
   For God gave to each only one mother!

          - By -

        PAUL L. COMPTON

FAITH!

Somewhere in the blue out yonder,

Somewhere beyond the sky,

Sometime we'll be united,

Never to say Goodbye!

Somewhere a voice is calling,

Somewhere a beckoning hand

Of someone loved and lost awhile

Will greet me on Tomorrow's Strand!

For somewhere they are waiting —

Our loved ones gone on before —

And some day we'll be welcomed

At the threshold of Eternity's Door!

— By —

PAUL L. COMPTON

MEMORIES!

In the garden of my memory
  There's a flower still in bloom,
In the garden of my memory
  That flower, dear, is you!

In the garden of my memory,
  I see you smiling there
With garlands of the Summer
  Entwined within your hair!

Though the years have been long and many
  Since last we parted, dear,
In that garden of my memory,
  Forever you'll be near!

And though the evening shadows lengthen
  In our garden made for two,
Always there you'll be with me
  And always smiling through!

For years, alone, cannot efface
  From memory's precious page
My thoughts of you when I look back
  Upon our golden age!

                        - By -

                   PAUL L. COMPTON

BACK IN THE OLD NEIGHBORHOOD

(No. 723 - 8th Street, N. E., between G & H - Years 1900 - 1901)

My steps wandered back
O'er life's beaten track -
    Back to the scenes of my boyhood;
And my feet once more strayed
Down the street where I played
    In those bygone days of childhood!

My memory cleared
As the old home I neared -
    A full minute I stood before it,
Recalling the past
Now gone, and alas!
    The joys that I once knew in it!

In fancy I saw
That dear one - our "Ma"
    At the front door calling my name:
"Leon, supper's now ready,
"Say Goodbye to Freddie
"And don't play so rough at that game!"

And beside her stood "Dad" -
The best a boy ever had -
    Just home from work on his bike;
He was one of us boys
In our "sorrows" and joys -
    A dad any lad would like!

And always so glad
To welcome home dad -
    In memory he frisked as of yore -
Just our pup, it is true,
But the time he well knew
    As, daily, he pawed at the door!

It was then with a pang
I recalled the "Old Gang" -
    Names half-forgotten, 'tis true;
It seemed sort of queer
That none should appear -
    The very thought made me feel blue!

In vision they danced,
Jumped, ran, and pranced -
    The sidewalk was crowded as of old
With wild, shouting boys
And their big, noisy toys
    And with "Indians" war-painted and bold!

There was Jim, long and lank,
Always up to some prank -
    His "heroes" - prize fighters of fame ;
There were Earl and Dick,
Brothers who'd stick,
    And "English" is their last name!

Their names brought to mind
A certain grape-vine
    That grew in their yard by the fence
And that peach tree of our's
Where we spent pleasant hours
    Swapping grapes for a peach - moments tense!

On the corner lived Will -
All called him "Bill" -
    His father - a genial soul,
For Neuland's by far
Was the street's favorite bar
    With frost on the eggnog bowl!

In memory there came
The same unknown Dame
    As, daily, the "Ladies Entrance" she sought,
With a pail on her arm
(Now was that any harm?)
    For 'twas only good lager beer she bought!

Down the block a few gates
Dwelled happy "Bill" Yates -
    Old Taylor School was his bane,
And a few doors away
And beloved to this day
    Lived, respected by all, Dr. Lane!

And the "shows" that we had -
Marionettes were the fad -
    Thinking back, I just had to grin
About the "wealth" that was made
With my brother's aid,
    Charging two pins to get in!

And the girls that we hauled -
Some laughed and some bawled -
    In wagons all 'round the square,
Up-setting a few
(And kissing 'em too)
    In "tunnels" as we pulled our fare!

And the shacks that we built
(For the winds to tilt)
    To house all the "clubs" we started!
And the fun that we had
O'er many a lad
    Before from the "gang" he parted!

And oft in the Spring
The street would ring
    With "music" by the hurdy-gurdy man;
And, Oh! what a treat
When they played on our street -
    Musicians of the "Little German Band"!

And, in memory, came night
And, Oh! what a sight!
    As those gay "lantern-wagons" paraded -
Made of designs neatly cut,
Colored tissued, lighted up -
    (Miller's shoe-boxes greatly aided!)

At this time of year,
I remembered quite clear
    How we boys had an added thrill,
For right on our street
With "passes" to treat,
    There roomed the ball-player, Lew Drill!

And to name others too -
Professionals we knew -
    Patton, Coughlin, and "Scoops" Carey would treat;
And, Oh! what a shame
When they lost any game -
    Those ball players who roomed on our street!

That Summer brought joy
To each girl and boy
    As we romped through the city's heat:
In sprinkling our lawn
(If you care for the yarn),
    I "hosed" a good cop on his beat!

In the chill Autumn days
Under Halloween's haze -
    "Tick-tacks", doorbell ringing and masks -
And the bonfires we started
With the leaves that we carted -
    Not work but real pleasure, such tasks!

And, My! what a thrill
Down Eighth Street hill!
    In Winter when snow covered all;
With a truck or a sled
(And no autos to dread) -
    Only to watch out for a fall!

In the long Winter's night
How we played by gaslight, -
    "Authors","parcheesi", "Old Maid" by the score
With loved ones now gone
But, in memory, live on
    As each dear face appeared as of yore!

And I'll forget not
When McKinley was shot -
   A day that stands out from the past,
The newsboys' loud cry,
The "extras" you'd buy,
   No radios, then, to broadcast!

And that first "stolen" smoke!
(I thought I would choke)
   At the store where that Indian of wood
In war paint so brave
And with countenance grave
   In all kinds of weather so patiently stood!

And the "five-centers" we read
(That went to the head!) -
   "Old King Brady", "Jesse James" and the rest -
Killings by the score
To obtain that rich "ore"
But "Elsie" books, the girls liked the best!

And what of our girls,
In pig-tails and curls,
   Oh! the parties they gave on that block!
I've been told by others
That some are grandmothers
   Who now sit and contently rock!

From memory's store
They shouted as of yore -
   Henrietta, Lucille, and Grace,
Marie and Anna,
Bessie and Ada,
   To see "Tootsie" and Mamie race!

And just 'cross the way
I heard laughter gay -
   My thoughts travelled back o'er the years
To one whose sweet smiles
And the cutest of wiles
   Made up for all the "gang's" jeers!

After pondering awhile,
I left with a smile
   And wended my way asof old
To the Madison School
Where some hours as a rule
   I wasted, if truth must be told!

I heard the same bell
The daily recess tell -
   Its tone seemed to roll back the years -
And the children at play
Little thought gave
   To one who would join in their cheers!

WAR ON THE HOME FRONT!

Father's sore and mother's mad -
  You can sense it in the air;
Brother John and Sister Anne
  Are speaking - well just rare!

Dear Aunt Mae and Uncle Ben,
  Happy in years gone by;
It's sad indeed to hear them
  Each heave a heavy sigh!

Cousin Kate and Cousin Jim
  Fight like cats and dogs;
Cousin Nell and Cousin Luke
  Call each other "hog!"

Grandpa Bill and Grandson Frank,
  Buddies tried and true,
Pass each other on the street
  As ne'er a smile breaks through!

Grandma Bess and the hired man
  Got along so well -
What's happened now you ask?
  God, alone, can tell!

Banker Smith and Lawyer brown
  Were comrades once they say,
But strangers now they seem to be
  And in each other's way!

The baby in her little crib
  Is crying all the time,
While the older children fiercely fight
  Each other for a dime!

Old Sport, our family pet,
  Has even bristled up,
As if to meet an enemy
  In every friendly pup!

And pretty parakeet,
  In his gilded cage,
When we start to teach him,
  Flies into a rage!

What changed all this?
  What happened here of late?
These questions now I answer:
  They settled (?) an estate!

      -- By --

    PAUL L. COMPTON

Lines to A. M. B. on his retirement from the Government Service

A. M. B. Is leaving us
   At three score years and ten
But 'er he goes and bids adieu,
   These few lines I'd pen!

A. M. B., we'll miss your aid
   In this here audit work,
Yes, you'll be missed by all you leave -
   You faithful Government clerk!

A. M. B., we'll miss that story
   As only you can tell -
The one about the Russian witness -
   You sure recite it swell!

A. M. B., what of that girl
   You are leaving with a broken heart?
"Where is she?", I hear you ask -
   Why, in most any room you dart!

No more she'll feel your wandering arms
   As you ask her for a date,
No more you'll gaze into her eyes
   Although your hour is late!

Yes, A. M. B., you are leaving us -
   The place won't seem the same,
Enshrined you are for evermore
   In our office Hall of Fame!

'Tis true we'll miss your hieroglyphics
   That you scribble upon a pad,
'Tis true some typist will have more time
   To spend upon her lad!

But, as you go to home and wife
   To live a life of ease,
Don't forget the office gang
   And visit us when you please!

- By -

Paul L. Compton

FROM OUT OF THE EAST

From out of the East, the cradle of dawn,
   Onto this Earth an infant was born -
Born like His brothers - no miraculous birth
   Ushered the Christ upon His mission on Earth!

From out of the East, like a clarion call
   Sounded His message for one and for all -
A message of love, eternal life -
   Then why o'er His birth this needless strife?

From out of the East, upon a cross
   They took His life, their's the loss!
Nor did He die for our souls' redemption
   But gave to each his own salvation!

From out of the East, there's a lesson to learn
   If, in the end, a Heaven you'll earn -
Forget His Birth - His Death as well
   AND LET HIS LIFE IN YOUR LIFE DWELL!

-- By --

PAUL L. COMPTON

"GRANDMA'S BOY"

Oh! for those days so long ago
    When life was in the Spring,
When all the things I heard and saw
    Had a joyful ring!

Care-free days and happiness
    Just from some little toy,
Playful ways and contentment
    When I was "Grandma's boy"!

Gone forever are those days
    When I was a tot and coy!
What would I give to bring them back -
    When I was "Grandma's boy"!

Turn back the clock!
    Return! O days of joy
To that time I love to dream about -
    When I was "Grandma's boy"!

And in that life hereafter,
    With nothing to annoy,
Her familiar voice will greet me -
    To welcome "Grandma's boy"!

- By -

PAUL L. COMPTON
3/14/56

(Affectionately dedicated to the memory of my
dear grandmother, Mrs. Lydia Hoyer, who passed
on in 1918, while I was oversea during the
First World War.)

IN MEMORY OF MY MOTHER!

"M ama", we cried, when, as children, we ran to you for comfort --

O nly that loving care such as you, mother dear, could give;

T ears were kissed away and hair brushed back by the tender

H ands of one "long gone and lost awhile" - mother mine!

E vening shadows lengthen as I look toward that setting sun

R eddening the path that one day, God willing, I shall tread
     to join you!

- By -

PAUL L. COMPTON

3-12-56

IN MEMORY OF MY FATHER!

F irst, a father, understanding, devoted, and wise;

A Master Mason, musician-composer, poet, writer, and printer;

T rustworthy, considerate, no bad habits, clean in body and mind;

H usband - faithful to his wife and family always; exemplary character;

E ver thoughtful of others; self-sacrificing, and kind;

R emarkable patience and fortitude during years of affliction;
   Rich in the good name he passed on to his children!

- By -

. PAUL L. COMPTON

3-12-56

IS MY HOUSE IN ORDER?

My guest awaits without –
   He is knocking at my door;
I must get my house in order –
   Clean the windows, scrub the floor!

I must clear away the rubbish –
   An accumulation of years,
I must polish all the silver
   And wash behind my ears!

I must discard all the old
   And replace it by the new,
I must make sure to have
   My very best on view!

I must pull up all the weeds
   In my garden grown
And guard well the roses –
   The few I really own!

I must be able to receive Him
   In a temple pure and fair
And have the banquet ready
   For Him who waits out there!

Is my house in order?
   Have I vanquished every sin?
Am I ready to receive Him? –
   To let my Savior in?

– By –

PAUL L. COMPTON

5/4/54

Paul L. Compton

Home of Paul L. and Eva Compton, Washington, DC

Eva Compton

(Images 1966)

About the Co-Author

Wendy Yessler graduated from Evangel University with a
B.S. in Social Work in 1988.

In 2000, she received a Master's in Biblical Studies from
Christian International School of Theology.

Between 1995-2001, she served as a deacon at the mega church,
Evangel Cathedral in Upper Marlboro, MD, under
Bishop Don Meares.

For two years she was co-leader of a women's mentoring group.

From 2001-2010 she was the Prince George's County coordinator for the
Strategic Prayer Network of Maryland.

Throughout this time, she homeschooled her two children between 1996 and 2013.
She has been mentoring people consistently since the mid-90s.

Her desire has been to see people experience a higher level of freedom in their lives,
and to see people freed from life controlling issues.

Other Books by

Wendy A. Yessler

Life Art Journal

Autumn Art Journal

Winter Art Journal

Spring Art Journal

Summer Art Journal

A Nostalgic Walk Through the Four Seasons:
A Coloring Book for Reminiscing

A Journey of Meditation on the Fruit of the Spirit

Check Amazon for more to come, or look for announcements on Instagram!

@Wendy_Yessler

Made in the USA
Middletown, DE
22 July 2022